The Presidents
of the United States
& the Jews

The Presidents of the United States

& the Jews

David G. Dalin & Alfred J. Kolatch

JD | JONATHAN DAVID PUBLISHERS, INC.
Middle Village, New York 11379

THE PRESIDENTS OF THE UNITED STATES
& THE JEWS

Copyright © 2000
by David G. Dalin & Alfred Kolatch

Jonathan David Publishers, Inc.
68-22 Eliot Avenue
Middle Village, NY 11379

www.jdbooks.com

2 4 6 8 10 9 7 5 3 1

Library of Congress Cataloging-in-Publication Data

Dalin, David G.
    The Presidents of the United States & the Jews / by David G. Dalin & Alfred J. Kolatch.
        p. cm.
    Includes bibliographical references and index.
    ISBN 0-8246-0428-8
    1. Presidents—United States—Relations with Jews. 2. Presidents—United States—History. 3. Jews
United States—History. 4. United States—Ethnic relations. I. Kolatch, Alfred J., 1916– . II. Title.
    E176.472.J47 D35 2000
    973'.04924—dc21
                                                 00-064526
                                                             CIP

Book design and composition by John Reinhardt Book Design

Printed in the United States of America

*For my children, Simona Sara Dalin
and Barry Simcha Dalin, with love,
D.G.D.*

*For Emily and Natalie,
A.J.K.*

Contents

Preface

A GREAT DEAL HAS BEEN WRITTEN ABOUT the history of the American Jewish experience generally, but little has been written on the subject of the U.S. presidency and the Jews. The literature does contain books and monographs analyzing a particular president's policies on matters of Jewish concern, and there are biographies and/or memoirs by American Jewish leaders—Mordecai Manuel Noah, Oscar Straus, Simon Wolf, Lewis Strauss, Philip Klutznick and Max Fisher, among them—that discuss the relationships between individual Jews and specific presidents. There is, however, no single book that devotes itself exclusively to the history of Jewish-presidential relations, presidential appointments of Jews, and presidential views and positions on issues of Jewish interest.

The Presidents of the United States & the Jews examines the role and experience of Jews in each administration, from George Washington to Bill Clinton, and discusses the relationship of each of the presidents to the American Jewish community at large and to individual Jews in particular. It provides biographical material on presidential appointments of Jews to Cabinet and major sub-Cabinet positions, ambassadorial posts, and the United States Supreme Court. The volume also presents significant presidential statements and positions relating to anti-Semitism abroad and to the plight of Jews denied religious and political freedom in Eastern Europe and elsewhere.

Written in a popular style for the lay reader, *The Presidents of the United States & the Jews* is intended to give an overview of the subject at hand. The reader will note that in the case of Jews who had associations with more than one president, in order to increase readability, some background material is repeated in the various chapters. Those seeking further information on a given individual or subject are encouraged to consult the bibliography.

A work of this scope of necessity requires the help and support of many. The librarians and staffs of the Jewish Theological Seminary, the American Jewish Archives, and the Library of Congress Presidential Archives were especially helpful. We also owe a debt of gratitude to John F. Rothmann of San Francisco, who gave us access to many out-of-print books and monographs contained in his vast private library. That material, especially in the areas of presidential biography and campaign literature and American Jewish autobiography, greatly helped facilitate our research.

For their generous assistance in obtaining the graphics that accompany the text of the book, our thanks to John McDugal of the New York Public Library, Sarah Jester of the Touro Synagogue General Archives, and the staffs of the American Jewish Archives, the Washington (D.C.) Jewish Community Center, the Washington Hebrew Congregation, and Congregation Rodef

Shalom of Pittsburgh, Pennsylvania. We would also like to express our appreciation to Cokie Roberts and Steve Roberts for sharing with us the photograph of their wedding, which was attended by President and Mrs. Lyndon B. Johnson, and to Rabbi Morris S. Friedman for providing the photographs of President Ronald Reagan's visit to North Woodmere, New York.

During the course of preparing our manuscript, we consulted with many colleagues, friends, and experts who took time out of their busy schedules to answer our questions and advise us, to share with us material relating to the subject of the book, and/or to read and comment on sections of the manuscript. We wish to acknowledge and thank each of the following individuals, whose sharing of their insights and expertise surely helped to make this a better book: Elliott Abrams, Joshua Boettiger, Professor Marshall Breger, Barbara Burstin, Sheldon S. Cohen, Stephanie Deutsch, Evelyn Erez-Kadosha, Douglas J. Feith, Rabbi Abraham Feldbin, Ira N. Forman, Rabbi Morris Friedman, Dr. Joseph R. Goldyne, Rabbi Emanuel S. Goldsmith, Professor Henry Graff, Rabbi Joshua Haberman, Larry Hackman, Rabbi Arthur J. Kolatch, William Kristol, Lisa Lenkiewicz, Ambassador Charles Lichtenstein, Professor L. Sandy Maisel, Morton J. Merowitz, Rabbi Avis Miller, Rabbi Stanley Rabinowitz, Steven Rabinowitz, Scott Roley, John Rothman, Professor Jonathan D. Sarna, and Raymond Teichman.

The staff of Jonathan David Publishers has been extremely helpful in seeing the manuscript through its various stages of development. For their special efforts we would like to thank Barbara Burke, Thelma Kolatch, Fiorella deLima, and Debra Danis Seiden.

Very special thanks are due Judy Sandman for her exemplary editing of the complete manuscript.

Finally, we are indebted to Professor Henry F. Graff, one of the country's preeminent presidential scholars, for writing the introduction to this volume.

DAVID G. DALIN AND ALFRED J. KOLATCH

Introduction

by Henry F. Graff
Professor Emeritus of History
Columbia University

WHEN THE FIRST JEWS ARRIVED ON THESE shores in the seventeenth century, they brought with them a habit they had internalized long since, namely to be ever watchful of the doings of their rulers. The history of their people had given them ample reason: vigilance was indispensable to their safety as well as to their freedom to worship as Jews. When monarchs gave way to presidents in 1789, the old attentiveness was as strong as ever, but already it had taken new form. Jews were still mysterious people to many fellow Americans— George Washington, for instance, insisted on referring to them in one famous document with the odd locution of "the stock of Abraham." Yet Jews were beginning to play a formative role in the new nation and had begun to feel physically and spiritually comfortable in the New World atmosphere, openly practicing their religion without a by-your-leave from anybody. President Franklin Pierce, for instance, felt highly pleased to sign the charter for the Washington Hebrew Congregation—the first synagogue in the District of Columbia. Before many presidential terms had passed, Jews were entering the sanctuary of political power and playing their role in the governance of the nation.

The story of this marvelous transition is the substance of this rich book, which chronicles the connections between Jews and the presidents, administration by administration. David Dalin and Alfred J. Kolatch have mined the historical record in order to give us a segment of presidential history that has lain, for the most part, untouched. The reward for the reader is the discovery on a large scale of how Jews and those closely associated with them have left a mark on every major epoch in the nation's history, beginning with Alexander Hamilton, who, as a boy, had attended the Jewish school on the Caribbean island of Nevis.

Not all of the Jews present in the book were heroes to the nation at large. Haym Salomon, for instance, the Polish-born American patriot who helped to finance the American Revolution, was never adequately recognized for his sacrifice and service by the public, or by Congress. Some were handicapped more than others for being Jewish, like Mordecai Manuel Noah, a journalist and lawyer, whose father was a patriot of the Revolution. Noah was sent as consul to Tunis in James Madison's administration, but after four years at his post he was summarily removed by Secretary of State James Monroe, because, it was said, Noah's being a Jew made him unsatisfactory to the Muslim community of Tunisia. (On top of this affront to Noah, it was hinted that his financial accounts were not in order.) Some members of the Jewish faith, like the brilliant Judah P. Benjamin, earned only obloquy from the nation for his role as secretary of state of the Confederacy. Some were figures in the early history of the republic whose labors were still being celebrated in the twentieth century, like the naval officer Uriah P. Levy, for whom a destroyer escort was named in the Second World War, and whose name lives today on the facade of the Jewish chapel at the Norfolk Naval Base.

These pages show how the range of tasks undertaken by Jews has been as wide as the opportunities various presidents found for them. Among the names Dalin and Kolatch have resurrected, for instance, is that of John Hays, a fur trader, who was appointed by Madison to be collector of internal revenue for the Illinois Territory. David Naar is another. He was named by President Polk to be the commercial agent of the United States in Saint Thomas, Naar's birthplace. (Naar was later mayor of Elizabeth, New Jersey.) And as the years rolled, and government became more complex and demanding of talent, Jews were serving almost everywhere, in Congress, on international missions, and finally on the Supreme Court of the United States—Louis D. Brandeis being elevated in 1916.

Today, no place seems unavailable to qualified Jews. As long ago as 1869, when General Grant was barely in the White House, he offered the post of secretary of the treasury to Joseph Seligman, who turned it down. Oscar Straus, appointed in 1906 by President Theodore Roosevelt to be secretary of commerce and labor, became therefore the first Jewish cabinet officer. Still, not until relatively recently has the appointment of Jews to the cabinet become so ordinary that it is no longer commented upon as remarkable by the mainstream media. The material to examine that whole transformation will be found in abundance in this book.

It is not too much to say that the presidents have shared in their youths in the culture of social anti-Semitism, and it is unlikely that until recently any of them grew up with Jewish playmates. So it is not a surprise that in their private conversations and writings they have sometimes uttered distasteful words about Jews. The examples are legion: Theodore Roosevelt angrily discussing Herbert Croly, author of *The Promise of American Life* and a founder of *The New Republic*; Harry Truman, on his way to the battlefront during the First World War, writing to his beloved Bess that he was in "Jew York"; Richard Nixon expressing on his infamous tapes hostility and scorn for his Jewish critics. Still, in their public performance the presidents have evidenced no such bigotry, not even Nixon, who made Henry Kissinger his secretary of state and Arthur F. Burns chairman of the Federal Reserve Board.

The protests of American presidents against so many major anti-Semitic outbursts abroad provide good evidence of admirable presidential humanity. The worst example of official anti-Semitism in American history may have been Ulysses S. Grant's now famous Order No. 11 during the Civil War, expelling "the Jews as a class" (who were accused of smuggling cotton and other contraband) from the Department of the Tennessee. The order was rescinded soon after it was issued through the intervention of President Lincoln. Grant, who was no bigot himself, in later years regarded the issuance of his order as the one public act of his that he most regretted.

It is a remarkable tribute to the authors' presentation as well as to their meticulous research that this is a "reading" book, as well as a work for the reference shelf. The biographies that stud the chapters, taken together, constitute a who's who of Jewish achievers in the political, military, and diplomatic history of the country. The roll call found here will, of course, always remain unfinished, for, as the line of the presidents lengthens, there will be new names to add and report upon, but scholars who write on the theme hereafter will be everlastingly in debt to this indispensable work.

The Presidents
of the United States
& the Jews

George Washington

Served from 1789 to 1797

Born on February 22, 1732, in Westmoreland County, Virginia

Member of the Episcopal denomination

Married Martha Dandridge Custis, a widow with two children,
on January 6, 1759

Had no natural children, two adopted children

Candidate of the Federalist Party

Vice president under Washington: John Adams

First Inaugural Address delivered on April 30, 1789, in New York City
Second Inaugural Address delivered on March 4, 1793, in Philadelphia

Died on December 14, 1799, in Mount Vernon, Virginia

First President of the United States

WHEN GEORGE WASHINGTON RAN FOR the presidency for the first time in 1789, he was so popular a figure that not one of the sixty-nine electors cast a vote against him. He carried ten states: Connecticut, Delaware, Georgia, Maryland, Massachusetts, New Hampshire, New Jersey, Pennsylvania, South Carolina, and Virginia. Of the three remaining states, New York had been unable to decide which electors to send, and Rhode Island and North Carolina had not yet ratified the Constitution. When Washington was unanimously reelected in 1793, he garnered the electoral votes of all thirteen states.

How does one account for the immense popularity of a man who had been in public life for more than twenty years before ascending to the presidency and who surely must have alienated many people during that time? The manner in which the first president of the United States of America conducted his life—that is, the way he treated both friend and adversary—is the answer to the enigma.

Early Years

Little is known about Washington's youth except that he was a child of his father's second marriage. The elder Washington was a wealthy businessman who was often away from home tending to business affairs in distant states as well as Britain. Interaction between the two was minimal and, sadly, when George was but eleven years old, his father died.

George grew into a large, strong man: In his prime he was 6 feet 2 inches tall and weighed upwards of 175 pounds. He preferred the soli-tude of an outdoor life and learned the art of surveying, which became his primary occupation.

On his twenty-first birthday George received an inheritance from his father's estate: several thousand acres of land, ten slaves, plus a portion of his father's personal property. Five years later, on January 6, 1759, George married Martha Dandridge Custis, a widow with two small children.

Entering the Public Arena

George Washington's introduction to public life began in 1749 when he accepted an appointment as surveyor of Culpepper County, in his home state of Virginia. In 1752 he received his first military appointment as a major in the Virginia militia. As a reward for admirable service, he was elevated to lieutenant colonel in 1754 and to full colonel in 1755. In December 1758, after being elected the previous July as one of Frederick County's two representatives to the House of Burgesses, forerunner of the U.S. Congress, he resigned from the militia. Washington served in the House of Burgesses until 1774, when he was elected to the First Continental Congress.

Washington was always eager to find common ground with Britain, but after a while saw that the British were unprepared to compromise on any of the issues dividing the two sides. The arbitrary imposition of taxes upon the colonists was one of many issues that led Washington to join the revolutionary forces that wanted to secure complete independence from the rule of Britain. War seemed inevitable, and on June 15, 1775, the Continental Congress turned to Washington to be commander in chief of the Continental Army.

By 1776, when the revolution had begun in earnest, there were comparatively few Jews in all of colonial America. In 1790, when the first federal census was taken, the Jewish population was between 1,300 and 1,500 souls out of a total population of 3,929,214. Between 300 and 350 of them lived in New York City, and most of the remainder resided in other port cities: Newport, Rhode Island; Philadelphia, Pennsylvania; Charles Town (later Charleston), South Carolina; and Savannah, Georgia. These cities were chosen by the newly arrived Jews because a great many were involved in the import-export business. Others, not involved in international trade, chose these port cities because they preferred to live among their own.

Some Jews, although comparatively few in number, did ultimately settle in towns with sparse Jewish populations. In *Golden Door to America*, historian Abraham J. Karp illustrates one of the problems encountered by an early settler in the 1790s. Rebecca Samuel of Petersburg, Virginia, wrote to her parents in Hamburg, Germany, in 1791: "You cannot know what a wonderful country this is for the common. One can live here peacefully." But at the same time, she lamented the poor condition of Jewish life: "I know quite well you will not want me to bring up my children like Gentiles. Here, they cannot become anything else. Jewishness is pushed aside here. There are here ten or twelve Jews, and they are not worthy of being called Jews . . . We do not know what the Sabbath and holidays are. On the Sabbath all the shops are open . . . . but ours we do not allow to open."

By and large the earliest Jewish settlers in America were satisfied with their lot, enjoying freedom and the rights of domicile, trade, and worship, although not the right to hold public office.

The wealthier Jews found British rule and the system of taxation overly burdensome and sided strongly with Washington's efforts to rid America of British domination. Perhaps more than anything else, however, what made the Jews of colonial America side with Washington was his reputation for being fair and honest. It was a belief shared by most of Washington's countrymen. It was the stuff from which myths grow.

The Tale of the Cherry Tree

Evidence of the positive impression Washington left upon most of the colonists was never better illustrated than by the efforts of one clergyman, Mason Locke Weems (1759–1825), also known as Parson Weems. He was a bookseller and an author who, in 1800, wrote a biography entitled *The Life and Memorable Actions of George Washington*. Critics found the book filled with inaccuracies and misinformation, but this did not bother Weems. His purpose was to set Washington on a pedestal so that he might serve as a moral model for the youth of America. Weems's biography sold well, and in 1806, when he issued the fifth edition of the book, he decided to enhance Washington's reputation even further by creating the "I cannot tell a lie" myth. One day, Weems wrote, George's father found that one of his cherry trees had been cut down. Suspecting that some innocent person might be accused falsely of perpetrating the foul act, George acknowledged that he was the culprit. This lesson in honesty, which grew out of dishonesty, has been used ever since by teachers and preachers, and was greatly appreciated by Jews because of its roots in the biblical Decalogue. A painting of the scene, created by artist Grant Wood more than a century later, helped keep the myth alive.

Washington Wins the Hearts of the Jews

Although General George Washington was not successful in all of his military engagements during the Revolutionary War, he did win the respect and admiration of members of the Continental Congress who appointed him commander in chief. He never used power to impose his personal will upon the colonists, always supporting the rulings of the Congress even when he was in disagreement. Humble and deferential in his dealings with people, Washington's modest demeanor was appreciated by the small Jewish population, as it was by the overall citizenry. Even those Jews who had emigrated from England, where they had been

A street in Jerusalem is named after the first president of the United States.

treated well and were now numbered among the British Tories or Loyalists to the Crown, valued the kindly American leader whose integrity was unimpeachable, despite the fact that he was fighting Britain.

Most Jews stood solidly behind Washington, and when he issued a call for volunteers, approximately one hundred responded by joining local and state militias. Considering that the total Jewish population at the time numbered less than two thousand, one hundred volunteers was substantial representation. One militia company in particular, situated in Charleston, South Carolina, consisted of such a preponderance of young Jews that it became known as "Jew Company."

Francis Salvador

One of the first Jews to join Washington's Continental Army was Francis Salvador (1747–1776) of South Carolina. Prior to his enlistment, he was the first Jew ever to hold elective office in the colonies, having served as a delegate to the Revolutionary Provincial Congresses of 1775 and 1776.

The Cherokee Indians had been recruited by the British to serve as scouts. They were very familiar with the terrain, which was totally strange to the colonist militias. In 1776, shortly after he donned his uniform, Salvador was captured, scalped, and murdered by the Cherokees.

Benjamin Nones

Benjamin Nones (1757-1826) was a French Jew who migrated to America from Bordeaux around 1772 and settled in Philadelphia. When the Revolutionary War broke out, he joined the Continental Army, serving in General Casimir Pulaski's legion. His abilities were quickly recognized, and before long he became a major on General Washington's staff. During the siege of Savannah, Nones distinguished himself for bravery.

After the war he became active in the antislavery movement while serving as president of Philadelphia's Congregation Mikveh Israel and an officer of the first organized charity, the Society of Ezrath Orchim.

David Salisbury Franks

One of the highest ranking Jews who fought in the Revolutionary War was David Salisbury Franks (c.1743–1793). Born in Philadelphia, he studied at what is now the University of Pennsylvania and, for a while, settled in Montreal, where he became a merchant and an active member of the Jewish community. In 1775 he was elected president of Montreal's Sephardic Congregation Shearith Israel. He left Canada in 1776 and returned to Pennsylvania, where he came to the attention of Brigadier General Benedict Arnold, a soldier acclaimed for his courage and heroism in battle. Franks became Arnold's aide-de-camp.

Despite the fact that Arnold had become an American hero, he was terribly disappointed when in 1777 Congress elevated five officers to the rank of major general and he was not among them. At that point Arnold wanted to leave the army, but George Washington, the supreme commander, persuaded him to stay.

In 1778 Arnold was assigned command of the troops in Philadelphia. He began spending money beyond his means and making sympathetic overtures toward the British. For his offense he was court-martialed. Although he was cleared and not punished, he was reprimanded for exercising poor judgment.

Offended at the lack of gratitude shown him for years of courageous service, Arnold harbored deep feelings of resentment. In 1780, after being appointed commandant of West Point, a fort on the western bank of the Hudson River that guarded New York City to the south, he began to correspond with the enemy and hatched a plot whereby he would surrender the fort to British general Sir Henry Clinton. The plot was uncovered before it could be executed, and Arnold fled to New York City, where he joined the British military forces with the rank of brigadier general.

Arnold's military aide, David Franks, was totally unaware of Arnold's doings but, nevertheless, was brought up on charges of espionage and collaborating with the enemy. Benedict Arnold wanted to shield the good name of his loyal aide, and on September 20, 1780, he wrote to George Washington attesting that Franks had no knowledge of his treasonous activities and should not be held accountable.

Despite Arnold's intervention, on October 2, 1780, Franks was arrested. He was tried the next day, but the evidence against him was weak, and he was found not guilty. Dissatisfied, Franks asked General Washington to appoint a court of inquiry to examine his record. Washington obliged, and on November 2, 1780, the court convened at West Point and exonerated Major Franks completely. The next year he was promoted to lieutenant colonel.

David Franks continued to serve the cause of the colonists. In 1781 he was sent by Superintendent of Finance Robert Morris to Europe with messages for John Jay (later the first chief justice of the U.S. Supreme Court) and Benjamin Franklin. Jay and Franklin were in France trying to negotiate loans from the French and Dutch to help finance the American Revolution. In 1785 Franks was appointed vice consul at Marseilles, and in 1789, upon retiring, and in recognition for his service to his country, David Franks was granted four hundred acres of land.

Haym Salomon

Of all the Jews in the colonial period who believed in George Washington, Polish-born Haym Salomon (1740–1785) is most noteworthy. Salomon immigrated to New York in 1772, at age thirty-two, and entered the brokerage business. When the war broke out he moved to Philadelphia, where he began dealing in the sale of Continental bills of exchange for hard Dutch and French currencies. The government needed funds for the purchase of supplies and ammunition, and although Salomon could have gouged the government, he was satisfied to earn a very modest one-quarter of one percent on his transactions. The Continental Congress appreciated Salomon's selflessness and appointed him official broker to the Office of Finance of the United States.

Throughout the eight years of struggle against the British, Salomon raised funds for Washington's revolutionary forces. Time and again, month after month and year after year, Washington turned to Salomon because Congress and the state assemblies were not forthcoming in allocating sufficient monies for supplies, ammunition, and salaries. Over many years Salomon advanced more than $200,000, often borrowing funds to satisfy Washington's needs.

The British were well aware of Salomon's innocent activities, yet, in September 1776, they arrested him as a spy. After being released, in August 1778, he was once again charged with espionage. He was arrested and sentenced to death, but escaped.

When Haym Salomon died on January 6, 1785, at age forty-five, leaving behind a widow and young children, it was reported that he owed financial institutions $638,000.

Salomon's role in saving the Revolution was never fully recognized by Congress or the American people. In 1941, a statue of George Washington was erected in Chicago, Illinois, in which the president is flanked by Robert Morris and Haym Salomon, small acknowledgment for the man who gave his fortune to save his country. But even this was not backed by the U.S. government; the Chicago statue was paid for by funds raised from the Jews of Chicago.

It wasn't until 1976, when America celebrated the centennial of the U.S. Postal Service, that a ten-cent stamp was issued to honor all of Salomon's efforts as a true patriot.

The Touro Family

It was during the visit of George Washington to the Touro Synagogue (originally called Kahal Kadosh Yeshuat Yisrael) in Newport, Rhode Island, in 1790 that the first president of the United States was able to express his appreciation for the backing and loyalty of Jews during the Revolution.

The Touro Synagogue was built and sustained by the family of Isaac Touro (1740–1784), a *chazzan* (cantor) who arrived in Newport from Curaçao in 1760. Isaac had two sons, Abraham (1774–1822) and Judah (1775–1854), both of whom grew extremely wealthy and were widely known for their generosity to Jewish and non-Jewish causes. Abraham settled in New Orleans, where he established a large shipping business. Subsequently, he moved to Boston. Judah settled in New Orleans and made a fortune in the import business.

Despite their departure from Newport, the city where they grew up, their loyalty to it and to the synagogue their father served never wavered. Judah in particular, a bachelor who outlived his brother by many decades, provided considerable funds for its maintenance.

President Washington visited the Touro Synagogue on August 17, 1790. One day after his visit, when he was ready to leave Newport, Moses Seixas, warden of the synagogue, along with a delegation from the congregation, called on the president and presented him with two letters of affection, expressing appreciation for his leadership. The more famous of the two reads:

> To the President of the United States
> of America
>
> Sir
>
> Permit the children of the Stock of Abraham to approach you with the most cordial affection and esteem for your person and merits and to join with our fellow-citizens in welcoming you to Newport.
>
> With pleasure we reflect on those days—

those days of difficulty and danger—when the God of Israel who delivered David from the peril of the sword shielded your head in the day of battle. And we rejoice to think that the same Spirit, who rested in the Bosom of the greatly beloved Daniel enabling him to preside over the Provinces of the Babylonian Empire, rests, and ever will rest upon you, enabling you to discharge the arduous duties of the Chief Magistrate in these states.

Deprived as we heretofore have been of the invaluable rights of free citizens, we now, with a deep sense of gratitude to the Almighty Disposer of all events, behold a Government erected by the Majesty of the People, a Government which to bigotry gives no sanction, to persecution no assistance, but generously

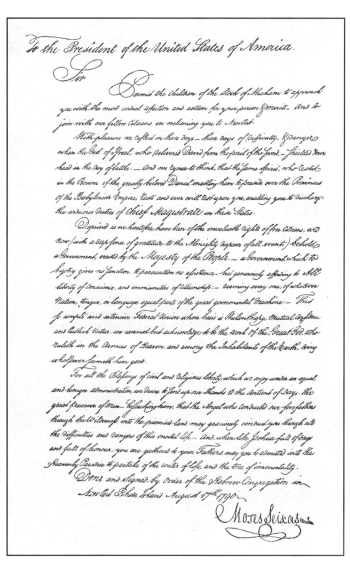

A facsimile of the letter delivered to George Washington on August 18, 1790, by a delegation of Jews led by Moses Seixas, warden of the Touro Synagogue.

affording to All liberty of conscience and immunities of citizenship, deeming every one, of whatever nation, tongue, or language equal parts of the great governmental machine. . . .

For all the blessings of civil and religious liberty which we enjoy under an equal and benign administration, we desire to send up our thanks to the Ancient of Days, the great Preserver of Men, beseeching him that the angel who conducted our forefathers through the wilderness into the promised land may graciously conduct you through all the difficulties and dangers of this mortal life. And when like Joshua, full of days and full of honor, you are gathered to your Fathers, may you be admitted into the Heavenly Paradise to partake of the water of life and the tree of immortality.

George Washington immediately responded to this warm letter with these words, some of which have become immortal:

Gentlemen:

While I receive with much satisfaction your address replete with expressions of affection and esteem, I rejoice in the opportunity of assuring you that I shall always retain a grateful remembrance of the cordial welcome I experienced in my visit to New Port from all classes of citizens. . . .

The citizens of the United States of America have a right to applaud themselves for having given to mankind examples of an enlarged

and liberal policy, a policy worthy of imitation.

All possess alike liberty of conscience and immunities of citizenship. It is now no more that toleration is spoken of, as if it was by the indulgence of one class of people that another enjoyed the exercise of their inherent natural rights. For happily the government of the United States, which gives to bigotry no sanction, to persecution no assistance, requires only that they who live under its protection should demean themselves as good citizens, in giving it on all occasions their effectual support.

It would be inconsistent with the frankness of my character not to avow that I am pleased with your favorable opinion of my administration and fervent wishes for my felicity.

May the children of the stock of Abraham who dwell in this land continue to merit and enjoy the good will of the other inhabitants, while every one shall sit in safety under his own vine and fig tree, and there shall be none to make him afraid.

May the Father of all mercies scatter light and not darkness in our paths, and make us all in our several vocations useful here, and, in his own due time and way, everlastingly happy.

G. Washington

In the months following his inauguration on April 30, 1789, Washington had received and responded warmly to messages of congratulations and support from rabbis and leaders of congregations in New York City, Savannah, Charleston, Richmond, and Philadelphia. He was praised for his opposition to religious bigotry and for furthering the principle of religious freedom for all citizens.

Alexander Hamilton's Jewish Connection

In times of war and peace no one was of greater support to Washington than Alexander Hamilton (c.1755–1804). He served as Washington's aide-de-camp during the Revolutionary War and later as the first secretary of the Treasury. He created the Bank of the United States, es-

The Touro Synagogue, in Newport, Rhode Island.

Alexander Hamilton

tablished a national currency, and secured the nation's credit here and abroad. But little is known about his Jewish "heritage."

Alexander Hamilton's mother, a non-Jew, was the daughter of a French physician. Her first marriage was to Michael Lavine, a Jew of Danish decent, but the union was unhappy and Lavine soon left. Soon thereafter Rachel met James Hamilton, a drifter of Scottish ancestry, and in 1752 the two began living together, although Rachel was still legally married to Lavine (they were not divorced until 1759). Alexander Hamilton was born in 1755 on the island of Nevis in the British West Indies, one of Britain's Caribbean possessions. So, it can be said that through his mother's first marriage Hamilton had a rather indirect Jewish connection.

Hamilton was aware, early on, of the fact that he was an illegitimate child, but he always insisted that "my blood is as good as those who plume themselves on their ancestry." Because of his tainted birth, he was denied early schooling in the Anglican parish in Nevis and instead received instruction in Nevis's Jewish school.

The anti-Semitism Hamilton encountered in his early youth was still prevalent when he became a leading figure in Washington's administration. As secretary of the treasury, when he introduced proposals to have the government fund war debts, he was attacked for having Jewish moneylending interests at heart.

Last Years

After leaving office on March 4, 1799, Washington and his wife, Martha, returned to his vast estate in Mount Vernon, Virginia, where he devoted himself to overseeing the many repairs required because of the years of neglect while he was serving the new nation. He received many guests and visitors, and Martha was a gracious hostess.

Washington was kept informed of important events by Secretary of War McHenry, especially because of the brewing tension between France and the United States and the possibility of a renewed military conflict. The situation became so acute that on July 4, 1798, Washington was commissioned lieutenant general and commander in chief of American forces. Fortunately, his services were not required.

On December 12, 1799, in snowy, freezing weather, Washington mounted his horse and spent five hours out-of-doors inspecting his plantation. The next day he developed chills and a sore throat, and began to experience difficulty in breathing. Three doctors attended him, but to no avail.

At ten o'clock P.M. on December 14 he whispered to his aide, Tobias Lear, "I am just going. Have me decently buried and do not let my body be put into a vault in less than two days after I am dead. Do you understand me?" "Yes, sir," replied Lear. "'Tis well," said Washington, and he expired.

Washington has often been characterized as nonreligious because he did not belong to any organized Christian denomination and was not affiliated with a particular church. It likewise has been pointed out that in his speeches and writings he did not express a belief in a personal God, but referred to God as Providence or the Almighty. To Washington God was an intangible, incorporeal, supernatural power that controlled men's lives. He fashioned for himself a moral code based upon a belief in what is right, and it is this code of conduct that governed his life and endeared him to the Jewish populace as well as to the entire citizenry of America.

[A.J.K.]

John Adams

Served from 1797 to 1801

Born on October 30, 1735, in Braintree (now Quincy), Massachusetts

Member of the Unitarian denomination

Married Abigail Smith on October 25, 1764

Father to one daughter and three sons; the eldest son,* John Quincy Adams,
later became the sixth president

Candidate of the Federalist Party

Vice president under Adams: Thomas Jefferson

Inaugural Address delivered on March 4, 1797, in Philadelphia

Died on July 4, 1826, in Quincy, Massachusetts

* Throughout the volume, only offspring who lived to maturity are included.

Second President of the United States

AFTER SERVING TWO TERMS AS GEORGE Washington's vice president (1789–1797), an office he considered not only boring but "the most insignificant office that ever the invention of man contrived or his imagination conceived." In the presidential election of 1796 John Adams pitted himself for the presidency against the popular Thomas Jefferson. Jefferson had served in Washington's Cabinet but subsequently resigned.

Supported by Washington, Adams won the electoral vote over Jefferson by 71 to 68, and, having come in second, Jefferson became vice president (as was the rule until 1804). The voters at large apparently favored the kind of strong central government advocated by Washington, and now by Adams, as opposed to placing power in the hands of the relatively inexperienced leaders of the individual states. Jefferson had proposed that states have the authority to reject the federal laws they deemed unconstitutional.

The country's small Jewish population favored Adams, although Adams had little if any direct contact with Jews and was probably unaware of their support. Adams's only knowledge of Jews, or interest in them, was derived from the Bible, and whatever association he had with Jews began only after he left office in 1801.

Growing Up

In physical makeup and intellectual prowess Adams and Washington were almost complete opposites. Whereas Washington was tall (6 feet 2 inches), well-built, and muscular, weighing variously between 175 and 200 pounds, Adams was short (5 feet 6 inches), stocky, and overweight.

And while Washington's schooling was limited to reading newspapers for the most part, Adams was a Harvard College graduate (1755) and a voracious reader who was proud of the fine personal library he had assembled. One of his regrets was that he did not have enough time "to learn Semitic tongues."

In an attempt to keep his portliness in check, Adams would walk as much as five miles at one time. While his efforts at keeping physically fit did not always yield the desired result, his nimble mind and intellectual prowess were appealing to the opposite sex.

In 1762, Adams met Abigail Smith, a pretty, petite, seventeen-year-old girl who forever had her nose in a book. A sickly child, she had never received a formal education. Ultimately, however, the self-taught Abigail would turn out to be one of the most learned of all first ladies.

On October 25, 1764, over the protestations of a distraught mother, who felt her daughter was wasting her life on an ill-mannered country lawyer, nineteen-year-old Abigail Smith married twenty-eight-year-old John Adams. They would be the first couple to occupy the White House, in 1800 called the President's House, when the seat of government was transferred from Philadelphia, Pennsylvania, to Washington, D.C.

The XYZ Affair

In 1797 French privateers began harassing American merchant ships, and war with France appeared imminent. President Adams sent a three-man mission to France to reduce the hostility and try to resolve the differences, but French foreign minister Talleyrand refused to receive the envoys and instead ordered three of his agents to demand what amounted to a $250,000 bribe before he would consider settling the conflict. Adams was deeply hurt at Talleyrand's unstatesmanlike conduct, and he proceeded to prepare for war. Refusing to believe that the situation was quite so serious, Jefferson and others asked to see the diplomatic dispatches.

On March 19, 1798, President Adams informed Congress of the failure of attempts to negotiate with France. He then made public all the documents but omitted the names of the bribe-seekers, substituting the letters XYZ. As a result of the revelations, anti-French sentiment mounted, and a general resentment of foreigners ensued.

To calm the unsettled mood in the country and end the strong clamor for war with France, Adams declared that May 8 was to be set aside as a day for prayer, fasting, and soul-searching. The Jews of New York City were called to assemble in their synagogue, where they heard a sermon delivered by the Reverend Gershom Mendes Seixas, who, like Thomas Jefferson, advocated a conciliatory approach in dealing with France, reminding his congregants that France was the first nation in Europe to grant citizenship to Jews. Not all rabbis adopted as pacifistic an approach.

Alien and Sedition Acts of 1798

In 1795, the year before Adams had become president, the third partition of Poland had taken place, and the country was divided among Russia, Prussia, and Austria. Thousands of additional Jews were now under Russian rule; conditions were oppressive, and many Jews wished to leave to join relatives in the United States. But the Alien and Sedition Acts of 1798—legislation that was encouraged in part by the XYZ Affair—would stand in the way of new immigration.

The first of the four-part legislation was the Naturalization Act. Although intended to limit French immigration, it made it more difficult for Jews to bring relatives to the United States from Russia and other parts of Europe. What disturbed American Jews was the inclusion in the Naturalization Act of the words "other foreigners," which they considered a euphemism for Jews.

Benjamin Nones

When Jews became aware that Adams, along with other Federalist Party members who advocated a strong federal government, backed the Naturalization Act (later to be repealed), they shifted their support from him to the anti-Federalist Republicans led by Thomas Jefferson. Quite likely, the Jewish vote helped sweep Jefferson into the presidency in 1800, after Adams had served but one term.

Benjamin Nones, a French Jew who had immigrated to America in the early 1770s and had served as a major on George Washington's staff during the Revolutionary War, was an ardent Jeffersonian. In August 1800 he participated in the Republican convention, held in Philadelphia, which chose Thomas Jefferson as its candidate for the presidency.

The city's leading Federalist newspaper, *The Gazette of the United States*, was critical of all who attended the Republican convention, singling out Nones as "a Jew, a Republican, and poor." Nones replied to the criticism immediately and passionately in the *Aurora*, the city's Jeffersonian newspaper, on August 11, 1800:

> . . . I am a *Jew*. I glory in belonging to that persuasion, which even its opponents, whether Christian, or Mahomedan [*sic*], allow to be of divine origin—of that persuasion on which Christianity was originally founded, and must ultimately rest—which has preserved its faith secure and undefiled, for near 3,000 years—whose votaries have never murdered each other in religious wars, or cherished the theological hatred so general, so unextinguishable among those who revile them. . . .
>
> I am a *Republican!* . . . I have not been so proud or so prejudiced as to renounce the cause for which I have *fought*, as an American, throughout the whole of the revolutionary war. . . .
>
> I am a Jew, and if for no other reason, for that reason I am a Republican. . . . In republics we have *rights*, in monarchies we live but to experience *wrongs*. . . .
>
> How then can a Jew but be a Republican? . . .
>
> But I am *poor*, I am so, my family also is large, but soberly and decently brought up.

They have not been taught to revile a Christian, because his religion is not *so old* as theirs . . .

Appreciation of Judaism

Although he lost the Jewish vote in his 1800 reelection campaign, John Adams's rational approach to religion, which he declared was "founded on the love of God and my neighbor," explains his appreciation for Judaism and the contribution of Jews to the making of a better world. This attitude is most evident in letters he wrote to Dutch jurist Francis Adrian Van der Kemp (1783–1825). In a communication dated December 31, 1808 (discovered in 1947 in the archives of the Historical Society of Pennsylvania by Rabbi Isidore S. Myer, who was the librarian of the American Jewish Historical Society), the then retired second president of the United States wrote that he was appalled at Voltaire's derogatory attitude toward the Bible and the Jewish people:

> Dear Sir:
>
> How is it possible this old fellow [Voltaire] should represent the Hebrews in such a contemptible light? They are the most glorious nation that ever inhabited this earth. The Romans and their empire were but a bauble in comparison to the Jews. They have given religion in three quarters of the globe and have influenced the affairs of mankind more and happily than any other nation, ancient or modern.
>
> Yours to the last,
> John Adams

And again, in a letter to Van der Kemp dated February 18, 1809, John Adams wrote:

> . . . In spite of Bolingbroke and Voltaire, I will insist that the Hebrews have done more to civilize men than any other nation. If I were an atheist and believed in blind eternal fate, I should still believe that fate had ordained the Jews to be the most essential instrument for civilizing nations. If I were an atheist of the other sect, who believe, or pretend to believe, that all is ordered by chance, I should believe

> that chance had ordered the Jews to preserve and propagate to all mankind the doctrine of a supreme, intelligent, wise, almighty Sovereign of the universe, which I believe to be the great essential principle of all morality, and consequently of all civilization. I cannot say that I love the Jews very much, nor the French, nor the English, nor the Romans, nor the Greeks. We must love all nations as well as we can, but it is very hard to love most of them.

Adams was sincere in his admiration for Jews and their contribution to civilization and would urge that Hebraic studies be a part of a classical curriculum.

Mordecai Manuel Noah

During the years of his retirement, Adams had considerable contact with prominent and aggressive Mordecai Manuel Noah (1785–1851). Born in Philadelphia in 1785, Noah was the son of a Sephardic mother and an Ashkenazic father who had fought in the Revolutionary War. Orphaned by age six, he was raised by his maternal grandparents in Charleston, South Carolina, but returned to Philadelphia to attend school, where he pursued a career in journalism and became involved in Democratic politics. He then joined the Pennsylvania militia and at age eighteen, in 1803, was appointed a major. This ambitious personality was later to serve briefly as consul to Tunis under President James Madison.

On May 28, 1818, Noah delivered an address at the consecration of New York's Mill Street Synagogue. He later sent a copy of the speech to John Adams, who replied as follows:

> I wish your nation [of Jews] may be admitted to all privileges of citizens in every country of the world. This country has done much. I wish it may do more, and annul every narrow idea in religion, government, and commerce. Let the wits joke, the philosophers sneer! What then? It has pleased the Providence of "first cause," the universal cause, that Abraham should give religion, not only to Hebrews, but to Christians and Mahometans [*sic*], the greatest part of the modern civilized world.

A portrait of President John Adams holding the Declaration of Independence.

THE PRESIDENTS OF THE UNITED STATES *&* THE JEWS

Despite the felicitous tone of Adams's response to Noah's communication, a follow-up letter dated March 15, 1819, was sent to Noah in which the ex-president made it clear that he hoped Jews would soon wear away some of the asperities and peculiarities of their character and possibly, in time, become liberal Unitarian Christians. It also was reported that in private Adams referred to Noah disrespectfully as "the Jew."

Last Days

Although disappointed in his failure to win re-election in 1800, outwardly Adams accepted defeat by Thomas Jefferson gracefully, saying, "Let me have my farm, my family and goose quill, and all the honors and offices this world has to bestow may go to those who deserve them better and desire them more. I court them not." Inwardly, critics say, he was so angry over his defeat that he refused to attend Jefferson's inauguration on March 4, 1801.

John Adams lived to see his son, John Quincy, elected president in 1824. On July 4, 1826, in Quincy, Massachusetts, on the fiftieth anniversary of the signing of the Declaration of Independence, John Adams died. On that very same day, just a few hours earlier, his successor, President Thomas Jefferson, also died.

[A.J.K.]

Thomas Jefferson

Served from 1801 to 1809

Born on April 13, 1743, in Shadwell, Virginia

Subscriber to the deist philosophy

Married Martha Wayles Skelton, a widow, on January 1, 1772

Father to two daughters

Candidate of the Democratic-Republican Party

Vice president under Jefferson: Aaron Burr (first term);
George Clinton (second term)

First Inaugural Address delivered on March 4, 1801
Second Inaugural Address delivered on March 4, 1805
Both addresses delivered in Washington, D.C.

Died on July 4, 1826, at Monticello Estate, Virginia

Third President of the United States

THOMAS JEFFERSON IS RECOGNIZED generally as having been the most talented and erudite president ever to have occupied the White House. President John F. Kennedy gave expression to this sentiment when, on April 29, 1962, he said to an assembled group of Nobel laureates:

> I think this is the most extraordinary collection of talent, of human knowledge, that has ever been gathered together at the White House, with the possible exception of when Thomas Jefferson dined alone.

Formative Years

Little is known of Jefferson's early childhood except that his father, Peter, was a prominent, successful landowner who was appointed executor of his friend John Randolph's estate. To fulfill this obligation, Peter moved his family from its home in Shadwell, Virginia, to Randolph's estate in Tuckahoe, Virginia, where for the next six years Thomas played with Randolph's children, read books, and hiked in the woods.

From age nine to fourteen, Thomas studied in Reverend William Douglas's school in Northam, Virginia, where he became proficient in French. From his fourteenth to sixteenth year, he pursued studies in the school of another reverend, Mr. Maury, a classical scholar.

In 1760, at age seventeen, Jefferson enrolled in the college of William and Mary at Williamsburg, where he proved to be a superior student. There, he studied law in addition to philosophy and, after a five-year apprenticeship, in April 1767, was admitted to the Virginia bar. He then rode the circuit from 1767 to 1769, practicing law in most of the counties in Virginia. Word of Jefferson's talents quickly spread, leading to an appointment to the House of Burgesses. In 1775 he became a member of the Continental Congress, of which John Hancock was president. Shortly thereafter, in 1776, Thomas Jefferson was appointed to the committee assigned the task of drafting a declaration of independence. Other members of the committee included John Adams and Benjamin Franklin.

Recognized by the committee as the most educated and literate of its members, as well as a master of prose, Jefferson was chosen to prepare the first draft of the declaration. He was urged to complete the task quickly, and this he did between June 11 and June 28, 1776.

John Adams was of the opinion that most of the ideas in Jefferson's draft were old—that in actuality they were drawn from the writings of John Locke. Nevertheless, Adams conceded that "the immortal phraseology of the preamble was strictly Jefferson's creation."

The Declaration of Independence

Despite the fact that the Declaration of Independence sets forth the fundamental human rights to which every citizen is entitled and proclaims that "all men are created equal" and that "they are endowed by their Creator with certain unalienable rights . . ." it does not condemn the inequality represented by the institution of slavery. The framers of the Declaration knew full well that if it included such a statement it would not pass muster with the Southern delegates. Each state had its own constitution, and each state dealt with the slavery problem as it saw fit.

Jefferson's critics point to the inconsistencies in his seemingly antislavery rhetoric by noting that he held hundreds of slaves, many of whom he inherited at age fourteen upon the death of his father, and 135 of which his wife, the widow Martha Wayles Skelton, brought to their marriage. Jefferson made no attempt to free those slaves, and it is reported that he acquired eight more while serving as president. Upon leaving office, it was by the toil of his black slaves that Jefferson built the mansion at Monticello.

Nonetheless, even Jefferson's most severe detractors, while faulting him for his seeming hypocrisy, did credit him with initiating the idea of legislation that would eliminate slave trade throughout the United States. Passionate about the democratic way of life, Jefferson recognized the need to protect the civil rights of the individual. He articulated this belief in a private letter to his friend Dr. Benjamin Rush during the 1800 campaign for the presidency. "I have sworn on the altar of God eternal hostility against every form of tyranny of the mind of men."

The Wall of Separation

In his home state of Virginia, Jefferson had fought long and hard to remove from its books a law on "disabilities for dissenters and Jews." As president, he continued the battle for civil rights for all citizens regardless of their religious persuasion, but he was careful not to allow his own religious beliefs to influence his conduct as president.

Jefferson was an acknowledged deist. He believed in a Creator, but not in a God who was involved in human affairs. He believed in reason, not Revelation, and he cared little about debating whether God does or does not exist (which led to his being branded an atheist). Jefferson believed that each individual is entitled to his or her own religious view. "It does me no injury," he once said, "for my neighbors to say that there are twenty gods or no God. It neither picks my pocket nor breaks my leg."

Thomas Jefferson made his feelings about the mixing of religion with affairs of state very clear when, upon becoming president in 1801, he broke with the practice established by Washington and Adams of proclaiming Thanksgiving Day "a day of national prayer." When implored by a clergyman to continue the custom of his predecessors, he replied: "I consider the government of the United States as interdicted by the Constitution from intermeddling with religious institutions [and it is not] for the interest of religion to invite the civil magistrates to direct its exercises."

Nonetheless, believing that a nation's leader must be a role model for all its citizens, Jefferson consciously set aside his religious doubts and attended church services. He could be seen on a Sunday morning going to church carrying a large red prayer book under his left arm. When a stranger once observed the president in this mode, he said to him, "Why, Mr. President, you don't believe a word of it!"

"Sir," Jefferson answered, "no nation has yet existed or been governed without religion. I, as the Chief Magistrate of this nation, am bound to give it the sanction of my example. Good morning, Sir."

There were approximately six thousand Jews in the country when Jefferson took office, and they found great comfort in his advocacy of religious freedom. They were particularly pleased that he insisted that the wall separating religion and government be maintained and respected, as guaranteed by the First Amendment to the Constitution.

To make the idea of "a wall of separation of church and state" a reality in Virginia, Jefferson wrote a bill that at first was turned down by the assembly but was adopted by the legislature in January 1786. The Ordinance of Religious Freedom, as it was called, later became the essence of the First Amendment to the U.S. Constitution. It guaranteed that "no man shall be compelled to frequent or support any religious worship . . . but that all men shall be free to profess, and by argument to maintain, their opinion in matters of religion."

Early Jewish Influence

While it is true that Jews in the first decade of the nineteenth century numbered fewer than three thousand, their influence was not insignificant. In fact, one prominent Jewish merchant, Solomon Simpson, became president of New York's Tammany Society, a powerful Democratic Club that had begun making its influence felt in local and national politics. It is significant that in the 1800 campaign of Jefferson vs. Adams, the Federalists who supported Adams were urged to choose "God—and a religious president" over "Jefferson—and no God." New York, which had the largest Jewish population (next to Charleston, which boasted five hundred Jews) and was politically more sophisticated and influential, cast all its twelve electoral votes for Jefferson.

First Jewish Appointee

When Jefferson assumed the presidency in 1801, he had had limited contact with Jews and knew little of their history, save that which he had learned from reading the Bible. It is not clear whether Jefferson was aware that when he appointed Reuben Etting (1762–1848) to a federal position, he was appointing a Jew. Etting's father, Elijah, had come to the United States from Germany in 1758. After Elijah's death, Etting's mother moved the family to Maryland. Etting became involved in politics as a Jeffersonian Republican and was a great patriot and admirer of the president.

When in 1798 war between the United States and France seemed imminent, Etting became the captain of a militia company. As a reward for his service, Jefferson named him U.S. Marshal for Maryland, an appointment he could not have received had it been offered by the state, because at the time the Maryland Constitution called for an "oath of support and fidelity to the state . . . and a declaration of belief in the Christian religion."

Uriah Phillips Levy

Although George Washington had some contact with Jews while in office, Jefferson, like Adams, had practically none. Whatever significant contact Jefferson had with a few individual Jews occurred after he left office.

Uriah Phillips Levy (1792–1862) was an admirer and supporter of Jefferson. Jefferson had just left office when young Levy began his naval career. Levy was particularly impressed by Jefferson's battle for equal rights and for his insistence on noninterference by the government in religious matters. Later in life Levy showed his admiration for the president by actually purchasing and refurbishing Jefferson's neglected and dilapidated home, Monticello. Jefferson had died in debt in 1826 and his heirs were unable to maintain the estate. Eventually it became a summer home for one of Levy's nephews, Congressman Jefferson M. Levy, and is now a national memorial. Uriah Levy's mother is buried on its grounds.

Mordecai Manuel Noah

One of the earliest contacts Jefferson had with a Jew after he left the presidency came via a communication he received from the ubiquitous Mordecai Manuel Noah. Noah sent the ex-president a copy of the address he had delivered on May 28, 1818, at the consecration of the Mill Street Synagogue in New York City, the same speech he had sent to John Adams. Responding, Jefferson wrote to Noah:

Sir:

I thank you for the discourse on the consecration of the Synagogue in your city, with

A drawing of the first synagogue in New York, the Mill Street building of Congregation Shearith Israel, erected 1729–1730.

which you have been pleased to favor me. I have read it with pleasure and instruction, having learnt from it some valuable facts in Jewish history which I did not know before. Your sect by its sufferings has furnished a remarkable proof of the universal spirit of religious intolerance inherent in every sect, disclaimed by all while feeble, and practiced by all when in power. Our laws have applied the only antidote to this vice, protecting our religious, as they do our civil rights, by putting all on an equal footing. But more remains to be done, for although we are free by the law, we are not so in practice; public opinion erects itself into an Inquisition, and exercises its office with as much fanaticism as fans the flames of an auto-de-fe.

Jacob de la Motta

Jacob de la Motta (1789–1845) was a prominent physician, Jewish communal leader, and politician in Savannah and later in Charleston, South Carolina. Having distinguished himself as an army surgeon in the War of 1812, he served as secretary of the Medical Society of South Carolina for ten years, as a trustee of the State Medical College, and as South Carolina's assistant commissioner of health. Long active in state politics and a leader of the Whig Party, he would run unsuccessfully for Congress during the 1830s and would be a leading supporter of William Henry Harrison's presidential candidacy in 1840.

In 1820 Jacob de la Motta wrote to Thomas Jefferson, informing him of the consecration of a new synagogue in Savannah. In response, Jefferson wrote that he was "happy in the restoration of the Jews to their social rights," and he hoped that soon "they will be taking their seats on the benches of science as preparatory to their doing the same at the board of government."

Isaac Harby

Isaac Harby (1788–1828) was a teacher, journalist, and playwright. In 1824 he played an important role in establishing the Reformed Society of Israelites in Charleston, after he and other members of Charleston's Congregation Beth Elohim petitioned the synagogue's board of directors unsuccessfully to permit sermons in English.

On the first anniversary of the establishment of the new congregation Isaac Harby delivered a speech outlining its aims. Harby sent a copy to Thomas Jefferson, who by that time had been long in retirement and was devoting all his efforts to the building of the University of Virginia, which he had founded and which opened in 1825. Harby's address emphasized that his group felt it no longer could be bound by blind observance. Jefferson, in acknowledging Harby's communication, wrote back:

> I am little acquainted with the liturgy of the Jews or their mode of worship but the reformation proposed and explained appears entirely reasonable. Nothing is wiser than that all our institutions should keep pace with the advance of time and be improved of human mind.

In 1826 Jefferson wrote to Harby once again, expressing regret for the inclusion in the curriculum of the University of Virginia a required course "in theological reading," which the consciences of Jews "do not permit them to pursue."

Jefferson on Judaism

Jefferson's support for Jewish religious and political equality, as reflected in his correspondence with Noah, de la Motta, and Harby, and his earlier opposition to Virginia's law on "disabilities for dissenters and Jews," did not suggest that he approved of Judaism as a religion. On the contrary, as scholars have pointed out, despite his commitment to the idea of religious freedom, Jefferson shared with other Enlightenment rationalists of his generation a decidedly negative view of the Jewish religion. Although Jefferson read widely, his knowledge of Judaism was minimal, and he believed that Judaism had not changed significantly since the time of Moses. As Egal Feldman has pointed out, Jefferson was "critical of Judaism's claim to a divine revelation . . . considered its biblical history distorted, its God and law cruel, its form of worship meaningless, and its morality ethnocentric." In a letter to John Adams, Jefferson wrote: "Ethics was so little understood among the Jews, that in their whole compilation called the Talmud, there is only one treatise on moral subjects. . . . It is impossible to collect from these writings a consistent series of moral doctrine."

Last Days

When Jefferson left Washington in 1809, he was twenty-four thousand dollars in debt. In 1815 he was forced to sell his sixty-five-hundred-volume library to the government for twenty-three thousand dollars. This collection became the nucleus for the new Library of Congress collection. The original Library of Congress had been destroyed in 1814, when the British burned the Capitol during the War of 1812.

On July 4, 1826, Jefferson breathed his last, just a few hours before John Adams died. Thus, the only two men who signed the Declaration of Independence and later were to become president died on the same day, the fiftieth anniversary of American independence.

[A.J.K.]

James Madison

Served from 1809 to 1817

Born on March 16, 1751, in Port Conway, Virginia

Member of the Episcopal denomination

Married Dolley Payne Todd, a widow with one son, on September 15, 1794

Candidate of the Democratic-Republican Party

Vice presidents under Madison: George Clinton (first term);
Elbridge Gerry (second term)

First Inaugural Address delivered on March 4, 1809
Second Inaugural Address delivered on March 4, 1813

Died on June 28, 1836, at Montpelier Estate, Virginia

Fourth President of the United States

W HEN JAMES MADISON WAS ELECTED in 1812 to serve a second term as president of the United States, Thomas Jefferson remarked: "I can say conscientiously that I do not know in the world a man of purer integrity . . . nor could I, in the whole scope of America and Europe, point out an abler head." Not all of Madison's political contemporaries agreed. Some thought of him as a mere "puppet of Jefferson." In fact, Madison was very much unlike Jefferson.

Jefferson was gregarious, while Madison was shy and reserved, requiring much privacy. Both, however, shared a love of learning. Madison was particularly taken with the ancient Greek and Latin classics, while Jefferson, much like the fox in Isaiah Berlin's essay "The Hedgehog and the Fox," was curious about all subjects.

After earning his Bachelor of Arts degree from Princeton University in 1771, Madison continued his studies there for one more year, concentrating on the Hebrew language. For a while he considered entering the ministry, but that was not to be. Like Jefferson, Madison built a very large personal library, consisting of many thousands of volumes, and he assisted Jefferson in creating the University of Virginia.

In a statement Madison made after leaving the presidency, he accentuated the importance of learning and of creating an educated electorate: "Knowledge will forever govern ignorance; and a people who mean to be their own Governors must arm themselves with the power which knowledge gives."

While professing to be a communicant of the Episcopal church and a devotee of its basic tenets, much like Jefferson, Madison doubted that man could really know the essence of God, the Divine Creator. Jefferson's deistic approach to religion was not altogether alien to Madison's thinking. The two men were in accord on the proper relationship of church and state. Both felt strongly that they should in no way be linked, Madison going so far as to oppose the appointment of a chaplain for Congress.

Jacob De La Motta

Among the many Jews who wrote to Madison and to whom he responded was Jacob de la Motta. On July 21, 1820, he delivered a speech at the dedication of the synagogue in Savannah in which he expressed, among other things, how aware Jews are of the measure of equality they enjoy in the United States as compared to the plight of "their brethren in foreign lands, writhing under the shackles of odious persecution, and wild fanaticism [sic]."

In his response the following month, Madison wrote:

> The history of the Jews must forever be interesting. The modern part of it is at the same time so little generally known, that every ray of light on the subject has its value. Among the features peculiar to the political system of the United States is the perfect equality of rights which it secures to every religious sect.

Mordecai Manuel Noah

In 1810 Mordecai Manuel Noah applied to the Madison Administration for a consular appointment. In his request, he wrote that, if appointed,

Mordecai Manuel Noah

"members of the Jewish nation" would be greatly encouraged to immigrate to the United States from Europe, and with their funds would show their gratefulness.

In 1811 President Madison replaced the current secretary of state, Robert Smith, with James Monroe. In 1813 Monroe appointed Noah as consul to Tunis, in North Africa, making this the first diplomatic post awarded to a Jew. In 1815, following two years in Tunis, James Monroe recalled him. At the time of Noah's appointment, said Monroe, the Department of State had not been informed of "the faith which you profess and that this would prove a diplomatic obstacle in a Moslem community."

Noah attacked Madison and his administration in a widely publicized letter to all of Noah's friends and political contacts. Deeply hurt, Madison, who was in the midst of campaigning for reelection in 1816, was forced to spend time placating and explaining his position to Jewish supporters.

Noah then returned to his career in journalism, and for a while he served as editor of the New York *National Advocate*. This provided him with a perfect vehicle through which he could

continue to attack Madison and Secretary of State Monroe. At the same time, Noah became active in New York's Mill Street Synagogue, which later became officially known as Congregation Shearith Israel and is sometimes popularly referred to as the Spanish and Portuguese Synagogue.

Despite the ill feeling that existed between Madison and Noah, the president realized the strong influence Noah exerted in Democratic politics. It is therefore not surprising that even after Madison left office, when Noah sent him a copy of the address he had delivered at the May 1818 consecration of the Mill Street Synagogue, the former president responded cordially as follows:

> Sir:
>
> I have received your letter of the 6th, with the eloquent discourse delivered at the consecration of the Synagogue. Having ever regarded the freedom of religious opinions and worship as equally belonging to every sect, and the secure enjoyment of it as the best human provision for bringing all, either into the same way of thinking, or into that mutual charity which is the only proper substitute, I observe with pleasure the view you give of the spirit in which your sect partake of the common blessings afforded by our Government and laws.

Uriah Phillips Levy

The unusual career of Uriah Phillips Levy began during the administration of James Madison. Its impact, however, was felt during the terms of office of five other presidents: James Monroe, Andrew Jackson, John Tyler, James Polk, and Abraham Lincoln. Levy's involvement and the positions he took in fighting injustice and inequity in the conduct of the naval establishment led his admirers to call him a "super patriot" and his defamers a "dirty Jew."

Levy was born in Philadelphia in 1792, the third of fourteen children of Michael and Rachel Levy. Rachel's father was Jonas Phillips, a leader of Congregation Mikveh Israel, to which Uriah's family also belonged. Michael Levy was a simple merchant, but his son Uriah had hopes of becoming a merchant marine. When he was but ten years old he signed up as a cabin boy on a ship carrying merchandise up and down the Atlantic, from Boston to Savannah.

Uriah's parents forgave him when, two years later, he returned home to prepare for his Bar Mitzvah. The call of the sea, however, could not be repressed, and when he was fourteen years old his parents apprenticed him for four years as a seaman to one of Philadelphia's leading ship owners. Thus began a naval career that lasted for more than fifty years.

When the War of 1812 began, Levy volunteered and, because of his decade of seagoing experience, was commissioned in June 1813 and given command of the brig *Argus* that was to carry the American minister to France through the British blockade. Levy accomplished his mission, but during a later action was captured by an enemy frigate and imprisoned for sixteen months.

He was released in December 1814, in the course of a prisoner-of-war exchange. He remained in the U.S. Navy and in April 1815 was assigned to the Philadelphia Naval Yard. At the Philadelphia Patriots Ball, in June 1816, a drunken naval lieutenant deliberately bumped him and his dancing partner three times. When he would not stop, Levy slapped the lieutenant's face. The next morning the lieutenant challenged Levy to a pistol duel. Levy tried to dissuade the lieutenant from engaging in an activity that was contrary to naval law. The lieutenant insisted on the duel and in the end was killed by Levy. Levy had to stand trial for murder, first before a naval court and then in a civilian court. He was acquitted twice on the grounds of self-defense.

John Hays

Among James Madison's other Jewish associates was New York-born John Hays (1766-1836), a fur trader who moved to Cahokia, the first permanent settlement in Illinois Territory. He later became its first postmaster and sheriff. On November 8, 1813, President Madison appointed him collector of internal revenue for the Illinois Territory.

In 1814 Madison appointed Hays as tax collector for the Indian Territory.

Last Years

After relinquishing the presidency to James Monroe, Madison retired to his large farm in Montpelier, Virginia, but his main interest was in helping Thomas Jefferson establish the University of Virginia. He served on the board of regents and succeeded Jefferson as rector in 1826.

After months of suffering from crippling rheumatism, Madison died on June 28, 1836. He had been hoping to be kept alive through stimulants so that he would die on July 4, the same day as had Jefferson (and John Adams) in 1826.

Like Jefferson, Madison believed that the perpetuation of slavery undermined the Union, but neither man took steps to free their slaves. When Madison died, one hundred of his slaves attended the funeral.

[A.J.K.]

James Monroe

Served from 1817 to 1825

Born on April 28, 1758, in Westmoreland County, Virginia

Member of the Episcopal denomination

Married Elizabeth Kortright on February 16, 1786

Father to two daughters

Candidate of the Democratic-Republican Party

Vice president under Monroe: Daniel D. Tompkins

First Inaugural Address delivered on March 4, 1817
Second Inaugural Address delivered on March 5, 1821

Died on July 4, 1831, in New York City

Fifth President of the United States

AN EVEN-TEMPERED MAN, JAMES MONroe had been deeply immersed in politics long before George Washington was elected president. Monroe served in diplomatic posts and elective office ranging from membership in the Virginia Assembly to the U.S. Senate. Under President James Madison, he served as secretary of state (1811 to 1817). His reputation was impeccable, and in 1787 Thomas Jefferson said of him: "Turn his soul wrong side outwards and there is not a spec on it."

The only blight on Monroe's reputation as far as the Jewish community was concerned was his association with Mordecai Manuel Noah, who had been appointed as consul to Tunis in 1813, when Monroe was secretary of state. At the time of the appointment, President Madison and James Monroe knew that Noah was Jewish, but they later claimed otherwise.

While serving as consul, Noah arranged for the release of twelve American sailors being held captive by Algerian pirates for a ransom of twenty thousand dollars. Noah was instructed by his superiors in the State Department to tell the pirates that the ransom money was coming from families of the captives, not the U.S. government. Noah did so, but was shocked to receive a reprimand from a State Department official who claimed that the payment had not been authorized.

This was followed by a note in 1815, from James Monroe himself, which stated:

> At the time of your appointment as Consul at Tunis, it was not known that the religion you profess would form any obstacle to the exercise of your Consular functions. Recent information, however, on which entire reliance may be placed, proves that it would produce a very

unfavorable effect. In consequence of which, the President [James Madison] has deemed it expedient to revoke your commission.

> I am, very respectfully, Sir,
> Your obedient servant,
> James Monroe

Not only did Noah take sharp offense at his dismissal, but many prominent Jews joined in the protest, believing the action to be a denial of the very Constitution itself. Isaac Harby, of Charleston, South Carolina, a prominent American Jew and the editor of the *Southern Patriot,* was most outspoken in his condemnation of what might be construed as an anti-Semitic act, although he found it difficult to conceive of Monroe as an anti-Semite.

In addition to the sharp editorials in his newspaper, Harby wrote directly to Monroe in 1816 expressing astonishment that Monroe saw Noah's Jewishness as ample reason to remove him from office. He reminded the then secretary of state that a man's religion is a matter between himself and his Maker.

Harby asked: "When was it discovered that religion disqualifies a man from the exercise of his political functions? . . . An objection on the score of religion would sound to them [the authors of the Constitution] most monstrous and unnatural . . . They know no religious distinctions."

In January 1817 the State Department admitted that it had made a mistake in recalling Noah, but he was not reinstated, nor did he ever again serve the federal government. This, however, did not end Noah's public career. Toward the end of Monroe's presidency he fathered a plan to create a city of refuge for persecuted Jews on Grand Island, in the Niagara River in upstate New York. In 1825 dedication ceremonies were held to mark the initiation of the project, but the city, named "Ararat," never was to materialize. European Jews who had been invited to settle there failed to arrive. American Jews derided Noah's scheme.

Uriah Phillips Levy

During Madison's presidency, when the War of 1812 erupted between the United States and Britain, Uriah Phillips Levy, with ten years of seagoing experience, had applied for a post as a noncommissioned officer in the U.S. Navy. His request was granted, and on October 23, 1812, he was placed in charge of a vessel that would carry the American minister to France through the British blockade.

On March 5, 1817, President Monroe recommended that Levy be made a lieutenant, and his nomination was confirmed by the U.S. Senate. Thus Uriah Phillips Levy became the second Jew to become a U.S. naval officer. (The first was Levi Charles Harby, who had been commissioned four months earlier).

From the time he assumed the role of officer, Levy became more and more disturbed by the flogging that was being administered to sailors as punishment for even minor offenses. He considered the beatings inhuman and unnecessary, and was determined to put an end to the widespread practice. He wrote articles about the barbarism of such conduct and spoke against it at every opportunity.

Levy's superiors and fellow officers were disdainful of his crusade, especially because Levy was a Jew who was critical of accepted naval tradition. Over a period of eleven years, Levy's adversaries had him court-martialed six times on petty charges, some of which were the result of fisticuffs he engaged in because he would not countenance anti-Semitic remarks directed at him. In every trial he was found guilty.

After his second court-martial, Levy was dismissed from the ship that he commanded. The court ruling was brought to the attention of President Monroe, who, after studying the evidence, was convinced that such severe punishment was not warranted. He set aside the verdict.

Nevertheless, Levy's detractors continued their crusade against him, and Levy was brought to trial several more times. After his sixth trial, in November 1827, he became so discouraged that he requested a six-month leave from active duty. The leave was extended incrementally for the next ten years.

During this time, Levy involved himself in the buying and selling of real estate in New York City. Before long he had accumulated great wealth, and then, after making his fortune, he left for France and spent several years there (1832–1834). While in Paris, he commissioned a French sculptor to fashion a bronze statue of his political idol, Thomas Jefferson. Levy brought the likeness back to the United States and asked Congress to accept it as a gift. They did so, and to this day it graces the rotunda of the Capitol in Washington, D.C.

Uriah Phillips Levy

Levy's admiration for Jefferson led him to purchase the ex-president's neglected estate, Monticello, for two thousand seven hundred dollars. He refurbished it and used it as a second residence. In 1923, a distant nephew, who had inherited the house, sold it to the Thomas Jefferson Association for five hundred thousand dollars.

Monroe's Legacy

Other than the Noah incident, which greatly disturbed the Jewish community, Jews generally felt well disposed toward Monroe, as did the rest of the nation, which labeled his eight years in office, from 1817 to 1825, the "Era of Good Feeling."

Monroe's outstanding achievement was introduced in a message to Congress on December 2, 1823. He proposed that the United States guarantee protection to all the independent nations of the Western hemisphere against European interference in their affairs. He opposed the establishment of new colonies anywhere in the Americas and forbade existing colonies from expanding. The main purpose of the proposal, which became known as the Monroe Doctrine, was to prevent interference in the Americas by the "Holy Alliance": Russia, Prussia, and Austria. The country rallied behind Monroe's proposal.

James Monroe died on July 4, 1831, the same date on which John Adams and Thomas Jefferson had died in 1826.

[A.J.K.]

John Quincy Adams

Served from 1825 to 1829

Born on July 11, 1767, in Braintree (now Quincy), Massachusetts

Member of the Unitarian denomination

Married Louisa Catherine Johnson on July 26, 1797

Father to three sons

Candidate of the Democratic-Republican Party

Vice president under Adams: John C. Calhoun

Inaugural Address delivered on March 4, 1825

Died on February 23, 1848, in Washington, D.C.

Sixth President of the United States

IN HIS DIARY, JOHN QUINCY ADAMS, SON OF the second president of the United States, John Adams, described his shortcomings: "I am a man of reserved, cold, austere and forbidding manners." He then added that his political adversaries called him "a gloomy misanthropist" while his personal enemies described him as "an unsocial savage."

Yet, these self-admitted character faults notwithstanding, John Quincy Adams was one of the most successful diplomats of his time. In 1797 George Washington said of him: "There remains no doubt in my mind that he will prove himself to be the ablest of our diplomatic corps."

John Adams had high hopes that his son would one day follow in his footsteps and become the occupant of the White House, and toward that end he groomed him from an early age. As president, John Adams took John Quincy along with him on diplomatic missions to Europe and, in fact, left him there for a time to enhance his education. As a result John Quincy mastered the classical languages—Greek and Latin—as well as French, Dutch, and even Spanish to some extent. Upon his return to America, John Quincy studied at Harvard, graduating in 1787 second in his class of fifty-one students.

From 1787 to 1790 he studied law and pursued interests from ancient history to modern literature. In July 1790 he was admitted to the bar in Massachusetts. Reputed to be one of the most learned men in America at that time, it was said of John Qunicy that he could write English with one hand while translating it into Greek with the other.

In keeping with a longstanding family tradition, John Quincy began to dabble in politics. Dedication to public service could be traced back to his great-grandfather, Colonel John Quincy (after whom he had been named), who had been speaker of the Massachusetts Assembly as well as a militia officer.

In 1794, only four years after John Quincy began practicing law, George Washington appointed him minister to the Netherlands. And three years later, when John Adams was president, he appointed his son minister to Prussia (Germany).

In 1801, when the first of John Quincy's three sons was born, he showed his appreciation for Washington's confidence by naming his son George Washington Adams. It was then that John Quincy began to turn his attention to elective office.

Elective Offices

Within a year of returning to the United States from his overseas assignment, John Quincy was elected to represent Suffolk County in the Senate of the state of Massachusetts. In 1803 he went on to win a seat in the U. S. Senate, where he served until 1808.

In 1809 President Madison appointed him as the first American minister to Russia, a position John Quincy held until 1814. From 1815 to 1817 he served as minister to Great Britain, and in 1817 President James Monroe selected John Quincy to be his secretary of state.

When Monroe completed his two terms in office at the end of 1823, John Quincy felt the time was ripe to make a run for the presidency. He realized that he faced a formidable opponent in popular war hero General Andrew Jackson, who was especially noted for beating back the British in 1814 when they attacked New Orleans. William H. Crawford of Georgia and Henry Clay of Tennessee also were serious contenders.

The winner of the 1824 presidential contest had to be determined by the House of Representatives. The law required that to be elected a candidate had to win a clear majority of the electoral votes, and none of the four candidates achieved the required total. Adams received 84 votes; Jackson 99; Crawford 41; and Clay 37. Despite Jackson's having received more votes, he failed to win a majority, and the House voted in favor of Adams. When Clay was later appointed secretary of state by Adams, Jackson's supporters accused Adams of bribing Clay to throw his votes to Adams. The resentment between Adams and Jackson never waned, and when Jackson took the oath of office on March 4, 1829, Adams refused to attend the inauguration.

Religious Beliefs

Adams was a religious man who read several chapters of the Bible before starting each day, and before retiring in the evening he recited the popular bedtime prayer beginning, "Now I lay me down to sleep . . ." He believed that Jesus was superhuman, but doubted his divinity. Neither was he able to accept the miracles of the Bible literally.

One of the most significant influences on John Quincy's life was Hannah Adams, a distant cousin on his father's side. She wrote many books on religion, including the notable two-volume *History of the Jews*. What perplexed her was why Jews persisted in rejecting Jesus so many centuries after he appeared on the scene. She made an effort to convert Jews by establishing the Female Society of Boston and the Vicinity for the Promotion of Christianity amongst the Jews, which included branches in New York City. Among its male supporters was President John Quincy Adams. He believed it was proper to introduce Jews to Jesus, the Savior, a gift that the Jews should appreciate.

John Quincy's alliance with forces advocating conversion of Jews was surprising inasmuch as he

had become well acquainted with some very affirmative, self-confident Jews as secretary of state under Madison. One such man was Mordecai Manuel Noah, who in 1820 had written to John Quincy Adams that he was proud of America, where everyone is guaranteed to follow his own religious dictates under the protection of the law:

> I have long been persuaded that this is the only country where Jews can be completely regenerated, where in the enjoyment of perfect civil and religious liberty . . . under the protection of the laws, their faculties could be developed, their talents and enterprises encouraged; their person and property protected and themselves respected and esteemed, as their conduct and deportment shall merit.

The Jewish Condition

It is estimated that between 1815, when Napolean met his defeat at Waterloo, and 1865, when the American Civil War ended, two million German-speaking Europeans left their homelands for America. Among them were many Jews, who fled from such regions as Bavaria and Baden, where they had been severely disenfranchised and barred from many occupations and professions.

American Jews wrote to their relatives in Germany and other central European countries about the beautiful lives they were leading in America, a new golden land of opportunity where Jews enjoyed the same freedoms as all other citizens. It is no wonder, then, that America looked so beckoning to many European Jews, and why tens of thousands reached its shores in the 1820s and 1830s.

Post-Presidential Career

The hallmark of John Quincy Adams's public life was not his presidency but his long service in Congress. After serving as president of the United Sates for one term, he lost the office to Andrew Jackson in 1828. Soon after Jackson was inaugurated in March of 1829, Adams left Washington for his hometown, Quincy, Massachusetts.

Immediately, he was pressed by citizens of his district to be a candidate for the House of Representatives.

Adams agreed reluctantly, but made it clear that he would not campaign for the office. Nevertheless, he won handily and, in 1831, at the age of sixty-four, he became a congressman. He was re-elected seven times, serving a total of seventeen years. John Quincy would die in office on February 23, 1848, during the presidency of James K. Polk.

The Slavery Issue

In Congress John Quincy Adams was a strong advocate of a myriad of antislavery petitions brought before it. He was outspoken in his opposition to slavery, which he considered an affront to God and humanity, although he believed this was a matter that had to be handled by each state and that the federal government did not have the right or power to intervene.

Perhaps the most dramatic example of Adams's opposition to slavery was the *Amistad* case, which he argued before the Supreme Court in 1841. A century and a half later, the case became front-page news once again when, in 1997, Steven Spielberg made a dramatic movie based on the event, starring Anthony Hopkins as defense attorney John Quincy Adams.

The movie portrayed the 1839 mutiny aboard the *Amistad*, a Spanish slave ship that was carrying slaves from Africa to be sold at auction in Cuba. Fifty-three of the African slaves rose in revolt and slaughtered all but two of their captors. (According to some accounts only thirty-nine mutineers were involved.)

Eventually, the ship landed in Long Island Sound. Cinqué, the leader of the rebellion, and the other slaves who participated, were brought to trial in New Haven, Connecticut. They were found guilty.

Ultimately, the case was brought on appeal to the Supreme Court in 1841, where the former president and now seventy-four-year-old congressman John Quincy Adams represented the defense. Despite the fact that six of the nine justices were

John Quincy Adams towards the end of his life.

slave owners, Adams won the case and the guilty verdict was overturned.

Final Years

After suffering a mild stroke in November 1846, Adams recovered sufficiently to resume his duties in Washington, D.C. The diary of John Hone has the following entry for February 24, 1848:

> John Quincy Adams is no more . . . He died as he must have wished to die, breathing his last in the Capitol . . . At twenty minutes past one o'clock on Monday the 21st, Mr. Adams, being in his seat in the House of Representatives (from which he was never absent during a session), attempted to rise (as one was supposed to in order to speak) but sank back upon his seat and fell upon his side . . .
>
> He rallied for an instant and spoke his last words: "This is the last of earth; I am content." He was then carried to the Speaker's room where he lay, with occasional indications of consciousness, until he breathed his last.

[A.J.K.]

Andrew Jackson

Served from 1829 to 1837

Born on March 15, 1767, in Waxhaw, South Carolina (now North Carolina)

Member of the Presbyterian denomination

Married Rachel Donelson Robards on January 17, 1794

Had no natural children; adopted one of Mrs. Jackson's nephews in 1801

Candidate of the Democratic Party

Vice presidents under Jackson: John C. Calhoun (first term), resigned in 1832; Martin Van Buren (second term)

First Inaugural Address delivered on March 4, 1829
Second Inaugural Address delivered on March 4, 1833

Died on June 8, 1845, in Nashville, Tennessee

Seventh President of the United States

ANDREW JACKSON WAS FIRST AND FORE-most a warrior. While a number of presidents felt ill-equipped to assume the responsibilities of the Chief Executive, none were more forthright than Andrew Jackson. In 1821, eight years before he was elected, he said: "I know what I am fit for. I can command a body of men in a rough way, but I am not fit to be president." Yet, in 1823 he fought bitterly for the presidency against John Quincy Adams.

William Cullen Bryant, editor of the *New York Evening Post*, did not agree with Jackson's assessment of himself. In 1836 Bryant wrote: "Faults he had, undoubtedly. . . . Notwithstanding this, he was precisely the man for the period in which he well and nobly discharged the duties demanded of him by the times."

Andrew Jackson was born in South Carolina in 1767 after the death of his father, and was named for him. His mother, a nurse, died when Jackson was fourteen years old. He always remembered the last cautionary words she imparted to him before leaving on her final nursing mission. She advised him not to lie or steal, but probably found it useless to encourage him to control his combative, quick temper.

By his twenty-first birthday Jackson was practicing law and within months would serve as public prosecutor in what would become Tennessee. In the years that followed he served in several elective offices, including U.S. senator (1797–1798). In 1798 he was appointed as a judge on the Tennessee Superior Court.

War of 1812

Jackson had begun his military career at age thirteen, when, along with his older brother, he joined the Continental Army and served as an orderly. By 1812 he had advanced to the rank of major general of the Tennessee volunteer militia, and by 1814 had been elevated to the rank of major general in the regular army.

One of General Jackson's major concerns was the defense of New Orleans, which the British were intent upon capturing. The British offered French privateer and smuggler Jean Lafitte (c.1780–c.1826) thirty thousand dollars and a captaincy in the Royal Navy if he would employ his men and fleet of ships in defense of Barataria Bay, an important approach to New Orleans.

Lafitte, a descendent of Sephardic Jews who were forced to convert to Christianity, maintained a covert loyalty to the Jewish faith. Though Lafitte pretended to support the British, his heart was with the new, free America. Consequently, he turned over all the military information confided in him by the British to Louisiana officials. As a result, the December 1814 to January 1815 battle ended in victory for the United States.

Many years later, when serving as president, Jackson would refer to the Battle of New Orleans and personally laud Lafitte as "one of the ablest men" in the battle.

Old Hickory

It was during the struggle to defend New Orleans that President Jackson acquired the nickname Old Hickory. Jackson was ordered to lead a contingent of 1,500 Tennessee Volunteers to bolster the defense of the city. The group traveled by foot, battling brutal weather conditions before reaching their destination. When they arrived, they were told their services were not needed. Instead of discharging his troops immediately, he marched

THE PRESIDENTS OF THE UNITED STATES & THE JEWS

them back to Tennessee in bitter winter weather. Because of his toughness, he was nicknamed Hickory. As he got older, he was referred to as Old Hickory.

Contact with Jews

In 1828 Jackson became the Democratic candidate for president, opposing the Republican incumbent John Quincy Adams. Jackson defeated him roundly. In 1832 Jackson won reelection against Republican candidate Henry Clay of Kentucky.

There appears to be no evidence of direct contact between Andrew Jackson and the Jewish community, although the influence of Mordecai Manuel Noah was felt as a subtle undercurrent during Jackson's administration, as it would be during the terms of office of subsequent presidents. Noah's absurd undertaking to create a safe haven for persecuted European Jews on Grand Island in upstate New York was a grand failure, but the Democratic Party found it useful to award patronage jobs to Noah. These included customs collector in New York as well as surveyor and sheriff.

Uriah Phillips Levy

The major activity in the tumultuous career of Uriah P. Levy took place under James Madison and James Monroe, but it was Andrew Jackson who, in 1837, promoted him from lieutenant to commander. This advancement came as a total surprise to Levy, who, after the many difficulties he had endured, had not expected recognition for his long service, let alone a promotion.

The Mood of the Country

Although not directly related to issues of states' rights, during the Jackson administration a number of cases arose regarding the rights of Sabbath-observant Jews. In 1830 the Supreme Court of South Carolina upheld the conviction of Alexander Marks for keeping his store open on Sunday in violation of an ordinance of the town council of Columbia, South Carolina. The court rejected the argument that the local law contravened the Constitution of the United States.

In 1831 the Supreme Court of Pennsylvania ruled that there was no reason to postpone a case simply because a Jewish, Sabbath-observant defendant would not be present in court.

One Kentucky congressman, Richard Mentor Johnson (1780-1850), who was later vice president under Martin Van Buren, thought differently about the rights of the Jewish minority. He stated before Congress in 1831 that "the Constitution regards the conscience of the Jew as sacred as that of the Christian, and gives no more authority to adopt a measure affecting the conscience of a solitary individual than that of a whole community."

Last Days

Although Jackson had suffered periodically since 1806 from a bullet that lodged precariously close to his heart—the result of a pistol duel with Charles Dickinson, a lawyer whom Jackson accused of maligning his wife—the president died of kidney and heart failure on June 8, 1845, in his home, the Hermitage, in Nashville, Tennessee. Yet, for more than one hundred years historians believed that Jackson's poor health was aggravated by doctors who overdosed him with medicine containing mercury. (This theory seems to have been disproved by an August 1999 report in the *Journal of the American Medical Association*.)

While Jackson was not a churchgoer, he did enjoy reading the Bible and considered himself a practicing Christian. His dying wish was that he would one day meet all his old friends again, both white and black. His last words were reported to be: "Do not cry. Be good children. We shall all meet in heaven."

[A.J.K.]

Martin Van Buren

Served from 1837 to 1841

Born on December 5, 1782, in Kinderhook, New York

Member of the Dutch Reformed denomination

Married Hannah Hoes on February 21, 1807

Father to four sons

Candidate of the Democratic Party

Vice president under Van Buren: Richard M. Johnson

Inaugural Address delivered on March 4, 1837

Died on July 24, 1862, in Kinderhook, New York

Eighth President of the United States

MARTIN VAN BUREN, ANDREW JACKSON'S vice president, had the misfortune of following a very popular two-term president who ranked high among the "near great" presidents of all time. Although Van Buren had a cheerful nature, he lacked Jackson's charisma and force of personality, and he was unable to win a second term in office. Through no fault of his own, two months after Van Buren assumed office, in March 1837, an economic depression descended upon the country, with nine hundred banks closing and the number of unemployed increasing steadily.

Martin Van Buren was born on December 5, 1782, in Kinderhook, in upstate New York. He was the first president to be an American citizen at birth, for his predecessors were born prior to the issuance of the Declaration of Independence and hence were British subjects.

Van Buren was a religious person who read the Bible regularly, attended church services, and joined heartily in the singing of hymns. But his attitude toward granting full equality to all Americans was less than wholehearted. He opposed the abolition of slavery in states where it already existed and, in his Inaugural Address, praised the wisdom of the Founding Fathers for not tackling the inequity in the institution of domestic slavery. He declared openly that he was an "uncompromising opponent of every attempt on the part of Congress to abolish slavery . . . against the wishes of the slaveholding states, and . . . interference with it in the states where it exists."

The above statement nothwithstanding, Van Buren did display a deep concern for injustice when an accusation of ritual murder was leveled against the local Jewish community of Damascus, Syria, in 1840.

The Damascus Affair

On February 5, 1840, Father Thomas, head of the Franciscan convent in Damascus, disappeared with his servant. The two had last been seen in the Jewish quarter, and fellow monks spread the rumor that Father Thomas had been slain by Jews for ritual purposes. The French consul in Damascus, an enemy of the Jews, used this occasion to search the Jewish quarter. Though nothing was found, a Jewish barber was coerced into confessing to the crime. He, together with a group of the city's most notable Jews, who also were forced to confess to the murder of the priest, were imprisoned and tortured. Pressure was put on Mohammed Ali to authorize the execution of the "murderers."

Jews around the world raised their voices in protest, and public meetings and rallies were held in London and Paris as well as in New York, Philadelphia, Charleston, Cincinnati, Savannah, and Richmond. Despite the fact that there were only fifteen thousand Jews in the United States at the time, Martin Van Buren heard their voices and saw fit to have his secretary of state, John Forsythe, issue the following condemnation of the Damascus Affair:

> In common with all civilized nations, the people of the United States have learned with horror the atrocious crimes imputed to the Jews of Damascus, and the cruelties of which they have been the victims. The President fully participates in the public feeling, and he cannot refrain from expressing surprise and pain that in this advanced age such barbarous measures be resorted to in order to compel the confession of imputed guilt. . . . The President has witnessed, with the most lively satisfaction, the effort of several of the Christian Governments

Sir Moses Montefiore

This famous windmill was built in Jerusalem in 1857 with funds provided by Sir Moses Montefiore.

of Europe to suppress or mitigate these horrors. . . . He has accordingly directed me to instruct you to employ, should the occasion arise, all those good offices and efforts which are compatible with discretion and your official character, to the end that justice and humanity may be extended to these persecuted people whose cry of distress has reached our shores.

Two prominent French Jews, lawyer Isaac Crémieux and Orientalist Salomon Munk, together with Sir Moses Montefiore of England, were sent to Alexandria to meet as mediators with Mohammed Ali. They succeeded in obtaining from him the unconditional release and exoneration of the nine prisoners (of the thirteen originally incarcerated) who were still alive.

The Isaac Adolphe Crémieux commemorative medallion.

Retirement Years

Van Buren's defeat by war hero William Henry Harrison in 1840 was a bitter one. The tireless campaigning of Daniel Webster and other well-known Whigs helped catapult Harrison and his running mate, John Tyler, to victory. The catchy slogan "Tippecanoe [the spot where Harrison defeated the Indians] and Tyler, Too!" resonated well with the public as did the cry, "Van, Van, Van/ Van Is a Used Up Man!"

When his term of office was over, Van Buren said: "As to the presidency, the two happiest days of my life were those of my entrance upon the office and my surrender of it." Yet, from the time of his retirement in 1841 until his death, he tried many times to regain the presidency, only to fail time after time.

Van Buren spent the last years of his life on his estate in Kinderhook, New York, where he died on July 24, 1862.

[A.J.K.]

William Henry Harrison

Served in 1841

Born on February 9, 1773, in Charles City County, Virginia

Member of the Episcopal denomination

Married Anna Tuthill Symmes on November 25, 1795

Father to five sons and four daughters

Candidate of the Whig Party

Vice president under Harrison: John Tyler

Inaugural Address delivered on March 4, 1841

Died in office on April 4, 1841

Ninth President of the United States

WILLIAM HENRY HARRISON DELIVERED the longest Inaugural Address on record (one hour and forty minutes), on March 8, 1841, but served for less time than any other president—a mere thirty-one days. Sixty-eight years of age when he became president, only Ronald Reagan was older when he took office. Foolishly, Harrison delivered his long address on a brisk, windy March day, without hat, gloves, or overcoat. He then rode his own horse in a long parade, still with no coat. Many conjecture that this was the beginning of the neglect that led to his early demise.

Born on February 9, 1773, in Charles City County, Virginia, Harrison was the last president to be born while the United States was still under British rule. His father, Benjamin Harrison, a wealthy farmer and politician, had been one of the signers of the Declaration of Independence and a governor of Virginia. At first William had decided to pursue a career in medicine, mostly to please his father, but when his money ran out after his father died, he decided, in August 1791, to join the army. He served from 1791 to 1798 and once again from 1812 to 1814, rising to the rank of major general.

In the intervening years, between 1798 and 1812, Harrison served as secretary of the Northwest Territory, an appointment made by President John Adams. Adams also appointed Harrison to be governor of the Indiana Territory, a position that he held from 1800 to 1812. He was elected to the U.S. House of Representatives from Ohio in 1816 and to the U.S. Senate in 1824.

When Harrison ran as the Whig Party candidate for president in 1840, he was perhaps best known for his military exploits, as the hero of the legendary battle of Tippecanoe. Tippecanoe was the name of the river in northern Indiana where, in 1811, Harrison had led his territorial militia in defeating a large-scale attack by the Shawnee Indians. The Battle of Tippecanoe had established Harrison's reputation as an Indian fighter, bringing him national fame. To accentuate his accomplishment, the Whig Party created one of the most memorable presidential campaign slogans, consisting of the euphonious, easy-to-remember words, "Tippecanoe and Tyler, Too!" John Tyler was Harrison's running mate.

Contact with Jews

It was while serving in Indiana that Harrison became friendly with a New York-born Jew named John Hays, a fur trader who had settled in nearby Illinois. President Madison had appointed Hays on November 8, 1813, to be collector of internal revenue for the Illinois Territory. Years earlier, in October 1801, then General Harrison presented Hays with the marriage certificate when he wed Mary Brocuillet in Vincennes, Indiana.

As governor of the Indiana Territory, Harrison also had a business relationship with Hyman (1776–1857) and Simon Gratz (1773–1839), Jewish merchants from Philadelphia, from whom he purchased food and supplies for his troops. On February 26, 1807, Harrison wrote the Gratz brothers from Vincennes:

> Please send me by George Wallace the following articles the amount of which shall be forwarded either to ourselves or to my friend Genl. Ino Wilkins, as soon as I receive your account viz.—one hundred pounds of coffee, one hundred Ditto Single refined loaf sugar,

six pounds best tea, ten gallons Madeira wine and fifty pounds of rice.

Probably the closest contact that Harrison had with a member of the Jewish community was with Jacob de la Motta, the Savannah, Georgia-born physician and Orthodox Jew. De La Motta opposed the Reform practices of Beth Elohim Congregation in Savannah and in the early 1840s founded and became president of Shearith Israel, a breakaway Orthodox synagogue.

When Harrison ran for president in 1840, de la Motta ran for Congress but lost. He had supported Harrison, and as a reward, in 1841, Harrison appointed him as receiver general for South Carolina.

Isaac Leeser

Mordecai Manuel Noah

Harrison could boast one other important Jewish connection as well. Although not personal friends, Harrison had close political ties to Mordecai Manuel Noah, the influential journalist and politician. As editor of the *New York Evening Star* and a vocal supporter of the new Whig Party, Noah had enthusiastically endorsed Harrison for the presidency in 1836, and had, most unrealisti-

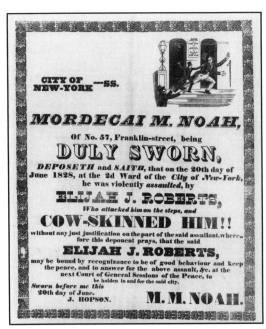

Public notice, dated June 20, 1828, reporting an assault on American Zionist, playwright, and editor Mordecai Manuel Noah.

cally, as it turned out, predicted certain victory at the polls. Indeed, in an embarrassing political blunder, the *Evening Star's* November 8, 1836, headline had pronounced "Harrison Elected," just as Martin Van Buren was declaring electoral victory.

In the 1840 presidential contest, Noah once again campaigned energetically for Harrison's election and mobilized the Whig Party's growing number of Jewish supporters on behalf of Harrison's candidacy. Noah also undertook to personally organize a group of Democrats for Harrison, part of a grand scheme to make Harrison the "Candidate of the Nation." Noah's active support for Harrison's presidential candidacy was rewarded when, in January 1841, he was appointed to a judgeship in New York.

Isaac Leeser's Eulogy

William Henry Harrison died on Sunday morning, April 4, 1841. The first president to die in office, he was succeeded by Vice President John Tyler. As the first vice president to become president upon the death of the incumbent, Tyler assumed all the prerogatives of the Chief Executive. The precedent he set has been followed by every vice president who has succeeded to the presidency.

President Harrison's untimely death occasioned the publication of a pamphlet, *Commemoration of the Life and Death of William Henry Harrison*, by Isaac Leeser (1806–1868), which was the first published eulogy for an American president by a Jewish clergyman. In commemorating the deceased president, Leeser, spiritual leader of Philadelphia's Mikveh Israel Congregation and editor of the *Occident*, the first English-language Jewish newspaper in America, expressed his great admiration for Harrison's military career, for his rise "from a humble standard-bearer to the chief command of the army and navy, and the presidency of the councils of his native land." In this historic eulogy, Leeser argues that the presidency is the highest station that "human ambition can look for," it being attained neither by the accident of birth nor wrested on the field of battle, but conferred "by a free people . . . [as] the highest honor within their gift." To Leeser, Harrison's life was "a lesson that virtue and moderation, joined to a straightforward line of conduct, are well calculated and will pre-eminently conduce to acquire for us the favour of God and man."

[D.G.D.]

John Tyler

Served from 1841 to 1845

Born on March 29, 1790, in Greenway, Virginia

Member of the Episcopal denomination; subscriber to the deist philosophy

Married Letitia Christian on March 29, 1813; died September 10, 1842
Married Julia Gardiner on June 26, 1844

Father to four daughters and three sons with Letitia
Father to five sons and two daughters with Julia

Candidate of the Whig Party

Assumed the presidency on April 4, 1841,
following the death of William Henry Harrison

Died on January 18, 1862, in Richmond, Virginia

Tenth President of the United States

AFTER SERVING AS VICE PRESIDENT FOR only one month, John Tyler ascended to the presidency upon the death of William Henry Harrison, who died unexpectedly on April 4, 1841. Tyler's sudden elevation led him to be nicknamed "The Ascendancy."

Born in Greenway, Virginia, on March 29, 1790, Tyler grew up in a family that was dedicated to public service. His father, also named John, served as governor of Virginia from 1808 to 1811, and like his father, the future president served as governor of Virginia from 1825 to 1827. He then resigned to run for a Senate seat as the Whig candidate, upsetting the incumbent Senator John Randolph.

At the national convention of the Whig Party, held in Harrisburg, Pennsylvania, John Tyler was selected as William Henry Harrison's vice-presidential running mate. On April 6, 1841, two days after Harrison's unitmely death, Tyler was sworn in as president; he served as the nation's leader until March 3, 1845. Since this was the first time that a vice president had become president as the result of the death of a sitting president, much controversy developed over the status and powers of the new Chief Executive. Tyler insisted that he was a president with the full powers of the office, not a "mere acting president," as some had maintained. Tyler's view prevailed, but he chose not to be a candidate in the election of 1844, and James K. Polk succeeded him.

Religious Affiliation

Although John Tyler was a member of the Episcopal church, like Jefferson he classified himself as a deist, a believer in the doctrine that God cre-

ated the world and its natural laws but is not involved in its day-to-day operation. Tyler believed in the separation of church and state, considering it harmful to mix religion and politics. Issues such as slavery, he felt, were not fit for discussion from the pulpit. Undoubtedly, this view was partially prompted by the fact that he came from a slave-owning family. It would also explain why he believed granting Congress the right to restrict the spread of slavery would lead to a civil war.

Welcoming Jews

In the 1840s, when the terms "Jew" and "to Jew" found their way into the vocabulary, many Jews were growing uncomfortable being part of a despised minority. It is estimated that about one-third of the grandchildren of Jews who lived during the American Revolution (roughly thirteen hundred to fifteen hundred people, according to the first United States federal census conducted in 1790) began abandoning the faith of their fathers.

President John Tyler's message to Congress in 1841, in which he encouraged immigration to the United States, may have been a factor in stemming the tide of assimilation, for it portrayed immigrants as valuable contributors to American life. In one of the first speeches Tyler made after taking office in 1841, he said:

The Hebrew, persecuted and downtrodden in other regions, takes up his abode among us with none to make him afraid. He may boast, as well he can, of his descent from the patriarchs of old—of his wise men in council and strong men in battle. He may even turn his

John Tyler early in his political career.

eye to Judea, resting with strong confidence on the promise that is made him of his restoration to the Holy Land, and he may worship the God of his fathers after the manner that worship was conducted by Aaron and his successors in the priesthood, and the aegis of the Government is over him to defend and protect him. Such is the great experiment which we have tried, and such are the happy fruits which have resulted from it; our system of free government would be imperfect without it . . .

Jesse Seligman

During the Tyler Administration, Jesse Seligman (1827–1894) landed penniless in New York. Later he would become a millionaire along with his brother Joseph, who was a senior partner in the Tri-Continental Corporation, one of the largest investment trusts in the United States. In a speech delivered fifty years later, Seligman described his first experience in America:

It was on a Monday morning [in 1841] that I landed . . . and at a time when immigrants were in great demand. I soon learned that the government had sent an official to me for the purpose of seeing whether my wooden box…contained anything that would be subject to the payment of duties. . . .

After ransacking the contents of my humble box . . . the official made a very serious face, and, fearful that he had discovered something that would compel him to retain it, I asked him the cause of his annoyance. He stated that he felt very much disappointed, indeed, in not finding a dress suit among the contents of my wardrobe. I told him that in my haste to get to this land of liberty and freedom, I had overlooked it.

Jacob Ezekiel

John Tyler's amiable disposition towards Jews was further expressed in two letters he sent to the Richmond, Virginia, Jewish communal leader Jacob Ezekiel. In the first, dated April 19, 1841, Tyler clarifies the meaning of the words "Christian people," which he used in his call for a national day of prayer to be held on May 14, 1841, to mark the death of President William Harrison. "I designed nothing," he wrote, "to exclude any portion of my fellow citizens from a cordial union in the solemnities of that occasion. In speaking in the first paragraph of the Christian people, I meant in no way to imply that similar duties should not be performed by all mankind. . . . The wisdom that flowed from the lips of your prophets has in time past, and will continue for all time to come, to be a refreshing fountain of moral instruction to mankind. . . ."

In a subsequent letter to Ezekiel dated July 10, 1842, Tyler stated his strong belief in a separation between church and state:

The United States have adventured upon a great and noble experiment which is believed to have been hazarded in the absence of all previous presidents—that of total separation of church and state. No religious establishment by law exists among us. The conscience is left free from all restraint and each is permitted to worship his maker after his own judgment.

Uriah Phillips Levy

Aside from anti-Jewish feelings that prompted antagonism toward Uriah Phillips Levy from his earliest days in the navy, his detractors were offended by his relentless effort to stop the cruel practice of flogging sailors for even minor infractions of naval rules.

In 1839, Levy had been given command of the war sloop *Vandalia*, a beat-up old ship that was thought to be irreparable. To everyone's surprise, within five months the ship was in impeccable shape, ready for sea duty. Several months later, when a young cabin boy on the *Vandalia* was accused of wrongdoing, rather than have him flogged, Levy chose a more humane method of punishment. The penalty seemed sufficient to teach the sailor the importance of obeying naval regulations.

Levy's abandonment of flogging as the punishment of choice was considered a violation of the naval code of conduct, and Levy again was court-martialed for dereliction of duty and dismissed from the service. When the case was brought before President Tyler for review, he set aside the court's verdict, arguing that Levy's se-

vere punishment was uncalled for, especially for an officer who had contributed so much in the course of his career to enhance the image of the navy. However, to placate the navy brass, Tyler did not disallow the court's ruling completely, instead reducing the sentence to "suspension without pay" for a period of twelve months.

In 1844, however, the president showed his admiration for Levy by recommending to the Senate that he be promoted from lieutenant to captain. The promotion was confirmed on May 31, 1844, although, ironically, Levy's suspension remained in effect.

Last Days

John Tyler left office on March 4, 1845, and settled down to practice law and work his twelve-hundred-acre plantation, Sherwood Forest, with the help of a few dozen slaves. It was there, with his young second wife, that he sired a new family of seven children.

In February 1861, on the eve of the Civil War, at the suggestion of the leaders of the state of Virginia, Tyler was called upon to see if he could effect a compromise in the pending North-South conflict. When his mission failed, he urged his state to secede, and in November was elected to the Confederate House of Representatives. John Tyler died, however, before he could take his seat.

[A.J.K.]

John Tyler

49

James K. Polk

Served from 1845 to 1849

Born on November 2, 1795, in Mecklenburg County, North Carolina

Member of the Presbyterian and Methodist denominations

Married Sarah Childress on January 1, 1824

Candidate of the Democratic Party

Vice president under Polk: George M. Dallas

Inaugural Address delivered on March 4, 1845

Died on June 15, 1849, in Nashville, Tennessee

Eleventh President of the United States

THE SON OF A FARMER, JAMES KNOX POLK was born in Mecklenburg County, North Carolina, on November 2, 1795. He graduated from the University of North Carolina in 1818 and within five years was elected to the state legislature, where he served from 1823 to 1825.

When Polk was ten, his father, Samuel, had moved the family from North Carolina to Tennessee, where he amassed great wealth in land speculation. To his son James, the future president of the United States, and his other nine children, Samuel left thousands of acres of land and fifty slaves. Having no children of his own, James Polk would leave the bulk of his estate to his wife, Sarah, specifying that all of his slaves be freed.

In 1825 James was elected by the sixth congressional district to the U.S. House of Representatives; in 1835 he was chosen to be Speaker of the House, a position he held until 1839. In 1844, although he had not sought it, Polk became the presidential nominee of the Democratic Party. In the presidential election he was the unexpected victor over the Whig candidate, the popular Henry Clay of Kentucky.

While Polk often was criticized for being excessively ambitious and an overachiever, he was well liked and usually emerged on the right side of conflicting issues. On the burning question of slavery, he refused to express opposition, thus gaining favor with voters in the Southern states.

David Naar

President Polk did not have many Jewish contacts, but his association with David Naar (1800–1880), who was born in Saint Thomas, the Danish West Indies (now the Virgin Islands), was signifi-

cant. As a teenager, David was sent by his father, a tobacco exporter, to New York to be educated. Because of Negro insurrections in the Caribbean and the poor economic prospects there, in 1834 the entire family moved to New York City. There, they continued to conduct their tobacco business.

David Naar was more interested in writing than in business, but as he pursued his journalism career, he became attracted to the world of politics. In 1838, after having purchased a farm in nearby Elizabeth, New Jersey, David became active in the local Democratic Party. While serving as a delegate to the state constitutional convention, he fought energetically for the right of Roman Catholics to vote and hold public office. Not long after, Naar came to the attention of President Polk, who appointed him commercial agent of the United States to Saint Thomas, a position he held from 1845 to 1848.

In 1849 Naar was elected mayor of Elizabeth, and he served in that capacity until 1853, when he moved to Trenton and purchased the *Daily True American*, a newspaper that promoted the interests of the Democratic Party. Naar edited the paper until 1870.

David Levy Yulee

A second Jew who figured prominently in the Polk Administration, although the president had no apparent direct contact with him, was David Levy Yulee (1810–1866). Yulee achieved notoriety that rivaled that of Naval Commander Uriah Phillips Levy, who made headlines during the Tyler Administration.

David Levy's grandfather was a Muslim named Jacoub ibn Youli, a prominent member of the court of the Sultan of Morocco from 1757 to 1790. During this period, Moroccan pirates captured Rachel Levy, the daughter of an English physician. Youli bought her as a slave, and she became part of his harem.

When Youli died in 1792, Rachel was pregnant with his child. Somehow, she managed to escape from the harem and find her way back to her family in England. There, she gave birth to a son, Moses Elias Levy.

Moses Elias married a Sephardic woman, and in 1810 they had a son named David. The entire family moved to Florida, where they became very wealthy in real estate. David, however, turned his attention to politics.

From 1841 to 1845 Levy was Florida's delegate to Congress, where he urged that Florida be admitted to the Union. In 1845, when Florida did finally join the Union, Levy was elected as the state's first senator, thus becoming the first Jew ever to hold a seat in the United States Senate. One year later, he married the beautiful daughter of the ex-governor of Kentucky. His wife was not pleased being known as Mrs. Levy and persuaded her husband to change his name. He assumed the surname Yulee, an approximation of the name of his Muslim grandfather, and agreed to bring up his children as Christians.

Moses Levy, David's father, was distraught over his son's denigration of their religious heritage, especially when he saw how David's children were being raised as Gentiles. He was also displeased with David's conservative political views, particularly his advocacy of secession and his belief that blacks constitute an inferior race, suited only to be slaves of the white man.

The views of Uriah P. Levy and David Levy Yulee came into sharp conflict in 1846 when David Levy Yulee became chairman of the Naval Affairs Committee of the U.S. Senate. He disagreed vehemently with the liberal Uriah P. Levy, who had been advocating legislation that would abolish flogging in the U.S. Navy.

David Levy Yulee was defeated in his Senate reelection bid in 1851, but was reelected in 1855. He served until 1861, at which time he resigned his seat.

David Naar

David Levy Yulee

Last Days

Early in his presidency, Polk announced that he would not seek a second term. When he left office on March 4, 1849, he declared: "I feel exceedingly relieved that I am now free of all public cares." And to his diary he confided, "I am sure I shall be a happier man in my retirement than I have been during the four years I have filled the highest office, the gift of my countrymen."

Unfortunately, James Knox Polk enjoyed only two and a half months of relief from public office. On June 15, 1849, after having been stricken with what doctors suspected was cholera, he died in Nashville, Tennessee, during a Southern speaking tour. A week before he died, Polk had been baptized a Methodist.

[A.J.K.]

James Polk as he appeared as a member of the House of Representatives from Tennessee (1825–1839).

Zachary Taylor

Served from 1849 to 1850

Born on November 24, 1784, in Orange County, Virginia

Member of the Episcopal denomination

Married Margaret Mackall Smith on June 21, 1810

Father to three daughters and one son

Candidate of the Whig Party

Vice president under Taylor: Millard Fillmore

Inaugural Address delivered on March 5, 1849

Died in office on July 9, 1850

Twelfth President of the United States

ZACHARY TAYLOR WAS PRESIDENT FOR ONLY sixteen months. He died unexpectedly at a time when the nation was in danger of being torn apart over the issue of slavery: The Northern states demanded an end to slavery, while those in the South battled to preserve their luxurious living styles and the maintenance of their expansive plantations through the use of slave labor. The nation believed that rough-and-tumble former general Zachary Taylor might be the best candidate to defuse the explosive situation, even though he had been a career soldier who never voted. The fact that he owned more than one hundred slaves made him acceptable to Southern voters.

Born on November 24, 1784, in Orange County, Virginia, Taylor had received only the most basic elementary education, earning a reputation as a poor speller. Aware of his limitations, Taylor once said of himself, "The idea that I should become president seems to me to be too visionary to require a serious answer. It has never entered my head, nor is it likely to enter the head of any sane person."

What propelled Taylor to the highest office in the land was the mark he made during his forty-year career as a military officer. Between 1808 and 1848, he rose from lieutenant to major general.

The future president's career began its upward spiral when, in 1811, after having been appointed commandant of Fort Knox at Vincennes in Indiana Territory, he restored order at that post. He proved his leadership qualities in successful campaigns during the War of 1812, the Black Hawk War of 1832, and the Mexican War of 1846. And in 1847, during the Mexican War, he showed his military prowess in a battle at Buena Vista, where he defeated the enemy who outnumbered his army by four to one. Taylor's courageous leadership earned him the affection of the nation and the sobriquet "Old Rough and Ready."

The Whig Party took advantage of Taylor's status as a national hero and nominated him as their candidate for the presidency in 1848. Millard Fillmore of New York was designated as his running mate.

The Jewish Condition

Because of Taylor's long association with the military and his brief service in office, he had little occasion to be in contact with individual Jews or to be privy to the concerns of the Jewish community. In fact, his interest in religion and religious affairs in general was probably no more than lukewarm, inasmuch as in his youth he never formally joined the church.

Zachary Taylor surely was unaware of the weakening of Jewish life during his brief presidency. The Jewish condition was such that the first ordained rabbi to serve a congregation in America, Rabbi Abraham Joseph Rice (1802-1862), a German immigrant who was elected leader of the Baltimore Hebrew Congregation in 1840, resigned his position in disgust in 1849. He then opened a dry goods store, because, as he wrote to a friend in Germany: "The religious life in this land is on the lowest level. Most people eat foul food and desecrate the Sabbath in public. . . . Thousands marry non-Jewish women. Under these circumstances, my mind is perplexed and I wonder whether it is even permissible for a Jew to live in this land."

Major General Zachary Taylor

August Belmont

One of the Jews Rabbi Rice may have had in mind in his pessimistic evaluation of Jewish life in America was German-born August Belmont (1816–1890), builder of the New York's race track, Belmont Park. Belmont was sent to New York in 1837 to be the agent of the wealthy European Rothschild banking family. After a time, Belmont himself became involved in the banking business and soon became very wealthy. He also began dabbling in politics and by 1860 had become treasurer of the Democratic National Committee.

Eager to be accepted by the Christian majority and the social elite, he had changed his name from Schönberg to Belmont, both meaning "beautiful mountain." He then converted to Episcopalianism and married the daughter of Commander (later Commodore) Matthew Perry. While he never denied his Jewish roots, Belmont did allow his children to be baptized, a practice not uncommon in the years before and after Taylor's presidency.

Belmont's status in high society would be deeply affected by accusations during the Civil War that he was buying Confederate bonds, thus showing disloyalty to the Union.

August Belmont

Sudden Death

On a hot Fourth of July, after only sixteen months in office, President Zachary Taylor suddenly took sick after attending a celebration at the Washington Monument, which was then under construction. Sitting under a broiling sun for two hours, he returned to the White House and devoured a large bowl of cherries and a pitcher of cold milk. This led to diarrhea, vomiting, and high fever.

The president's health continued to decline, resulting in his death on July 9, 1850. Zachary Taylor was succeeded in office by Vice President Millard Fillmore who, unlike Taylor, favored the extension of slavery to the North.

[A.J.K.]

Millard Fillmore

Served from 1850 to 1853

Born on January 7, 1800, in Locke, New York

Member of the Unitarian denomination

Married Abigail Powers on February 15, 1826; died March 30, 1853
Married Caroline Carmichael McIntosh on February 10, 1858

Father to one son and one daughter with Abigail

Candidate of the Whig Party

Assumed the presidency on July 10, 1850, following
Zachary Taylor's death on July 9, 1850

Died on March 8, 1874, in Buffalo, New York

Thirteenth President of the United States

MILLARD FILLMORE SUCCEEDED TO THE presidency upon the death of Zachary Taylor in 1850, the second vice president to reach the White House without having been elected. Fillmore was the first vice president, as well as the first president, to be born in the nineteenth century. The last of the Whig Party presidents, Fillmore remains the only incumbent president in American history to fail to be renominated by his own party.

Fillmore was born in a log cabin on January 7, 1800, in Cayuga County, New York, to a poor frontier farmer. After teaching school for a while, he read law in the office of a local county judge and, at the age of twenty-three, was admitted to the bar. Entering politics in 1828, Fillmore won election to the New York State Assembly and, in 1830, moved to the growing town of Buffalo, where he established a successful law practice. While a New York legislator, Fillmore played a leading role in developing his state's public school system and was instrumental in enacting the legislation abolishing imprisonment for the nonpayment of debts. Elected to Congress from Buffalo in 1832 as the candidate of the newly formed Whig Party, Fillmore would serve five terms in the House of Representatives. When the Whigs gained control of Congress under President Tyler, Fillmore served for a brief period as chairman of the powerful House Ways and Means Committee. After retiring from Congress, he ran unsuccessfully for governor of New York in 1844. Two years later he was elected comptroller of New York State.

At the Whig national convention of 1848, Fillmore, an opponent of slavery, emerged as the compromise vice-presidential candidate, receiving the Whig Party's vice-presidential nomination to balance the ticket headed by the southern slave owner Zachary Taylor. In the close election of 1848, Fillmore's vice-presidential candidacy helped win New York's crucial electoral vote for the Whig ticket.

The Compromise of 1850

As vice president in 1849, Fillmore presided over the historic Senate debates that led to the group of legislative measures known as the Compromise of 1850, which he would later sign into law as president. The signing and enactment of the epochal Compromise of 1850, which averted the Civil War for eleven years, was the most significant event of the Fillmore presidency. As part of this Compromise, Fillmore signed and tried to enforce the Fugitive Slave Law, which the Southerners demanded and the Northern abolitionists deplored. Although a Northerner and a vocal opponent of slavery, Fillmore signed the Compromise (and its Fugitive Slave Law) because he believed that in so doing he would best be able to preserve peace and the Union. Nonetheless, he and other moderate Whigs, like Daniel Webster and Henry Clay, who supported the Compromise, were condemned by radical abolitionists as apostates and traitors.

Millard Fillmore and the Jews

In 1850, the Fillmore Administration negotiated a commercial treaty with Switzerland that granted full rights to American Christians traveling or working in the country but permitted Swiss cantons to deny entry to American Jews. When

American Jewish leaders wrote to President Fillmore and his secretary of state, Daniel Webster, protesting U.S. government participation in this discriminatory treaty and urging its nonratification by the Senate, Fillmore agreed to oppose it. In his message to the Senate, President Fillmore expressed "decisive objection" to the treaty on the grounds that "neither by law, nor by treaty, nor by any other official proceeding is it competent for the government of the United States to establish any distinction between its citizens founded on differences in religious beliefs." President Fillmore's strong objection to the treaty, together with the equally vocal opposition of Webster and the Senate Foreign Relations Committee chairman Henry Clay, prompted the Senate to refuse to ratify the treaty.

Judah P. Benjamin

Millard Fillmore has the distinction of being the first president to offer a seat on the U.S. Supreme Court to a Jew, Judah P. Benjamin (1811-1884), then a U.S. senator from Louisiana. Benjamin had been born into an old Sephardic family in the British West Indies in 1811. His family moved to North Carolina two years later, and Benjamin received his early education at the Fayetteville Academy, one of the state's finest preparatory schools. After attending Yale University, one of the first Jews to do so, he settled in New Orleans and in 1832, at the age of twenty-one, was admitted to the bar. Specializing in commercial law, he soon became the leading commercial lawyer in New Orleans and one of the preeminent attorneys in the state.

Active in politics, Benjamin won election to the Louisiana State Legislature in 1842. Two years later, he was selected as a delegate to the Louisiana Constitutional Convention, where he played an important role in founding the state university that later became Tulane. In February 1852 Benjamin entered national politics, winning a seat in the United States Senate, the first professing Jew to do so. (David Levy Yulee, who had been elected to the U.S. Senate from Florida in 1845, had been born Jewish, but changed his name from Levy to Yulee, publicly renounced Judaism, and converted to Christianity.)

Several months later, in the fall of 1852, President Fillmore offered Benjamin a seat on the U.S. Supreme Court. Benjamin, however, declined Fillmore's appointment, preferring to remain in the Senate, where he soon established a reputation as one of the chamber's greatest orators, often being compared to Daniel Webster and John Calhoun. When Louisiana seceded from the Union in February 1861, Benjamin, a passionate Southerner, resigned his seat and joined Jefferson Davis's Cabinet as, successively, attorney general, secretary of war, and secretary of state of the Confederacy. Besides being the greatest nineteenth-century American Jewish statesman, Judah P. Benjamin enjoys another historic distinction as well. He is the only American Jew who appears on a piece of currency: the Confederate two-dollar bill.

Judah P. Benjamin appears on the Confederate two-dollar bill.

Modernization of the White House

One of Fillmore's enduring contributions to the presidency was the modernization of the White House. During his brief tenure, a new cast-iron cooking stove was installed in the kitchen to replace the open-hearth fireplace that heretofore had been used in preparing meals. The Fillmores installed the first bathtub with running water in the Executive Mansion. With a grant from Congress, Fillmore's wife, Abigail, also established the first White House Library, in the upstairs Oval

Room, purchasing the works of her favorite authors, including Thackeray and Dickens. There had not been so much as a Bible or dictionary in the White House when the Fillmores arrived.

Although Southern Whigs wanted Fillmore as their presidential candidate again in 1852, the Northern abolitionist faction of the party, whom he had alienated by signing the Fugitive Slave Law, actively opposed his renomination. Under pressure from its abolitionist wing, the Whig Party decided to dump Fillmore from the ticket and nominate in his stead a celebrated war hero, General Winfield Scott. Scott and the Whig Party were overwhelmingly defeated by the Democratic presidential candidate Franklin Pierce in the 1852 election. Soon thereafter, the Northern abolitionist Whigs began to switch to the new Republican Party, which actively opposed slavery, and by the late 1850s the Whig Party had ceased to exist. Millard Fillmore was thus the last of the four Whig Party presidents.

Post-Presidential Years

On a bitterly cold day in March 1853, Fillmore turned over the presidency to his successor, Franklin Pierce. At the inauguration, Abigail Fillmore caught a bad chill, which soon developed into bronchial pneumonia; she died a few weeks after leaving the White House. Following the Pierce inauguration and the death of his wife, Fillmore retired to Buffalo to resume his law practice.

In 1856, Fillmore accepted the presidential nomination of the anti-Catholic American, or Know-Nothing, Party, whose platform sought to exclude immigrants from holding public office in the United States. He received the nomination of the remnants of the Whig Party as well. In the election, Fillmore received only 21 percent of the vote, running a poor third behind the Democratic candidate, James Buchanan, and the Republican Party nominee, John C. Frémont. Fillmore carried only one state, Maryland.

In retirement, Fillmore soon became Buffalo's leading citizen. His law practice prospered, and he also became the first chancellor of the University of Buffalo. In 1858 he married Mrs. Caroline Carmichael McIntosh, the wealthy widow of a prominent businessman, who was thirteen years younger than Fillmore and who survived him by several years.

In 1861, the former president entertained President-elect and Mrs. Lincoln in Buffalo, on their way to the inauguration. In 1864, however, he supported Lincoln's opponent, McClellan, for the presidency. Although Fillmore supported the Union cause during the Civil War, he was widely criticized for his signing of the Fugitive Slave Law while president. After the Civil War, during Reconstruction, he supported President Andrew Johnson.

Millard Fillmore died on March 8, 1874, and was buried in Buffalo's Forest Lawn Cemetery, where there now stands a memorial to him and his family.

[D.G.D.]

Franklin Pierce

Served from 1853 to 1857

Born on November 23, 1804, in Hillsborough, New Hampshire

Member of the Episcopal denomination

Married Jane Means Appleton on November 19, 1834

Father to one son

Candidate of the Democratic Party

Vice president under Pierce: William R. King

Inaugural Address delivered on March 4, 1853

Died on October 8, 1869, in Concord, New Hampshire

Fourteenth President of the United States

A NORTHERN DEMOCRAT WHO SUPPORTED the extension of slavery, Franklin Pierce was the Democratic Party's dark-horse presidential nominee in 1852. It was hoped that he would win both Northern and Southern votes. A politician's politician, the handsome, genial Pierce had never lost an election, serving at different times as a popular congressman, U.S. senator, and governor of New Hampshire. Pierce can boast one of the most literate campaign biographies in the history of presidential politics. His was written by Bowdoin College classmate and lifelong friend, novelist Nathaniel Hawthorne. That Pierce was a master at getting along with people is evidenced by the fact that he is the only president in history who served out a complete term in office without having to make a single change in his Cabinet.

At the same time, however, Franklin Pierce was one of our worst chief executives, who badly misjudged the temper of the times. He regarded the abolitionists as a lunatic fringe who should be ignored, and, in signing the Kansas-Nebraska Act and the repeal of the Missouri Compromise, he unwittingly exacerbated the sectional conflicts that led to the Civil War. Overly fond of the bottle and well beyond his depth in the sectional quagmire and political turmoil of the 1850s, he was, as one commentator aptly put it, "a pleasant mediocrity at a time that demanded political giants in the White House."

The Capital's First Synagogue

Pierce has the unique distinction of being the only president whose name appears on the charter of a synagogue. Until 1856 the laws of the District of Columbia discriminated against the establishment of Jewish houses of worship. To put an end to this, Congress, which had sole jurisdiction over the District of Columbia, enacted legislation proclaiming that "all the rights, privileges and immunities heretofore granted by law to the Christian churches in the City of Washington, be, and the same hereby are, extended to the Hebrew Congregation of said city." When President Pierce put his signature on this bill, he made possible the establishment of the first synagogue, Washington Hebrew Congregation, in the nation's capital.

August Belmont

Franklin Pierce also has the distinction of having appointed August Belmont, the influential Jewish financier, to the post of U.S. Minister to The Hague. Belmont was the first Jew to hold this rank in the American diplomatic service. Throughout his long career in Democratic Party politics, Belmont would raise more money for presidential candidates than any other nineteenth-century American Jew. Although Belmont did not deny that he was Jewish, he dissociated himself from the Jewish community and permitted his children to be baptized in the Church.

Julius Bien

President Pierce helped launch the government career of Julius Bien (1826–1909), one of the world's greatest cartographers and lithographers. Bien had studied the graphic arts in his native Germany, prior to immigrating to America in

Franklin Pierce in uniform during the Mexican War.

1849. He set up a successful lithographic business in New York City in 1850, and his work received increasing public recognition in Washington, bringing him to the attention of President Pierce. At a meeting with Pierce, the president suggested that Bien apply for work with then Secretary of War Jefferson Davis. Bien was soon commissioned to make maps for the war department's transcontinental railway surveys. His map of the territory beyond the Mississippi River would remain the standard map of the American West for more than twenty-five years. From the time of his commission until his retirement, there was scarcely a major geographical or geological publication issued by the federal government for which the maps and illustrations were not engraved and printed by Bien.

Post-Presidential Years

Having not been nominated for a second term, Pierce's post-presidential years were bitter. Asked what a president should do after leaving office, Pierce answered: "There's nothing left . . . but to get drunk." Pierce took his own advice and would begin to drink even more heavily after the death of his wife in 1863. In 1860 he proposed his former secretary of war, Jefferson Davis, for the Democratic Party's presidential nomination, and, with the onset of the Civil War, Pierce publicly opposed the use of force by the North and denounced the Emancipation Proclamation as unconstitutional. He came to be regarded as a traitor of sorts and was shunned by his former friends. In his native New Hampshire he became so un-

Julius Bien

popular that a half-century went by after his death in 1869 before the citizens of Concord saw fit to erect a statue in his honor.

During the Civil War, Nathaniel Hawthorne, against the advice of his publishers, dedicated one of his books to the former president and included in it an open letter to his old friend that was full of praise. Ralph Waldo Emerson bought Hawthorne's book but cut out both the dedication and the letter before reading it.

[D.G.D.]

James Buchanan

Served from 1857 to 1861

Born on April 23, 1791, in Cove Gap, Pennsylvania

Member of the Presbyterian denomination

Candidate of the Democratic Party

Vice president under Buchanan: John C. Breckinridge

Inaugural Address delivered on March 4, 1857

Died on June 1, 1868, in Lancaster, Pennsylvania

Fifteenth President of the United States

JAMES BUCHANAN WAS THE ONLY PRESIDENT who never married. In addition to being our nation's only bachelor president, Buchanan enjoys two other distinctions. He was the last American president born in the eighteenth century and, at age sixty-five, the oldest man to become Chief Executive until the inauguration of Ronald Reagan in 1981.

The first of eight children, James Buchanan was born on April 23, 1791, in a log cabin at Cove Gap, just outside Mercersberg, Pennsylvania, where his family moved when he was five years old. After attending Dickinson College, Buchanan moved to Lancaster, Pennsylvania, where he studied law and was admitted to the bar in 1812.

Buchanan had a long, distinguished political career before entering the White House. Following service in the War of 1812, he was elected to the Pennsylvania State Legislature as a member of the Federalist Party. In 1820 he was elected to the U.S. House of Representatives, where he served until 1831. With the disintegration of the Federalist Party during the 1820s, Buchanan became a member of the new Democratic Party led by Andrew Jackson. Prior to his election as president in 1856, Buchanan would subsequently serve as a U.S. senator, U.S. Minister to Russia and Great Britain, and secretary of state.

Buchanan and the Jews

Shortly after taking office in 1857, President Buchanan met with a delegation of prominent American Jewish leaders to discuss their opposition to a United States commercial treaty with Switzerland that discriminated against American Jews. Originally negotiated by the Fillmore administration in 1850, the treaty with Switzerland, while granting full rights to American Christians traveling or working in their country, permitted Swiss cantons to deny entry to American Jews. In response to protests from the Jewish community, President Fillmore had agreed to oppose the treaty, which the Senate had then refused to ratify. In 1855, however, a second draft of the Swiss Treaty was ratified by the Senate. When, in 1857, an American Jewish merchant was ordered to leave the Swiss canton of Neuchâtel solely because he was a Jew, protest meetings denouncing the treaty were organized in Jewish communities throughout the U.S., and Jewish leaders met with President Buchanan to discuss their opposition to the treaty. Buchanan supported the Jewish community's position and advised the U.S. minister to Switzerland, Theodore S. Fay, to work for the removal of the discriminatory clause. At Buchanan's behest, Fay wrote a lengthy protest note to the Swiss government. On the eve of the Civil War, Fay claimed that his note had changed official Swiss opinion on the issue, and he confidently predicted a removal of the treaty's anti-Jewish restrictions. Despite the efforts of the Buchanan administration, the anti-Jewish restrictions would not be lifted until 1866.

The Mortara Case

The following year, American Jewish leaders met with President Buchanan again, requesting that he intercede with the Vatican on their behalf in the Mortara affair, which had aroused worldwide protest. In June 1858 papal authorities had abducted six-year-old Edgar Mortara from the home of his Jewish parents in Bologna, Italy, over which the Vatican ruled, claiming that the child had been secretly baptized at the request of a Catholic servant of the Mortaras and thus should be raised as a Catholic. Although Buchanan sympathized with the Jewish community's request, he believed it inappropriate for the United States to intervene in the "internal affairs" of another government, in this case the Papal States. That President Van Buren had intervened earlier in the Damascus Affair in 1840 did not influence Buchanan. His mind was focused on the slavery debate; it was consuming much of his time and also was weakening Democratic Party unity. As a Democrat, Buchanan did not want to divide the Democratic Party further by antagonizing Northern Irish Catholic voters who supported the papacy's position.

August Belmont

During his presidency, James Buchanan had close contacts with two prominent Jewish politicians, August Belmont and Judah P. Benjamin. Belmont, the influential German-Jewish financier who had married the daughter of Commodore Matthew C. Perry and was at the center of New York society, was one of the leaders of New York's Democratic Party and one of Buchanan's close political confidants. In 1852, Belmont had been the New York manager of Buchanan's unsuccessful presidential campaign. The following year, Buchanan had helped persuade President Franklin Pierce to offer Belmont the major diplomatic post of U.S. Minister to The Hague, which Belmont held throughout the Pierce administration.

After raising considerable money for Buchanan's successful presidential campaign in 1856, Belmont turned down offers of diplomatic appointments from Buchanan, but continued to advise Buchanan throughout his administration, while resuming his banking career on Wall Street. In 1860, Belmont would be named chairman of the Democratic National Committee, a position that he would hold for more than a decade.

COURTESY OF THE NEW YORK PUBLIC LIBRARY

James Buchanan towards the end of his career.

Judah P. Benjamin

Benjamin, the flamboyant U.S. Senator from Louisiana and future secretary of state of the Confederacy, who had been offered a seat on the Supreme Court by Millard Fillmore, was Buchanan's most important political supporter in the Jewish community. One of the first Jews to attend Yale University, Benjamin had settled in New Orleans in 1828 and had established a reputation as one of the most prominent attorneys and politicians in the state, winning election to the U.S. Senate in 1852. Benjamin played an especially influential role in Buchanan's presidential campaign in 1856 as one of the leaders of the "Buchaneers," a group that took over the Democratic National Convention to nominate Buchanan for president. After his election, Buchanan offered Benjamin the ambassadorship to Spain, which Benjamin turned down, preferring to remain in the Senate. Throughout his presidency, Buchanan would consult Benjamin on a regular basis, particularly on policies relating to the issues of slavery and states' rights.

Presidency and Post-Presidential Years

James Buchanan entered the White House hoping to resolve the acrimonious debate that was dividing his Democratic Party, and the nation, in the years before the Civil War. In this objective his presidency was a failure. Although devoted to the Union, Buchanan's pro-Southern policies as president had helped bring on the Civil War. He supported the Fugitive Slave Act, the admission into the Union of Kansas as a slave state, and the Supreme Court's infamous Dred Scott decision, declaring that Congress could not prohibit slavery in U.S. territories. In 1860 Buchanan supported his vice president, John C. Breckinridge, a pro-slavery Democrat from Kentucky, for president. As the secession crisis intensified during the last months of his administration, Buchanan's main objective was to postpone the outbreak of fighting until he left office. In this goal he was successful. When Buchanan turned the government over to Abraham Lincoln on March 4, 1861, he is reported to have said: "If you are as happy in entering the White House as I shall be in returning to Wheatland [Pennsylvania], you are a happy man indeed."

Although content in his retirement in Pennsylvania, as a former president Buchanan was the subject of continuing public criticism. He and his administration were vilified for bringing on the Civil War, and it was alleged by some that his Cabinet had committed treason. Throughout the Civil War, however, Buchanan remained a loyal supporter of Abraham Lincoln and his administration, and subsequently of the Reconstruction policy of Lincoln's successor, Andrew Johnson.

Shortly before his death in 1868, Buchanan told a friend: "I have always felt and I still feel that I discharged every public duty imposed on me conscientiously. I have no regret for any public act of my life, and history will vindicate my memory."

Such faith was misplaced. History never did vindicate him, and historians have, over the years, continued to rank Buchanan as one of our worst presidents.

[D.G.D.]

Abraham Lincoln

Served from 1861 to 1865

Born on February 12, 1809, in Hardin (now Larue) County, Kentucky

No formal religious affiliation but attended Presbyterian services

Married Mary Todd on November 4, 1842

Father to three sons

Candidate of the Republican Party

Vice presidents under Lincoln: Hannibal Hamlin (first term);
Andrew Johnson (second term)

First Inaugural Address delivered on March 4, 1861
Second Inaugural address delivered on March 4, 1865

Assassinated on April 15, 1865 in Washington, D.C.

Sixteenth President of the United States

*I*N A POLL TAKEN IN 1962, HISTORIANS RANKED Abraham Lincoln first among all presidents who had served to date. Yet, in the opinion of many of his contemporaries, Lincoln was an unlikely choice for Chief Executive.

In a July 19, 1887 letter to a friend, William Henry Herndon, who became Lincoln's junior law partner in 1844 and who knew his colleague well, described Lincoln as "six feet and four inches tall in his stocking feet; consumptive by build, and hence more or less stoop-shouldered. He was tall, thin, and gaunt. When he rose to speak to the jury or to crowds of people, he stood inclined forward, was awkward, angular, ungainly . . ."

Novelist Nathaniel Hawthorne, who saw Lincoln in Washington, D.C., in the spring of 1862, wrote in his *Tales, Sketches, and Other Tales*: "There is no describing his lengthy awkwardness nor the uncouthness of his movements. . . . If put to guess his calling and livelihood, I should have taken him for a schoolmaster as soon as anything else."

Jews, however, saw only the stately side of Lincoln. He was a hero of unsurpassed stature and distinction, so much so that his memory evoked warm, positive feelings for more than a century after his passing. This feeling was demonstrated in 1968 when James Myers, a descendant of Jewish shopkeepers Morris and Katherine Myers, joined with several friends to purchase a dilapidated building in Springfield, Illinois, where Abraham Lincoln had practiced law. They restored the interior of the building as faithfully as possible, and it became a favorite tourist attraction.

What impelled James Myers to undertake this memorial to the slain president was the recollection of how affected his ancestors had been by the assassination of Lincoln. At the very moment that Morris and Katherine Myers were moving into Springfield from nearby Athens, they happened across the president's funeral procession, which was on its way to the cemetery. Together with their four young children, Morris and Katherine Myers fell into line and witnessed Lincoln's coffin being lowered into the ground as piercing rifle volleys filled the air.

This emotional experience left an indelible impression on the Myers family in 1868, feelings that were still reverberating in James Myers over one hundred years later.

Lincoln's Jewish Contacts

During Lincoln's years in office, he cultivated many Jewish friends who supported him while he endured difficult and trying times. He had no family to call upon for advice, comfort, or support. His wife, Mary Todd, while refined and well-educated, was also contentious and subject to temper tantrums. Once Lincoln was elected president and she became first lady, the pressures of public life were more than she could handle. She reached the breaking point in 1862 when their twelve-year-old son, Willie, died. The unhappy event left her terribly distressed and increased the president's bouts with depression. Many of Lincoln's Jewish friends and confidants helped him navigate through his personal and public travails—particularly the dissolution of the Union.

There is no record of Lincoln's having had contact with Jews in his formative years, but it is evident that from his reading of Scripture he was impressed by how readily God showered his blessing upon the Israelites in times of peril. Among the Jewish friends, supporters, and admirers of Lincoln who influenced his political life and supported him during the difficult Civil War period were five men of note: Abraham Jonas, Abraham Kohn, Isachar Zacharie, Simon Wolf, and Adolphus S. Solomons. Other Jews also had an impact on Lincoln's life although they did not always stand firmly behind him. Lincoln had met one such individual, Henry Greenbaum, at the home of "Long John" Wentworth, mayor of Chicago. After their meeting, Greenbaum commented on Lincoln's "congeniality," "mental endowment," and "sense of humor." But when Lincoln asked Greenbaum at that meeting for his backing in the campaign against Stephen A. Douglas, Greenbaum told Lincoln that he had already committed himself to Douglas and could not go back on his word. Lincoln appreciated Greenbaum's integrity.

Abraham Jonas

One of Lincoln's early friends, and one of the first to suggest that he seek the presidency, was Abraham Jonas (1801–1864). Jonas was born in Exeter, England, one of twenty-two siblings. He immigrated to the United States in 1817 and settled in Cincinnati, Ohio. There, together with his brother Joseph (1792–1869), who had arrived in Cincinnati earlier, he established the state's first synagogue. Abraham moved several times, finally settling permanently, in 1838, in Quincy, Illinois, where he was admitted to the bar, established a law practice, and became acquainted with Abraham Lincoln.

Jonas aspired to political office but failed in two attempts, in 1842 and 1844, to win a seat on the Illinois State Legislature. Nevertheless, he remained active in politics, joining the Republican Party of Lincoln and supporting him in his campaigns against Douglas for the presidency.

Lincoln appreciated the efforts of Jonas and in a February 3, 1860, letter called him "one of my most valued friends . . ." In 1862, Lincoln appointed Jonas postmaster of Quincy, a position he held until his death on June 2, 1864.

Being a person of noble character, Jonas never

took advantage of his friendship with the president. Even when one of Jonas's sons, Charles, who had been serving in the Confederate Army, was captured and sent to a Union prisoner-of-war camp, Jonas did not ask the president to intercede on his behalf. It was only when Jonas was on his deathbed that his wife asked Lincoln to intercede so that his son might be at his bedside when his father passed away. Lincoln issued the order, and Charles reached his father's side just moments before he drew his last breath.

Abraham Kohn

Abraham Kohn, who in 1842, at the age of twenty-three, left his Bavarian village to seek his fortune in America, was one of Abe Lincoln's devoted supporters and admirers. Within two years of arriving in America, Kohn had established a successful business in Chicago and become one of the leaders of Chicago Jewry and founder of the Kehillath Anshe Ma'Arav (K.A.M.) synagogue. In 1860, the year Lincoln was elected to the presidency, Kohn was elected city clerk of Chicago. He was characterized by his detractors as "one of the blackest Republicans and abolitionists."

Learning of Lincoln's love for the Bible, upon the president's election Kohn sent him a painted replica of the American flag that he had personally decorated and upon which he had inscribed these Hebrew words from the Book of Joshua (1:3,5-6): "Every place that the sole of your foot shall tread, I have given to you, as I promised to Moses . . . I will not fail you or forsake you. Be strong and of good courage . . ."

It is reported that whenever Kohn and Lincoln met, they spent more time talking about the Bible than about politics.

Isachar Zacharie

In the late summer of 1862 Lincoln was introduced to British-born podiatrist Isachar Zacharie. The president, who had been having trouble with his feet, learned that such luminaries as Henry

Clay and William Cullen Bryant had suffered from similar ailments and that Dr. Zacharie had treated them with good results. The doctor's successful treatment of Lincoln earned him the president's praise, and this led to Zacharie's appointment as White House chiropodist.

Lincoln expressed his confidence in the ability and wisdom of Zacharie in yet another matter, this one of great national import. In January of 1863, only four months after having met Zacharie, the president sent the doctor to New Orleans to appraise the military situation and to sound out the prospects for entering peace negotiations with the Confederacy. In a letter to Lincoln dated January 14, 1863, Zacharie indicated that conditions were not ripe for such discussions but that the local population was pleased that General Nathaniel Banks had replaced General Benjamin Butler, who had treated the local residents poorly.

General Banks got along well with Zacharie and in July of 1863 wrote a letter to Secretary of State Seward praising Zacharie's efforts. Mean-spirited General Butler, however, who had not fared well with the local community of New Orleans or its affluent Jewish minority, accused Jewish soldiers under his command of displaying cowardice in battle. Butler's superior, General George B. McClellan, rejected the accusations and wrote to the local newspaper, the *Jewish Record*: "My attention [was] never called to the peculiarities of Jewish soldiers when I was in command . . . I have never had reason to suppose them inferior to their comrades of other races and religions."

Simon Wolf

Among the immigrants who had fled Germany in the mass exodus of 1848 was Simon Wolf (1836–1923). He and his family settled in Ulrichsville, Ohio. In 1862, after studying law, Simon, who was intensely interested in politics, moved to Washington, D.C. By age twenty-four he had been selected to serve as a delegate to the Democratic Party conventions held in Charleston in 1856 and Baltimore in 1860. Liberal-minded and antislavery, Wolf was attracted to

A street in Jerusalem bears the name of the sixteenth U.S. president.

Lincoln's philosophy and in 1860 switched to the Republican Party.

Wolf's association with Lincoln was widely publicized in 1861 after Wolf, who lived in Ohio, received a message that a local Jewish boy who was accused of desertion was to be shot the following morning at sunrise. Together with Ohio Congressman Thomas Corwin, Simon Wolf went to see the president to plead for the life of the soldier. The soldier was not a deserter. He had simply left camp without permission to visit his dying mother.

Lincoln told the duo he could do nothing for the boy because Secretary of War Stanton threatened to resign if he pardoned another deserter. Appealing to the compassionate nature of Lincoln, Wolf then asked the president:

> What would you have done in the boy's place? If your dying mother had summoned you to her bedside to receive her last message before her soul would be summoned to its Maker, would you rather have been a deserter to her who gave you birth or a deserter in law but not in fact to the flag to which you had sworn allegiance?

Deeply touched, Lincoln rang a bell, summoning his secretary, John Jay, and ordered that a telegram be sent to halt the execution.

Subsequently, the soldier returned to his regiment and in the 1864 battle of Cold Harbor was killed while leading a charge with an American flag held aloft in his hand. When the president learned of the soldier's heroism, he said: "I thank God for having done the right thing."

In 1864 the poet William Cullen Bryant, who was editor of the *New York Evening Post* and considered the dean of the American press, printed biased articles critical of Jews and their loyalty to America. After Wolf responded, saying that "ignorance is the foundation of prejudice and intolerance," Lincoln came to the defense of the Jews, saying: "No class of citizenship in the United States was superior in patriotism to those of the Jewish faith."

Adolphus Simeon Solomons

One particular Jew who Lincoln admired and respected for his gentlemanly character and devoted loyalty was Adolphus S. Solomons (1826–1910). Born in the United States, Solomons became a prominent Washington businessman. He also was a photographer, ran a publishing house, and served as a leader in many social and welfare agencies, especially the Red Cross. During the presidency of Millard Fillmore, Secretary of State Daniel Webster had appointed Solomons special bearer of dispatches to Berlin.

Solomons took an active part in planning the inauguration of every president from Abraham Lincoln to William Taft. His influence with Lincoln and with the Republican leadership in Congress was profound. Although Jews were a very small minority, he was able to arrange for Rabbi Morris J. Raphall (1798–1868), of Congregation B'nai Jeshurun in New York City, to have the privilege of being the first rabbi to deliver an invocation at a morning session of Congress. At a later date, Solomons was able to arrange a meeting between Lincoln and Raphall so that the rabbi might ask a favor of the president.

The story behind this meeting was revealed by Solomons many years later when, in a 1903 speech at a Lincoln birthday celebration given under the auspices of the Hebrew Educational Society of Brooklyn, New York, he made the following statement:

> The day that Lincoln issued one of his early war proclamations I chanced to be at the White House with a distinguished New York rabbi, Dr. Morris J. Raphall, who came to Washing-

ton to ask for the promotion of his son, Alfred, from a second to a first lieutenancy in the army. The White House was closed for the day when we got there, but upon sending up my card we gained admittance, and after Lincoln had heard the rabbi's request he blurted out, "As God's minister is it not your first duty to be at home today to pray with your people for the success of our arms as being done in every loyal church throughout the North, East and West?"

> The Rabbi, evidently ashamed at his faux pas, blushingly made answer: "My assistant is doing that duty."

> "Ah, said Lincoln, "that is different."

> The President then drew forth a small card and wrote the following upon it: The Secretary of War will promote Second Lieutenant Raphall to a First Lieutenancy.

> And then, handing the card to the rabbi, the President said: "Now, doctor, you can go home and do your own praying."

In *Reminiscences of Abraham Lincoln*, an informative book Solomons wrote about Lincoln and their relationship, the author describes how he asked the president if he would sit for a new picture in the photographic department of his publishing house situated at 911 Pennsylvania Avenue. Solomons reports: "The president came on Sunday April 9th and wore a troubled expression. The negative did not show up well and Lincoln caught the disappointment on Adolphus's face. He agreed to pose again saying, 'Solomons, tell me one of your funny stories, and we will see if I can't do better.'"

This was the last picture ever taken of the president. Five days later he would be assassinated.

Uriah Phillips Levy

After Uriah Phillips Levy's suspension from the Navy without pay by President Tyler, between 1845 and 1855, he tried persistently to return to active duty, but all efforts at reinstatement failed. The excuse given in 1855, during the presidency of Franklin Pierce, was that it was due to an effort "to improve the efficiency of the Navy." Finally, in November and December of 1857, Levy was given an opportunity to present his case personally before a court of inquiry held in Washington, D.C.

Offering a very emotional defense, Levy condemned the anti-Jewish sentiment prevailing in the Navy and insisted that he was entitled to equal treatment even as he had been careful to treat fairly every Christian sailor under his command. He presented statements by George Bancroft, secretary of the Navy, to the effect that anti-Semitism was a contributing factor motivating those opposed to his reinstatement.

Public protest in favor of Levy followed the proceedings of the court of inquiry, and on January 29, 1858, he was reinstated as a naval captain. Three years later, when the Civil War broke out, Levy, at age sixty-nine, tried unsuccessfully to persuade the Navy secretary to send him back to sea. Levy appealed to President Lincoln, but according to an unconfirmed legend the president reminded Uriah that he was "a mite too old" for such duty. The president then suggested that since Uriah had survived a few courts-martial in his day, "all that experience ought not go to waste. I think you will be useful serving on the Courts-Martial Board here in Washington."

Levy served on the board from November 1861 to March 1862, when he caught a cold that developed into pneumonia. He died on March 22, 1862. He regarded the outlawing of corporal punishment in the U.S. Navy to have been the greatest achievement of his life. He reflected that feeling when he left instructions that his tombstone be engraved with the following words: "Uriah P. Levy, Captain in the United States Navy, Father of the law for the abolition of the barbarous practice of corporeal punishment in the Navy of the United States."

Uriah P. Levy was buried in New York's Shearith Israel's synagogue cemetery in Cypress Hills, Brooklyn, New York. During World War II, a destroyer was named in his honor, and in 1959 the Jewish Chapel at the Norfolk Naval Base was designated the Uriah Phillips Levy Chapel.

Other Jewish Supporters

By 1861, many of the Jews who had come from Germany to the United States had become active in the Republican Party, which encouraged middle-class business entrepreneurs. Included among these was Moses Aaron Dropsie (1821–1905), a Philadelphia lawyer whose father was Jewish and mother Christian. At age fourteen, Moses had favored Judaism and become a devout Jew; he would bequeath funds to establish Dropsie College for Hebrew and Cognate Learning. Dropsie was a founder of the Republican Party in Philadelphia which strongly supported Lincoln.

Another ardent Lincoln supporter was Moritz Pinner (1828–1909) of Missouri, who, together with Lewis N. Dembitz (1833–1907) of Kentucky, was one of the three delegates at the Republican convention in 1860 who placed Lincoln's name in nomination. Pinner was the editor of the outspoken abolitionist newspaper, the *Kansas Post*. When Lincoln wanted to repay Pinner for his support by offering him a consular post, Pinner declined, choosing to enlist in the Union Army, as did many of his coreligionists.

Another unsung hero of the Lincoln Administration was Joseph Seligman (1819-1880), who, together with his brothers, had prospered as international bankers and developed a close relationship with General Grant during the Civil War. They purchased and encouraged others to buy war bonds, so essential for the waging of war. Seligman sought no reward for his loyalty, and when later, as president, Grant wished to appoint him secretary of the Treasury, he declined the honor.

The Chaplaincy Battle

Lincoln's gratefulness for the loyalty of his Jewish friends and admirers was nowhere more evident than in the struggle to have rabbis officially recognized as chaplains in the armed forces. While army chaplains of the Christian faith had been serving in the armed forces of the United States as far back as the Revolutionary War, it was not until the Civil War that sufficient influence was brought to bear to grant Jewish chaplains the right to serve.

As pointed out by David Max Eichhorn in *Rabbis in Uniform*, the American army had thirty chaplains at the start of the Civil War, none of them Jewish. A congressional act of July 22, 1861, allowed each regiment one chaplain who had to be an ordained Christian clergyman. He was to receive the pay and allowances of a captaincy of cavalry.

This did not mean that a Jewish chaplain could not serve if he did not seek recompense, and so Colonel Max Freedman, commanding officer of the sixty-fifth Regiment of the Fifth Pennsylvania Cavalry, selected Michael Allen, a young Philadelphia Hebrew teacher and student of Rabbi Isaac Leeser, to be their chaplain. When it was discovered that Allen was neither a Christian nor an ordained clergyman, a vehement protest ensued, and he was forced to resign on September 23, 1861.

Upset by this unfair treatment, Colonel Freedman persuaded a rabbi from New York, Arnold Fischel, a duly ordained clergyman, to apply for a commission as chaplain of his regiment. The application was turned down on October 23 by the secretary of war because Fischel was not "a minister of some Christian denomination."

This action upset not only the Board of Delegates of American Israelites, organized in 1859 to fight for Jewish rights, but Congressman Clement L. Vallandigham of Ohio as well. Maintaining that the rights of the Jewish people were being violated, Vallandigham proposed that the act be amended and that words such as "some religious society" be substituted for the words "some Christian faith."

The Board of Delegates then urged Rabbi Fischel to travel to Washington to discuss the matter directly with the president. Proper arrangements were made, and on December 11 Fischel met with Lincoln. Two days later, Fischel received the following note from the president:

> I find there are several particulars in which the present law in regard to Chaplains is supposed to be deficient, all which I now design presenting to the appropriate committee of Congress. I shall try to leave a new law broad enough to cover what is desired by you in behalf of the Israelites.

Rabbi Fischel was terribly disappointed, not only because his mission had failed, but because the Jewish community did not sufficiently appreciate his effort and did not reimburse him for the expenses he had incurred during his stay in Washington. Later, in 1862, he returned to Holland, the country of his birth.

True to his promise, Lincoln submitted to Congress a list of proposed changes in the chaplaincy law. After much debate, the proposed changes passed the Senate on March 12, 1862, and the House on July 17, 1862.

Upon the recommendation of the Board of Ministers of the Hebrew Congregation of Philadelphia, President Lincoln then appointed the Reverend Jacob Frankel (1808–1887), of Rodeph Shalom Congregation, to serve as the first Jewish military chaplain. The Jewish community was gratified over Lincoln's swift action.

Abram Jesse Dittenhoefer

Motivated by a strong belief that Jews in particular should oppose the institution of slavery, Abram Dittenhoefer (1836-1919) found it necessary to rebel against his family's loyalty to the pro-slavery Democratic Party. The son of Isaac and Babette Dittenhoefer, Abram was born in Charleston, South Carolina, on March 17, 1836, and brought to New York when he was four years old. By age nineteen, he had graduated from Columbia College and begun practicing law. He dabbled in politics by associating himself with the abolitionist Republican Party, and by 1864 he had risen to be one of New York's electors on the Lincoln ticket. Dittenhoefer would act as chairman of the General Republican Central Committee for twelve terms.

In his memoir *How We Elected Lincoln—Personal Recollections and Men of His Time*, Dittenhoefer recalls frequent interviews he had with President Lincoln and his "well-considered estimate of the Great Emancipator's character and personality." Most appreciative of Dittenhoefer's continued support, in 1863 the president offered to appoint him judge of the district court of South Carolina, his native state. However, Dittenhoefer's

President Lincoln expresses his support for a Jewish state in a conversation with Henry Monk, a prominent Christian Zionist.

increasing business in the city of New York, and his wife's disinclination to move to South Carolina, "compelled me to decline the honor."

Grant's Order No. 11

Lincoln's appreciation for Jewish support was displayed most meaningfully perhaps by his revocation of General Ulysses S. Grant's Order No. 11, issued on December 17, 1862, which read: "The Jews, as a class, violating every regulation of trade established by the Treasury Department and also departmental orders, are hereby expelled from the Department [of the Tennessee] within twenty-four hours." With Tennessee Jews falsely accused of bribing officers to allow them to smuggle cotton, a scarce commodity, from the South to the North, Jewish businessmen strongly protested Grant's order.

The Assassination

President Lincoln was in a festive mood on Friday, April 14, 1865, as was the entire city of Washington. One week earlier, on April 9, General Robert E. Lee had surrendered to General Ulysses S. Grant at Appomattox Court House, Virginia. The war was over and, in accordance with Lincoln's instructions, generous terms were granted. Confederate soldiers were allowed to go home with their horses, and officers were permitted to retain their side arms. For Jews it was a doubly joyous time; they were also celebrating Passover, commemorating freedom from Egyptian enslavement several millennia earlier.

Lincoln and his wife, Mary, along with several friends, went to Ford's Theatre that evening to watch the performance of the comedy *Our American Cousin*. When they arrived at 8:30, the show had already begun. As soon as the president entered his box, the entire sixteen-hundred-person audience stood and cheered while the orchestra played "Hail to the Chief."

Ninety minutes later, during a scene that had the audience rocking with laughter, John Wilkes Booth, a twenty-six-year-old frustrated and deranged actor, shot the president in the back of the head, rendering him unconscious. Mary Todd Lincoln would later recall the president's expressed desire, just minutes before he was shot: to consider planning a visit to the Holy Land.

Instead of celebrating the Passover of 1865 joyfully in their homes and synagogues, Jews grieved for their fallen hero. Not the least among the mourners was Dr. Charles Henry Lieberman, one of the sixteen doctors summoned to try to save the life of the wounded president. But neither he nor any of the other doctors could help. The bullet that entered the president's left ear had tunneled through to his brain. At 7:22 A.M. on April 15, 1865, the sixteenth president of the United States was pronounced dead.

Rabbinic Supporters and Detractors

Jews were immensely saddened by the president's untimely death. Many congregations in the North expressed their grief by draping their galleries and entrance doors with black hangings and reciting memorial prayers, and Congregation Ohabei Shalom of Boston went so far as to express its sorrow by adopting the following resolution: "That the synagogue shall be draped in mourning for 30 days, and that a prayer for the dead shall be chanted every Sabbath and Mondays and Thursdays [days when the Torah is read] during that time."

The action of the Jews of Boston accurately represented the feelings of Jews generally. The death of the president was felt as keenly as though they had lost a member of their immediate family.

The eulogies delivered for the slain president were heart-rending. Rabbis of all denominations were profuse in their praise of Lincoln. Even those who were critical of his policies and often demeaning in their characterization of him now viewed him from a different perspective. Among

these was Rabbi Morris J. Raphall, who had never failed to chastise Lincoln from the pulpit for his advocacy of abolition. From 1861 onward, in sermon after sermon, Raphall's preachments were aimed at convincing his flock and all Americans that slavery was sanctioned by the Bible and that those opposed to slavery had no right to condemn those who were slaveholders.

In an 1861 sermon entitled "The Bible View of Slavery," Raphall wrote: "When you remember that Abraham, Isaac, Jacob and Job—the men with whom the Almighty conversed . . . were slaveholders, does it not strike you that you are guilty of something very little short of blasphemy?" The sermon, which was widely distributed, was aimed at Henry Ward Beecher and other abolitionists who were preaching that slavery is a sin.

Raphall had only kind words for the slain Abraham Lincoln.

Isaac Mayer Wise

In the 1850s and 1860s, Rabbi Isaac Mayer Wise (1819–1900), the esteemed rabbi of Cincinnati's Reform congregation B'nai Yeshurun and a staunch Democrat with pro-Southern leanings,

Isaac Mayer Wise

did not hesitate to preach pro-slavery sentiments to his predominantly Republican membership. He particularly angered many members of his congregation as well as the readers of the *Israelite*, a newspaper he edited, when he urged that Jews vote the Democratic ticket and support the Dred Scott decision, which held that Congress had no right to prohibit slavery in the territories.

At one point, after observing Lincoln at a pre-inaugural stop in Cincinnati in 1861, Wise wrote in his newspaper: "Poor old Abe Lincoln who has the quiet life of a country lawyer, has been elected President of the United States . . . We have no doubt he is an honest man . . . but he will look queer in the White House with his primitive manner."

Only after Lincoln's assassination did Rabbi Wise have a change of heart and begin to express an appreciation for Lincoln's contributions to the United States. It was reported that in a eulogy delivered by Rabbi Wise five days after the assassination he said: "Brethren, the lamented Abraham Lincoln believed himself to be bone from our bone and flesh from our flesh. He supposed himself to be a descendant of Hebrew parentage. He said so in my presence." Regretfully, scholars have not been able to substantiate the accuracy of the report.

David Einhorn

David Einhorn and Benjamin Szold

Reform rabbi David Einhorn (1809-1879), of Har Sinai Temple in Baltimore, Maryland, had come to the United States from Germany in 1848, the same year that a large influx of German Jews migrated to America. Eighteen forty-eight was a watershed year, the time when most German Jews became convinced that there was no future for them in their homeland, where the hope for the establishment of a liberal parliamentary system of government was fading.

Einhorn had long attacked Morris Raphall for his anti-abolitionist sermons, reminding him that to enslave human beings created in the image of God constituted a rebellion against God. Most rabbis agreed with Einhorn in opposing slavery, but his call for its immediate eradication was considered too extreme. Instead they favored a gradual dissolution of the institution.

In one of his most dramatic sermons, Einhorn called slavery "the cancer of the Union," then went on to say:

> Does the Negro have less ability to think, to feel, to will? Does he have less of a desire to happiness? Was he born not to be entitled to all these? Does the Negro have an iron neck that does not feel a burdensome yoke? Does he have a stiffer heart that does not bleed when . . . his beloved child is torn away from him? . . . Slavery is immoral and must be abolished.

In time, Einhorn so displeased a sufficient number of his influential congregants that he was forced to leave town and seek a pulpit elsewhere. He ended up in Philadelphia, where he was at liberty to espouse his views, although even there many disagreed with him.

While Einhorn had admired Lincoln greatly,

Solomon Schechter

he had not hesitated to fault him for his leniency toward the South. He wanted the president to condemn secessionists and slaveowners as "rebels against the Almighty," deserving of severe punishment. Yet, in his eulogy for Lincoln, Einhorn sang only the praises of the president, referring to him as "the Messiah of his people" and "the High Priest of Freedom."

Rabbi Einhorn's more traditional colleague in Baltimore was Benjamin Szold (1829–1902), a strong supporter of the president. In his eulogy for Lincoln, Rabbi Szold (the father of Henrietta Szold, a founder of Hadassah) said:

> To us Jews Lincoln has a special meaning. In the course of history we found many fatherlands. We never knew freedom. It was here in the United States that we found freedom. It was Lincoln, who was so devoted to freedom, that we may, indeed, consider him a son of

Israel . . . Because of his love for freedom, we Jews must honor his memory.

Sabato Morais and Solomon Schechter

Italian-born Sabato Morais (1823–1897), who officiated as a rabbi in London from 1846 to 1851 and then came to America to succeed Rabbi Isaac Leeser (1806-1868) at the Sephardic Mikveh Israel congregation in Philadelphia, was one of Lincoln's most ardent supporters and an outspoken abolitionist. He would become one of the founders of New York's Jewish Theological Seminary of America and its first president.

In his eulogy for Lincoln, Morais compared the president to Hillel, the outstanding first-century B.C.E teacher who was motivated by the golden rule of Leviticus 19:18: "And thou shalt love thy neighbor as thyself."

One of the most moving tributes to Lincoln was that of Romanian-born Solomon Schechter (1847–1915), who was only a teenager when Lincoln was murdered. Though comfortably ensconced for many years in a teaching position at Cambridge University in England, Schechter had been hoping to come to America, where he might enjoy closer contact with a Jewish environment and Jewish scholars. In 1901 he was appointed president of the Jewish Theological Seminary of America, and soon afterwards expressed his fascination with the freedom Lincoln had advocated for all the citizens of the United States, regardless of race. In his *Seminary Addresses and Other Papers*, Schechter articulated these feelings about the Great Emancipator: "We may be grateful to God for having given us such a great soul as Lincoln, who, under God, gave this nation a new birth of freedom, and to our dear country, which by its institutions and its people rendered possible the greatness for which Abraham Lincoln shall stand forever."

Mourning a Martyr

Issac Leeser, one of the more prominent rabbis, scholars, and journalists of the mid-nineteenth century, arrived in the United States from Germany at age eighteen and became a great admirer of President Lincoln. For twenty-five years he served as editor of the *Occident and American Jewish Advocate*, which he had founded in 1843 and which was the most popular and influential Jewish publication of the period.

When the untimely death of America's beloved president was announced, Leeser wrote an essay entitled "How to Mourn," in which he counseled Jews how to grieve for their fallen hero—the martyred president of the United States. The Jews, perhaps more than any other segment of the American population, took the untimely death of the president as though it were a death in their own family.

[A.J.K.]

Andrew Johnson

Served from 1865 to 1869

Born on December 29, 1808, in Raleigh, North Carolina

Occasionally attended Methodist services with his wife,
but belonged to no church

Married Eliza McCardle on May 17, 1827

Father to two daughters and three sons

Candidate of the Democratic Party

Assumed the presidency on April 15, 1865, following
the assassination of Abraham Lincoln

Died on July 31, 1875, in Carter County, Tennessee

Seventeenth President of the United States

ANDREW JOHNSON WAS, IN MANY RESPECTS, a unique figure in the history of the American presidency. One of the few presidents to have had no formal education, his wife, Eliza, taught the future leader how to read and write, and how to do simple arithmetic. Johnson, who had been apprenticed to a tailor at the age of ten, was the only tailor ever to occupy the White House, and he was fiercely proud of his craft. He made his own clothes until he moved to Washington as a congressman. As governor of Tennessee, he still tailored his own clothes, and made a suit for the governor of Kentucky as a gesture of friendship. Even after Andrew Johnson became president, he almost never passed a tailor shop without dropping in for a chat. Although he rose rapidly in life after entering politics, he never forgot his humble origins. "Andy Johnson," said people in East Tennessee, "never went back on his raisin'."

The only Southern senator to oppose secession, Johnson responded to the hatred and vilification of secessionists in Tennessee and elsewhere with courage and defiance. He was the first president to be impeached and exonerated, and was also the first former president to return to Washington as a United States senator. Regrettably, Andrew Johnson was unique in another way as well: He was one of the few American presidents to have made overtly anti-Semitic public statements as a rising politician on the road to the White House.

An Andrew Jackson Democrat, Johnson was first elected to Congress at the age of thirty-four. He served four terms in the House and then went on to win election as Governor of Tennessee in 1853. "I have reached the summit of my ambition," Johnson said, when the Tennessee legislature elected him to the U.S. Senate in 1857. In the Senate, Johnson remained a good Jacksonian Democrat, attacking secession as "hell-born and hell-bound." To secessionists he was a "Southern traitor," and there were many threats on his life when he returned home to Tennessee after Abraham Lincoln's inauguration. In Knoxville, Memphis, and Nashville, Johnson was hanged and shot in effigy. Refusing to bow to threats and intimidation, he stumped the state to fight the movement for secession. Johnson's courageous efforts to keep Tennessee in the Union were ultimately in vain. In June 1861 Tennessee voted to join the Confederacy, and Johnson had to flee Tennessee for Washington. After northern troops seized western and central Tennessee in 1862, Lincoln appointed Johnson military governor of the state. Soon thereafter, Johnson persuaded the Tennessee legislature to rescind the ordinance of secession and to end slavery in the state forever.

In June 1864, when Johnson was nominated for vice president to run with Lincoln on the National Union Party ticket, people who disliked Lincoln ridiculed Johnson as well. "The age of statesmen is gone," lamented the *New York World* of the Lincoln-Johnson ticket; "the age of rail-splitters and tailors, of buffoons, boors and fanatics has succeeded . . ." The presence of a Jackson Democrat on the Union ticket, however, helped Lincoln win a large majority over his Democratic opponent, General George McClellan.

On the day of the Lincoln inauguration, March 4, 1865, Johnson was ill and had wanted to skip the inaugural ceremonies. To steady his nerves, he drank some whiskey beforehand and, as a result, embarrassed himself and his friends by talking too much and rather incoherently at the inaugural proceedings. When some people suggested to Lincoln that he should ask for his vice president's resignation, the president good-humoredly answered: "I have known Andrew Johnson for many years. He made a bad slip the other day, but you need not be scared; Andy ain't no drunkard."

When Johnson became president after Lincoln's assassination in April 1865, the Radical Republicans in Congress had high hopes for him, assuming that he would support their plans for a "radical" reconstruction of the Southern states, which included enfranchising the former black slaves and barring most of the ex-Confederates from government. However, they were disappointed in these expectations: It soon became clear that Johnson, like Lincoln, favored a milder reconstruction policy than that desired by the Radical Republicans. Johnson was not ready to disenfranchise former Confederate leaders or guarantee the freed slaves their complete rights as citizens. In the aftermath of the Congressional elections of 1866, in which the Radical Republicans won an overwhelming victory, they instituted a new and harsher Reconstruction program for the South over Johnson's vetoes, and enacted the Tenure of Office Act, limiting the president's power to remove federal appointees from office.

Believing this act to be unconstitutional, Johnson removed Secretary of War Edward M. Stanton, a Radical Republican who had been undermining the president's policies in his Cabinet. In response, in February 1868 the House of Representatives voted to impeach the president for "high crimes and misdemeanors." In the subsequent Senate trial, which lasted for over two months, Johnson was narrowly acquitted, with his opponents failing by only one vote to secure the necessary two-thirds for conviction.

Indirectly, one Jew played a part in the Andrew Johnson impeachment proceedings. Throughout the 1860s, and for decades to come, Adolphus S. Solomons, a friend and confidant of both Abraham Lincoln and Ulysses S. Grant, would play an active part in planning the inauguration ceremonies of every president from Lincoln to William Howard Taft. Upon his arrival in Washington in 1859, Solomons founded the successful printing and publishing firm of Philip and Solomons, which became a major supplier of stationery and office supplies to the U.S. Congress and which, for many years, until the establishment of the Government Printing Office, was given all government contracts for printing. In 1868 Solomons's firm printed the tickets to Andrew Johnson's congressional impeachment trial.

Andrew Johnson and Anti-Semitism

In February 1861, while still a senator from Tennessee, Johnson made several scurrilous attacks against two prominent Jews in government. Both were fellow Southern senators who, unlike Johnson, resigned from the Senate when their states seceded from the Union. While speaking to Charles Francis Adams, son of John Quincy Adams, about the secession of Florida, Johnson went out of his way to berate David Levy Yulee, Florida's senator. Yulee, who Johnson apparently blamed for Florida's secession from the Union, was called the "Florida fire-eater," because of his passionate proslavery oratory and staunch defense of the Confederate cause. Said Johnson to Adams:

> There's that Yulee, miserable little cuss! I remember him in the House—the contemptible little Jew—standing there and begging us—yes! Begging us to let Florida in as a State. Well! We let her in, and took care of her... and now that despicable little beggar stands up in the Senate and talks about her rights.

Ironically, Yulee, whom Johnson so publicly despised as a Jew, had renounced Judaism several years prior to Johnson's anti-Semitic remarks. Having changed his name from Levy to Yulee, he had converted to Christianity and thereafter claimed that he was not Jewish at all but descended from a Moroccan prince.

Charles Francis Adams also recounted to his son, Charles Francis Adams, Jr., how Johnson spoke disparagingly of Louisiana's Jewish senator, Judah P. Benjamin, who later served as attorney general, secretary of war, and secretary of state of the Confederacy. "There's another Jew," exclaimed Johnson, "that miserable Benjamin! He looks on a country and a government as he would on a suit of old clothes. He sold out the old one; and he would sell out the new if he could in so doing make two or three million!"

Moreover, in a speech delivered on the floor of the Senate later in 1861, while lashing out at a number of Southern senators for dividing the Union, Johnson was especially harsh in his attack on Benjamin for abandoning the Union cause:

> Mr. Benjamin of Louisiana, one that understands something about the idea of dividing garments; who belongs to that tribe that parted the garments of our Savior, and in this venture cast lots—went out of this body [the U.S. Senate] and was made Attorney General [of the new Confederate government], to show his patriotism and disinterestedness.

"Toward Jews," noted Adams, "Johnson felt a strong aversion.

Johnson and the Jews of Nashville

Despite these anti-Semitic attacks, Andrew Johnson had many Jewish friends and political supporters in Nashville, Tennessee. Several years after leaving office, in 1874, Johnson was the keynote speaker at the dedication of Nashville's Vine Street Temple. Prior to the ceremony, he rode in a carriage with Rabbi Isadore Kalisch of the Nashville congregation and with Rabbi Isaac Mayer Wise, the leader of Reform Judaism in America, and was accompanied by them to the pulpit. After introductory addresses by Rabbis Kalisch and Wise, Johnson spoke to the congregation, stating that no one felt a deeper interest in their success and prosperity or that of their temple than did he. In concluding, he expressed the hope that the Vine Street Temple "would ever remain a monument to the industry, prosperity, and welfare of the Jewish citizens of Nashville."

Judah P. Benjamin

Post-Presidential Years

After leaving the White House in March 1869, Andrew Johnson returned to Tennessee, but not to retirement. Anxious to vindicate his reputation, so tarnished by the impeachment proceedings, he reentered politics, running for Congress in both 1869 and 1872. Although he lost these elections, in 1874 the Tennessee legislature elected him to his old office of U.S. senator; he triumphantly returned to Washington in March 1875 as the only former president ever elected to the Senate. Johnson made only one speech in the Senate, reaffirming his belief in the milder Reconstruction policies that he had attempted to institute as president and denouncing the policies that had been imposed on the nation by the Radical Republicans. He felt vindicated by the applause that greeted him in the very Senate chamber that had tried to convict him seven years earlier.

After serving as senator for less than five months, the former president died of a stroke on July 31, 1875, at the age of sixty-six.

[D.G.D.]

Ulysses S. Grant

Served from 1869 to 1877

Born on April 27, 1822, in Point Pleasant, Ohio

Member of the Methodist denomination

Married Julia Boggs Dent on August 22, 1848

Father to three sons and one daughter

Candidate of the Republican Party

Vice presidents under Grant: Schuyler Colfax (first term);
Henry Wilson (second term)

First Inaugural Address delivered on March 4, 1869
Second Inaugural Address delivered on March 4, 1873

Died on July 23, 1885, in Mount McGregor, New York

Eighteenth President of the United States

ORN TO A WELL-TO-DO TANNER IN POINT Pleasant, Ohio, on April 27, 1822, Ulysses S. Grant was actually christened Hiram Ulysses Grant (Hiram for his maternal grandfather and Ulysses for the hero of Greek mythology). When Representative Thomas L. Hamer arranged to have him enroll in West Point, the congressman mistakenly recorded Grant's name as Ulysses Simpson Grant, Simpson being the maiden name of Grant's mother, Hannah Simpson. When Grant graduated from West Point in 1843, his diploma read Ulysses S. Grant, and he stated flatly: " I adopted it and have so signed my name ever since."

After four undistinguished years at West Point, Grant served in the Mexican War and then, in 1854, he resigned from the army. When the Civil War began, he rejoined the army as a colonel because "I could not endure the thought of the Union separating." Having demonstrated strong leadership, Grant was elevated by President Abraham Lincoln to the rank of lieutenant general and, in 1864, was assigned to command the Union armies. On April 9, 1865, he received Lee's surrender at Appomattox, a small village near Lynchburg, Virginia. He did so without braggadocio.

Although Ulysses S. Grant did not hold organized religion in high regard, he valued the Bible and its teachings. He took seriously the cautionary words in the Book of Proverbs (24:17), "When your enemy has fallen, do not exalt; if he trips, let your heart not rejoice," as evidenced by his halting the action of soldiers who had begun "firing a salute of a hundred guns in honor of the victory."

Shy and self-effacing, Grant disdained pageantry and undeserved honors. In 1866 he even went so far as to decline a share of his father's inheritance because, Grant stated, he had not contributed to the success of the family tanning business, which he detested and worked at for only one year.

Ulysses S. Grant displayed the same sense of correctness later in life. In his second Inaugural Address, on March 4, 1869, he did not hesitate to express his displeasure with the pro-slavery South:

> Social equality is not a subject to be legislated upon, nor shall I ask that anything be done to advance the social status of the colored man, except to give him a fair chance to develop what there is good in him, give him access to the schools, and when he travels, let him feel assured that his conduct will regulate the treatment and fare he will receive.

It is a credit to Grant that the fifteenth amendment to the Constitution, guaranteeing in precise language that "the right of citizens of the United States to vote shall not be denied or abridged by the United States or by any State on account of race, color, or previous condition of servitude," was ratified in 1870, during his tenure. A century would pass before "the fair chance" of which Grant spoke would be realized during the administrations of Presidents John F. Kennedy and Lyndon B. Johnson.

Order No. 11

In 1862 Grant was in command of the so-called Department of Tennessee, which included northern Mississippi and parts of Kentucky. The entire area was the center of a boom in the sale of cot-

President and Mrs. Grant (right) and their party, including Grant's former secretary Orville Babcock (left).

In a matter of days, a telegram was sent to President Lincoln, signed by leading Jewish businessmen and industrialists including D. Wolff and the brothers C. F. and J. W. Kaskel, expressing outrage at the inhuman treatment, "which made Jews look like outlaws before the entire world."

On January 3, one of the Kaskel brothers went to Washington to see the president. Initially, it appears, neither the president nor Stanton, his secretary of war, believed that Grant would have issued "an order so absurd and ridiculous." Kaskel then produced an official copy of the document, convincing the president that the allegation was true. Immediately, Lincoln revoked Order No. 11. As a consequence, most Jews harbored no resentment toward Grant, as was proven by his close friendship with Jews when he became president.

ton, which was badly needed in the North. As a result, hordes of speculators swarmed into Grant's territory and made tremendous profits by buying cotton at a cheap price and then taking it up North to sell at a huge profit. Jewish as well as non-Jewish traders were involved in these dealings, often resorting to smuggling and illegal profiteering. From ten cents a pound in December 1860, the price of cotton jumped to sixty-eight cents a pound in December 1862.

False charges were circulated that it was Jews who were involved in these crimes and that they alone bribed officers to smuggle out goods that were a much-needed wartime commodity. No reference was made to other speculators. As a consequence, on December 17, 1862, Major General Grant issued his notorious Order No. 11, by which all Jews were expelled from the entire Department of Tennessee and were given twenty-four hours in which to leave. It was further stipulated that any Jew who returned to the area would be summarily arrested.

Grant's Antagonists

Not all Jews, however, forgave what they called Grant's lack of sensitivity to the Jewish population. Prominent among them was the outspoken Reform leader Rabbi Isaac Mayer Wise, who was born in Bohemia and immigrated to the United States in 1846. After serving as rabbi of a synagogue in Albany, New York, Wise eventually moved to a new pulpit in Cincinnati, Ohio, where he gradually modified the service and turned it into a leading Reform congregation. In 1873 he organized the Union of American Hebrew Congregations (UAHC), and in 1875 he founded Hebrew Union College (HUC), which was dedicated to the training of Reform rabbis.

A longtime Democrat, Wise urged Jews to defeat Republican Grant in his 1868 run for the presidency. Wise argued that "no one in the nineteenth century, in civilized countries, has abused and outraged the Jew" more than Grant. "If there are," he continued, "any among us who lick the feet that kick them about like dogs, run after him who has whipped them; if there are persons small enough to receive indecencies and outrages without resentment . . . we hope their number is small." Clearly, Wise had Order No. 11 in mind.

Other prominent Jews also voiced strong sentiments against candidate Grant during the 1868 race. Herman Hellman of Los Angeles, founder of the Merchants National Bank, announced that he could not vote for someone with Grant's history. Charles Moses Strauss, who then lived in Memphis, organized the Jews of Tennessee to defeat Grant. Strauss later moved to Arizona and became mayor of Tucson.

Grant's Support of Jewish Interests

While a number of Jewish leaders considered Grant insensitive to Jewish needs, many considered him fair and forthcoming. Actually, Grant appointed more Jews to public office than any president before him, and when called upon by American Jews to intervene with foreign powers in whose countries the safety of Jews was threatened, the president did not hesitate to use his influence. In 1869, when it was called to Grant's attention that the expulsion of twenty-thousand Jews from an area in southwestern Russia was contemplated, he intervened with the czarist government, and the expulsion order was rescinded.

One year later, when Romanian Jews needed support, Grant took the unusual step of appointing a Jew as consul to the newly independent country so that he might monitor the situation more closely.

The Peixotto Appointment

In 1847 New York City-born lawyer and communal leader Benjamin Franklin Peixotto (1834-1890) settled with his family in Cleveland, Ohio. There, in 1863, while engaged in the clothing business, he was elected president of B'nai B'rith. Seven years later, at the urging of the Seligman brothers (Joseph and Jesse) and Simon Wolf, the president appointed Peixotto as the first U.S. consul to Romania. That country had only recently gained its independence from the Turkish empire; in the wake of independence a series of attacks were perpetrated by the local population against the Jews of Romania. The consular position was an unpaid one; B'nai B'rith agreed to defray all expenses for five years.

In the letter that Grant sent with Peixotto to be presented to the ruling powers of Romania, he wrote:

> The bearer of this letter, Mr. Benjamin Peixotto, who has accepted the important, though unremunerative, position of U.S. consul to Romania, is commended to the good offices of all representatives of this Government abroad.
>
> Mr. Peixotto has undertaken the duties of this present office more as a missionary work for the benefit of the people he represents than for any benefit to accrue to himself—a work in which all citizens will wish him the greatest success. The United States, knowing no distinction of her own citizens on account of religion or nativity, naturally believes in a civilization the world over which will secure the same universal views.

In February 1871, when Peixotto arrived in Bucharest to present the letter from the president of the United States to Prince Charles, the Jews of Romania were ecstatic. Upon receipt of the

Benjamin Franklin Peixotto

communication, the prince expressed his confidence in "our Romanian Jews." However, while attacks against Jews declined, during Peixotto's five-year tenure in Bucharest Prince Charles proved unable to stem the anti-Semitic sentiment that prevailed, and because he was unwilling to offend Austria, and particularly Russia, Romania remained committed to denying political and civil rights to its Jews.

H. Z. Sneerson

Among the prominent Jews who had urged President Grant to appoint Peixotto as consul to Romania was H. Z. Sneerson, a resident of Jerusalem who traveled to Australia, France, England, and the United States to raise funds to resettle Jews in Palestine. In 1870 Grant and Secretary of State Hamilton Fish agreed to meet with Sneerson, who urged them to remove the incumbent American consul in Jerusalem, a man he considered an anti-Semite. A few months later after returning to Palestine, Sneerson contacted President Grant once again, urging him to appoint his loyal friend Peixotto as consul to Romania.

Joseph Seligman

Joseph Seligman (1819-1880) was one of Grant's staunchest supporters, even as he was one of Abraham Lincoln's. In fact, it was at the suggestion and urging of Seligman that General Grant was appointed commander of the Union armies— a gesture for which Grant was surely eternally grateful.

Seligman came to the United States from Bavaria in 1837, during a great depression. Starting out as a backpack peddler, trudging from farmhouse to farmhouse in Pennsylvania, he saved his earnings and brought his three younger brothers to the United States (several more siblings would follow). Together, they prospered in business and later, as international bankers headquartered in New York, established branches in New Orleans, San Francisco, London, Paris, Berlin, Frankfurt, and Amsterdam.

Seligman's first contact with Grant dates back to the 1840s, when two of Joseph's brothers opened a general store in Sackett's Harbor, New York, where young lieutenant Ulysses Grant was stationed. Grant became a regular customer, and a friendship developed with the Seligmans, particularly with the oldest brother, Joseph.

Their friendship intensified when Seligman expended great effort and resources to sell and buy war bonds during the Civil War. Abraham Lincoln was grateful for Seligman's efforts, as was General Grant. Some historians considered Seligman's successful fundraising efforts crucial to the winning of the war.

Seligman sought no reward. He loved his adopted country with all his heart. When Grant wished to appoint him secretary of the treasury, Seligman declined. His only desire was to do good for the United States and its leaders. His sincerity was never more apparent than when he used his influence to prevail upon President Grant to approve a three-thousand-dollar annual pension for President Lincoln's widow, who was practically penniless after her husband's assassination.

Despite Seligman's selfless devotion to the United States, in 1877, when he attempted to register in the elite Grand Union Hotel in Saratoga Springs, New York, he was refused. The hotel was owned by the wealthy A. T. Stewart, who had been offered the post of secretary of the Treasury after Seligman had turned it down. The Senate refused to confirm Stewart because of his connection with the corrupt New York politician "Boss" William Tweed. Disappointed and angered, Stewart took out his frustration on Seligman and all Jews by banning them from his hotels.

Simon Wolf

Simon Wolf, perhaps the closest to the American presidents of all nineteenth-century Jewish leaders, came to the attention of Ulysses S. Grant during the presidential campaign of 1868 when he defended Grant against accusations that he was anti-Semitic, charges stemming, of course, from the infamous Order No. 11 of 1862.

Wolf had good reason to believe in Grant's innocence, as he wrote in an article in the *American Hebrew*, which appeared on November 24, 1905, entitled "Fifty Years at Home and Abroad":

> After his [Grant's] election, I had a long and interesting conversation with him, and then for the first time he told me that he had absolutely nothing to do with said Order [No. 11], and that it had been issued from headquarters upon the report made by General Sherman who had complained that there were a large number of citizens, especially Jews, who were violating the rules of war in running the blockade and in purchasing cotton contrary to the law. . . . The Order was made by one of the staff officers, but unfortunately bore the name of General Grant.

Wolf believed that Grant was sincere and campaigned for him in 1868, thus helping Republican Grant to carry the Jewish vote. Grant appointed Wolf recorder of deeds for the District of Columbia, a post he would hold until 1877.

In 1869, Wolf brought a delegation of B'nai B'rith leaders to the White House to request that the president appeal to the czar to halt harsh treatment and the expatriation of some two thousand Jewish families from their homes in Russia. The president willingly complied and immediately dictated a letter to the czar.

President Grant manifested his warm friendship with Wolf and his appreciation for Wolf's support by accepting an invitation to serve as *kvater* (godfather) at the *brit milah* (circumcision) of Simon's son, who was born in 1869. Wolf, in turn, showed his appreciation by naming the child Adolf Grant Wolf.

In another gesture of friendship toward the Jewish community, President Grant, along with his son and other prominent personages of his administration, attended the dedication of Adas Israel Congregation, in Washington, D.C., in 1876.

mander in chief, Grant had to resign his commission in the army reserves and was not entitled to a pension. To change that provision, an act of Congress was required. When the measure was brought up for a vote, the Senate approved, but the House of Representatives, which included twenty-five former Confederate officers, voted it down. Grant's estate had no assets at the time, and his widow would have been left destitute had it not been for the $450,000 Grant's memoirs earned in royalties.

Grant was devastated by the action of the House, and as he looked back upon his life, he regretted that he allowed the Republican Party in 1868 to persuade him to be a candidate for the presidency. "I did not want the presidency," he said, "and I have never forgiven myself for resigning the command of the army to accept it . . . war and politics are so different." He continued: "It was my fortune, a misfortune, to be called to office of Chief Executive without previous training . . ."

On July 23, 1885, four days after he completed writing his memoirs, Ulysses S. Grant died of cancer in Mount McGregor, New York. Although he had been gravely ill for more than a year, his family had not decided where the eighteenth president of the United States was to be buried. More than two weeks were to elapse before he was finally buried, on August 8, 1885, in a temporary site in New York City while a permanent resting place was being prepared. It was estimated that one million people participated in the funeral procession.

In 1897 President William McKinley dedicated Grant's Tomb, an imposing structure on Riverside Drive in New York City, overlooking the Hudson River, opposite Riverside Church and two blocks west of the Jewish Theological Seminary of America.

[A.J.K.]

Final Days

Under Article II, Section I, Paragraph 7 of the Constitution, upon becoming president and com-

Rutherford B. Hayes

Served from 1877 to 1881

Born on October 4, 1822, in Delaware, Ohio

Subscribed to no denomination but was baptized a Presbyterian and attended
Episcopal services; later attended his wife's Methodist church

Married Lucy Ware Webb on December 30, 1852

Father to four sons and one daughter

Candidate of the Republican Party

Vice president under Hayes: William A. Wheeler

Inaugural Address delivered on March 5, 1877

Died on January 17, 1893, in Fremont, Ohio

Ninteenth President of the United States

I
N ONE OF THE GREAT PARADOXES OF PRESI-
dential politics, Rutherford Birchard Hayes,
one of the most honest men ever to occupy
the Oval Office, became president following one
of the most corrupt, and certainly the most controversial, presidential elections in American history.

When the balloting was over, on November 7,
1876, the Democratic candidate, Samuel J. Tilden,
appeared to have won the election: Tilden had
received 247,448 more popular votes than Hayes
out of more than eight million cast, and 184 electoral votes to Hayes's 165, only one short of victory.

Tilden was sure he had won; even Hayes went
to sleep on election night assuming he had lost.
Republican Party leaders, however, claimed that
Southern blacks had been denied access to voting booths in South Carolina, Florida, and Louisiana, and challenged the electoral returns from
these states, and from Oregon as well. The twenty
electoral votes in dispute held the key to the 1876
election: If the electoral votes of all four states,
claimed by the Republicans, were awarded to
Hayes, it would give him a one-vote margin of
victory.

With the country in a quandary over the issue,
the House of Representatives appointed a fifteen-
member electoral commission consisting of eight
Republicans and seven Democrats from the
House of Representatives, the Senate, and the
Supreme Court to decide the outcome. When the
members of this supposedly impartial commission voted eight-to-seven, along strict partisan
lines, to award the disputed electoral votes to the
Republican candidate, Hayes was declared the
winner. As outraged Democrats were accusing the
Republicans of "stealing" the election, party lead-

ers, behind closed doors, negotiated a deal that
induced Tilden and his supporters to accept
Hayes's victory. As part of the deal that gave him
the presidency, Hayes ended Reconstruction by
withdrawing federal troops from the South, thus
leaving local government in the hands of Southern whites, the majority of whom were Democrats. As president, Hayes pursued a policy of
conciliation toward the South. He appointed so
many Democrats to office and backed so many
bills for internal improvements in the South that
northern newspapers began protesting the "loot-
ing of the treasury for the former rebels."

To many it seemed that Rutherford B. Hayes
had the makings of a great president. A decorated war hero, praised by Ulysses S. Grant for
"conspicuous gallantry" in combat, who had risen
to the rank of major general, Hayes had been an
effective congressman and the only three-term
governor in Ohio history. And yet, the circumstances under which Hayes came to the presidency
made it impossible for him to obtain wide political support and succeed in office. Most historians concur that, in terms of policies and programs,
his administration was generally a lackluster one.

Rutherford Hayes was one of the most deeply
religious occupants of the Oval Office. Morning
prayers and nightly "hymn sings" were introduced, and profanity, tobacco, and liquor were
banned. Many people blamed Mrs. Hayes, called
"Lemonade Lucy" by her detractors, for the un-
popular ban on liquor, but Hayes assumed the
responsibility himself. Although not a prohibi-
tionist, Hayes had long supported the temperance
movement. And while he allowed wine to be
served at the first official White House function,
a dinner for two Russian grand dukes, it was never
served again. "It seemed to me," Hayes explained,

"that the example of excluding liquors from the White House would be wise and useful, and would be approved by good people generally. I knew it would be particularly gratifying to Mrs. Hayes to have it done." It was less gratifying to many of the guests who dined at the White House during the Hayes years. After one official dinner, Hayes's secretary of state, William M. Evarts, would remark: "It was a brilliant affair; the water flowed like champagne."

President Hayes also established a precedent that would be of special interest to religiously observant Jews. Hayes was the first president to guarantee the right of federal civil servants to observe the Sabbath. He personally intervened in a job appointment to the Department of the Interior of an applicant who refused to work on Saturday. The president was quoted as saying that anyone who would rather forgo a job than violate the Sabbath was a good citizen and worthy of the appointment.

Simon Wolf's Disappointment

Hayes's major political supporter in the Jewish community was Simon Wolf, the politically influential Washington, D.C., lawyer and Jewish communal leader who had been a staunch supporter and confidant of Presidents Lincoln and

Simon Wolf

Grant. Wolf campaigned actively for Hayes in 1876, accepting an invitation to stump Ohio, Indiana, and New York for the Republican presidential nominee. In New York, especially, Wolf worked diligently, mobilizing Jewish support on Hayes's behalf.

After the 1868 election, Wolf's efforts in support of Ulysses S. Grant's candidacy had been rewarded by his appointment to the newly created federal post of recorder of deeds for the District of Columbia. Wolf held this office throughout the Grant Administration. Wolf assumed that he would be reappointed to this post by President Hayes, having played an active role in his campaign. To his surprise and chagrin, Hayes asked for Wolf's resignation, to become effective in April 1878.

Wolf always attributed his fall from political grace to Hayes's support for the temperance movement, which Wolf opposed. Because he was a leader in a German-American social club, in which the consumption of alcoholic beverages was common, Wolf believed that the prohibitionists had initiated a campaign to have him removed from office. Deeply hurt by this turn of events, Wolf wrote to President Hayes with unbridled frankness: "I did, during the last campaign, everything possible to have you elected, and I find it perfectly logical that I should be punished, for no doubt had I opposed you, I might have been elected to the Cabinet." When Hayes subsequently offered Wolf a minor diplomatic post, Wolf turned it down, feeling that a "second-class consulate" was beneath his dignity. Three years later, he would accept a more important diplomatic post, as U.S. consul general in Egypt, when it was offered by President-elect James A. Garfield.

Support of Benjamin Franklin Peixotto

A former national president of B'nai B'rith and a leading Jewish Republican who had served as U.S. consul to Romania for five years during the Grant Administration, Benjamin Franklin Peixotto was another of Hayes's important supporters in the Jewish community. A distinguished Jewish communal leader and skillful orator, Peixotto spent several months campaigning for Hayes in Ohio and New York, helping to mobilize Jewish support on behalf of Hayes's candidacy. When Hayes took office in 1877, he nominated Peixotto as U.S. consul to Saint Petersburg, the first American Jew to be appointed to a major diplomatic post in czarist Russia. Before Peixotto could assume his new post, however, the czarist government refused to accept him as U.S. consul because of the avowed anti-czarist sentiment he had expressed in an American lecture tour on Romania. Hayes then offered him the post of U.S. consul to Lyons, France, in which Peixotto continued to serve throughout the Garfield and Arthur administrations, until 1885.

Post-Presidential Years

After leaving the White House in 1881, Hayes retired to Spiegel Grove, his estate in Fremont, Ohio. Living quietly, Hayes loyally supported Republican presidential nominees while devoting himself to charitable causes and serving as a trustee of Ohio State University and other Ohio colleges. After suffering a heart attack, he died on January 17, 1893, at Spiegel Grove. The presence of Democratic President-elect Grover Cleveland at Hayes's funeral led some to conclude that the Democratic Party had finally accepted the disputed election of 1876.

[D.G.D.]

James A. Garfield

Served in 1881

Born on November 19, 1831, in Orange, Ohio

Member of the Disciples of Christ denomination

Married Lucretia Rudolph on November 11, 1858

Father to four sons and one daughter

Candidate of the Republican Party

Vice president under Garfield: Chester A. Arthur

Inaugural Address delivered on March 4, 1881

Assassinated on September 19, 1881, in Washington, D.C.

Twentieth President of the United States

THE LAST PRESIDENT TO BE BORN IN A LOG cabin, James Abram Garfield grew up in poverty on a frontier farm in rural Ohio where, as a child, he dreamed of becoming a sailor. Although he never fulfilled his childhood dream of going to sea, at the age of sixteen he worked briefly on a canal boat, before resuming his education. Inspired by the preaching of a Disciples of Christ evangelist, Garfield was baptized into the faith in 1850 and, the following year, entered Hiram College, a small Disciples of Christ school in Ohio. In 1854 he transferred to Williams College, in Williamstown, Massachusetts, from which he graduated in 1856. After a brief stint as professor of Greek and Latin at Hiram, Garfield became president of the college at the age of twenty-six, and two years later was elected to the Ohio State Senate. With the outbreak of the Civil War, Garfield commanded an Ohio regiment of infantry volunteers, becoming the youngest general in the Union Army at the age of thirty.

While still on active duty in 1862, Garfield was elected to Congress, and in December of 1863 he resigned his commission and took his seat in the House of Representatives. In his seventeen years in Congress, he became the leader of the Republican Party in the House and one of the foremost orators of the day.

In June 1880, as head of the Ohio delegation, Garfield went to the Republican National Convention in Chicago committed to the presidential candidacy of his Ohio friend, Secretary of the Treasury John Sherman. The Republican convention of 1880 was a drawn-out, contentious affair in which Sherman and several other candidates tried independently to stop the nomination of ex-President Ulysses S. Grant. After his eloquent nominating speech for Sherman, for which he

received a standing ovation, momentum grew for the selection of Garfield as a possible compromise candidate. The convention dragged on, hopelessly deadlocked through thirty-three ballots. On the thirty-fourth ballot, however, Wisconsin suddenly cast its sixteen votes for Garfield, and after Sherman supporters rallied to his banner, Garfield was nominated on the thirty-sixth ballot.

The 1880 presidential campaign was in some ways humiliating for Garfield. His Democratic opponent, Major General Winfield Scott Hancock, a hero of the Battle of Gettysburg, made a major issue of whether Garfield had been involved in the scandals that had tarnished Congress during the Grant Administration. Among other things, the Democrats alleged that in 1868 Garfield had accepted a bribe of $329 from the Crédit Mobilier, a construction company formed by the directors of the Union Pacific Railroad. Although a congressional investigating committee had decided that there was no conclusive evidence that Garfield had ever taken bribes for political favors, suspicions lingered and were revived in 1880. By September, the figure 329 began appearing throughout the country: on sidewalks, streets, doors, fences, hats, and napkins, as well as on the steps of the Garfield home in Washington. Garfield narrowly won the election despite the attacks on his character but seems not to have taken much pleasure in his victory. "My God!" he would exclaim after only a few weeks in the White House. "What is there about this place that a man should ever want to get into it!"

As a devout Christian and a lay preacher of the Disciples of Christ, Garfield was expected to maintain high standards of morality in the White House. After taking his oath of office in March 1881, he turned and kissed his aged mother, the first woman ever to witness the inauguration of her son as president.

Garfield Appoints Simon Wolf

Simon Wolf, the politically influential Washington lawyer and Jewish communal leader had been named recorder of deeds for the District of Columbia by Ulysses S. Grant in 1869, a minor presidential appointment that he held throughout the Grant Administration. Wolf, who had actively campaigned for Garfield, as he had earlier for both Grant and Hayes, had hoped for a diplomatic post when Garfield took office. He was finally rewarded for his many years of service to the Republican Party when he was named consul general to Egypt by President Garfield on July 1, 1881, just one day before the Chief Executive was to fall mortally wounded to an assassin's bullet. For Garfield, who read the Bible daily and was well aware of the Jewish experience in ancient Egypt, it was of historic import that he was appointing a Jewish consul general to Egypt, at the very time when Jerusalem was under Egyptian control. In making this appointment, Garfield's last words to Wolf were:

> I hope you will have a pleasant trip and find the land of your forefathers all that you expect. I am happy to name a descendant of a people who had been enslaved by the Egyptians as a representative to that country from a great free land . . . there is still a God in Israel; I hope you will have a good time, be strengthened in mind and body; and pluck the mystery out of Egypt.

As the first American Jew to be appointed to a diplomatic post in Cairo, Wolf was delighted to be compared to the biblical Joseph, as President

Portrait of James A. Garfield in uniform.

COURTESY OF THE NATIONAL ARCHIVES & RECORDS ADMINISTRATION

Garfield had implicitly done in his comment concerning the Egyptian enigma.

The Garfield Assassination

James A. Garfield was the second American president to be killed by an assassin. On the morning of July 1, 1881, Garfield went to the Baltimore and Potomac railroad station in Washington, D.C., to board a train to Massachusetts. As he walked across the waiting room with Secretary of State James G. Blaine, Charles J. Giteau, a mentally disturbed and disgruntled political supporter who had been rebuffed in his efforts to obtain a job from the State Department, fired two shots at Garfield, striking him in the arm and back. The wounded Garfield was carried back to the White House, where he remained in critical condition for several weeks. In early September, to escape the Washington heat, President Garfield was moved to a seaside cottage in New Jersey, where he died on September 19, 1881, eighty days after the shooting. His assassin, Giteau, was tried, sentenced to death, and hanged on June 30, 1882.

Adolphus S. Solomons and Garfield Memorial Hospital

President Garfield was not cared for in a hospital because, at the time, there was no institution in the nation's capital to which he could be taken. After Garfield's death, at a special prayer service in his memory in Washington, D.C., Adolphus S. Solomons (1826–1910), one of the preeminent Jewish communal leaders in Washington, D.C., and one of the founders of the American Red Cross, proposed that the city establish a hospital to be named for Garfield as a memorial for the slain president.

Solomons, like Simon Wolf, was an important figure in American Jewish public life throughout the late nineteenth century. A friend and confidant of Presidents Lincoln and Grant, Solomons played a major part in the inauguration ceremonies of every president from Lincoln to Taft. A religiously devout Jew, Solomons had declined President Grant's offer to appoint him governor

Adolphus S. Solomons

of the District of Columbia because he felt that his faithful observance of the Sabbath would conflict with the duties of office.

The District of Columbia adopted Solomons's idea, and Solomons chaired the successful effort to raise funds for Garfield Memorial Hospital. At his urging, the first two financial contributions toward the opening of the hospital, which later was incorporated into the Washington Hospital Center, came from Washington, D.C.'s two synagogues, Washington Hebrew Congregation and Adas Israel.

[D.G.D.]

Chester A. Arthur

Served from 1881 to 1885

Born on October 5, 1829, in Fairfield, Vermont

Member of the Episcopal denomination

Married Ellen Lewis Herndon on October 25, 1859

Father to one son and one daughter

Candidate of the Republican Party

Assumed the presidency on September 20, 1881, following
the assassination of James A. Garfield

Died on November 18, 1886, in New York City

Twenty-First President of the United States

WHEN JAMES ALAN GARFIELD DIED and Chester A. Arthur became president, one leading Republican exclaimed: "Chet Arthur President of the United States. Good God!" His shock was understandable. Prior to his election as vice president in 1880, Chester Arthur had never held elective office. Known as the "Gentleman Boss" of the Republican Party in New York City, Arthur was a behind-the-scenes politician, closely associated with Roscoe Conkling's corrupt political machine that distributed political patronage. And yet, when Arthur became president, his friend Governor Foster of Ohio predicted that people "will find that Vice President Arthur and President Arthur are different men." He was correct. To the surprise of his detractors, Arthur turned out to be an honest and effective president.

After passing the bar in 1854, Arthur began to practice law in New York City and soon became active in the new Republican Party, campaigning for John C. Frémont for president in 1856 and for Abraham Lincoln in 1860. During the Civil War, Arthur served as New York's quartermaster general, with the rank of brigadier general, in charge of equipping and transporting the volunteer troops being organized in the state.

Returning to his law practice and Republican Party politics after the war, Arthur rose to political prominence as the second most powerful person in the New York State Republican political machine headed by Senator Roscoe Conkling. As chairman of the political organization, Arthur worked diligently for the presidential nomination and election of Ulysses S. Grant in 1868. He was rewarded for his successful efforts when president Grant appointed him Collector of the Port of New York, the most important federal patronage job in the city. In this plum post, Arthur was able to dispense patronage widely, as he controlled the appointment of more than one thousand employees of the New York Custom House. Holding this position for eight years, he was able to build a loyal and powerful political machine of his own.

In 1879, President Hayes, in his zeal to reform the civil service, asked for Arthur's resignation. When Arthur refused to resign, he was dismissed from office.

At the Republican National Convention in 1880, Arthur was a member of the New York delegation, led by Conkling, that supported Ulysses S. Grant for a third term. When Garfield defeated Grant for the presidential nomination, to appease Conkling and insure the New York delegation's support for the presidential ticket, Arthur was nominated for vice president.

As president, Arthur surprised his critics, and his old associates in the Conkling political machine as well. Arthur himself had been a product of the corrupt spoils system, whereby federal jobs were awarded on the basis of political patronage rather than merit. In the White House, however, President Arthur became an advocate of civil service reform and, in 1883, signed the Pendleton Civil Service Act, which established the Civil Service Commission that instituted a merit system for the awarding of federal jobs. Besides civil service reform legislation, the Arthur Administration is best remembered for its advocacy of a modernized and up-to-date navy, and for the president's refusal to squander surplus revenues then pouring into the federal treasury.

Judge Brady administering the presidential oath to Vice President Arthur upon the death of President Garfield.

THE PRESIDENTS OF THE UNITED STATES *&* THE JEWS

President Arthur and Simon Wolf

Arthur's closest acquaintance and political confidant in the Jewish community was Simon Wolf, the influential Washington, D.C., attorney and Jewish communal leader who had known Arthur since the early 1870s. When Wolf resigned his diplomatic post as U.S. consul general in Egypt, to which he had been appointed by President Garfield, Arthur accepted his resignation with great reluctance, hoping that he would change his mind. Upon Wolf's return to the United States in May 1882, President Arthur publicly praised his tenure as consul general in Egypt and invited Wolf for the first of several visits to the White House. As Wolf noted in his memoir, *The Presidents I Have Known*, he had "the honor and privilege" of meeting with Arthur often and to discuss with him "matters of importance affecting the Jewish people." Also, recounts Wolf, Arthur graciously made appointments of Jewish candidates to West Point and Annapolis on Wolf's recommendation.

Adolphus S. Solomons and the Red Cross

President Arthur encouraged American participation in international political, cultural, and scientific conferences and convened a conference of representatives of all the countries of the Western Hemisphere to seek new ways to prevent war. Arthur became the first president to affirm American support for the Treaty of Geneva, establishing the International Red Cross, and appointed Adolphus S. Solomons and Clara Barton as the first delegates representing the U.S. government to the International Conference of the Red Cross held in Geneva in 1884.

Solomons, the Washington, D.C., Jewish leader who had been a political confidant of Presidents Lincoln and Grant, and who had been instrumental in establishing the capital's James A. Garfield Memorial Hospital, had been one of the original founders of the American Red Cross. The first meeting of that organization had taken place in Solomons's home in Washington, D.C., and Solomons had served as one of its two vice presidents and as its first treasurer.

Post-Presidential Years

One of the last public ceremonies in which Arthur took part as president was the dedication of the Washington Monument on February 21, 1885. After attending Grover Cleveland's inauguration, which took place a couple of weeks later, Arthur retired to his home in New York City and resumed the practice of law. Declining health, however, forced him to retire from his law practice after only a few months. While still president, Arthur had been diagnosed as suffering from Bright's disease, a then fatal kidney disorder. He died at his home in New York City on November 18, 1886.

[D.G.D.]

Grover Cleveland

Served from 1885 to 1889 & 1893 to 1897

Born on March 18, 1837, in Caldwell, New Jersey

Member of the Presbyterian denomination

Married Frances Folsom on June 2, 1886

Father to three daughters and two sons

Candidate of the Democratic Party

Vice presidents under Cleveland: Thomas A. Hendricks (first term);
Adlai E. Stevenson (second term)

First Inaugural Address delivered on March 4, 1885
Second Inaugural Address delivered on March 4, 1893

Died on June 24, 1908, in Princeton, New Jersey

Twenty-Second and Twenty-Fourth President of the United States

GROVER CLEVELAND IS THE ONLY PRESIDENT in American history to have served two nonconsecutive terms in the White House: First elected in 1884, he was defeated in 1888, and then made a comeback, being reelected to a second term in 1892. He also was the first Democrat to be elected president after the Civil War.

Born in Caldwell, New Jersey, to a Presbyterian minister, Cleveland was one of nine children. He attended schools in Fayetteville and Clinton, New York, where his father held pastorates, but concluded his formal education at the age of sixteen in order to help support his family. At the age of eighteen, Cleveland decided to head to Cleveland, Ohio, a city founded by a distant relative. When he stopped in Buffalo, New York, to visit an aunt and uncle, he was offered a job on his uncle's farm and decided to stay. With his uncle's help, he obtained a clerkship at a local law firm. After passing the bar at the age of twenty-two, Cleveland established a prosperous law practice and became active in Democratic Party politics. In 1881 he won election as the reform candidate for mayor of Buffalo, promising to clean up corruption in Buffalo's city government. Soon thereafter, he was elected as the reform candidate for governor of New York. As governor from 1882 to 1884, he stood up to the corrupt political bosses of Tammany Hall, insisting that political appointments be based on merit, not party patronage. He also signed into law the state civil service reform bill sponsored by a dauntless young assemblyman named Theodore Roosevelt.

At the Democratic National Convention of July 1884, Cleveland's reputation for honesty made him the favorite, and he was nominated on the second ballot to run for the presidency.

Just ten days after his nomination, a Buffalo newspaper revealed that eleven years earlier Cleveland had fathered a son by a woman he did not marry. Asked by his political handlers how to respond to the charges, Cleveland insisted that they tell the truth. His candid admission was accepted by the electorate, although the Republicans made it a favorite theme of their campaign, and came up with the chant:

Ma, Ma, where's my Pa?
Gone to the White House, ha, ha, ha!

Cleveland defeated his Republican opponent, James G. Blaine, in one of the closest presidential elections in history.

Cleveland lost a close bid for reelection in 1888 to Benjamin Harrison. When his term ended on March 4, 1889, Cleveland claimed that there was "no happier man in the United States" than he when he left the White House. His wife, Frances, however, whom he had married in the White House on June 2, 1886, was sure that he would return. On the morning of Harrison's inauguration, she cautioned the White House staff "to take good care of all the furniture and ornaments in the house, and not let any of them get lost or broken, for I want to find everything just as it is now, when we come back again." When asked when that would be, she confidently replied: "We are coming back just four years from today." She was right. In 1892 Cleveland defeated Harrison and returned to the White House.

No Tolerance for Anti-Semitism

During his first term in office, when the Austrian government refused to accept John Kieley as

From left to right: Ambassador Straus, Mrs. Straus, and former vice president Fairbanks in Constantinople in 1910.

It was during Cleveland's second term that czarist Russia's discriminatory treatment of American Jews became an issue. Oscar Straus and other Jewish leaders close to Cleveland protested the fact that Russian consular officials in the United States were denying Jews the right to travel or visit relatives in Russia. In response to this protest, Cleveland instructed his secretary of state to send a note to the czar's government protesting this "religious inquisitorial function."

In the latter part of Cleveland's second term, during the height of the mass Jewish immigration to the United States from czarist Russia and Poland, Congress passed a law providing for a compulsory educational test for immigrants. At the urging of Straus and others, Cleveland promptly vetoed the bill as discriminatory.

In 1903, in the aftermath of the Kishinev pogroms, former President Cleveland would address a public protest meeting at New York City's Carnegie Hall, expressing outrage over the resurgence of anti-Semitism in czarist Russia.

Cleveland's minister-designate because Kieley's wife was Jewish, President Cleveland denounced the refusal and publicly stated that the United States would not tolerate such religious discrimination. Cleveland preferred to leave the post vacant throughout his administration rather than yield to an act of anti-Semitism.

One year into his second term, in 1893, Cleveland paid tribute to the B'nai B'rith organization on its golden jubilee, writing:

> A society formed for the furtherance of such noble purposes as that of B'nai B'rith should not only excite the enthusiasm of its members, but should also inspire the good wishes of all who desire to see humanity bettered and the higher instincts of our nature cultivated. Accept for your Order my sincere wish that the gratifying results which have followed its effort for good in the half century that has passed may be multiplied in the years to come.

> Every American human sentiment has been shocked by a late attack on the Jews of Russia—an attack murderous, atrocious and in every way revolting. As members of the family of mankind, and as citizens of a free nation, we are here to give voice to the feeling that should stir . . . every American worthy of the name. There is something intensely horrible in the wholesale murder of unoffending, defense-less men, women and children. . . . Such things give rise to a distressing fear that even the enlightenment of the twentieth century has neither destroyed nor subdued the barbarity of human nature, nor wholly redeemed the civilized world from "man's inhumanity to man."

The Straus Brothers

Grover Cleveland's most influential Jewish political supporter and adviser was Oscar S. Straus

(1850–1926). Oscar was born in Bavaria on December 23, 1850, the youngest of Lazarus and Sara Straus's three sons. The family came to the United States in the early 1850s, settled in Georgia, and lived there until the end of the Civil War. They then moved to New York City, where Oscar studied at Columbia University Law School.

After graduating from Columbia, Oscar Straus practiced law for several years before working briefly for L. Straus and Sons, his family's china and glassware business. With the financial help of his brothers Isidor (1845–1912) and Nathan (1848–1931, who in 1888 became partners in, and later sole owners of, the R. H. Macy Department Store), Straus was able to devote his life to scholarship and public service. In 1882 he entered politics as leader of a citizen's movement dedicated to municipal reform, which worked to reelect William R. Grace mayor of New York. Two years later, Straus played an active role in the presidential campaign, speaking widely on behalf of Cleveland's candidacy.

In 1887 President Cleveland appointed Straus U.S. minister to Turkey, the second Jew to hold this rank in the American diplomatic service. At first, when the appointment was announced, there was some opposition. As its detractors pointed out, the ambassador's chief role in Constantinople was the protection of Christian missionaries and Christian colleges.

Several Protestant clergy actively supported Straus's appointment, including the enormously popular Brooklyn preacher Henry Ward Beecher, who wrote to President Cleveland: "The bitter prejudice against Jews, which obtains in many parts of Europe, ought not to receive any countenance in America. It is because he is a Jew that I would urge his appointment as a fit recognition of this remarkable people who . . . deserve and should receive from our government such recognition."

Straus was an immensely successful and popular ambassador. His gift for diplomacy enabled him to win an invitation from the sultan to arbitrate a business dispute between the Turkish government and Baron Maurice de Hirsch, the Jewish financier and philanthropist who had built the first railroad connecting Constantinople and the cities of Europe.

Although Straus resigned his ambassadorship following Cleveland's defeat for reelection in 1888, he remained a close friend and political confidant of President Cleveland throughout his life. He was a frequent guest at the White House during the second Cleveland Administration, advising the president on monetary policy and on immigration issues of Jewish concern.

Oscar's older brothers Isidor and Nathan built New York City's famed Macy's department store into the largest department store in the world. Active in Democratic party politics and a close friend and supporter of Grover Cleveland, Isidor Straus helped reelect Cleveland in 1892 and later influenced the president to back the gold standard. Cleveland had hoped to appoint Isidor Straus secretary of the Treasury, but other political obligations made that impossible. Cleveland did offer him the position of postmaster general, which Straus turned down in order to run for Congress. With Cleveland's strong support, Isidor Straus was elected to the House of Representatives, where he served one term (1894–1895). In

Isidor Straus

Nathan Straus

April 1912 Isidor and his wife, Ida, sailed aboard the ocean liner *Titanic* on its maiden voyage across the Atlantic. After the ship struck an iceberg, Ida repeatedly was offered a seat on one of the lifeboats available for women and children. She refused to leave her husband, and they died together when the *Titanic* went down.

Post-Presidential Years

After leaving the White House for good in 1897, Grover Cleveland retired to Princeton, New Jersey. He became a popular lecturer at Princeton Uni-

versity, a trustee of the university in 1901, and president of the board of trustees three years later. In 1906, he was hired as a consultant to reorganize the Equitable Life Assurance Society. The following year, he became president of the Association of Presidents of Life Insurance Companies.

Cleveland remained in close contact with his friends Oscar and Isidor Straus. They and their wives continued to socialize with the Clevelands, at each other's homes in New York and Princeton, and Oscar Straus continued to send the former president a case of matzah each year, as he had done annually since the 1880s.

On November 20, 1905, at a Thanksgiving Day

celebration of the 250th anniversary of the settlement of Jews in the United States, held at New York City's Carnegie Hall, former President Cleveland gave a major address in which he assured his listeners that Jews had "been more influential in giving shape to the Americanism of today" than any other group. "It is time," continued Cleveland, "for the unreserved acknowledgment that the toleration and equal opportunity accorded the Jews of the United States have been abundantly repaid to us. . . . I know that human prejudice—especially that growing out of race or religion—is cruelly inveterate and lasting. But wherever in the world prejudice against the Jews still exists, there can be no place for it among the people of the United States, unless they are heedless of good faith, rec-

reant of the underlying principles of their free government, and insensible to every pledge involved in our boasted equality of citizenship."

Early in June 1908, the former president invited Isidor Straus to visit him in New Jersey, desirous of having a leisurely talk with him. It proved to be the last time that Cleveland would speak to anyone outside of his immediate family, for he died two weeks later, on June 24. The Straus families attended the small, private funeral service for Cleveland two days later, having received a personal note from Mrs. Cleveland requesting their presence.

[D.G.D.]

Benjamin Harrison

Served from 1889 to 1893

Born on August 20, 1833, in North Bend, Ohio

Member of the Presbyterian denomination

Married Caroline L. Scott on October 20, 1853; died October 25, 1892
Married Mary Scott Lord Dimmick on April 6, 1896

Father to one son and one daughter with Caroline
Father to one daughter with Mary

Candidate of the Republican Party

Vice president under Harrison: Levi P. Morton

Inaugural Address delivered on March 4, 1889

Died on March 13, 1901, in Indianapolis, Indiana

Twenty-Third President of the United States

BENJAMIN HARRISON WAS BORN INTO ONE of America's most venerable political dynasties. A decade after the first Harrison (also named Benjamin) arrived in Virginia in the early 1630s, he was elected to the House of Burgesses, establishing the longest unbroken line of politicians in American history. In each subsequent generation, a Harrison would be elected to public office. Named for his great-grandfather, who had been one of the signers of the Declaration of Independence and a governor of Virginia, Benjamin Harrison was the grandson of William Henry Harrison, hero of the battle of Tippecanoe and the nation's ninth president. Benjamin's father, John Scott Harrison, served two terms as a U.S. congressman from Ohio during the 1850s.

By virtue of his distinguished ancestry, Harrison, who was born in North Bend, Ohio, on August 20, 1833, seemed destined for a career in politics; politics and public service were in his genes. Admitted to the bar in 1854, Harrison settled in Indianapolis, Indiana, where he opened a law practice and soon became active in the new Republican Party. He was elected city attorney of Indianapolis in 1857 and reporter of the Indiana Supreme Court in 1860. During the Civil War, Harrison commanded a regiment of Indiana volunteers, rising from second lieutenant to brigadier general.

Returning to Indianapolis at the end of the war, Harrison resumed his office of reporter of the State Supreme Court, having been reelected while still at the front in 1864. In 1876, as the Republican candidate for governor of Indiana, he was narrowly defeated. As the chairman of the Indiana delegation to the Republican National Convention in 1880, Harrison was instrumental in securing the presidential nomination for James A. Garfield, who offered him a Cabinet post. Harrison declined, preferring to serve in the U.S. Senate, to which he was elected by the Indiana legislature in January 1881. In the U.S. Senate from 1881 to 1887, Harrison became known as the "soldier's legislator," because of his continuing support of pensions for Civil War veterans.

At the Republican National Convention that met in Chicago in June 1888, Benjamin Harrison was nominated for president on the eighth ballot. Lew Wallace, the bestselling author of *Ben Hur*, was commissioned to write Harrison's 1888 campaign biography, *Life of General Benjamin Harrison*, which was a big success. As one wit aptly put it, "He did so well on *Ben Hur* that we can trust him with *Ben Him*." In the November election, President Cleveland, who had been renominated by the Democrats, outpolled Harrison by nearly one hundred thousand popular votes, only to lose in the Electoral College. Forty-eight years to the day after his grandfather had become president of the United States, Benjamin Harrison took the oath of office as president on March 4, 1889.

In the era of political corruption and robber barons known as the Gilded Age, Benjamin Harrison was one of the most principled and ethical political leaders. Presbyterian Church elder and Sunday school teacher, he also was one of the most deeply religious of American presidents, believing that the purpose of all human activity was to serve God. As a devout Presbyterian, he would be especially sympathetic to the Christian Zionist aspirations of Presbyterian clergy, such as William E. Blackstone, who, during Harrison's presidency, would petition the U.S. government to adopt a resolution in favor of a Jewish homeland in Palestine.

Jewish Supporters and Appointees

Benjamin Harrison's leading supporter and closest political confidant in the Jewish community was Simon Wolf, American Jewry's unofficial spokesman in Washington, D.C., and self-appointed advisor to every Republican president from Lincoln to Wilson. Wolf had first met and campaigned for Harrison when Harrison had run for governor of Indiana in 1876. They maintained a cordial friendship over the next decade, and, following Harrison's election, Wolf was made a member of the committee that planned and organized the presidential inauguration in March 1889. Harrison subsequently offered Wolf the diplomatic post of U.S. consul general to Egypt, which Wolf declined so as to be able to resume his private law practice.

Upon Simon Wolf's recommendation, Benjamin Harrison appointed Solomon Hirsch (1839-1902), a Republican merchant and state legislator from Oregon, to succeed Oscar Straus as U.S. minister to Turkey. A native of Württemberg, Germany, who had settled in Portland in the late 1850s, Hirsch built up one of the largest mercantile establishments in the West and played a prominent role in Jewish communal life, serving as president of Congregation Beth Israel in Portland for several years. Entering politics in 1872, Hirsch represented Portland in the Oregon State Senate, serving as president of the State Senate from 1880 to 1882. Hirsch served as U.S. minister to Turkey from 1889 to 1892.

Concern for Russian Jews and Zionism

As president, Benjamin Harrison expressed public concern and sympathy for the worsening predicament of the Jews in czarist Russia and was willing to protest to the czarist government in Saint Petersburg on their behalf. As the pogroms and anti-Semitic expulsions of Jews escalated in 1890 and 1891, a delegation of Jewish leaders that included Simon Wolf, Oscar Straus, Jacob Schiff, Jesse Seligman, and Louis Marshall met with President Harrison in the White House in

Joseph Seligman

Jacob Henry Schiff

April of 1891 to discuss the state of czarist anti-Semitism and what the United States government might do to alleviate the plight of Russian Jews.

The group suggested that President Harrison appoint a special commission, to be headed by John B. Weber, U.S. commissioner of immigration at Ellis Island, to travel to Russia and investigate and report on the Russian Jewish situation firsthand. Several months later, Weber issued a damning report of Russian anti-Jewish edicts and persecutions. Jewish leaders, as well as Harrison himself, were outraged by the findings, and Harrison requested that Congress adopt a strong resolution calling upon the U.S. State Department to officially protest Russia's anti-Jewish persecutions. In his Annual Message to Congress of December 9, 1891, Harrison expressed his sympathy for the Jews of Russia in the most unequivocal of terms:

> The Government has found occasion to express, in a friendly spirit, but with much earnestness, to the Government of the Czar, its serious concern because of the harsh measures now being enforced against the Hebrews in Russia. . . . By the revival of anti-Semitic laws, long in abeyance, great numbers of these unfortunate people have been constrained to abandon their homes and leave the empire by reason of the impossibility of finding subsistence within the pale to which it sought to confine them . . .
>
> The Hebrew is never a beggar; he always kept the law—lives by toil—often under severe and oppressive civil restrictions.is also true that no race, sect or class has more fully cared for its own.

On March 5, 1891, Benjamin Harrison received a petition urging him to call an international conference "to consider the condition of the Israelites and their claims to Palestine as their ancient home, and to promote, in all other just and proper ways, the alleviation of their suffer-ing condition." Issued six years before Theodor Herzl convened the first Zionist Congress, this petition, initiated and circulated by Reverend William E. Blackstone, a prominent Presbyterian clergyman and Zionist, was signed by many of the leading figures in American government and public life, including J. Pierpont Morgan; Melville Fuller, Chief Justice of the Supreme Court; Congressman William McKinley, the future president; Thomas Reed, Speaker of the House; and John D. Rockefeller.

Post-Presidential Years

Fifty-nine years old when he left the White House, Harrison accepted an invitation to deliver a series of law lectures at Stanford University in 1894, after which he returned to Indianapolis to practice law. Between 1897 and 1899 he was employed as counsel for the government of Venezuela in a dispute with Great Britain over its boundary with British Guiana. In arguing the case for Venezuela, Harrison filed an eight-hundred-page brief and presented twenty-five hours of oral argument over five days. In 1900 President William McKinley appointed Harrison to the newly established Permanent Court of International Justice in The Hague. After Harrison's death, President Theodore Roosevelt would appoint Oscar Straus to succeed Harrison as the American representative on this international tribunal.

Harrison's wife had died a few days before the election of 1892, and in 1896, at the age of sixty-two, Harrison married her thirty-seven year old niece Mary, who had served as her aunt's assistant in the White House. Mary survived Harrison by nearly fifty years. Together they had a daughter, Elizabeth. On March 13, 1901, Benjamin Harrison died at his home in Indianapolis.

[D.G.D.]

William McKinley

Served from 1897 to 1901

Born on January 29, 1843, in Niles, Ohio

Member of the Methodist denomination

Married Ida Saxton on January 25, 1871

Candidate of the Republican Party

Vice presidents under McKinley: Garrett A. Hobart (first term);
Theodore Roosevelt (second term)

First Inaugural Address delivered on March 4, 1897
Second Inaugural Address delivered on March 4, 1901

Assassinated on September 14, 1901, in Buffalo, New York

Twenty-Fifth President of the United States

ONE OF THE MOST POPULAR PRESIDENTS IN American history, William McKinley was reelected to a second term as president with a larger plurality of popular votes than Abraham Lincoln or any other previous Chief Executive. The third president of the United States to be killed by an assassin, he was also the last Civil War veteran to be elected to the White House.

Born in Niles, Ohio, in 1843, McKinley enlisted in the Twenty-third Ohio Volunteer Infantry at the outbreak of the Civil War in 1861. His commanding officer was another future president, Rutherford B. Hayes. Beginning his military service as a commissary sergeant, McKinley was cited for bravery at the Battle of Antietam and was promoted to second lieutenant. He served with distinction in several other battles, receiving three more promotions, to first lieutenant, captain, and brevet major.

After the war, McKinley studied law and, on being admitted to the bar in 1867, opened a practice in Canton, Ohio, where he became active in local Republican Party politics. He campaigned actively for his old commanding officer, Hayes, and when Hayes was elected president in 1876, McKinley was elected to Congress, where he would serve, with the exception of one term, until 1891. In 1891, McKinley was elected governor of Ohio by a narrow margin but was reelected by a large majority two years later. In 1895 a group of wealthy Ohio businessmen led by industrialist Mark Hanna began a movement to secure the presidential nomination for McKinley in 1896. At the Republican National Convention in June of that year, McKinley was easily nominated on the first ballot.

The presidential campaign of 1896 centered on the question of whether U.S. monetary policy should be based on a gold standard or a silver standard. After nominating William Jennings Bryan, the radically vocal free-silver advocate from Nebraska, the Democrats came out for the free unlimited coinage of silver, at a ratio of sixteen ounces of silver to one ounce of gold. McKinley and the Republicans upheld the gold standard and "sound" money, and in so doing won the support of President Grover Cleveland and many other conservative Democrats, including the Jewish diplomat and Cleveland confidant Oscar Straus.

The Spanish-American War and the Annexation of Hawaii

It is one of the ironies of American history that William McKinley, who entered the White House believing that "peace is preferable to war in almost every contingency," is remembered primarily for taking the nation into the Spanish-American War. "We want no wars of conquest," he proclaimed in his Inaugural Address. "We must avoid the temptation of territorial aggression. Wars should never be entered upon until every contingency of peace has failed."

And yet, thirteen months after William McKinley's inauguration, America was at war with Spain. In 1895, when Cuban insurgents had begun a revolution against Spanish rule of their island, President Cleveland had managed to keep America out of the conflict. Although President McKinley had hoped to act as a mediator between Spain and the Cuban rebels, he was not as successful. More than anything else, the sinking of the U.S. battleship *Maine* in Havana Harbor on

February 15, 1898, in which many of the 350-member crew were killed, was the precipitating event that caused President McKinley to ask Congress to declare war on Spain in April 1898.

The Spanish-American War, which lasted only four months, ended in August 1898 with freedom for Cuba and the surrender of Puerto Rico, Guam, and the Philippines to the United States. In July 1898 President McKinley had reversed the policy of the previous administration and signed a joint congressional resolution annexing the Hawaiian Islands.

American Jews and the Spanish-American War

American Jews generally were supportive of U.S. involvement in the Spanish-American War. In May of 1898, Isaac Mayer Wise's weekly newspaper, *American Israelite*, reported: ". . . No sector of the people have exhibited a more fervent patriotism than the Jewish Americans and none have responded quicker or in larger numbers, pro rata, to President McKinley's call for volunteer soldiers." Several Jews served with Theodore Roosevelt's famous Rough Riders and took part in the regiment's dramatic charge up San Juan Hill. For Isaac Mayer Wise and many other Jewish leaders, Jewish support for Cuban independence from Spain was linked to Spain's mistreatment of the Jewish people during the Spanish Inquisition.

The *American Israelite* was "uniformly critical" of Spain and her allies during the Spanish-American War, repeatedly characterizing Spain as a barbaric, decadent country and, quoting a London newspaper, observed that ". . . a state's mistreatment of its Jewish population has throughout history served as a moral barometer." The editors of other Jewish periodicals concurred with Wise in supporting America's war against Spain, reflecting widespread American Jewish opinion that Jewish support for the Cuban rebels was just comeuppance for Spain's historic sins against the Jewish people.

This Jewish opinion was further reflected the following year when Theodore Roosevelt ran for governor of New York. Yiddish handbills were distributed throughout New York's Lower East Side, urging Jews to vote for Roosevelt, "who was so instrumental in fashioning the defeat of Spain" in the Spanish-American War. In arguing that "every true Jew must and will vote for . . . Theodore Roosevelt," these handbills pointed out that:

> In Spain our ancestors were good and useful citizens. They made rich Spain's treasury . . . and gave Spain the power that made her a mighty nation. How did Spain reward them? Spain took away everything the Jews had, and she sent her Jews to the dungeons of the Inquisition and the fires of the auto-da-fé. . . . The cruelty and tyranny that Spain set loose, did not remain in its own land. Spain brought it to the new world. . . . And until Theodore Roosevelt charged up San Juan Hill, there still rang in our ears the crimes and screams of Spain's brutality. The long felt Jewish desire to see Spain fall was finally fulfilled. The Republican Party through its president gave the word that Spain should move out of the New World and. . . . Theodore Roosevelt was one of the chief instruments of the late war. . . . Spain now lies punished and beaten for all her sins. . . . Vote for Theodore Roosevelt. . . . Vote to express your approval of Spain's defeat.

At the Republican National Convention held in Philadelphia in June 1900, William McKinley was unanimously nominated for a second term as president. Theodore Roosevelt, the youthful governor of New York and the hero of the Spanish-American War, was nominated for vice president, as McKinley's running mate. In the November election, McKinley once again defeated William Jennings Bryan, by almost a million popular votes and by an electoral vote total of 292 to 155.

McKinley and Simon Wolf

President McKinley enjoyed the friendship and staunch political support of Simon Wolf, the preeminent Washington attorney, politician, and Jewish communal leader. Wolf actively campaigned for McKinley in the presidential elections of 1896 and 1900. A frequent guest at the McKinley White House, Wolf was offered presidential appointments as postmaster of Washington, D.C., and commissioner of the District of Columbia, both of which he declined. Wolf was appointed a member of the inaugural committee that planned and organized President McKinley's inauguration ceremonies in March 1897. As chairman of its committee on medals, Wolf "had the honor and pleasure of pinning the gold medal on his [President McKinley's] coat at the head of the stairs of the Reviewing Stand," prior to the president's delivery of his Inaugural Address.

When, after the inauguration, Wolf sent McKinley a copy of his book *The American Jew as Patriot, Soldier and Citizen*, President McKinley wrote back to Wolf, in a letter addressed to "My Dear Friend," as follows:

> I received the copy of your memorable book, "The American Jew, as Patriot, Soldier and Citizen," and I thank you sincerely for the privilege of reading the same. I consider it a masterly treatment of the subject, and you have rendered not only to your people, but to all people a great service. No better class of citizens than the Jewish exists in our country, many of whom have been and are my personal friends.

At Wolf's suggestion, President McKinley was invited to attend the laying of the cornerstone of the Washington Hebrew Congregation, which was held on September 16, 1897. To the delight of the congregation, President McKinley arrived with his entire Cabinet. As the ceremonies commenced, a local drum corps, thirty strong, played "Hail to the Chief." An enthusiastic welcome was given to President McKinley by the large audience in attendance. Following remarks by Simon Wolf, President McKinley concluded the program with a congratulatory address to the congregation. The chair on which President McKinley sat during the ceremonies, marked with a brass plaque, is treasured by the Washington Hebrew Congregation to this day, and remains a historic reminder of the first and only time in American history that a president and his entire Cabinet were in attendance together at an American synagogue.

Appointment of Oscar Straus

Another of McKinley's strongest Jewish supporters was Oscar Straus, a descendant of the New York merchandising family that owned Macy's, who had served as U.S. minister to Turkey under Grover Cleveland. Having resigned his diplomatic post after Cleveland's defeat for reelection in 1888, Straus had devoted himself to Jewish scholarship and public service, serving as the first president of the American Jewish Historical Society and on a committee of leading Jews who met with President Benjamin Harrison to urge him to actively protest czarist Russia's mistreatment of Russian Jews. Throughout the 1890s, Straus remained a close friend and political confidant of Grover Cleveland, helping to renominate Cleveland at the Democratic National Convention in Chicago in 1892 and serving as a member of Cleveland's kitchen cabinet during his second term of office. As an advocate of sound money and of the gold standard that the Republican Party upheld, Straus opposed the nomination of William Jennings Bryan and broke with the Democratic Party by actively campaigning for William McKinley in 1896.

With McKinley's election, Straus had easy access to the White House and advised McKinley on a variety of issues relating to international diplomacy and foreign affairs. In early 1898, as war with Spain over the question of Cuban independence loomed on the horizon, McKinley welcomed a proposal from Straus that endeavored to resolve the Cuban imbroglio peacefully, without U.S. military intervention. But, amidst the growing clamor for war in Congress and in the press, and with the sinking of the battleship *Maine*, the Straus plan was ignored in Washington, and on April 25, 1898, an eager Congress declared war on Spain.

Later, in 1898, McKinley asked Straus to accept appointment as U.S. minister to Turkey, the same diplomatic post Straus had held under Cleveland. In the aftermath of the Turkish massacre of Armenians, which had shocked the civilized world the previous year, American relations with Turkey had deteriorated, with the Turkish sultan refusing American claims for property destroyed during the massacres and American citizens in

President William McKinley and his entire Cabinet at the laying of the cornerstone of Washington Hebrew Congregation, September 10, 1897.

Turkey calling for American warships to back up their claims. In offering him the appointment, McKinley told Straus, who enjoyed the respect of the Turkish sultan, that it was his duty to return to Turkey as American minister, as he was "the only man in the United States who could save the situation."

Although he was at first reluctant to accept the nomination, Straus concluded that "my destiny" was to return to Constantinople, and he wrote to McKinley that "I deem it my patriotic duty to you and to the country to accept." His nomination was quickly confirmed by the Senate on June 3, and Straus remained as U.S. minister in Turkey for more than two years, until December of 1900.

Jacob Hollander: Treasurer of Puerto Rico

William McKinley's other major Jewish appointee was Jacob Hollander, a distinguished young economist who was named the first treasurer of Puerto

Rico's new government in 1900. In 1895, a year after completing his doctorate, Hollander received an appointment at Johns Hopkins University, where he eventually became chairman of the Economics Department, the first Jew to hold such a position at a major American university. After receiving President McKinley's appointment in 1900, Hollander drew up a revenue system for the new Puerto Rican government, which was subsequently known as the Hollander Law and which continued to serve Puerto Rico for several decades. In 1905 President Roosevelt would send Hollander to Santo Domingo as U.S. special commissioner to investigate the public debt. Perhaps the most distinguished American Jewish economist of the pre-1950s era, Hollander would become the first American Jew elected to the presidency of the American Economic Association.

The Assassination

On September 5, 1901, President McKinley gave a major public address at the Pan American Exposition in Buffalo, New York. The following day, as he stood in a receiving line at the Temple of Music on the exposition grounds, a young anarchist named Leon Czolgosz approached McKinley with his right hand wrapped in a handkerchief. As McKinley extended his hand to greet him, Czolgosz shot him with a gun concealed under the handkerchief. Horrified, people nearby grabbed the assassin, knocked him down, and pinned him to the floor. Over the next few days, McKinley suffered greatly, rallied briefly, and finally succumbed to his fatal wounds on September 14. Shortly before he died, he whispered to his wife, Ida: "It is God's Way. His Will be done," and repeated some lines from his favorite hymn, "Nearer, my God to Thee, Nearer to Thee." The nation was stunned and shocked by a third presidential assassination in less than forty years. William McKinley was as deeply and widely mourned as were Abraham Lincoln and James A. Garfield, whose presidencies had earlier tragically been cut short by assassins' bullets. A biography published soon after McKinley's death described the mood of the country: "A universal spasm of grief passed from end to end of the land . . . . Never was there a crime more without purpose, more without possible good effect."

[D.G.D.]

Theodore Roosevelt

Served from 1901 to 1909

Born on October 27, 1858, in New York City

Member of the Dutch Reformed denomination

Married Alice Hathaway Lee on October 27, 1880; died February 14, 1884
Married Edith Kermit Carow on December 2, 1886

Father to one daughter with Alice
Father to four sons and one daughter with Edith

Candidate of the Republican Party

Assumed the presidency on September 14, 1901, following the assassination
of William McKinley; elected to a full term on November 8, 1904

Vice president under Roosevelt: Charles W. Fairbanks (second term)

Inaugural Address delivered on March 4, 1905

Died on January 6, 1919, in Oyster Bay, New York

Twenty-Sixth President of the United States

THE FEARLESS, BRAWNY, ROBUST TWEN-ty-sixth president of the United States, who in the 1898 war with Spain organized the Rough Riders and courageously led the charge up San Juan Hill, near Santiago de Cuba, was daring enough to appoint a Jew to his Cabinet, a first in the American history.

Born in New York City on October 27, 1858, asthmatic and nearsighted, Roosevelt described himself as "a sickly boy, nervous, and timid," but determined to "train himself painfully and labo-riously," which he did by taking boxing lessons, lifting weights, and hiking for miles.

The product of an old Dutch family whose first member arrived in America in 1644 and pros-pered in New Amsterdam, Roosevelt was in a position to be tutored privately. By the time he was sixteen, he was sufficiently advanced aca-demically to be accepted as a student at Harvard College, from which he graduated in 1880.

The Teddy Bear

As part of his regimen to build up his physical health, Theodore Roosevelt engaged in march-ing over rough terrain and hunting. For four days on one bear-hunting expedition, Roosevelt had no luck; on the fifth day of his safari, one of his companions, feeling sorry for the president, caught a bear cub and tied it to a tree so it would be an easy mark. The president refused to shoot the bear under such unfair conditions. When the public learned of his compassion for the cuddly cub, they began to think of him as a gentle, cuddly human being, despite his bravado and love of hunting.

No one was more impressed by the president than Rose Michtom and her husband, Morris, two recent Jewish immigrants to America from Russia. When the Michtoms opened a notions store, they added to their line of merchandise stuffed animals that Rose created. Because of her affection for the president, she designed a stuffed bear that she named Teddy—the Teddy Bear.

Rose sent the first copy to President Roosevelt and asked for permission to use his nickname. Roosevelt readily agreed. He loved the toy, as did his brood of children, who enjoyed endless hours playing with it. When Morris began displaying copies of the teddy bear in the window of his shop, it was an immediate bestseller and has remained so for one hundred years.

The Michtoms were not the only Jews who admired and respected Theodore Roosevelt. In the introduction to his popular book *For 2¢ Plain*, Harry Golden, editor and publisher of the *Carolina Israelite*, wrote: "Two of the most beloved Christians in the history of the American-Jewish community were Enrico Caruso and Theodore Roosevelt. I doubt whether anyone else, before or since, has ever enjoyed the same degree of rev-erence and devotion."

First Contact with Jews

Born and raised in a New York City brownstone on East 20th Street, about a mile from the Lower East Side where the "huddled masses" of Jewish immigrants would settle, Roosevelt would become acquainted with the newly Americanized Jews who were his neighbors. In 1872 and 1873, while taking a tour of the Middle East, one of his stops was the Holy Land, which gave him another op-portunity to get to know many Jews personally.

Roosevelt's positive feelings towards Jews surfaced in 1895 when he became police commissioner of New York City. In his autobiography he writes:

> While I was Police Commissioner, an anti-Semitic preacher from Berlin, Rector Ahlwardt, came over to New York to preach a crusade against the Jews. Many of the New York Jews were much excited and asked me to prevent him from speaking and not to give him police protection. This, I told them was impossible; and if possible would have been undesirable because it would have made him a martyr. The proper thing to do was to make him ridiculous. Accordingly I detailed for his protection a Jew sergeant and a score or two of Jew policemen. He made his harangue against the Jews under the active protection of some forty policemen, every one of them a Jew.

After serving as police commissioner for two years, President McKinley appointed him to be assistant secretary of the Navy. He served in this capacity until 1898 and was then elected governor of the state of New York. After two years in office, in 1900 he was elected vice president on the Republican ticket with William McKinley. When McKinley was assassinated in 1901, Roosevelt became president. In 1904, he was elected on his own; oddly enough, he failed, by 60,000 votes, to carry the East Side of New York City, where he had grown up.

After his election in 1904, Roosevelt received a communication from British-born Rabbi Henry Pereira Mendes (1852-1937), of Shearith Israel in New York City, asking the president to provide more adequately for the religious needs of Jewish servicemen. Roosevelt was quick to act and issued the following order: ". . . commanding officers [are to] be authorized to permit Jewish soldiers to be absent for attendance at services on the Jewish holy days."

This was in keeping with Theodore Roosevelt's basic religious philosophy, which he expressed in these words: "The religious man who is most useful is not he whose sole care is to save his own soul, but the man whose religion bids him strive to advance decency and clean living and to make the world a better place for his fellows to live in."

Oscar Straus

Of all the Jews to whom Roosevelt turned for counsel and support, Oscar Straus, the younger brother of Isidor and Nathan Straus, who had built Macy's Department Store into the largest department store in the world, stands out above the rest. In 1906 Oscar became the first Jew ever to occupy a Cabinet post. After having served previously as U.S. minister and ambassador to Turkey, Roosevelt appointed him secretary of commerce and labor.

Prior to making this appointment, at lunch one day in 1906 Roosevelt turned to Oscar Straus and said:

> I don't know whether you know it or not, but I want you to become a member of my Cabinet. I have a very high estimate of your character, your judgment and your ability, and I want you for personal reasons. There is still a further reason: I want to show Russia and some other countries what we think of Jews in this country.

Oscar Straus

When Straus told McKinley of his intention to resign his diplomatic post and return to private life, the president informed him that he could not resign without accepting a higher post. Shortly after McKinley was assassinated, when Secretary of State John Hay seemed about to resign for reasons of poor health, McKinley had seriously considered appointing Straus to succeed Hay. Hay remained in office, however, and McKinley shared with Straus his plans to appoint him to another high post, the recently established Permanent Court of International Justice in The Hague. President McKinley, however, was assassinated before the appointment could be made. In 1902 McKinley's successor, Theodore Roosevelt, appointed Straus to a six-year term on the international court, a prestigious appointment that would be renewed four times, by three presidents, in the years ahead.

When Theodore Roosevelt left the presidency in 1909, Straus remained one of Roosevelt's closest political confidants and advisers. In 1912, when Roosevelt formed the Progressive Party and ran against Taft, the Progressive Party candidate for president, Straus actively supported Roosevelt's candidacy. At Roosevelt's urging, Straus accepted the Progressive Party nomination for governor of New York. Although defeated in a three-way race, Straus ran well, receiving 4,000 more votes than Roosevelt in New York State.

The day following the 1912 election, Roosevelt wrote to Straus: "Dear Oscar, I count myself fortunate in having run on the same ticket with you and in having the privilege of supporting you. You are the kind of American who makes one proud of being an American."

The Kishinev Pogrom

In 1902 Plehve Vyacheslav became Russia's minister of the interior and announced that the socialist revolution that had begun to spread would be crushed and drowned in Jewish blood. He made good on his promise when, in the spring of 1903, the whole civilized world was shocked by the bloody pogrom that took place in Kishinev, in the province of Bessarabia. Jews had lived there

in relative peace for a century, but beginning with the 1903 pogrom, which was inspired and backed by the ministry of the interior and supported by local governmental officials, including the chief of police, a wave of pogroms took place in numerous towns throughout Russia.

In Kishinev alone close to fifty Jews were killed and hundreds of others were seriously wounded. In addition, fifteen hundred shops and homes were plundered. As a result, between 1903 and 1906, tens of thousands of Jews fled the country to seek safety in such faraway countries as the United States, South Africa, and Palestine.

Along with other world leaders, President Roosevelt sent a note of concern to Czar Nicholas II but was fearful of upsetting the delicate balance that had been arrived at in U.S.-Russian relations. Likewise, the leading figures of American Jewry were relatively silent. These leaders were of German descent and had little contact with the Jewish communities of Eastern Europe. Numbered among these American leaders were Oscar Straus, Louis Marshall, Cyrus Adler, Jacob Schiff, and Mayer Sulzberger.

It was not until 1906 that these men began to mobilize their forces and use their influence to help the beleaguered Jews of Russia. On November 11 of that year they founded the American Jewish Committee to help their coreligionists financially and to pressure U.S. elected officials to demand that the Russian leadership put a halt to its widespread anti-Semitic campaign.

The Romanian Saga

Concurrent with the troubles of Jews in Russia, the situation of Jews in Romania was equally hazardous. An anti-Semitic league that was organized there in 1895 was using every means possible to render the condition of the Jews unbearable and to force them out of the country. In 1902 Roosevelt directed his secretary of state, John Hay, who had been appointed in 1901 and was concerned with the plight of Jews, to send a stiff note to the government of Romania. Hay's communication read:

למתים על קדוש השם בקישינוב

Dedication page of Sbornik *by Maxim Gorki, in memory of the victims of the Kishinev Pogrom.*

The political disabilities of the Jews in Rumania, their exclusion from the public service and the learned professions, the limitations of their civil rights and the imposition upon them of exceptional taxes, involving as they do wrongs repugnant to the moral sense of liberal modern peoples, are not so directly in point for my present purpose as the public acts which attack the inherent right of man as a breadwinner in the ways of agriculture and trade. The Jews are prohibited from owning land, or even from cultivating it as common laborers. They are debarred from residing in the rural districts. Many branches of petty trade and manual production are closed to them in the overcrowded cities, where they are forced to dwell and engage, against fearful odds, in the desperate struggle for existence. This government cannot be a tacit party to such an international wrong. It is constrained to protest treatment to which the Jews of Rumania are subjected, not alone because it has unimpeachable ground to remonstrate against the resultant injury to itself, but in the name of humanity.

For his efforts on behalf of the Jews of Romania, Hay, like Roosevelt, was greatly admired by American Jews. Rabbis praised him in their sermons, and the note to Romania was read from the pulpit in many synagogues just before congressional elections. Hay was so widely praised by Jews that his friend Henry Adams once said to Mrs. Hay: "I'm so glad John loves the Jews." When Hay died in 1905, Jews went into mourning, and one large Philadelphia synagogue even consecrated a stained-glass window to his memory.

Presidential Praise

Throughout his career, Theodore Roosevelt showed how deeply he empathized with the Jewish condition and the welfare of the Jews. Nowhere, however, did he express his concern more eloquently, particularly his support of continued Russian immigration, than in a November 20, 1905, communication to Jacob H. Schiff. The occasion was the Thanksgiving celebration, in New York's Carnegie Hall, marking the 250th anniversary of the settlement of Jews in the United States. Roosevelt wrote:

My Dear Sir:

I am forced to make a rule not to write letters on the occasion of any celebration. . . . I make an exception in this case because of the lamentable and terrible suffering to which so many of the Jewish people in other lands have been subjected. . . . I am glad to be able to say, in addressing you on this occasion, that while the Jews of the United States, who now number more than a million, have remained loyal to their faith and their race traditions, they have become indissolubly incorporated in the great army of American citizenship, prepared to make all sacrifice for the country, either in war or peace, and striving for the perpetuation of good government and for the maintenance of the principles embodied in our constitution. They are honestly distinguished by their industry, their obedience to law, and their devotion to the national welfare.

Retirement Years

Theodore Roosevelt, as he had promised, served only one full four-year term; on March 4, 1909, he handed the staff of leadership to his own hand-picked successor, William Howard Taft. Roosevelt had hoped that Taft would continue his philosophy of liberal government. After returning from a yearlong African safari, however, Roosevelt was disappointed in Taft's leadership and once again declared his candidacy for the Republican nomination. He lost, bolted the Republican Party, and formed the Progressive or Bull Moose party, thus dividing the Republican party and enabling Democrat Woodrow Wilson to win the presidency in 1912.

Roosevelt lived out his seven remaining years on his Sagamore Hill estate in Oyster Bay, New York, plagued with many illnesses. He died on January 6, 1919.

[A.J.K.]

William H. Taft

Served from 1909 to 1913

Born on September 15, 1857, in Cincinnati, Ohio

Member of the Unitarian denomination

Married Helen Herron on June 19, 1886

Father to two sons and one daughter

Candidate of the Republican Party

Vice president under Taft: James S. Sherman

Inaugural Address delivered on March 4, 1909

Died on March 8, 1930, in Washington, D.C.

Twenty-Seventh President of the United States

WILLIAM HOWARD TAFT HAS THE unique distinction of having been the only person to serve as both president of the United States and chief justice of the U.S. Supreme Court. Taft never really wanted to be president. In fact, he once said, "Politics when I am in it, makes me sick." Possessing a judicial temperament, his greatest aspiration was to serve on the Supreme Court, a dream that he finally realized eight years after leaving the White House.

Born on September 15, 1857, in Cincinnati, Ohio, Taft was the son of a prominent attorney and Republican politician, Alphonso, who had served in the Cabinet of President Ulysses S. Grant, first as secretary of war and then as attorney general. Alphonso Taft later would be appointed ambassador to Austria-Hungary by President Chester Arthur.

After graduating from Yale College and the University of Cincinnati Law School, William Taft began practicing law in Cincinnati and, in 1887, was appointed a judge of the Ohio Superior Court. In 1890 he resigned his judgeship to accept an appointment by President Benjamin Harrison to be solicitor general of the United States, the federal government's attorney before the Supreme Court. Two years later, at the age of thirty-four, Taft was appointed by President Harrison to a federal judgeship on the Sixth U.S. Circuit Court of Appeals, where he served with distinction until 1900. In that year, President William McKinley asked Taft to chair a new presidential commission being formed to govern the recently annexed Philippine Islands. Although reluctant to leave the bench, Taft accepted when McKinley promised him an eventual appointment to the Supreme Court. In 1901 Taft became the first civilian governor of the

Philippines and, three years later, joined President Theodore Roosevelt's Cabinet as secretary of war.

From 1906 on, it became apparent that Theodore Roosevelt had handpicked Taft as his successor. Taft's mother gave him no encouragement, writing: "I do not want my son to be president. His is a judicial mind and he loves the law." Although Taft's fondest aspirations were still for an appointment to the Supreme Court, he succumbed to the ambitions of his wife and brothers, who urged him on toward the White House. At the Republican Convention in Chicago in 1908, on the first ballot, Taft won the presidential nomination by acclamation. Running against William Jennings Bryan, who had lost to William McKinley in 1896 and 1900, Taft won an easy victory, defeating Bryan by more than 1,200,000 popular votes and by an electoral vote of 321 to 162.

Taft's administration had many notable accomplishments to its credit. Postal savings and parcel post services were established. The civil service was greatly expanded, and an eight-hour workday was granted to all government employees. New Mexico and Arizona were admitted to the Union, as the forty-seventh and forty-eighth states. And the Sherman Anti-Trust Act was strenuously enforced: More antitrust suits were prosecuted by the federal government under Taft than had been under Theodore Roosevelt.

Although Taft would easily be renominated as the Republican Party's presidential candidate in 1912, his former mentor and friend, Theodore Roosevelt, openly opposed him. When Taft received the Republican nomination, Roosevelt's supporters bolted the Republican Convention and organized the Progressive (Bull Moose) Party,

President Taft (in back seat of car, with straw hat), arriving in May 1909 to speak at Congregation Rodef Shalom, in Pittsburgh, Pennsylvania.

nominating Roosevelt as its candidate for president. The Democratic Party nominated Woodrow Wilson, the urbane governor of New Jersey and former president of Princeton University. Although he campaigned in more than five hundred cities and towns, Taft could not hope to win the "three-cornered" race, with the still enormously popular Teddy Roosevelt splitting the Republican vote and taking away much of what should have been Taft's traditional Republican support. Wilson's victory on November 5 came as a surprise to no one. Taft was badly defeated for re-election, receiving the fewest popular votes of the three candidates and the electoral votes of only two states, Utah and Vermont.

Isaac Mayer Wise and Adolph Marix

More than most American presidents, William Howard Taft counted several prominent Jewish leaders among the personal friends and confidants with whom he corresponded and socialized on a regular basis. During his presidency, he attended a Passover Seder, the first sitting president to do so. Also, shortly after taking office, he spoke from a synagogue pulpit during Sabbath services, a first for an American president: On Saturday, May 29, 1909, Taft addressed the Sabbath worshippers from the pulpit of Congregation Rodef Shalom in Pittsburgh.

Taft's close association with American Jewish life began while growing up in his native Cincinnati, where Isaac Mayer Wise, the rabbi of Cincinnati's largest synagogue, B'nai Yeshurun, and the founder of Reform Judaism in America, was a friend of his father and would become a friend of Taft's as well. The Taft family attended a church across the street from Wise's temple, and Taft would sometimes accompany his father to listen to Wise's sermons. Over the years, the Wise and Taft families dined at each other's homes.

Taft often spoke of his family's friendship with Isaac Mayer Wise, as well as his own friendship with Wise and with other American Jews, such as Adolph Marix (1848-1919). During his tenure as governor of the Philippines, Taft had befriended

Navy Commander Marix, an 1868 graduate of the Naval Academy at Annapolis, who had been promoted for "eminent and conspicuous conduct" in battle during the Spanish-American War. On becoming president, Taft appointed Commander Marix rear admiral, the first Jew to attain such high rank in the U.S. Navy.

During his administration and thereafter, Taft was on especially friendly terms with three of the most important Jewish communal leaders of his era: Simon Wolf, Mayer Sulzberger, and Julius Rosenwald.

Simon Wolf

Simon Wolf had known Taft's father during the Grant Administration. Wolf subsequently befriended William Howard Taft during his years in Washington, D.C., when Taft served as solicitor general of the United States and later as secretary of war, prior to his election to the presidency. Wolf, who met with President Taft often, both at social functions and in the White House, enjoyed Taft's respect and friendship throughout his presidency and in the years following his retirement from office.

When Wolf died in 1923, William Howard Taft, then chief justice of the Supreme Court, paid tribute to Wolf in a memorable eulogy:

> He was a leader in Israel, and had the interests of his people deeply at heart. He labored much for them. He was a man of intellectual force, of conviction and courage of expression. He was greatly respected by all who knew him, and this included all the prominent men in Government for many decades of his long and honored life. In his death, the country loses a patriot, and the Jewish people a strong man.

Mayer Sulzberger

William Howard Taft enjoyed an especially close personal friendship with Judge Mayer Sulzberger (1843-1923), an eminent figure in American Jewish public life. One of the founders of the Jewish Publication Society and an important early leader of Conservative Judaism in America, Sulzberger had played a pivotal role in organizing the American Jewish Committee and served as its first president. A pillar of the Republican Party, in 1895 Sulzberger had been elected a judge of Philadelphia's Court of Common Pleas, the city's principal judicial tribunal, on which he would serve with distinction for twenty years, the last fourteen as its president judge. Taft, who had known and admired Sulzberger since his days as a federal court judge in the 1890s, had long considered Sulzberger to be one of the most distinguished and scholarly jurists in the country. Their extensive correspondence, which has been preserved in the Taft Papers at the Library of Congress, continued for several decades until Sulzberger's death in 1923.

Shortly after taking office in 1909, Taft offered Sulzberger the ambassadorship to Turkey, the diplomatic post that had been held by Oscar Straus during the Cleveland and McKinley administrations, and by Solomon Hirsch when Benjamin Harrison was president. To many, the American embassy at Constantinople had come to be considered a "Jewish" diplomatic post, to which a prominent Jewish communal leader should be appointed. At the age of sixty-six, Sulzberger felt that he was too old to accept this new assignment. Preferring to remain on the bench and not leave his beloved Phildelphia, Sulzberger graciously declined Taft's offer. At Taft's and Sulzberger's urging, Oscar Straus was prevailed

Mayer Sulzberger

upon to return to Turkey for a third tour of duty. Writing to Sulzberger in April 1909, President Taft indicated that he understood his friend's disinclination to accept the appointment:

> I was very sorry that you concluded that you could not accept the appointment to be Ambassador to Constantinople. The Embassy is one of the pleasantest in Europe from a mere physical standpoint, because we there furnish the Ambassador with a suitable home and with a vessel for sailing on the Bosphorus. Still, I can understand how a gentleman like yourself, in love with your work on the Bench, should decline to be torn up by his roots, so to speak, and sent abroad.
>
> I am glad, however, to have had the opportunity to express my high appreciation of your learning and culture as a man, and your high ideals of patriotism as a citizen.

Julius Rosenwald

Taft also enjoyed the political support and friendship of Julius Rosenwald (1862-1932), president of Sears, Roebuck and Company, and one of the preeminent Jewish philanthropists in America. A stalwart of the Republican Party, and one of the most influential Jewish Republicans in America, Rosenwald had strongly supported Taft's presidential candidacy in 1908 and would remain one of his most loyal supporters in the Jewish community. Rosenwald was one of the few Jewish communal leaders to actively support Taft's reelection campaign against Teddy Roosevelt and Woodrow Wilson in 1912. Indeed, it was rumored that Rosenwald would become secretary of commerce in Taft's Cabinet if the president were reelected. When asked by a newspaper reporter about this rumor, Rosenwald was quoted as saying:

> I know nothing about it except what has been written in today's papers, and have received no communication from the President or anyone else on the subject; of course, I feel highly complimented to be mentioned for such an honor, but there is not an office in the gift of the President, or the people that I would accept—all I ask is to keep my good health and to be allowed to live in Chicago among my

friends. I greatly enjoy the work in which I am engaged.

In February 1912 President Taft invited Rosenwald to visit him at the White House, and Rosenwald spent two days there. While several other Jewish leaders had been invited to various presidential dinners and receptions, Julius Rosenwald was the first American Jew to be an overnight guest at the White House. Writing to his wife on White House stationery on the evening of February 28, Rosenwald confided: "Just think of it. Here I find your best fellow going to bed in the White House. I didn't dream of it....Good night, my dear girl. I wish you were here with me to enjoy the experience. Maybe some day we will be here together as guests during the [president's] second term."

Abrogation of the Russo-American Commercial Treaty

Beginning in 1908, Mayer Sulzberger, Simon Wolf, and other Jewish leaders with close ties to Taft began a campaign to bring about the abrogation of the Russo-American Commercial Treaty of 1832, because of the Russian government's refusal to recognize U.S. passports when American Jews wished to travel freely in czarist Russia. During the late nineteenth century, the czarist government had begun to utilize clauses in this treaty to subject American Jews visiting Russia to the same harsh restrictions under which their Russian coreligionists lived. Despite repeated objections from the American government, the Russian regime remained adamant.

During the presidential campaign of 1908, the issue of Russia's refusal to recognize the rights of American Jewish passport holders led Sulzberger, as president of the American Jewish Committee, to urge Taft to secure Jewish electoral support by making an explicit statement on the passport question. On July 17, 1908, Sulzberger wrote to Taft, who had been nominated one month earlier as the Republican Party candidate for the presidency, strongly urging that he do so. Outraged by the czarist government's discrimination against American Jews, and also concerned lest his Democratic rival capture the Jewish vote by promising to pressure the Russians to recognize American Jewish passports, Taft responded favorably to his friend Sulzberger's entreaties and spoke out forcefully on the issue in his campaign speeches and later in his Inaugural Address, committing his new administration to solving the Russian passport problem. "No humane government," Taft declared, "could look with favor on a member of the family of nations which permitted such acts within its borders."

Throughout his years in the White House, Taft met and corresponded frequently with Sulzberger, Wolf, and other Jewish Republican leaders to discuss their ongoing efforts to seek congressional abrogation of the treaty. When, in December of 1911, both Houses of Congress passed a joint resolution instructing President Taft to notify the czarist government of American intention to abrogate the treaty, and when Taft subsequently conveyed that official notification, Sulzberger promptly sent a personal letter of congratulations to the president. Taft would later say with pride that it was the first time in American history that a treaty had been rescinded because of religious persecution—a historic governmental action in response to anti-Semitism that would ensure the religious liberty of American Jews traveling abroad.

Post-Presidential Years

Upon leaving the White House, Taft became a professor at Yale Law School, where he taught for the next eight years. He also lectured throughout the country, wrote articles for national magazines, and served with distinction as president of the American Bar Association. All the while, he still had high hopes of achieving his lifelong ambition of serving on the U.S. Supreme Court.

On several occasions Taft displayed his concern for Jewish rights in the United States and abroad by expressing his abhorrence of anti-Semitism. In a widely discussed article entitled "Progressive World Struggles of the Jews for Civil Equality," which he wrote for the *National Geographic* magazine in July 1919, Taft responded to the anti-Semitic restrictions against Jews in postwar Russia and Romania. Quoting Mirabeau's suggestion that Jews could be made full

contributors to the modern state only by being granted full economic and political rights, Taft asserted that when given such equality, Jews have made notable contributions to the countries in which they reside: "Jews are unique in that for eighteen hundred years they have had no country . . . and have, whenever there was any pretense of equality of opportunity for them, forged their way ahead into positions of prominence, influence and power in business, professions, in philosophy, in art, in literature, and in government."

In December 1920, in a speech before the Anti-Defamation League of B'nai B'rith in Chicago, Taft publicly attacked Henry Ford's virulent anti-Semitic campaign initiated earlier that year with a series of articles on "The International Jew" in Ford's Michigan newspaper, the *Dearborn Independent*. Deflating the charge that all Jews were capitalists by pointing out that many of them lived in poverty, Taft also exposed the falsity of The *Protocols of the Elders of Zion*, upon which Ford's allegations of an international Jewish conspiracy had been based. Denouncing both the Protocols and the *Dearborn Independent*, Taft unequivocally condemned the resurgent American anti-Semitism of which Ford's diatribes were a part:

> There is not the slightest ground for anti-Semitism among us. It is a vicious plant. It is a noxious weed that should be cut out. It has no place in free America, and the men who seek to introduce it should be condemned by public opinion.

In 1920 Taft had actively supported the presidential candidacy of his friend Warren G. Harding. When Chief Justice Edward D. White died shortly after Harding's inauguration, Taft was appointed to fill the vacancy, thus becoming the only man to serve as both president and chief justice. His last nine years, serving on the Supreme Court, were the happiest of his life. Because of failing health, however, Taft was forced to resign from the Supreme Court in February 1930. He died in Washington, D.C., a few weeks later at the age of seventy-two.

[D.G.D.]

Woodrow Wilson

Served from 1913 to 1921

Born on December 28, 1856, in Staunton, Virginia

Member of the Presbyterian denomination

Married Ellen Louise Axson on June 24, 1885; died August 6, 1914
Married Edith Bolling Galt, a widow, on December 18, 1915

Father to three daughters with Ellen

Candidate of the Democratic Party

Vice president under Wilson: Thomas R. Marshall (both terms)

First Inaugural Address delivered on March 4, 1913
Second Inaugural Address delivered on March 5, 1917

Died on February 3, 1924, in Washington, D.C.

*P*ERHAPS MORE THAN ANY OTHER PRESI-
dent, Woodrow Wilson had the utmost
respect and admiration for the Jewish
people. He once remarked: "Here is a great body
our Jewish citizens from whom have sprung men
of genius in every walk of our varied life; men
who have conceived of its ideals with singular
clarity; and led enterprises with spirit and sagac-
ity. . . . They are not Jews in America, they are
American citizens."

In his formative years, Wilson seems to have
had no contact with Jews. His father, Joseph
Ruggles Wilson, was a Southern Presbyterian minister with strong Christian theological convictions;
his mother's father, Thomas Woodrow (whose
name the president bore, having dropped the Thomas), was likewise a Presbyterian minister. In fact,
Wilson's entire family was immersed in biblical
study and the spread of biblical values.

As a dedicated Presbyterian, Woodrow would
kneel to pray morning and evening, say Grace
before meals, attend Wednesday prayer services,
and read the Bible each day. A firm believer from
an early age in predestination, he was convinced
that he would become president of the United
States, and when that happened Wilson hoped to
be instrumental in restoring the Jews to their ancient homeland, as per the teachings of the Bible.

Oddly enough, this future president of Princeton University did not start his formal education
until he was nine years old, when the Civil War
ended. He was a slow learner, having had difficulty in reading until he was eleven. However, in
the years that followed, he more than made up
for his late start; by the time he was seventeen he
was ready for college. In 1873 he enrolled in
Davidson College, a Presbyterian school in North
Carolina.

Because of ill health, Wilson had to drop out
of college before completing his freshman year,
and when he was ready to resume his studies, he
chose Princeton College, in New Jersey. After a
poor academic start at Princeton, his work began to improve, and in 1879 he was graduated
thirty-eighth in his class of one hundred and six.

Deciding to pursue a career in law, he then
entered the University of Virginia Law School and,
after graduating in 1882, opened a law office in
Atlanta, Georgia. Unable to attract clients, he
closed his practice and went to Johns Hopkins
University in Baltimore, Maryland, to do graduate work in history and politics. In 1886 he was
awarded a doctorate.

For the next several years Wilson taught in
small colleges with great success. His reputation
spread, and Princeton University invited him to
be professor of jurisprudence. In 1902 he was
elected president of the university.

Then, politics beckoned: The Democratic Party
in New Jersey selected Woodrow Wilson as their
candidate for governor. He developed into a good
campaigner and in 1910 was swept into office. His
impressive victory earned him national recognition, and in 1912 the Democrats put him up as
their candidate for the presidency. Fortunately for
him, the Republican vote was split between Taft
and Roosevelt, and Wilson emerged victorious.

Louis D. Brandeis

Without doubt, the greatest Jewish influence in
Wilson's life was Louis D. Brandeis (1856-1941),
a brilliant lawyer whose parents had escaped religious persecution in Bohemia by coming to
America in 1848. They settled in Louisville, Ken-

tucky, where Louis was born on November 13, 1856. During the Civil War, Brandeis later recalled, his parents, who felt that the South had been unjustified in seceding from the Union, would carry food and clothing in the darkness of night to Union troops camped nearby. The battle against injustice, which governed his life, was imbued in him at an early age.

In 1872 the Brandeis family visited Europe, and Louis stayed to complete his education at the Annen Realschule in Dresden. In 1875, at the suggestion of his favorite uncle, attorney Lewis Dembitz, whose surname he would later adopt as his middle name, Louis returned to the United States and enrolled in Harvard Law School, graduating first in his class. As a Supreme Court justice, he would always select the Harvard student who graduated first in his class to be his law clerk.

Brandeis opened a law office in Boston, where he took on cases involving the defense of labor unions. He did much pro bono work, earning him

Louis Brandeis

the sobriquet "The People's Attorney."

The manner in which he conducted his law practice attracted national attention. His celebrity was further enhanced upon the publication in 1914 of his book *Other People's Money*. It was reported that the book came to the attention of President Woodrow Wilson and had a strong impact upon his thinking. Wilson was particularly impressed by Brandeis's insistence on the importance of creating a highly competitive society through reducing protective tariffs, a concept that blended well with Wilson's New Freedom platform, on which he campaigned successfully in 1912.

Brandeis Supports Zionism

Although Brandeis's uncle Lewis Dembitz was an ardent Zionist, Brandeis did not embrace the Zionist cause until 1911, when he met Jacob de Haas (1872–1937), editor of Boston's *Jewish Advocate*, who had served as Theodor Herzl's secretary when Herzl visited London.

Like de Hass, Brandeis was impressed by the dedication and vision of Herzl. After having been elected president of the World Zionist Organization in August 1897, Herzl had written in his diary: "At Basle I founded the Jewish state. If I said this out loud today, I would be answered by universal laughter. Perhaps in five years, and certainly in fifty, everyone will know it."

Horace Kallen (1882–1974), a professor of philosophy at Harvard University, also encouraged Brandeis's nascent Zionist feelings. In 1913 Kallen sent Brandeis many articles that he had authored. Kallen emphasized the importance of Palestine as a cultural center for Jews. Some of Kallen's views on the place of Palestine in the hearts of American Jews were echoed by Brandeis in remarks such as: "Multiple loyalties are objectionable only if they are inconsistent."

After delving more deeply into the writings of Zionist leaders, Brandeis said: "My sympathy with the Zionist movement rests primarily upon the noble idealism which underlines it, and the conviction that a great people, stirred

Supreme Court portrait. Louis Brandeis is seated on the left in the first row.

by enthusiasm for such ideals, must bear an important part in the betterment of the world."

The Immigration Surge

By the end of the eighteenth century and in the early decades of the nineteenth century, the Socialist Party had dedicated itself to the alleviation of the harsh and horrifying conditions to which workers were subjected in the factories of the larger cities in the United States. Most of the 3.5 million Jews living in the United States prior to World War I had emigrated from Russia, Poland, Romania, Austria-Hungary, and other Eastern European countries, where the persecution of Jews was relentless and unending.

Some of the newcomers who swamped the shores of the United States seeking a "golden" life turned to peddling to make a living. Those who had come with some savings opened small retail stores, selling clothing, notions, and general household goods. But the vast majority could find employment only in factories manufacturing clothing of various sorts. Most of these factories were located in New York City, where the preponderance of immigrants settled. Conditions under which they were forced to work were deplorable, even inhuman. Doors were locked and guarded so no one could enter or leave unobserved, thus making sure there was no thievery.

In most of these factories, employees worked over nine-and-a-half hours each day, six days a week, for an average salary of $15.40 per week. To use toilet facilities, they had to go outside, through steel doors, but not before receiving permission from a supervisor.

Efforts were being made to unionize these shops, but even with the support of the International Ladies' Garment Workers' Union (ILGWU), founded in 1900, the power of the bosses to crush strikes was formidable. On the Lower East Side of New York, the United Hebrew Trades Union was formed to improve working conditions, but it met with failure. It was only after the Triangle Shirtwaist Factory fire of 1911 that a change was brought about.

The factory employed one thousand workers, mostly Jewish women. The fire broke out near the front entrance, and with the heavy iron exit door in the back locked to ensure that no employee could leave unobserved, all crowded the front entrance. In the crush, one hundred forty-six workers perished.

A bitter three-month strike ensued, the workers demanding that conditions in factories be improved and their unions recognized. Louis Brandeis, along with the most prominent Jewish leaders of the time, including Jacob Schiff, Louis Marshall, and Rabbi Judah Magnes, were called in to adjudicate the conflict between labor and management. In the end, an agreement was hammered out calling for a fifty-hour workweek, and time-and-a-half for overtime. There were to be ten paid legal holidays, workmen's compensation, and the enforcement of stricter fire regulations.

Credit for the final enactment of the legislation went to the future senator from New York, Robert F. Wagner, and Assemblyman Alfred E. Smith, the future governor of New York State.

Supreme Court Nominations

In 1916 President Wilson nominated Louis Brandeis for the Supreme Court, sending Washington and Wall Street into convulsions. Brandeis was criticized on all sides for his "radicalism," his "liberalism," and his "pro-unionism." Last but not least was the fact that Brandeis was Jewish and considered unworthy of being a Supreme Court justice. He was accused of being "a Jew with a reformist bent." One of President Wilson's friends remarked, "Isn't it a shame, Mr. President, that a man as great as Mr. Justice Brandeis should be a Jew?" To which the president responded: "But he would not be Mr. Brandeis if he were not a Jew!"

Many special interest groups were opposed to Brandeis's nomination. Having worked closely with Brandeis, and knowing first-hand of his brilliance and sterling character, Wilson was not prepared for the opposition that emerged. But Wilson would not give in, even to members of his own political party. "He is a friend of all just men and a lover of the right; and he knows more than how to talk about the right—he knows how to set it forward in the face of its enemies," stated President Wilson about Brandeis.

In a more elaborate statement, Wilson spelled out his reasons for advocating the appointment of Brandeis to the highest court in the land:

> I cannot speak too highly of his impartial, impersonal, orderly and constructive mind, his rare analytical powers, his deep human sympathy, his profound acquaintance with the historical roots of our institutions and insight into their spirit, or of the many evidences he has given of being imbued to the very heart of our American ideals of justice and equality of opportunity; of his knowledge of modern economic conditions and the way they bear upon the masses of the people . . . . The friend of justice and of men will ornament the high court of which we are so justly proud.

Finally, after four months of struggle, Wilson managed to marshal sufficient support in the Senate to win the battle. On June 1, 1916, by a vote of forty-seven to twenty-two, fifty-nine year-old Brandeis was confirmed; he would serve with distinction until his retirement in 1939.

Several years after his retirement, Brandeis was reminded of the bitter struggle that ensued over his appointment to the Supreme Court. One rainy evening, when he was taking his pre-dinner walk, a portly gentleman bumped into him and then stopped short. Brandeis looked up, and before he could say anything, the heavyset man offered his hand and said: "Isn't this Mr. Brandeis? I am Mr. Taft. I once did you a great injustice, Mr. Brandeis. I am sorry." "Thank you, Mr. Taft," Brandeis responded softly and then continued on his walk.

A Call to War

Although a firm believer that the only path to peace is a resolution of conflicts through compromise, when in February 1917 Germany repeatedly violated an understanding that it would not attack merchant shipping in the Atlantic, Woodrow Wilson broke off diplomatic relations with the Kaiser's government. One month later, German submarines sank five American merchant ships. Wilson's hope for peace completely evaporated, and on April 2, 1917, he asked Congress to declare war. On April 6, Congress complied, hoping, as did Wilson, that this would be a war to end all wars and bring democracy to the world.

Chaim Weizmann, British Savior

While Brandeis was unequalled in influencing President Wilson on matters relating to Zionist aspirations, on the other side of the Atlantic no one was the match of Chaim Weizmann (1874-1952) in bringing Zionist hopes to fruition.

Russian-born Weizmann left his native village, near Pinsk, to study chemistry first in Berlin and later in Switzerland. In Berlin he began to associate with other Zionist intellectuals, including Ahad Ha-Am (1856–1927) an advocate of cultural Zionism. In Switzerland he met Theodor Herzl (1860–1904). After Weizmann completed his doctorate, he was invited in 1906 to teach biochemistry at Manchester University, in England.

In 1910, after cultivating many friendships with influential people in Britain, Weizmann became a British citizen. Most prominent among these celebrities was Arthur Balfour, leader of the Conservative Party, and Winston Churchill. He also drew close to C. P. Scott, editor of the *Manchester Guardian*, who introduced him to David Lloyd George, who would serve as British prime minister from 1916 to 1922.

Britain entered World War I at the end of 1914. By 1916 it was having a difficult time fending off attacks by the Germans, who had learned how to manufacture high explosives. Acetone was the key ingredient, and the Germans had cornered the market on this highly desirable chemical. The British military turned to Chaim Weizmann, who had earned a reputation as a brilliant chemist, to find a substitute for acetone.

After a year of testing and experimentation, Weizmann had discovered a formula for extracting acetone from chestnuts. Before long, children all over Britain were scouring the countryside for chestnuts so badly needed to wage the war.

Weizmann was hailed by Prime Minister David Lloyd George as a national hero. Years later, Lloyd George would write in his memoirs:

> I felt a debt of gratitude, and so did all the Allies, to the brilliant scientific genius of Dr. Weizmann. When we talked to him, and asked him: "What can we do for you in the way of honours?" he replied: "All I care for is an opportunity to do something for my people."
>
> It was worth anything to us in honor, or in coin of the realm, but all he asked for was to be allowed to present his case for the restoration of his people to the old country which they had made famous throughout the world.

The Balfour Declaration

While Weizmann's celebrity in England played an important part in the effort to have Palestine recognized as the Jewish homeland and the fulfillment of the Zionist dream, there was a long row to hoe before that dream became a reality. Weizmann's friendly contacts with British Foreign Secretary Arthur James Balfour and Prime Minister Lloyd George would make possible the issuance in 1917, of the famous Balfour Declaration, which was communicated to Lord Rothschild by Balfour.

This breakthrough, which thrilled Jews the world over, came after many months of arduous negotiations and consultations in London and Washington. Involved in the process in America were President Wilson and his White House staff, as well as Louis Brandeis and Rabbi Stephen S. Wise.

In the spring of 1917, Brandeis arranged to have Chaim Weizmann come to the United States to meet with President Wilson. The meeting went well. On May 6 Brandeis himself met with Wilson and discussed the details of the declaration

Three of the most prominent Zionists in the 1920s were philanthropist Nathan Straus (left), U.S. Supreme Court Justice Louis Brandeis (center), and Rabbi Stephen Wise.

being proposed. Wilson expressed his accord with the overall content of the document, so much so that when Wilson met with Stephen S. Wise the following month, he said: "Whenever the time comes, and you and Justice Brandeis feel that the time is ripe for me to speak out, I shall be ready."

But when Wilson's secretary of state, Robert Lansing, and other members of the State Department expressed opposition to the idea, Wilson backed off.

Back in London, on July 18, 1917, Chaim Weizmann and other British Zionist leaders met with government officials to construct a formal working draft of what would become the Balfour

Declaration. It was then cabled to Cecil Spring-Rice, Britain's ambassador to the United States, who gave it to Brandeis. Brandeis took it to Colonel Edward House, President Wilson's aide, for review. House, who had never been well disposed to Zionist goals, nor particularly fond of Jews, showed the document to Secretary of State Lansing. They persuaded President Wilson that it was unwise to endorse such a document because it might offend the Ottoman Empire, which controlled Palestine and Syria.

When the president followed their advice, Brandeis called Wilson and persuaded him otherwise. He also convinced Colonel House that it was in America's best interest to endorse the proposed Balfour Declaration. After a meeting between House and the president, Wilson assured Brandeis that he was "in entire sympathy" with the proposed declaration.

In Britain, Lloyd George, Arthur Balfour, and their staffs met again to refine the document and satisfy all legitimate objections that had been raised. The Balfour Declaration finally was made public on November 2, 1917. It read:

> I have much pleasure in conveying to you, on behalf of His Majesty's Government, the following declaration of sympathy with Jewish Zionist aspirations which has been submitted to, and approved by, the Cabinet.
>
> "His Majesty's Government view with favour the establishment in Palestine of a national home for the Jewish people, and will use their best endeavours to facilitate the achievement of this object, it being clearly understood that nothing shall be done which may prejudice the civil and religious rights of existing non-Jewish communities in Palestine, or the rights and political status enjoyed by Jews in any other country."
>
> I should be grateful if you would bring this declaration to the knowledge of the Zionist Federation.

Sometime later, President Wilson confided to Rabbi Wise: "How proud I am that because of the teachings instilled in me by my father, it has been my privilege to restore the Holy Land to its rightful owners."

Stephen S. Wise

Next to Louis Brandeis, Rabbi Stephen S. Wise (1874–1949) was probably the American Jew closest to President Wilson. It was Wise, along with Brandeis, who influenced the wavering president to accept the contents of the Balfour Declaration despite the heavy opposition by high-ranking members of his own administration, and it was to Wise that Wilson sent an open letter to be shared with the public announcing his approval of the Balfour Declaration.

Stephen S. Wise was born in Budapest, Hungary, and was brought to the United States when he was seventeen months old. After graduating from Columbia University in New York at age eighteen, Wise studied for the rabbinate and in 1893 was ordained by Adolph Jellinek of Vienna.

Wise's first pulpit was Congregation B'nai Jershurun in New York City. He was then called to Temple Beth Israel in Portland, Oregon, where he served for six years. Upon returning to New York, he was offered the post as rabbi of the prestigious Reform Temple Emanu-El. But being of independent mind, when the president and the board of directors of the congregation would not guarantee him freedom of the pulpit—the right to speak his mind on current issues—he turned down the offer and in 1907 founded the Free Synagogue of New York. In 1922, Wise founded the Jewish Institute of Religion in New York City. In 1950 it would merge with the Hebrew Union College, founded by Isaac Mayer Wise in Cincinnati, Ohio, in 1875.

Stephen Wise, who was well known for his oratorical skills and booming voice, had come to Woodrow Wilson's attention as far back as 1898, when Wise became secretary of the newly established Federation of American Zionists, which in 1918 would become the Zionist Organization of America (ZOA). Wise also was one of the founders of the American Jewish Congress. Having developed a warm friendship with Wilson, Wise was able to acquaint Wilson with Zionist goals and aspirations.

Wise and Wilson developed so close a relationship that in October 1917, when the British government sent President Wilson a copy of the proposed Balfour Declaration for his private consideration, Wilson asked Wise to evaluate the document. Wise was disturbed over the wording expressing British intentions to create "a national haven for Jews." He suggested that the document read "a national home for the Jewish people." Wilson agreed and transmitted the suggestion to the British government. The amendment was accepted.

Anti-Zionist Jews

As grateful and delighted as Wise and Brandeis were over the issuance of the Balfour Declaration, many Jews were displeased. They feared that if they were supportive of the Jewish homeland, they would be charged with harboring dual loyalty. The leaders of Reform Judaism and most of their followers shared this anti-Zionist bias.

When Wise reminded President Wilson that he might be severely criticized for taking a pro-Zionist position, Wilson responded: "My wastebasket is big enough to take care of all such letters."

In fact, in March 1919 Julius Kahn (1861–1924), a Republican congressman from California, presented Wilson with a petition signed by three hundred anti-Zionist American Jews, including bankers, judges, rabbis, and playwrights, expressing opposition to a Jewish homeland in Palestine and the fear that the Balfour Declaration might lead to "a denial of full citizenship and human rights in all lands." Wilson paid little heed to it, consigning it to his wastebasket as he had promised Wise.

Bernard Baruch

Multimillionaire Bernard Baruch (1870-1965) was born in Camden, South Carolina, where his family had settled after coming to America from Germany. His father, Simon, was a well-known Confederate army surgeon.

Baruch's family moved to New York City in 1881, and in 1884 Bernard enrolled in City College. After graduation he worked as an office boy

in a Wall Street firm for three dollars a week. He quickly learned how to play the market.

By 1902 he had amassed a fortune of over three million dollars and had begun cultivating an interest in politics. For many years he had admired Wilson, and when the New Jersey governor became the Democratic nominee for president in 1910, Baruch contributed generously to his campaign.

When Baruch was asked by a friend why he would vote for Woodrow Wilson, a Democrat, rather than for Theodore Roosevelt, for whom he had voted in 1904, Baruch responded:

> Remembering my own college days, when the fact of being a Jew had been enough to bar me from fraternities, I admired [Woodrow] Wilson's blunt attack of the [eating] clubs [at Princeton]. Moreover, his two years as governor of New Jersey had marked him as an imaginative and effective leader; and the New Freedom he talked about touched in me an awakening, though still ill-defined, political philosophy.

Impressed by Baruch's devotion and impressive accomplishments in the world of finance,

Bernard Baruch

President Wilson brought him into his inner circle of advisers in 1915. Sensing that America would soon be drawn into the war raging in Europe, Baruch urged that the United States strengthen its military and industrial capabilities. In 1916 Wilson appointed him a member of the advisory commission of the Council of National Defense. With America's actual entry into the war in 1917, Baruch was appointed chairman of the War Industries Board. In 1919 he would accompany Wilson to Paris for the peace conference, where he helped shape the economic language of the peace treaty.

Having married an Episcopalian, and having agreed to raise their children in that faith, Baruch let it be known that he considered himself an American first and a Jew second. While at first he was openly anti-Zionist and opposed to the establishment of Israel as an independent state, in the end he rallied to the Zionist cause, when in 1947 the United Nations debated the issue. In subsequent years, however, his support of Israel waned once again.

When Wilson retired from the presidency, after having served for two terms, Baruch helped him finance the Georgian-style brick house at 2340 S Street in Washington, D.C., on which the president and his second wife, Edith Bolling Galt, had made a deposit of five thousand dollars. Donors were solicited for ten shares at one thousand dollars apiece. Baruch, who paid for a share, also bought the lot adjacent to the house so that the Wilsons might have complete privacy. The former president would not get to enjoy his new home for very long, however. He would die less than a year after leaving office.

Henry Morgenthau

When Woodrow Wilson's political career began to flourish, Henry Morgenthau (1856-1946), like Bernard Baruch, was attracted to him even as were some prominent, wealthy, Jewish Republicans, including Jacob H. Schiff.

Born in Germany, Morgenthau was brought to the United States in 1865, at age ten, at the close of the Civil War. The Morgenthau family settled in New York City, where Henry received his education, first at City College and then at Columbia Law School, from which he graduated in 1877.

In the 1880s Morgenthau began to devote himself to real estate investments, from which he became very wealthy. He backed Stephen S. Wise when he established the Free Synagogue of New York. Morgenthau felt compelled to resign his affiliation with the synagogue in 1919, however, because of profound ideological differences with Stephen Wise over the issue of Zionism.

Morgenthau served as chairman of the Democratic National Committee's finance committee during Wilson's 1912 and 1916 campaigns for the presidency. In 1913 President Wilson appointed him ambassador to Turkey, a post he held until 1916. In 1919, when Wilson was using the full weight of his office to persuade the Senate to vote in favor of joining the League of Nations, Morgenthau stood foursquare behind him, though the effort failed. That same year Morgenthau became one of the prime movers in establishing the International Red Cross.

Morgenthau's son, Henry Morgenthau, Jr., (1891–1967), would later follow in his father's political footsteps and, under Franklin D. Roosevelt, serve as secretary of the treasury from 1934 to 1945.

Paul M. Warburg

Born in Hamburg, Germany, Paul Warburg (1868–1932), scion of the German-Jewish banking family, would achieve renown as one of the architects of the U.S. Federal Reserve System.

After studying finance in London and Paris, Warburg became a partner in the family banking house M.M. Warburg & Co. That same year he married Nina Loeb, daughter of Solomon Loeb, one of the founders of the Wall Street investment banking firm Kuhn, Loeb & Co. In 1902 Warburg immigrated to the United States and became a partner in his father-in-law's firm.

Several years later, Warburg worked closely with Senator Nelson W. Aldrich in drafting congressional legislation that would create the Federal Reserve System. When enacted into law in

December 1913, The Federal Reserve Bill provided for twelve regional Federal Reserve Banks and a Federal Reserve Board based in Washington, D.C., whose members would be appointed by the president.

In 1914 Warburg was nominated by President Wilson to serve as a member of the newly created Federal Reserve Board. From 1917 to 1918, he served as the Board's vice-chairman. Warburg wrote several influential books about the U.S, banking system, including *Federal Reserve System, Its Origin and Growth*, published in 1930.

The Paris Peace Conference

When Germany and the Central Powers realized that their war was lost, they sued for peace. In 1918, on the eleventh hour of the eleventh day of the eleventh month, an armistice was signed. (Some saw the event forecast in First Kings 11:11, where Solomon is admonished for violating the word of God.) The German Kaiser and the crown prince fled to Holland, and the stage was set for peace talks.

In January 1919, two months after the armistice was signed, President Wilson led an American delegation to the Paris Peace Conference to be conducted in nearby Versailles, the site of the magnificent palace built by Louis XIV. Wilson came convinced, as he stated in an address to the Senate on January 22, 1919, that if peace is to be established, "it must be a peace without victory . . . Only a peace between equals can last."

Wilson invited Jewish representatives to be part of his delegation so that they could make their case for the establishment of a Jewish homeland in Palestine. In fact, Stephen S. Wise was one of the speakers who addressed the conference in Versailles. When Wise concluded his dramatic presentation, Wilson said: "Don't worry, Dr. Wise, Palestine is yours." And to the other American Jewish delegates at the conference the president offered this assurance: "I am persuaded that the allied nations, with the fullest concurrence of our Government and people, are agreed that in Palestine there shall be laid the foundation of a Jewish commonwealth."

The Fourteen Points

President Wilson came to Versailles with a fourteen-point program that he was convinced was fair and equitable and could be the basis for a realistic settlement of the variety of claims and conditions that would be set forth by the various nations. On January 8, 1918, he delivered his fourteen-point peace program, which called for the formation of an association of nations that would guarantee political independence and territorial integrity to all countries and nationalities, large and small.

To Jews, this meant not only a guarantee to ensure the viability of the newly created states of Eastern Europe, but a return of Jews to Palestine, their ancestral homeland. But the conference itself did not place its stamp of approval on the establishment of a Jewish homeland. Arab delegates contested the Zionist interpretation of Wilson's proposal, and many European countries sided with them. Even the French premier poked fun at Wilson's idealism, roaring: "Who is the man who comes to us with fourteen points? God Almighty never had more than ten!"

Nonetheless, on June 28, 1919, the Treaty of Versailles with Germany was signed, based for the most part upon Wilson's Fourteen Points. Among other concessions, Germany agreed to give up her overseas colonies and to pay fifty-six billion dollars in reparations. In addition, at the urging of Wilson, the delegates agreed to establish the League of Nations. For all his efforts, President Wilson earned the Nobel Peace Prize in 1919.

Final Trip

On June 29 Wilson set out to return to the United States, conscious of the strain that had begun to affect his health. He felt that he had succeeded in his mission, but learned soon enough that there was strong opposition in Congress, led by Senator Henry Cabot Lodge of Massachusetts, to his proposal that the United States join a league of nations. Lodge was not displeased with the concept of a league of nations, but was vigorously opposed to article ten of the covenant of the league, which obliged all members to defend any other member who came under attack. He felt that the United States should not "commit ourselves to [declaring] war at the pleasure of other nations."

Wilson, who had labored so hard for the covenant that the nations had agreed upon, refused to compromise, declaring: "The hand of God led us this way. We cannot turn back." Whereupon, he embarked upon a whistle-stop tour of the West, eager to win popular support for his position. The president gave hour-long speeches twice a day. En route from Colorado to Kansas he suffered a stroke and collapsed. He never fully recovered, and his effort to have the United States join the League of Nations failed to win the two-thirds vote of the Senate required to ratify a treaty.

Wilson's stroke partially incapacitated him. His second wife, Edith Galt, whom he had married in December 1915, took charge and screened all communications addressed to her bedridden husband. She vigorously denied offering advice on how matters of government were to be disposed, but admitted that she passed on to him only those matters she deemed worthy of his attention.

Summing Up

After leaving office on March 4, 1921, and retiring to the Washington, D.C., house for which Bernard Baruch had helped the Wilson's obtain financing, Woodrow Wilson's health continued to fail, and he died on February 3, 1924.

On November 11, 1923, he had summed up his philosophy of life and politics: "I am not one of those that have the least anxiety about the triumph of the principles I have stood for. I have seen fools resist Providence before, and I have seen their destruction, as will come upon these again, utter destruction and contempt. That we shall prevail is as sure as that God reigns."

Wilson likely had in mind his predecessor, William Howard Taft, who in 1916 criticized Wilson as "a ruthless hypocrite . . . an opportunist, who hasn't the convictions that he would not barter at once for votes." And surely, Wilson was also thinking of the criticism leveled at him by Theodore Roosevelt, who in 1919 said of him that he is a leader who "hasn't a touch of idealism in him" and whose "advocacy of the League of Nations no more represents idealism on his part than advocacy of peace without victory."

To many Jews, however, President Wilson was a hero and a savior, a man of principle and ethical uprightness. He was a leader who was relentless in the struggle to overcome anti-Semitism, as he demonstrated by his battle to have Louis D. Brandeis confirmed as Supreme Court justice, an action opposed even by members of his own administration. And the importance of Woodrow Wilson's support of the Balfour Declaration would be fully appreciated three decades later when the homeless survivors of the Holocaust finally found a haven of refuge in the homeland promised the Jewish people on November 2, 1917.

It is predicted that Wilson's legacy will loom large in the annals of Jewish history.

[A.J.K.]

Warren G. Harding

Served from 1921 to 1923

Born on November 2, 1865, in Corsica (now Blooming Grove), Ohio

Member of the Baptist denomination

Married Florence Mabel Kling DeWolfe on July 8, 1891

Father to one illegitimate daughter

Candidate of the Republican Party

Vice president under Harding: Calvin Coolidge

Inaugural Address delivered on March 4, 1921

Died in office on August 2, 1923

Twenty-Ninth President of the United States

HE RESULTS OF THE 1920 ELECTION, in which Republican candidate Warren Gamaliel Harding roundly defeated his Democratic opponent, James M. Cox, revealed, among other things, how unfavorably Americans viewed Wilson's advocacy of United States' participation in the League of Nations.

The son of a doctor perpetually in debt, Harding did not model himself after his father. After working hard, first as a teacher and later as an insurance salesman, he finally found his niche in journalism. He acquired the *Marion Star*, a failing Ohio newspaper, and built it into one of the most successful newspapers in the state.

Harding's mother likewise was a doctor. But, unlike her husband, she was a deeply religious woman who, in middle age, converted from Methodist to Seventh-Day Adventist. Warren, however, rejected the religious doctrines to which his mother was addicted. During his studies at Ohio Central College, he had been introduced to Darwin's theories, which led him to doubt divine creation. (Abraham Lincoln shared similar doubts about God's role as Creator of the world and manager of all man's affairs.)

After achieving success as a publisher and accumulating some wealth, Harding felt inclined to enter the political arena. To get a taste of the public mood, he visited cities and towns throughout the state, where he would deliver speeches. His handsome physical stature and his oratorical skills were quite impressive, and he was encouraged by the reception accorded him. At the same time, he was learning that to succeed in politics he would have to tone down his unconventional religious convictions.

This latter lesson was especially impressed upon Harding when he read an 1845 statement by Lincoln that appeared in the *Illinois Gazette*. Lincoln is reported to have said that although he belonged to no church, "I have never spoken with intentional disrespect of religion in general, or of any denomination of Christians in particular. . . . I do not think I could myself be brought to support a man for office whom I knew to be an open enemy of, and scoffer at, religion."

After Harding became the Republican nominee for president in 1920, he declared: "It is my conviction that the fundamental trouble with the people of the United States is that they have gotten too far away from Almighty God."

A Political Career Begins

In 1884, having settled in Marion, Ohio, and having acquired full control of the *Marion Star*, Harding made his first bid for office—that of county auditor—but lost in the highly Democratic Marion County.

In 1899 he made another try, this time for the Ohio State Senate, and he succeeded. After serving two terms, in 1903 Harding was elected lieutenant governor of Ohio. In 1914 he was elected United States senator from that state; he served for six undistinguished years and was present for less than one-third of the roll-call votes. Nevertheless, with Harry Daughtery as his campaign manager, Harding was easily victorious in his campaign for the presidency in 1920, defeating Democratic candidate James M. Cox and his running mate, Franklin Delano Roosevelt, 61 percent to 35 percent. Socialist candidate Eugene V. Debs came in third with 3 percent of the vote.

The Jewish vote in the 1920 presidential election was estimated at 43 percent for Harding, 38 for Debs, and 19 percent for Cox.

Popular entertainer Al Jolson (1886-1950) demonstrated his affection for Harding by composing and singing this ditty on the campaign trail:

> We need another Lincoln
> to do this country's thinkin.'
> Mis-ter Harding,
> you're the man for us.

Although he did not always satisfy the Jewish interest in a number of areas, Harding's true feelings toward Jews was made manifest in a 1923 statement he sent to the Union of American Hebrew Congregations when it was celebrating its Golden Jubilee:

> One of the marvels of humanity's story has been the strength and persistence of the Jewish faith and the continuing influence and power of the Jewish people. I cannot but feel that these things are in large measure owing to the Hebrew conception of a personal God and of the individual accountability of men and women.

Wilson's Ridicule

Woodrow Wilson belittled Harding's victory over his Democratic opponent, when in his third year in office Harding admitted to being confused and overhelmed by the job. Harding complained: "I listen to one side and they seem right, and—God—I talk to the other side, and they seem just as right! I can't make a damn thing out of this problem."

After this admission, Wilson observed: "How can he lead when he doesn't know where he is going!" Later, Harding tacitly agreed, admitting: "I am not fit for this office and should never have been here." Harding was much more at home playing cards with his "poker Cabinet," which included War Secretary John W. Weeks, Attorney General Harry Daugherty, and Interior Secretary Albert B. Fall. Harding would have preferred to spend his time yachting and fishing, watching baseball games and boxing matches.

Zionist Associations

When Chaim Weizmann, revered scientist and Zionist statesman, came to the United States in 1921 to launch his Keren Hayesod drive—to raise funds for Jewish settlements in Palestine—he brought with him from Germany fellow scientist Albert Einstein, who had earned worldwide acclaim and had been the recipient of the Nobel Prize in physics that year. Einstein came aboard to raise funds for the Hebrew University.

When the boat carrying the two internationally celebrated dignitaries docked in New York City in March 1921, they were greeted by police launches and fireboats, and were whisked to City Hall where they were given the key to the city by Mayor James Hylan and Fiorello La Guardia, president of the New York City Board of Aldermen.

Later, they visited Washington, where President Harding presented to the two men awards from the National Academy of Sciences. Undoubtedly,

Chaim Weizman

one reason the president was so gracious in his reception of the two prominent leaders was that Jews had supported him in his campaign for the presidency. Evidently, Jews had forgotten that, while a senator, Harding had voted against the appointment of Louis D. Brandeis to the Supreme Court.

Immigration Legislation

Jewish disillusionment with Harding set in when, shortly after he took office, he called Congress into session especially for the purpose of enacting legislation that would greatly curtail immigration into the United States (a similar bill had been introduced a year earlier and Wilson had pocket-vetoed it).

The Emergency Quota Act of 1921, also known as the Johnson Act because it was introduced by Alfred Johnson of Washington, was promptly signed by President Harding. The bill limited the number of immigrants admitted in any one year to 3 percent of their ethnic stock present in the United States in 1910. A shocking blow to the interests of the Jewish community, it reduced the number of Jews entering the United States from eastern and southern Europe to a trickle. Some senators went so far as to complain that the legislation had not set the quota low enough.

Immigrant Jews from other countries, such as those in northern Europe and England, had a much easier time reaching American shores. In their book *The Jewish American Family Album*, Dorothy and Thomas Hoobler describe the recollection of twelve-year-old Rachel Gerson's experience when she came to America from England in 1921. She writes: "We traveled tourist. That's like third class. We weren't in steerage with the immigrants from other countries like Russia. They were on a deck below us."

She then continues to describe the experience on Ellis Island where each immigrant was examined thoroughly because they would not pass anyone who had trachoma or lice. She concludes: "They really gave you a thorough examination. That was the most horrible place I have ever been."

Rising Anti-Semitism

From the time Harding had his eye on the presidency, he began cozying up to men of great celebrity, such as Thomas Edison, and men of great influence and affluence, such as automobile magnate Henry Ford. He furthered their interests by keeping the minimum wage and taxes low and by turning a deaf ear to the demand of union bosses.

Anti-Semitic activity, which had been relatively dormant during the Wilson Administration, percolated and bubbled over in the 1920s while Harding was in office. Increasingly, quotas were imposed upon the admission of Jewish students to colleges and universities, and schools refused to appoint Jews to their faculties.

In 1922, as the proportion of Jews at Harvard College began to exceed 21 percent, President Abbott Lawrence Lowell approved the establishment of a quota that would limit the number of Jews admitted. He argued that this would reduce anti-Semitism. Soon thereafter, other colleges adopted similar policies.

But it was the racist attacks by the Ku Klux Klan (KKK) that Jews found most unsettling. The organization had been reorganized in 1915 by Colonel William J. Simmons and was spewing out hate against Jews, Catholics, and blacks, claiming that they were denigrating the social and moral fabric of America. Moreover, to the deep disappointment of American Jewry, it was the celebrated and popular tycoon Henry Ford who subscribed to these racist views.

The Dearborn Independent

In 1920, a weekly Detroit, Michigan, newspaper, the *Dearborn Independent*, which Henry Ford had acquired, began to publish a series of almost one hundred articles entitled "The International Jew." It also ran the text of the fictitious *The Protocols of the Elders of Zion* and other anti-Semitic articles based on it. At its peak, Ford's weekly would reach a circulation of approximately half a million Americans who were being fed the old anti-Semitic myth that the Jews were plotting to

President Warren G. Harding and his wife, Florence Mabel Kling de Wolfe, standing in front of one of Henry Ford's early models.

dominate the world. Ford hammered away at this libel in his weekly column, "Mr. Ford's Page," written for him by journalist William J. Cameron.

The origin of this type of fictitious story has been traced to a satire on Napoleon III of France, who in 1864 was accused of planning to dominate the world. The same scenario surfaced later, only this time the Jewish Elders of Prague were accused of hatching a plot of world domination.

Henry Ford's newspaper specifically targeted wealthy financiers and philanthropists such as Felix Warburg, Jacob Schiff, Morris Loeb, and Simon Guggenheim. All were accused of conspiring to control American industry and corrupting American culture by their "depraved Hollywood films" and other offensive activities. *The Dearborn Independent* also dredged up rumors that President Wilson had taken secret orders over the phone from Judge Brandeis, and that the Federal Reserve, established by Wilson in 1913, of which Paul Warburg, the brother of Felix, was a member, was created so that Jews would have an unfair financial advantage over Christians.

Attorney Louis Marshall (1856-1929), one of the founders in 1906 of the American Jewish Committee, an organization dedicated "to prevent the infraction of the civil and religious rights of Jews in any part of the world," was singled out for ridicule by Ford and his underlings. As the leading spokesman of American Jewry, Marshall constantly was lambasted as the "evil genius" behind Wilson's pro-League of Nations stance at the Paris Peace Conference. To the delight of Ford, despite Wilson's efforts in 1921 to promote the League of Nations to the American people, the Senate failed to ratify the treaty, and America never joined the League.

To counter the anti-Jewish propaganda being spewed by the *Dearborn Independent*, the Jewish community fought back by boycotting Ford automobiles. Ford was attacked as an ignoramus who was being taken in by bigots. This was followed by a "manifesto," spearheaded by President Wilson and former President Taft and was signed by one hundred nineteen prominent Americans, condemning the automobile manufacturer.

Although Ford was weakened and demeaned by all the adverse publicity, it would not be until 1925, when faced with a million-dollar lawsuit instituted by Aaron Sapiro (1884-1959), a San

Francisco lawyer who was highly regarded by Presidents Harding and Coolidge, as well as by Herbert Hoover, who was secretary of commerce from 1921 to 1928, that Ford realized how dire the consequences of his actions would be.

Scandal-Ridden Administration

Before Harding took office on March 4, 1921, he pledged to the American people, who had experienced a horrendous world war, that if elected he would institute "a return to normalcy." Harding was elected, but the nation did not return to normalcy. In fact, after serving for only two years, Harding was overwhelmed by revelations that scandalous activity was brewing in various departments of his administration. Some of his Cabinet selections, including Herbert Hoover as secretary of commerce, were excellent, but many of Harding's choices to head departments or serve as counselors to the president were ill-advised, and some were downright corrupt.

One of Harding's top appointees was Colonel Charles Forbes, selected to head the Veterans Bureau. Forbes was convicted of and served a two-year jail sentence for selling to bootleggers and narcotics dealers drugs and alcohol that belonged to veterans hospitals,. His aide, Charles Cramer, who was involved in the corrupt practices, committed suicide.

Harding's alien property custodian, Thomas Miller—overseer of property belonging to German nationals that had been confiscated during the war—was convicted of accepting bribes, and Jesse Smith, bagman for Miller and a personal aide to Attorney General Daugherty, committed suicide when Harding asked for his resignation.

Teapot Dome

The most devastating, ego-shattering event during Harding's term of office occurred when the president learned, while on a tour of the West and Alaska, that his close friend, secretary of the Interior Albert B. Fall, had accepted more than four-hundred-thousand dollars in 1922 for illegally leasing federally-owned oil reserves to business associates, some of whom were close friends of the president.

Terribly worried and depressed by the scandal brewing among some of his most trusted aides, appointees, and companions, Harding headed for home. During a stop in San Francisco, he took sick and developed pneumonia, from which he died there on August 2, 1923.

According to historian Robert K. Murray, Harding's early demise was a certainty, for Harding had for some time been suffering from high blood pressure and an enlarged heart. Murray reports that when the famed Jewish heart specialist Dr. Emanuel Libman of New York saw the president at a dinner early in 1923, he predicted that the leader of the nation "would be dead from heart disease within six months."

Harding Eulogized

On August 10, 1923, Harold Standish Corbin, one of the active freelance writers for the Chicago, Illinois, Loyal Order of Moose, penned moving words memorializing the life of the twenty-ninth president of the United States. He compared the passing of Harding to that of Moses, who died on Mount Nebo before entering the Promised Land. "His path," wrote Corbin, "terminated suddenly at the grave. He has joined the choir invisible of those immortal dead who live again in minds made better by their presence."

While the record reveals little connection between Harding and individuals of the Jewish community, Corbin went on to praise the president in these laudatory words: "In administering the affairs of the country, he knew no difference between Protestant, Catholic, and Jew."

Most historians rank Harding among American's ten worst presidents. Future president Herbert Hoover, Harding's secretary of commerce, said of Harding: "He was not a man with either the experience or the intellectual quality that the position [of president] needed."

[A.J.K.]

Calvin Coolidge

Served from 1923 to 1929

Born on July 4, 1872, in Plymouth, Vermont

Member of the Congregationalist denominiation

Married Grace Anna Goodhue on October 4, 1905

Father to two sons

Candidate of the Republican Party

Assumed the presidency on August 3, 1923, following the death
of Warren G. Harding; elected to a full term on November 4, 1924

Vice president under Coolidge: Charles G. Dawes (second term)

Inaugural Address delivered on March 4, 1925

Died on January 5, 1933, in Northampton, Massachusetts

Thirtieth President of the United States

ESPITE THE TEAPOT DOME SCANDAL and others that left a stain on the presidency of Warren G. Harding, the turmoil did not carry over into the Coolidge Administration. Calvin Coolidge served out the remaining two years of Harding's term of office and was then reelected in 1924 for a full term.

Prosperity was in the air, and Coolidge's policy of avoiding involvement in international conflicts sat well with most Americans, as did his policy of noninterference in the affairs of business and industry. Jews apparently were not overly pleased with the reelection of Coolidge because of his negative attitude toward immigration. They showed their apprehension by giving the Democratic candidate for the presidency, John W. Davis, 51 percent of the vote over 27 percent for Coolidge. The general population gave Coolidge 54 percent to Davis's 29 percent.

No sooner was President Coolidge sworn into office than he signed the Immigration Act of 1924. This act further reduced considerably the number of Jews who would be able to enter the United States as immigrants from southern and eastern Europe under the Emergency Quota Act of 1921.

Early Years

Calvin Coolidge, whose reserved and quiet nature earned him the sobriquet "Silent Cal," was actually named John Calvin Coolidge. However, so as not to be confused with his father, who shared the same name, Calvin dropped the John.

Born on July 4, 1872, in Plymouth, Vermont, Calvin's father was a prosperous farmer who had dabbled in politics. From 1891 to 1895, Calvin attended Amherst College. In 1892, during his

An early photograph of "Silent Cal," who decided not to run for a second term.

From left to right: Harry Firestone, President Calvin Coolidge, Henry Ford, Thomas A. Edison, and Grace Coolidge.

sophomore year, he became interested in politics and campaigned for the reelection of President Benjamin Harrison.

After graduating from college, Calvin studied law and was admitted to the bar in 1897, after which he became more deeply involved in the Republican Party. From 1899 onward, he served in elective offices that extended from city councilman to mayor of Northampton, to state senator, to lieutenant governor, to governor of Massachusetts.

In September 1919 Coolidge attracted national attention when, as governor, he called out the National Guard to quell two days of rioting after the Boston police had gone on strike. "There is no right to strike against the public safety by anybody, anywhere, any time," he declared. As a result, he became known as the "law and order man from Massachusetts," which, in large measure, led to his being nominated for the vice-presidency by the 1920 Republican National Convention.

As vice president Coolidge presided quietly over the Senate, rarely interjecting from the chair. Then suddenly, while vacationing at his father's home in Plymouth Notch, Vermont, he was noti-

fied on August 3, 1923, that President Harding had died. At 2:47 A.M., Coolidge was sworn into office by his father, a justice of the peace and a notary public.

According to legend, Calvin Coolidge promptly went back to sleep.

Contact with Jews

With the exception of Adolph Simon Ochs (1858–1935) and Louis Marshall (1856–1929), Calvin Coolidge had little, if any, contact with Jews. He took no part in the debate that continued to rage during his administration over the calumniation of Jews by Henry Ford. But Coolidge did befriend Ochs and Marshall.

After a successful career in Chattanooga, Tennessee, as a newspaper publisher, Ochs left for New York, where in 1896 he purchased *The New York Times*, then on the verge of bankruptcy. Under his management, and later, with the assistance of his son-in-law, Arthur Hays Sulzberger (1891–1968), he saved the paper, which went on

Calvin Coolidge participating in the cornerstone-laying ceremony of the Washington Jewish Community Center, on May 3, 1925.

to become the most influential publication in the world.

In a February 13, 1924, letter, President Coolidge thanked Mr. Ochs for two very positive editorials that appeared in the *Times* supporting his tax-reduction program. And in a February 21, 1924, communication, Adolph Ochs thanked the president for an invitation to stay at the White House the following Monday when he planned to be in Washington.

Although prominent attorney Louis Marshall, a communal leader and founder of the American Jewish Committee, requested an interview with the president in January 1924, he was refused. Marshall had hoped to convince President Coolidge how detrimental to Jewish life it would be if the immigration bill, pending before Congress, was passed. Much to Marshall's chagrin and the

disappointment of the Jewish community, when the Johnson-Reed Act was passed, Coolidge promptly signed it. As a consequence, in the fiscal year 1924–1925, less than ten thousand Jews from all countries entered the United States.

Nevertheless, Marshall swallowed his pride, and when the president spoke laudatory words about the Jewish presence in America, Marshall was extremely pleased. Coolidge, who had been invited to speak at the laying of the cornerstone for Washington's Jewish Community Center, offered these noble sentiments:

> It will be at once a monument to the achievement of the past and a help in the expansion of these achievements into a wider field of usefulness in the future . . . .
>
> The Jewish faith is predominantly the faith of liberty. From the beginnings of the conflict

Calvin Coolidge (seated center) is shown here with his first Cabinet, which was composed mostly of holdovers from the Harding era.

between the colonies and the mother country, they were overwhelmingly on the side of the rising revolution. . . .

It is easy to understand why a people with the historic background of the Jews should thus overwhelmingly and unhesitatingly have allied themselves with the cause of freedom. From earliest colonial times, America has been a new land of promise to this long-persecuted race . . .

Every inheritance of the Jewish people, every teaching of their secular history and religious experience, draws them powerfully to the side of charity, liberty, and progress.

In a May 5, 1925, letter to the president, Marshall expressed his profound appreciation for the president's words on that occasion:

It was a memorable utterance and has brought balm to our hearts. It will do much to dispel the mists of suspicion and misunderstanding which have been spread by propagandists, either through ignorance or malice, against the Jews. Your words will never be forgotten, because, as I can assure you, the Jews are a grateful people.

The president responded to Marshall's letter on May 6:

My Dear Mr. Marshall:

I have been greatly pleased to receive your letter of May 5th, with its very generous references to my address of Sunday. It gratifies me profoundly to know that you feel that which I said may be helpful. I am deeply appreciative of your thought in writing and thank you most sincerely.

Very truly yours,
Calvin Coolidge

Ford's Apology

The fact that not only Jews, but numerous Gentiles—individuals and firms—were boycotting Ford products was an important consideration in Ford's decision in 1925, during the Coolidge Administration, to settle the lawsuit by Aaron Sapiro of San Francisco. This called for an apology from Ford and a written statement that read as follows: "I deem it to be my duty as an honorable man to make amends for the wrong done to the Jews as fellow-men and brothers, by asking their forgiveness for the harm that I have unintentionally committed. . . ."

Apparently, however, Ford died in 1947 unrepentant, claiming that his signature on the document had been forged.

Final Days

Without explanation and to the surprise of almost all political pundits, on August 1, 1927, after having served successfully in office since 1923, President Calvin Coolidge announced flatly: "I do not choose to run for President in 1928." He and his wife, Grace, both of whom were in ill health, retired to Northampton, Massachusetts, where Coolidge wrote his autobiography as well as articles for a number of magazines. He died peacefully on January 5, 1933, in Northampton.

[A.J.K.]

Herbert Hoover

Served from 1929 to 1933

Born on August 10, 1874, in West Branch, Iowa

Member of the Quaker denomination

Married Lou Henry on February 10, 1899

Father to two sons

Candidate of the Republican Party

Vice president under Hoover: Charles Curtis

Inaugural Address delivered on March 4, 1929

Died on October 20, 1964, in New York City

Thirty-First President of the United States

ERBERT CLARK HOOVER WAS THE FIRST Quaker president of the United States and the first president born west of the Mississippi River. The son of a blacksmith, Hoover was born in West Branch, Iowa, on August 10, 1874. His father died when Herbert was six years old; his mother died three years later. Hoover was raised by an uncle and aunt in Newberg, Oregon, where he attended a Quaker secondary school. A precocious student who had read the entire Bible by the age of ten, Hoover received one of the best formal educations of any president up to that time.

Admitted to the first class of California's Stanford University, Hoover graduated in 1895 and became a mining engineer. He began working for the London-based firm Bewick, Moreing and Company in Coolgardie, Australia, where he was responsible for inspecting and evaluating prospective mines prior to purchase. In 1902 he began to develop highly lucrative zinc and silver mines, from which, over the next decade, he made a considerable fortune. In 1908 he formed his own engineering firm, which was engaged in unearthing natural resources throughout the world, including important oil deposits in Russia.

Hoover gained international attention and renown as a humanitarian during World War I, with his highly efficient leadership in distributing food, clothing, and medical supplies to war-ravaged Europe. In 1914 he became chairman of the American Relief Committee in London, which assisted 120,000 Americans who had been stranded in Europe at the beginning of the war to return to their homes in the United States. As the First World War intensified in Europe, Hoover organized and then led the Commission for the Relief of Belgium, which provided desperately needed food to the more than nine million Belgian and French citizens threatened with starvation, who were trapped between the German army and the British navy. Hoover's emergency undertaking evolved into one of the greatest humanitarian enterprises in world history and brought Hoover into international prominence.

When the United States entered the war in 1917, President Woodrow Wilson appointed Hoover head of the United States Food Administration, a specially created wartime agency of the federal government, whose task was to administer and guarantee the necessary supply of food to feed the American and Allied armies. As U.S. food administrator (and a member of the president's War Cabinet), Hoover supervised food conservation and production, while successfully creating surpluses of exportable food for the American and Allied armies, who faced privation and even starvation if the necessary supplies were not delivered to them through the German submarine blockade. The Allied Food Council, which Hoover also chaired, coordinated the allocation and distribution of millions of tons of food to civilians across Europe during the final months of the war.

After the war, in November 1918, Hoover again took charge of humanitarian relief for Europe, when President Wilson named him director of the newly created American Relief Administration (ARA), whose job was to organize and administer a vast relief program designed to feed the people and restore the economy of the war-ravaged European continent. Under Hoover's highly efficient direction, in 1919 and early 1920, the Paris-based ARA distributed over thirty million tons of supplies to twenty-three countries throughout war-devastated Europe, helping to alleviate widespread sickness and starvation. By the time he returned to the United States in 1920, Hoover was hailed as "the great humanitarian" and was regarded by many as a leading candidate for the Republican presidential nomination that year.

After Warren G. Harding received the Republican nomination for president, however, Hoover actively campaigned on Harding's behalf. Hoover was appointed secretary of commerce in the Harding Administration and continued as commerce secretary in President Coolidge's Cabinet as well. When, during the summer of 1927, Coolidge announced that he would not run for reelection the following year, Hoover emerged as front-runner for the Republican presidential nomination. At the Republican National Convention in June 1928, Hoover was nominated for president on the first ballot.

The Democratic presidential candidate in 1928 was Governor Al Smith of New York, the first Catholic to be nominated for the presidency. While religion didn't decide the 1928 election, it was a major issue throughout the campaign. Anti-Catholic literature was circulated throughout the country, especially in the South, and Ku Klux Klansmen attacked the Democratic nominee, claiming that "A Vote for Al Smith is a Vote for the Pope." For many if not most voters, however, the health of the economy was a more salient issue than Smith's Catholicism. Hoover and his Republican Party were given credit for the country's robust economy. As Hoover himself aptly put it: "General Prosperity was on my side."

In the November election Hoover swept the country, winning in a landslide. He won 58 percent of the popular vote to Smith's 41 percent. Carrying forty states, Hoover also won overwhelmingly in the Electoral College, 444 to 87 votes, the largest electoral vote margin since the election of Ulysses Grant.

Herbert Hoover testing the newly-introduced telephone.

COURTESY OF THE NEW YORK PUBLIC LIBRARY

Hoover's Jewish Supporters

Although Al Smith received close to 80 percent of the Jewish vote in the presidential election of 1928, Hoover enjoyed the friendship and active support of several prominent Jewish leaders, including Lewis Strauss, Julius Rosenwald, Louis Marshall, Herbert Straus, Harry Guggenheim, and Felix Warburg.

Lewis L. Strauss

The influential Wall Street investment banker Lewis L. Strauss (1896-1974), who would become chairman of the Atomic Energy Commission during the Eisenhower Administration, had served as Hoover's private secretary during his tenure as U.S. food administrator and director of the ARA, and would remain one of Hoover's closest friends and political confidants until the end of Hoover's life. As his private secretary, Strauss was Hoover's right-hand-man and acted as Hoover's personal representative at several post-war diplomatic conferences. Strauss, moreover, with Hoover's support, worked closely with Felix Warburg and the leadership of the Jewish Joint Distribution Committee, which had been organized in 1915 to help alleviate the suffering of European Jews during the war. Strauss was instrumental in keeping Hoover informed of anti-Semitic incidents in Eastern Europe, in response to which Hoover frequently would protest or intercede. When, in March 1919, with war raging between Poland and the Soviet Union, anti-Semitic Polish troops that had captured the city of Pinsk massacred thirty-seven Jews in a local synagogue, Hoover immediately wrote in outraged protest to Polish Prime Minister Paderewski and met in person with him to demand "that the most vigorous investigation should be made at once." Throughout the 1920s and early 1930s, and in his post-presidential years, Hoover frequently would consult Strauss on issues relating to the Jewish community, anti-Semitism, and Jewish political concerns.

In 1919, after working as Hoover's secretary for two years, Strauss accepted a lucrative offer to join the Wall Street investment banking firm of Kuhn, Loeb & Co., of which Strauss would become a partner in 1929. While on Wall Street, however, Strauss remained one of Hoover's closest political strategists and advisers. When Hoover first sought the Republican presidential nomination in 1920, Strauss was one of his most fervent Jewish supporters, actively campaigning for his nomination and mobilizing Jewish support on behalf of his candidacy. In 1928, when Hoover made his next bid for the presidency, Strauss enthusiastically threw himself into the campaign, raising twenty thousand dollars to help Hoover win the Republican nomination and seeking to convince other Jewish leaders to endorse his candidacy. It was a "patriotic duty" to support Hoover, Strauss argued, for he was "better qualified than any living American to guide the country."

Julius Rosenwald

The president of Sears, Roebuck and Company and one of the preeminent Jewish philanthropists in America, Julius Rosenwald (1862–1932) was also a close friend, political confidant, and major financial supporter of Hoover. Rosenwald gave millions of dollars to a wide range of charitable institutions, including the University of Chicago, the Chicago Museum of Science and Industry, Chicago's Associated Jewish Charities, the Tuskegee Institute established by Booker T. Washington, and hundreds of black schools throughout the rural South. Increasingly concerned about the worsening plight of the Jews of Eastern Europe during World War I, he helped organize the American Jewish Relief Committee for War Sufferers, under the auspices of the Jewish Joint Distribution Committee, and soon became the single largest American contributor to east European Jewish war relief, eventually donating 10 percent—more than a million dollars—of all the money collected for that effort.

It was through Rosenwald's involvement with Jewish war relief that his close working relationship and friendship with Herbert Hoover, then the director of the Commission for the Relief of Belgium, had begun. Subsequently, in 1917, as a member of President Wilson's Advisory Commission of the Council of National Defense, Rosenwald worked closely with Hoover, who chaired the council's committee on food supply and prices. During the devastating Russian famine in the aftermath of World War I, moreover, Rosenwald had applauded the work of the ARA, which, under Hoover's direction, had given $100 million for the distribution of food and medical supplies in eastern Europe, undertaking to feed tens of thousands of Russian Jews as part of its general relief work to combat the Russian famine and supplementing Jewish philanthropic efforts to save these Russian Jews from perishing from mass starvation.

Rosenwald, who grew up in Springfield, Illinois, one block west of the home of Abraham Lincoln, was a lifelong Republican whose support for the Republican Party never waivered. No Jewish leader of Rosenwald's era contributed as much money as he did to the presidential campaigns of the Republican Party. During the 1928 presidential campaign, Rosenwald contributed fifty thousand dollars to Hoover's campaign fund and worked assiduously to gain support for Hoover's candidacy throughout the country. Long impressed with Hoover's relief work during and after World War I, and his record as secretary of commerce, Rosenwald believed that Hoover's "organizing ability and humanitarian experience" would make him "one of the greatest American presidents." Rosenwald praised Hoover's candidacy enthusiastically, regarding Hoover "as fitted beyond any man of his generation for the presidency," and "the best equipped man ever nominated by any party at any time for president of the United States, not excluding Lincoln and Washington." Indeed, Rosenwald would go so far as to write that, "I yield to no one in my devotion and affection for Abraham Lincoln, who was a fellow citizen of mine in Springfield, but without detracting in the least from his ability, I feel that . . . neither [Lincoln nor Washington] when they took office were in any sense as well equipped for the duties that confronted them, either by training or experience, as is Mr. Hoover."

Louis Marshall

Another influential Jewish supporter was Louis Marshall, the distinguished constitutional lawyer and president of the American Jewish Committee, who actively campaigned throughout the country on Hoover's behalf. Marshall's friendship with Hoover, like Rosenwald's, had begun through his involvement with Jewish war relief work in Europe during and after World War I, and through his work as president of the Committee of Jewish Delegations to the Paris Peace Conference in 1919, which Hoover also attended as one of Woodrow Wilson's advisors. Like Rosenwald and Strauss, Marshall, perhaps the preeminent Jewish Republican in America, had actively supported Hoover's quest for the Republican presidential nomination in 1920. "There is no one in public life today," Marshall had written to Samuel Koenig, the Jewish chairman of the New York County Republi-

can Committee, "who possesses the qualities that are most needed [for the presidency] at this time. . . . The work that [Hoover] did in Belgium was marvelous . . . As the head of the American Relief Administration, he practically kept the people of Poland, Lithuania, Roumania, Czechoslavakia and Yugoslavia alive . . . He is a man who thinks and studies and understands the problems with which the next President will have to struggle . . . what we require is a sound man of affairs, and Hoover meets the requirement better than any other man whom I know."

During the presidential campaign of 1928, Marshall gave "complete and warm" support to Hoover's candidacy and served as a member of the executive committee of the National Hoover-Curtis Lawyers Campaign Association. Recognizing that many Jewish voters might be influenced in favor of the Democratic nominee, Al Smith, as a reaction to the strong prejudice against Smith's Catholicism, Marshall tried to repudiate allegations of Republican bigotry and to eliminate the religious issue from the campaign. Speaking to large Jewish audiences in Boston, Brooklyn, and elsewhere, Marshall praised Hoover's humanitarian job of administering war relief activities after World War I, during which Hoover had displayed "supreme indifference to religion," and the subsequent record he had achieved as secretary of commerce.

Throughout the campaign, Marshall made a special effort to speak to Jewish audiences about the help he had received from Hoover when Marshall had served as the president of the Committee of Jewish Delegations to the Paris Peace Conference in 1919. The Republican National Committee responded favorably to suggestions that Marshall publish a statement concerning "Mr. Hoover's interest in the Jewish people and . . . the assistance rendered by him to Mr. Marshall and others" during the framing of the Treaty of Versailles, with its recognition of Jewish minority rights. Such a statement, it was suggested to the chairman of the Republican National Committee, would be "a great benefit" in Hoover's campaign for Jewish votes.

Other Jewish leaders actively supported Hoover's 1928 presidential candidacy as well.

Daniel Guggenheim, the influential head of the ever-expanding Guggenheim family business empire, who had established the Daniel and Florence Guggenheim Foundation and the Daniel Guggenheim Fund for the Promotion of Aeronautics, was an enthusiastic supporter of his friend Hoover's candidacy, as was Guggenheim's wife, who served for many years as treasurer of the Women's National Republican Club. Together, they made a sizable contribution to Hoover's campaign fund. Their son, Harry Frank Guggenheim (1890–1971), who also actively campaigned on Hoover's behalf and who subsequently served as ambassador to Cuba during Hoover's administration, joyfully cabled Hoover after his election: "Your victory constitutes the greatest vindication of democracy in the history of the world. . . . Its result will mark a new epoch in human progress." Albert M. Greenfield, the Philadelphia real estate developer and merchant prince, who made one of the nominating speeches for Hoover at the 1928 Republican Convention, was also a major Jewish supporter of Hoover during his 1928 campaign. So was Herbert Nathan Straus, the vice president of Macy's and the nephew of Oscar Straus, President Theodore Roosevelt's secretary of commerce and labor. Straus, who held leadership positions within the New York State Republican Party, was the founder and president of Republican Business Men, Inc., an organization that played an important role in Hoover's 1928 presidential campaign.

President and Mrs. Herbert Hoover

Hoover's Jewish Appointments

Hoover had wanted to appoint his friend Julius Rosenwald as secretary of commerce in his administration. Rosenwald, however, declined the appointment because of age and failing health, and his preference to remain in Chicago. Hoover also had wanted to appoint his protégé and friend Lewis Strauss to a Cabinet position. Although Strauss played a major role in Hoover's presidential campaign and with his wife was among the honored guests at Hoover's inaugural festivities in March 1929, Strauss also declined offers of several posts in the Hoover Administration.

Hoover did, however, succeed in appointing a number of Jews to other positions, including ambassadorships and presidential task forces and commissions. He appointed Rabbi Abba Hillel Silver (1892–1963), the prominent American Zionist leader and the preeminent Republican in the American rabbinate, to a national advisory committee on unemployment relief. Hoover also appointed Harry Frank Guggenheim, heir to the Guggenheim family mining and industrial fortune, and a major financial supporter, to the National Advisory Committee for Aeronautics, on which Guggenheim served for almost a decade (1929–1938). Guggenheim, who had served since 1926 as the president of the Daniel Guggenheim Fund for the Promotion of Aeronautics, through which he had established projects to win public support for safe, commercially feasible passenger travel by air, was subsequently offered the position of assistant secretary of the navy for aeronautics by President Hoover. Guggenheim turned it down, however, hoping for a diplomatic post, preferably in Latin America, which he received when Hoover appointed him ambassador to Cuba and in which he would serve until 1933.

The Appointment of Benjamin Cardozo

One of the most acclaimed appointments of Hoover's presidency was that of Benjamin N. Cardozo (1870–1938) to the United States Supreme Court in 1932, upon the retirement of Justice Oliver Wendell Holmes, Jr. When Holmes announced his resignation from the Court on January 15, 1932, there was a groundswell of support, from legal scholars and politicians alike, for the nomination of Cardozo, chief judge of the New York Court of Appeals, a man widely considered to be one of America's most brilliant jurists. In nominating Cardozo, Herbert Hoover became the second president to appoint a Jew to the Supreme Court.

Benjamin Cardozo

Cardozo, who had been born in New York City in 1870 and was a descendant of Rabbi Gershom Mendes Seixas, the Revolutionary War patriot who had spoken at George Washington's inauguration, was a member of one of America's most prominent Sephardic families. His father, Albert Jacob Cardozo, had been the first Jew to become a justice of the Supreme Court of the State of New York. Privately tutored by Horatio Alger, the author of popular books for young readers, Benjamin Cardozo graduated at the top of his class at Columbia College and studied for two years at Columbia Law School, prior to being admitted to the bar in 1891.

After a distinguished career as a lawyer, he was elected to the New York State Supreme Court in 1913 and, shortly thereafter, was appointed to the New York Court of Appeals, the state's highest court, of which he became chief judge in 1927. That same year, President Coolidge offered Cardozo an appointment to the International Court of Justice at The Hague, which he declined. In addition to Cardozo's stature as one of the country's most distinguished and influential jurists, whose appeal crossed party and ideological lines, he also was renowned for his stylistically beautiful works of scholarship, such as *The Nature of the Judicial Process*, which had won him wide acclaim.

A lifelong member of New York City's venerable Spanish-Portuguese Synagogue, Cardozo also had been involved in Jewish communal affairs, serving on the boards of governors of the Friends of the Hebrew University and the American Jewish Committee, and enjoyed the close friendship of several Jewish leaders, such as Rabbi Stephen S. Wise, who played a prominent role in mobilizing Jewish leaders to lobby President Hoover and members of the U.S. Senate on behalf of the Cardozo nomination.

Cardozo's most influential supporter in the U.S. Senate was William E. Borah, the Republican senator from Idaho and influential chairman of the Senate Foreign Relations Committee. Though Cardozo was a Democrat who had supported Al

Smith in 1928, Borah successfully urged Hoover to nominate Cardozo, despite the fact that many in their party were pressing Hoover to appoint a Republican. Of the six presidents who have appointed a Jewish justice to the Supreme Court, only Hoover so transcended partisan considerations and nominated a Jewish candidate who was not of his political party. In nominating Cardozo, Hoover also should be credited with having ignored the objections of those who opposed having two Jewish justices on the Supreme Court at the same time, Cardozo and Justice Louis Brandeis.

Meeting with Hoover the day before the president had indicated that he would announce his Supreme Court nominee, Senator Borah had reassured Hoover that he should appoint Cardozo despite the fact that, as those opposing the nomination pointed out, "there is a great deal of anti-Semitism in the country and this appointment would mean two Jews on the Bench." "Such an opportunity may never again come to you, Mr. President, to strike a blow at anti-Semitism," Borah is reported to have told Hoover. Ignoring the anti-Semitic tirades of Justice James McReynolds, who had urged Hoover not "to afflict the Court with another Jew," Hoover did indeed "strike a blow at anti-Semitism" that Jewish leaders, Democrats and Republicans alike, widely applauded. Hoover's nomination of Cardozo sailed through the Senate with no opposition. Unique among the seven Jewish appointees to the Supreme Court, Cardozo's nomination was "confirmed by virtual acclamation," without even a debate or roll-call vote in the Senate.

When, on March 15, 1932, Benjamin N. Cardozo took his seat on the United States Supreme Court, President Hoover was widely praised for his appointment. "Seldom, if ever, in the history of the Court," commented *The New York Times*, "has an appointment been so universally commended." One Democratic senator called Hoover's appointment of Cardozo "the finest act of his career as president." History would concur that it was one of Hoover's greatest and most enduring presidential achievements.

Justice Cardozo died in 1938, after only six years on the Court. Although his tenure was brief, he authored more than one hundred opinions, many of which were landmark decisions in American constitutional history. In 1937 he spoke for the Court in upholding several key provisions of the historic Social Security Act of 1935. It was Cardozo who wrote what constitutional scholars have called "the most significant basic decision ever pronounced by the Court on behalf of the application of the federal Bill of Rights to the several states," the celebrated "incorporation" case of *Palko v. Connecticut*. Cardozo has been ranked by American legal scholars, along with John Marshall, Joseph Story, Louis D. Brandeis, and Oliver Wendell Holmes, Jr., as one of the ten greatest justices in the history of the United States Supreme Court.

The Great Depression

"The poorhouse is vanishing among us, " Hoover had optimistically predicted during the presidential campaign of 1928. "We in America today are nearer to the final triumph over poverty than ever before in the history of the land. . . . We shall soon with the help of God be in sight of the day when poverty will be banished from this nation."

In his Inaugural Address of March 1929 Hoover waxed similarly optimistic about the country's "economic progress toward prosperity and the further lessening of poverty." Seven months later, however, the stock market crash of October 1929 turned this dream into a nightmare. The Great Depression that followed was the worst in America's history and shattered Hoover's reputation for administrative skill and humanitarian concern. Twelve million Americans were unemployed and thousands of businesses bankrupt.

As president, Hoover in fact took concrete measures to cope with the economic depression. It was at his urging that Congress established the Reconstruction Finance Corporation, with a budget of two billion dollars, to lend money to banks, industries, and state and local governments. But this and the policies he pursued—such as expanding public works programs in the hope that the building industry would absorb the unemployed—did not succeed in stemming the tide of financial disaster. Hoover opposed direct federal relief to the millions of unemployed, and, as the Great Depression worsened, Hoover's popularity continued to plummet. It reached its low point in the summer of 1932, when thousands of World War I veterans and their families, who had marched on Washington in the hope of persuading Congress to appropriate funds for veterans' bonuses were, at Hoover's instruction, ordered by the army to move out of Washington. Hoover's role in having them turned out of the city at the point of bayonets struck many Americans as especially cruel and inhumane.

In November of 1932, Hoover was defeated for reelection by the Democratic Party candidate, Franklin D. Roosevelt, in a landslide of similar proportions to the one by which Hoover had come into office: FDR received over seven million more popular votes than Hoover, while winning 472 electoral votes to Hoover's 59. The vast majority of American Jews—82 percent—voted for Roosevelt with only 18 percent going to Hoover.

Post-Presidential Years

Herbert Hoover remained active in public affairs for many years after he left the White House in 1933 and retired with his wife to their home in Palo Alto, California, near the Stanford University campus.

During his administration and after, Hoover strongly supported the goals of the Zionist movement in Palestine. As a guest speaker at a Zionist function, he stated:

> I have watched with genuine admiration the steady and unmistakable progress made in the rehabilitation of Palestine which, desolate for centuries, is now renewing its youth and vitality through the enthusiasm, hard work, and self-sacrifice of the Jewish pioneers who toil there in a spirit of peace and social justice.

Among the causes with which he publicly associated himself during the 1930s was the plight of German Jews seeking refuge from Hitler. As the persecution of Jews in Germany increased, Hoover added his name to a public protest:

> I am glad to again evidence my own indignation and to join in an expression of public protest at the treatment of Jews in Germany.
>
> It is the duty of men everywhere to express our indignation not alone at the suffering these men are imposing on an innocent people, but at the blow they are striking at civilization.

In November 1938, when the Federal Council of Churches in the United States condemned the *Kristallnacht* pogrom unleashed by the Nazis against German Jewry as "the day of the Inquisition in Germany," Hoover joined in the forceful denunciation, publicly condemning the Nazis for "taking Germany back four hundred and fifty years in civilization to Torquemada's expulsion of the Jews from Spain." When legislation was introduced in Congress in 1939 to permit twenty-thousand German refugee children to enter the United States, outside of the prevailing quota, Hoover was an outspoken advocate of the plan, going against the nation's anti-immigration consensus. He maintained that every American should support the measure. "There can be no criticism that this action adds distress to our unemployed," Hoover said. "It befits the American wish to aid the suffering. It answers the appeal to every American heart for the protection of children."

Together with Bernard Baruch, the financier and adviser to Democratic presidents, and Lewis Strauss, Hoover worked simultaneously on another plan to resettle Jewish refugees from Hitler, a plan to establish a haven for Jewish refugees in central Africa. Although sympathetic to the reclamation efforts of Zionist settlers in Palestine, Hoover believed that "local Arab hostility constituted an insurmountable obstacle to the settlement of large numbers of Jewish refugees there." As an alternative, Hoover proposed, these Jewish refugees from Nazi Europe could be resettled "on the uplands of central Africa, embracing parts of Northern Rhodesia, Tanganyika, Kenya and the Belgian Congo." An internationally renowned engineer prior to his career in politics, Hoover expressed his readiness to "visit the new country and organize its communications, its transport, and the development of its resources."

In July 1939, at Hoover's behest, Strauss sailed for England to advance their resettlement plan directly with officials of the British government, which owned most of the desired territory in central Africa. The trip proved disappointing, and the Hoover-Baruch plan died when the British secretary of state for colonies and other foreign office personnel refused to discuss any resettlement of Jewish refugees in Africa, indicating to Strauss that the desired British territory in central Africa would be unavailable for their project.

More than a decade after retiring from the presidency, Herbert Hoover reentered public life at the invitation of President Truman, who named him chairman of the Famine Emergency Commission, an organization to prevent starvation of Europeans in the aftermath of World War II. In 1947 Hoover accepted Truman's appointment as chairman of the Commission on Organization of the Executive Branch of the Government. Known as the Hoover Commission, this group recommended major structural changes in the Federal government. In 1953 President Eisenhower named Hoover as head of a similar federal commission that recommended further structural changes in the government.

Herbert Hoover died in New York City at the age of ninety on October 20, 1964.

[A.J.K.]

Franklin D. Roosevelt

Served from 1933 to 1945

Born on January 30, 1882, in Hyde Park, New York

Member of the Episcopal denomination

Married Anna Eleanor Roosevelt on March 17, 1905
Father to one daughter and four sons

Candidate of the Democratic Party

Vice presidents under Roosevelt: John N. Garner (first and second terms);
Henry A. Wallace (third term); Harry S. Truman (fourth term)

First Inaugural Address delivered on March 4, 1933
Second Inaugural Address delivered on January 20, 1937
Third Inaugural Address delivered on January 20, 1941
Fourth Inaugural Address delivered on January 20, 1945

Died in office on April 12, 1945

Thirty-Second President of the United States

ORN INTO AN ARISTOCRATIC FAMILY IN idyllic Hyde Park, New York, Franklin Delano Roosevelt enjoyed a sheltered childhood. His father was a successful lawyer and financier whose antecedents had come to America from Holland in 1644 and settled in New Netherland (later named New York), along the Hudson River. Franklin's mother, Sara Delano Roosevelt, was the daughter of a merchant who made his fortune in trade with China. She had grown up in Newburgh, New York.

Franklin accompanied his parents on their frequent trips. On one occasion, his father, who had strong Democratic ties, took the boy along on a visit to the White House. President Grover Cleveland, who was feeling the stress of the presidency, patted five-year-old Franklin on the head and said: "My little man: I am making a strange wish for you. It is that you may never be president of the United States."

Early Education and Marriage

An above average student, Franklin attended the elite Groton School (1896–1900) in Massachusetts. At his graduation in June 1900, a commencement address was delivered by Governor Theodore Roosevelt, Franklin's fifth cousin. From 1900 to 1904, Franklin attended Harvard University, where he majored in political history and government. He attended Columbia Law School from 1904 to 1907 and was admitted to the bar in 1907. Upon entering Columbia at age twenty-two, although he was a Democrat like his father, Franklin chose to cast his vote for the Republican presidential candidate, Theodore Roosevelt.

One year later, in 1905, Franklin married Anna

Eleanor Roosevelt, a fifth cousin once removed and the niece of President Theodore Roosevelt. Teddy Roosevelt gave the bride away.

Like her distant cousin Franklin, Eleanor, as she was popularly known, was born into a distinguished New York family on October 11, 1884. She bore Franklin six children, of whom one daughter and four sons lived to maturity.

After his marriage, with the support of Eleanor, Franklin's interest in politics began to take hold. He served as a New York State senator before being appointed assistant secretary of the navy in 1913. In 1920 he was chosen to run as vice president on the Democratic ticket with James M. Fox. The Democrats were defeated by Warren G. Harding, whose running mate was Calvin Coolidge.

In 1921 Franklin contracted polio and was crippled for life. While his upper torso was muscular and strong as a result of strenuous exercising, his lower limbs were totally incapacitated: he was unable to stand without braces or walk even a short distance without crutches or canes. The tragedy brought Eleanor and Franklin closer, and she, more than anyone else, encouraged him to remain active in the political arena despite the hopeless infirmity that kept him wheelchair-bound. In 1928 the effort paid off, culminating in Franklin's election to the governorship of New York, the largest state in the Union, and four years later he defeated incumbent Republican Herbert Hoover, becoming the thirty-second president of the United States. Roosevelt was reelected three times, becoming the first and only president ever to win the presidency in four consecutive presidential elections.

While Roosevelt's political victories were enormous accomplishments, he sometimes made light of them, commenting offhandedly: "If you had spent two years in bed trying to wiggle your big toe, then anything else seems easy."

Relationship with the Jewish Community

Roosevelt endeared himself to rank-and-file Jewish New Yorkers from the moment he assumed the governorship in 1928. He was greatly appreciated both for developing programs to help the needy and for his advocacy of old-age pensions to help the elderly during the Great Depression.

Jews demonstrated their deep affection for their governor by helping him gain the presidency in 1932. It is estimated that 82 percent of the Jewish vote went to Roosevelt while only 18 percent went to the Republican, Herbert Hoover. In Roosevelt's bid for a second term in 1936, he was supported by an even greater number of Jews: Alfred M. Landon received 15 percent of the Jewish vote while Roosevelt received 85 percent. In the 1940 election the margin of victory was greater still: 90 percent for Roosevelt, 10 percent for Wendell Willkie. The same margin of victory was repeated in 1944 when Roosevelt defeated Thomas E. Dewey.

The elation felt by most Jews over Roosevelt's presidency was best expressed by Judge Jonah Goldstein after Roosevelt won election in 1932 and the New Deal program was announced: "The Jews have three velten [worlds]: die velt [this world], *yeneh velt* [the world to come], and Roosevelt."

FDR's Brain Trust

When Franklin Delano Roosevelt assumed the presidency in 1933, the nation was still struggling to emerge from the Depression, which had begun with the stock market collapse of October 29, 1929, known as "Black Tuesday." The president's success in curbing the Depression can be largely attributed to the counsel of his "Brain Trust," which was comprised of individuals nearly all of whom were or had been college professors

and many of whom were Jews. Dorothy Rosenman, wife of Samuel Rosenman, one of Roosevelt's close advisers, observed in her book *Presidential Style*: " I do not believe Franklin Roosevelt, in considering a man's suitability for appointment to office, cared anymore about his religion than he did about the color of his hair."

Stephen S. Wise

An intimate friend and adviser of presidents from Wilson to Truman, Rabbi Stephen S. Wise was especially close to Franklin Roosevelt, so close in fact that they were on a "Steve-Boss" basis.

A liberal spirit, Wise was an ardent supporter of the labor movement. In 1909 he helped found the National Association for the Advancement of Colored People (NAACP) and in 1911, after the tragic New York City Triangle Shirtwaist Factory fire, Wise argued that "the life of the lowest worker in the nation is most sacred." In 1917 President Woodrow Wilson had called upon Wise to help in the formulation of the Balfour Declaration, which favored "the establishment in Palestine of a national home for the Jewish people."

Stephen Samuel Wise

As governor of New York from 1929 to 1933, Franklin Roosevelt was greatly impressed by Rabbi Wise's efforts on behalf of the underdog. He was particularly struck by the admiration that organized labor expressed for the rabbi because of his advocacy of social legislation to improve the living conditions of the average American. Governor Roosevelt could foresee how, with Wise's help, he could garner support of the New York delegation at the upcoming Democratic National Convention.

But when Wise and his close friend, Reverend John Haynes Holmes, asked the governor to remove the corrupt New York City mayor Jimmy Walker from office, Roosevelt balked. He did not want to antagonize Walker, who controlled Tammany Hall, the powerful Democratic base in New York City. The clergymen persisted, however, and during Roosevelt's first term as president, Wise would be *persona non grata* at the White House.

In 1935, with new elections one year away, Roosevelt believed it prudent to mend fences with Rabbi Wise. Some Jews believed that Roosevelt was paying scant attention to the precarious situation of Jews in Nazi Germany, so Roosevelt invited Wise to visit with him at the Roosevelt estate in Hyde Park, New York, to see if their differences could be resolved and a reconciliation effected.

Felix Frankfurter

Felix Frankfurter

Outstanding among the members of Roosevelt's Brain Trust was Felix Frankfurter (1882-1965), who *Fortune* magazine once characterized as "the most influential single individual in the United States." When Eleanor Roosevelt met Frankfurter for the first time, before she had overcome the anti-Semitism of her early upbringing, she said: "An interesting little man, but very Jewish."

Born in Vienna, Felix Frankfurter was raised as a practicing Jew. "As a boy," he recounted, "I was religiously observant. I wouldn't eat breakfast until I had done the religious devotions in the morning." In 1894, at age twelve, he came to the United States with his family, settling on the Lower East Side of New York City. In 1902 he graduated from City College with honors, as he would be several years later from Harvard Law School. In 1914 he was appointed law professor at Harvard, a position he held for twenty-five years. It was there that he earned a reputation as being not only a liberal, but a radical.

During the Taft Administration, having been appointed personal assistant to Secretary of War Henry L. Stimson, Frankfurter drew close to Louis D. Brandeis, who in 1916 had been appointed to the Supreme Court. Brandeis influenced Frankfurter to become involved in the Zionist cause, and in 1919 Frankfurter attended the Paris Peace Conference as legal adviser to the Zionist delegation. It was there that he collaborated closely with Chaim Weizmann, who was negotiating with Emir Feisal, son of Sharif Huessein of Mecca, the leader of Arab nationalism, at Aqaba. Feisal pledged support of Zionist aims in Palestine on condition that Arab nationalist aims were met in Syria and Iraq.

As Woodrow Wilson's assistant secretary of the navy, Roosevelt became acquainted with Frankfurter. Roosevelt recognized the Harvard professor's brilliance and was particularly impressed by his original interpretations of the Constitution, by his ingenuity in devising wage-and-hour and other labor laws, as well as his struggle for the rights of the common man in civil liberties cases. So it was not surprising that in 1939, after Supreme Court Justice Benjamin Cardozo died, Roosevelt would appoint Frankfurter to fill the so-called "Jewish seat" on the Supreme Court.

Arthur Hays Sulzberger, always fearful that Jews might be too prominent in public affairs, counseled Roosevelt not to name Frankfurter to succeed Cardozo. Sulzberger worried that it would look as if there must always be a Jew on the court, "whether qualified or not." At the end of their meeting, President Roosevelt said to Sulzberger, "I agree with you completely." Ignoring Sulzberger's counsel, Roosevelt then went ahead and nominated Frankfurter anyway. Frankfurter would serve on the court until 1962, when a stroke would force him to retire.

Commenting on Frankfurter's deep affection for Roosevelt, Robert A. Burt of Yale Law School wrote in *Two Jewish Justices*: "Two days before his death, Frankfurter told his chosen biographer, 'Tell the whole story. Let people see how much I loved Roosevelt, how much I loved my country, and let them see how great a man Roosevelt really was.'"

During his tenure on the Supreme Court, many of Frankfurter's former students became influential in the Roosevelt Administration. They had assimilated their mentor's passion for social justice and enhancement of the quality of life for the average American. And they were instrumental in fostering and implementing the two major elements in Roosevelt's recovery program: the National Recovery Act, which provided

for the construction of bridges, roads, and public buildings, all of which provided employment for millions of unemployed Americans; and, second, the National Recovery Administration, which helped stimulate competition, and would prove beneficial to producers and consumers alike. The measures they proposed became known as the New Deal.

Henry Morgenthau, Jr.

After Rabbi Stephen Wise and Felix Frankfurter, Henry Morgenthau, Jr., had the closest personal relationship with President Roosevelt of any Jew. American-born, Morgenthau followed in the footsteps of his father, Henry Morgenthau, Sr., in devoting his life to public service. The elder Henry had served as U.S. ambassador to Turkey from

Left to right: President Roosevelt, Herbert H. Lehman, and Alfred E. Smith.

1913 to 1916 under Woodrow Wilson, and Henry Jr. served as Roosevelt's secretary of the treasury from 1934 to 1945, after having been active in public life as conservation commissioner.

The Morgenthau family grew close to the Roosevelts when they were neighbors in Dutchess County, in upstate New York, which was not too distant from Hyde Park. When Roosevelt began his race for public office, the wealthy Morgenthau family, which had become prosperous from their activities in banking and real estate, supported Roosevelt's campaigns generously. As secretary of the treasury, Morgenthau was responsible for arranging financing for America's war effort and developing New Deal programs, although it was the wise old man of politics, the affluent Bernard Baruch, who had a hand in fashioning much of the New Deal.

However, most of Henry Jr.'s involvement in Jewish communal affairs began after the conflict in Europe was over. From 1947 to 1950 he was chairman of the United Jewish Appeal, and from 1951 to 1955 he served as chairman of the Israel Bond Drive in the United States.

Rosenman and Niles

Samuel Rosenman (1896–1973), another close friend and trusted adviser of Franklin Roosevelt, was educated at Columbia University. Rosenman served for four years as a member of the New York State Legislature, and when Roosevelt was elected governor of New York, Rosenman joined his staff in Albany as a speech writer and special counsel. While serving as a New York State Supreme Court justice from 1934 to 1943, Rosenman, who coined the term "New Deal," continued to advise Roosevelt on an informal basis and, as Patrick Anderson has pointed out, "was increasingly called upon as presidential troubleshooter in the early war years."

In August 1941, Roosevelt asked Rosenman to draft a reorganization plan to prepare the government for wartime production. Subsequently, Roseman played a major role in creating the National Housing Authority, the Office of War Information, and the Office of Economic Stablization.

In September 1943, Rosenman resigned his judgeship to serve on the White House staff as special counsel to the president. Upon Roosevelt's death, Rosenman continued as special counsel to President Truman for a year before returning to private law practice in New York.

Also a close Roosevelt confidant and adviser was David K. Niles (1890–1952), who had been appointed labor assistant to Harry Hopkins, director of the Works Progress Administration and later secretary of commerce in 1935. He joined the White House staff as assistant to the president in 1942. Sometimes referred to as Roosevelt's "House Jew," Niles was the president's unofficial liaison to the Jewish community, advising the president, as Michael J. Cohen has noted, "which Jewish leaders to receive and which might be rejected politely without causing too much political damage." Like Rosenman, Niles continued on the White House staff as an assistant to President Truman.

Other Close Advisers

Other Jewish advisers and political confidants of Roosevelt included Justice Louis D. Brandeis, who helped draft New Deal legislation while serving on the Supreme Court; attorney Benjamin V. Cohen (1894–1983), a former student of Felix Frankfurter at Harvard Law School, who served as a speechwriter for Roosevelt and also played a major role in drafting the Securities Act of 1933, the Securities Exchange Act of 1934, and other important New Deal legislation; and Judge Joseph Proskauer (1877–1971), who had been Al Smith's campaign manager during the 1928 presidential election and who, during the 1940s, was the influential president of the American Jewish Committee. Roosevelt's Jewish entourage also included Herbert Lehman (1878-1963), arguably New York's most popular Jewish political figure, who had been Roosevelt's lieutenant governor and succeeded him as governor of New York when Roosevelt was elected president, and his brother, Irving Lehman (1876–1945), a respected federal court judge and Jewish communal leader in New York.

FDR with Winston Churchill (right).

were introduced, revoking Jewish citizenship. The Jews of Germany were now at the mercy of an undertow of anti-Semitic feeling that had been relatively latent in pre-Hitler Germany. For a while most Jews were complacent, convinced that this was but a passing bad dream, hopeful that the severe restrictions placed upon their rights would be rescinded or would evaporate with time. Franklin D. Roosevelt fell victim to this baseless optimistic view and allowed it to guide him as he tried to fashion American policy.

Prelude to World War Two

While Franklin Roosevelt was devoting his time and energies to formulating policy and structure for his New Deal program, German nationalists, who continued to feel deeply humiliated over their defeat in World War I, were strengthening their fascist political party: The National Socialist German Workers' Party, better known as the Nazi party.

By 1932 the Nazis had won 230 seats in the Reichstag elections. In January 1933, when Hitler became chancellor and head of the German government, he systematically eliminated all opposition. One of his first acts was to ban political meetings and outlaw publications that did not subscribe to his program of nationalism, racism, and rearmament.

On March 10, 1933, one week after Roosevelt delivered his first Inaugural Address, the first concentration camp was established at Dachau, near Munich, where 40,000 persons would be killed, the vast majority being Jews. On April 26, 1933, the Nazis took full control of the Gestapo, the state secret police, and by July of 1933, with Adolf Hitler at its helm, the Nazi Party became the only legal political entity in Germany.

Two years later the infamous Nuremberg Laws

Nazi Deception

Roosevelt, like many others, was convinced that the Nazi threat was not as grave as portrayed. In a meeting with Rabbi Stephen S. Wise, he tried to convince the rabbi that the situation of the Jews in Germany was not as dire as many claimed. The president described a report that he personally had received from two people who had recently toured Germany and found "the synagogues crowded" and apparently "nothing wrong with the situation at present."

Like millions of Americans, Roosevelt was misled by the display of calm and coexistence conjured up in 1936 for the Olympic Games that were to be held in Germany. Hitler and his cohorts had carefully removed all signs that might lead visitors to believe that anti-Semitism was a national policy. The Nazis even pretended to allow Jews to participate in the athletic competition, when in fact only one German athlete with two Jewish parents, the hockey player Rudi Ball, was allowed to compete on a German team.

Roosevelt, like the editors of the liberal American publication *The Nation*, had been taken in by this feigned display of harmony and goodwill. This was evident from an essay that appeared in *The Nation's* August 1, 1936, issue:

> [One] sees no Jewish heads being chopped off, or even roundly cudgeled. . . . The people smile, are polite and sing with gusto in beer

gardens. Board and lodging are good, cheap, and abundant, and no one is swindled by grasping hotel and shop proprietors. Everything is terrifyingly clean and the visitor likes it all.

When Roosevelt did take the initiative, in July 1938, to call a conference on the refugee problem in the resort town of Évian-les-Bains, France, none of the thirty-two nations that participated, with the exception of the Dominican Republic, offered to accept sizable numbers of refugees. The United States agreed with Great Britain that a discussion about allowing Palestine to become a haven for persecuted Jews was out of place, lest any concession made by the British be considered an offense to Arab nations.

Kristallnacht

On November 7, 1938, a half-crazed young Jew named Herschel Grynszpan, whose family had been caught in the no-man's land between Germany and Poland, burst into the German embassy in Paris and fatally shot German First Secretary Ernst von Rath. In response, Hitler allowed the hitherto marginally contained hatred against Jews to be fully unleashed, resulting in *Kristallnacht*, when Nazi Party members smashed windows and looted shops owned by Jews in Germany and Austria. Teams were sent out to plunder and burn down synagogues. To all this Roosevelt reacted mildly, recalling American ambassador Hugh Wilson to demonstrate U.S. displeasure.

Disillusionment with Roosevelt

Even early on it was evident to Jews, including Roosevelt's staunch supporter Rabbi Stephen S. Wise, that the president was not addressing the plight of European Jewry with sufficient energy. As president of the American Jewish Congress, Wise organized protest meetings urging the administration to declare a boycott on the import of German goods. But while Roosevelt would issue a sympathetic statement, he did not battle

vigorously for the relaxing of immigration laws that would facilitate the entry of oppressed Jews to the United States.

The St. Louis Debacle

Six months after *Kristallnacht*, in May 1939, a boatload of more than 900 German Jewish refugees arrived at Cuban shores aboard the St. Louis. Most of the passengers held visas, but they were refused entry into Havana by the new Cuban government on the grounds that their entry permits were invalid. For days, the St. Louis was docked in Havana's harbor, and no amount of bribery could change the situation.

When the ship left Havana and attempted to land in Florida, the U.S. Coast Guard fired warning shots. Finally, the *St. Louis* was forced to return to Europe, where passengers were admitted to England, Belgium, Holland, and France.

This incident was a turning point for some American Jews, who would ultimately hold Roosevelt responsible for the tragic event. And it may explain why in July 1942, when twenty-thousand Jews attended a rally at New York's Madison Square Garden to protest Nazi atrocities, Roosevelt felt it necessary to send a message to the assembly in which he condemned German acts of violence against Jews. The American people "will hold the perpetrators of these crimes to strict accountability in a day of reckoning which will surely come," the president declared.

But future events proved Roosevelt's sentiments empty.

The Jan Karski Message

Probably the most crushing evidence to sustain the view that Franklin Roosevelt was not sympathetically attuned to the precarious situation of the Jews of Europe was the short shrift he gave to twenty-eight-year-old Jan Karski. A Polish diplomat who was deeply affected by the cruelty exhibited by the Nazis, Karski was sent by the Jewish resistance movement in Poland to alert the highest authorities he could reach in London and

Henry Morgenthau, Jr., with David Ben-Gurion (right).

Washington to the dire plight of European Jews and to try to convince them and the world that Hitler's plot to exterminate the Jews was for real—and ongoing. Karski had secretly crossed Nazi-occupied Europe four times to gather firsthand, eyewitness accounts of the atrocities perpetrated against Jews.

In June 1943, Karski arrived in Washington and met with Supreme Court Justice Felix Frankfurter, who, after hearing Jan's story, although not completely convinced of its veracity, brought him to the White House on July 28 to meet with Roosevelt so that he might apprise the president of the terrible situation the Jews of Europe were facing.

Roosevelt listened and asked questions, but not a single one probing the Jewish condition. After a meeting that lasted an hour and twenty minutes, the president shook Karski's hand without actually reacting to the story Karski had brought him. Just as he was being ushered out of the Oval Office, the Polish emissary turned to Roosevelt and said: "Mr. President, I am going back to Po-

land. People will know that I was received by the president of the United States. Everybody will ask me: What did President Roosevelt tell you? What am I to tell them?"

The president responded: "You will tell the leaders that we shall win this war! You will tell them that the guilty ones will be punished. Justice and freedom shall prevail. You will tell your nation that they have a friend in this house."

Upon his return to Poland, Karski continued to bear witness to the systematic Nazi extermination of the Jews, risking his own life to report the unspeakable atrocities. And when the war was over, he devoted himself to protecting the memory of the victims of the Holocaust and combating anti-Semitism.

In April 2000, at a United Nations reception, eighty-six-year-old Jan Karski, a resident of Chevy Chase, Maryland, was one of four surviving heroes (out of a total of sixty-five from twenty-two countries) who were honored for saving more than three hundred thousand Jews. In an interview, Karski explained:

> I wanted to be helpful to the Jews, the oppressed people. I saw terrible, terrible things happening to the Jews. There was poverty, despair—the Jews were treated worse than cattle. They could not travel or walk the streets but were confined to ghettos and concentration camps.

As to the attitude of President Roosevelt, he commented generously:

> President Roosevelt was one of the greatest men in the twentieth century, but he was not a Jewish or Polish president, he was an American president [who looked out] for American interests.

Jan Karski, a Righteous Gentile, died on Thursday, July 13, 2000.

The Holocaust and FDR

During the years of Nazi persecution of the Jews of Germany and neighboring countries, the ma-

Members of the U.S. Supreme Court in 1939. Felix Frankfurter is pictured in the top row, second from right.

jority of American Jews had faith in Roosevelt's leadership, as evidenced by the large number of Jews who supported him during each of his four races for the presidency.

Journalist Arthur Morse, author of *While Six Million Died: A Chronicle of American Apathy* (1967), was one of the first to suggest that Roosevelt had been more dedicated to winning the war against Hitler than in rescuing the victims of his persecution, although privately Roosevelt had continued to assure his Jewish friends and supporters that by his policies he was easing the suffering of their fellow European Jews. Morse's best-selling book was followed by the publication of in-depth analyses of the subject, including Henry L. Feingold's *The Politics of Rescue: The Roosevelt Administration and the Holocaust* (1980) and David S. Wyman's *The Abandonment of the Jews: America and the Ho-*

locaust, 1914–1945 (1984). These works provided new evidence to substantiate Morse's indictment that—Roosevelt's many Jewish appointees and advisers notwithstanding—the president did much less than he might have to rescue European Jewry during the time of their greatest peril. His apparent unwillingness to take the official steps necessary to rescue the Jewish victims of Nazism was, according to these and other critics, an unforgivable moral failure of Roosevelt and his administration. David Wyman characterizes Roosevelt's "abandonment of the Jews" as "the worst failure of his presidency."

The serious questions raised by these studies of Franklin D. Roosevelt and the Holocaust have transformed the attitudes of many American Jews toward Roosevelt, forcing them to reassess their once uncritical view of Roosevelt as a hero and as the greatest friend of the Jewish people. Indeed, even as Arthur Schlesinger, Jr., a defender of Roosevelt's role during the Holocaust, has noted, some Jews today view Roosevelt "not as a hero, but as the president who might have saved millions of Jews from Hitler and instead abandoned them to a terrible fate."

Why Auschwitz Was Never Bombed

One of the most serious indictments leveled against the Roosevelt Administration was over its failure to bomb the gas chambers and crematoria of Auschwitz and the railroads leading to the Nazi death camp. Wyman and Feingold demonstrate conclusively that by the spring of 1944 the bombing of Auschwitz would have been feasible for the Roosevelt Administration. In 1944, however, the U.S. War Department rejected out of hand several appeals to bomb Auschwitz and the railroads leading to it, claiming that such actions would divert essential air power from decisive operations elsewhere. In rejecting one such request, Assistant Secretary of the Army John J. McCloy, a close friend and political supporter of Roosevelt, callously noted that "such an operation . . . would in any case be of such doubtful efficacy that it would not warrant the use of our resources." Yet, during the very months the government was turning down such pleas, numerous American bombing raids took place within fifty miles of Auschwitz. Moreover, during the spring and summer of 1944 American bombers were already striking industrial targets within the Auschwitz complex itself, only five miles from the gas chambers. Had they been permitted to bomb the railroads to Auschwitz and the gas chambers therein, the lives of tens of thousands of Hungarian and Slovakian Jews who had been deported to Auschwitz in 1944 might possibly have been saved.

Last Years in Office

Toward the end of March 1944, Roosevelt received a complete physical examination at the Bethesda Naval Hospital. The results were not revealed, but his doctors suggested that he take time out for complete rest. As a consequence, he was invited by his old friend Bernard Baruch to recuperate at the financier's large estate in Hobcaw, South Carolina. Roosevelt spent one month there, sleeping twelve hours each night. On May 6 he returned to the White House feeling refreshed.

A year later, on March 30, 1945, the president went to his retreat in Warm Springs, Georgia, for another period of rest and recreation. On April 11 he was visited by his old friend Henry Morgenthau, Jr. They had a meal together, reminisced about old times—even about their youth in Hyde Park—and shared gossip about some of the influential people in Washington.

The next morning, April 12, Roosevelt sat up in bed and had a hearty breakfast. Before lunch was to be served at 1:15 P.M., he complained of a severe headache, slumped back in his chair, and died.

FDR's Jewish Great-Grandson— Studying to Be a Rabbi

In September 2000, Joshua Adler Boettiger, the great-grandson of President Franklin D. Roosevelt, began seminary studies at the Reconstructionist Rabbinical College in Philadelphia. He is the first and only known descendant of an American president to study for the rabbinate.

Joshua Boettiger is a grandson of Anna Roosevelt, the daughter of Franklin and Eleanor Roosevelt, who married John Boettiger, a reporter for the *Chicago Tribune*, in 1935. John and Anna Roosevelt Boettiger's son, John, married a Jewish woman, Janet Adler. Janet grew up in Frankfurt, Indiana, where she and her family were the only Jews in town; they moved to Miami Beach when Janet was a teenager. Although Janet Adler did not grow up in a religiously observant home, she and her parents belonged to a Reform congregation, where they attended High Holiday services. When she married John Boettiger, who did not convert to Judaism, Janet Adler Boettiger raised her children as Reform Jews.

Joshua Adler Boettiger grew up in western Massachusetts where, as a child, he attended High Holiday services with his parents at a Reform congregation. During his high school and college years, Joshua became increasingly interested in Judaism, and visited Israel on three separate occasions. As an undergraduate at Bard College, he took courses in Judaic studies and majored in religion.

During the 1999-2000 academic year, Boettiger studied Hebrew Bible and Mishnah at Jerusalem's Pardes Institute, a nondenominational institute for advanced Jewish studies. While studying in Israel, where he became more religiously observant, Boettiger applied and was accepted for admission to the Reconstructionist Rabbinical College.

An Evaluation

The final chapter has not yet been written on the presidency of Franklin D. Roosevelt in light of the Holocaust. On the one hand, historians feel that Jews, on the whole, were satisfied with the president's performance in dealing with the Nazis, considering the political climate in which he had to work and the ironclad immigration laws that would not allow a massive inflow of refugees from war-torn Europe. They point to the fact that in 1944, at the height of the Nazi terror, when concentration camps were fully operative and the gas chambers were performing with great efficiency, American Jews still voted for Roosevelt's reelection to a fourth term, giving him ninety percent of their votes to ten percent for Thomas E. Dewey his Republican opponent.

Many historians, however, believe that Roosevelt was not being forthright with the Jewish people when he played down legitimate, authentic reports documenting the horrors that were transpiring in Europe. They pointed out that before the Chief Executive would act to establish the War Refugee Board with special powers to rescue Hitler's victims, secretary of the Treasury Henry Morgenthau, Jr., had to present conclusive proof that the State Department was sabotaging efforts to rescue Jews.

In 1999 a report surfaced that on December 8, 1942, a delegation of Jews had met with President Roosevelt in the White House and presented to him vivid details of the plight of Eastern European Jewry. The report reveals that the American government was aware of the mass murder of Jews at Auschwitz as early as 1942, and that although Roosevelt relayed the information to London, the British government filed it away without further comment. The president took no direct action to aid the Jews of Europe at that time either.

Whether or not Franklin Delano Roosevelt did enough to alleviate the suffering of the Jews of Nazi Europe is open to conjecture. On this matter of historical import, the jury is still out.

[A.J.K.]

Harry S. Truman

Served from 1945 to 1953

Born on May 8, 1884, in Lamar, Missouri

Member of the Baptist denomination

Married Elizabeth Virginia Wallace on June 28, 1919

Father to one daughter

Candidate of the Democratic Party

Assumed the presidency on April 12, 1945,
following the death of Franklin D. Roosevelt;
elected to a full term on November 2, 1948.

Vice president under Truman: Alben Barkley (second term)

Inaugural Address delivered on January 20, 1949

Died on December 26, 1972, in Kansas City, Missouri

Thirty-Third President of the United States

On April 12, 1945, four-term U.S. president Franklin Delano Roosevelt died in Warm Springs, Georgia, and Vice President Harry S. Truman was sworn in as president of the United States. Many politicians believed that he was ill-equipped for the job, and Truman often concurred in this estimate. But, as he remarked, he had a job to do and he would do it to the best of his ability.

Truman learned quickly that he had to be an independent thinker who would not be unduly influenced by anyone in his administration. Such an attempt was made by the clearly anti-Zionist Department of State, led by Secretary Edward R. Stettinius, Jr. Five days after Franklin Roosevelt's death, Stettinius sent Truman the following note:

> It is likely that efforts will be made by some of the Zionist leaders to obtain from you at an early date some commitments in favor of a Zionist program. . . . The question of Palestine is . . . a highly complex one and involves the questions which go far beyond the plight of the Jews in Europe. . . . as we have interests in the area which are held vital to the United States. We feel that this whole subject is one that should be handled with the greatest care and with a view to the long-range interests of this country.

The new president took offense at the patronizing tone of the note and in his usual direct and uninhibited manner minced no words with his associates: "Don't ever trust those goddam sons of bitches in the State Department." That is the manner in which Truman conducted his presidency.

Early Years

Harry Truman was born in Lamar, Missouri, on May 8, 1884, to John Anderson Truman and Martha Ellen Young Truman. Named Harry after his mother's brother, Truman's parents could not agree on a middle name: Should they choose Solomon, after his maternal grandfather, Solomon Young, or Shipp after his paternal grandfather, Anderson Shipp Truman? They compromised by simply using the letter S.

Truman's formal education was limited. He attended public schools in Independence, Missouri, and after high school graduation applied to West Point, but was rejected because of poor eyesight. In 1901 he began working at a series of jobs, including one as timekeeper on the Santa Fe railroad in Kansas City and another as a bank bookkeeper. At age twenty-two, following his father's death, Turman went back to work on the family farm. During that period of time, from 1906 to 1917, he also served as a member of the Missouri National Guard, advancing to the rank of first lieutenant.

In April 1917 the United States declared war against Germany, and the thirty-three-year-old Truman, although two years beyond the age of conscription set by the Selective Service Act, felt duty-bound to volunteer. By war's end, he had been promoted to major.

Eddie Jacobson

In basic training, Truman was in charge of the regimental canteen, selling cigarettes, candy, and sundry articles to soldiers in his unit. His second-in-command was Sergeant Edward ("Eddie") Jacobson, whose prewar experience as a clerk in a Kansas City clothing store came in handy. Unlike other units, which ran at a loss, Harry and Eddie's canteen turned a profit and was widely praised. As a result, the two formed a fast friendship that lasted a lifetime.

In one of his daily letters to his childhood sweetheart, Bess, whom he would marry in 1919, Truman wrote: "I have a Jew in charge of the canteen by the name of Jacobson and he is a crackerjack."

When the war ended, Truman looked up his old army buddy, and in 1922 he and Eddie opened a haberdashery in Kansas City. Despite their high hopes, by 1924 the enterprise had failed. The two, however, remained good friends.

Entry into Politics

During the years following the war, Truman was determined to concentrate on improving his education. Between 1923 and 1925 he attended the Kansas City Law School, a move that proved rewarding. In 1922 he was elected to a county judgeship, and in 1926 he was elected presiding judge of Jackson County, a position he held for two consecutive four-year terms—from January 1927 to January 1935.

In 1935, chiefly because of the backing of Thomas J. Pendergast, Democratic party boss of his district, a man who ruled the party with an iron hand, Truman won election to the U.S. Senate. In 1940 he ran for office once again and was elected to a second six-year term, which he did not complete, for in 1944 the Democratic Party selected him to be Franklin D. Roosevelt's running mate.

Often during the 1944 campaign Truman was portrayed as a failed haberdasher who "couldn't even make good selling shirts." Additionally, because of his association with Eddie Jacobson, and because he had a grandfather named Solomon, a rumor spread that Truman was part Jewish. Truman responded that he was not Jewish, but even if he were, he would never be ashamed of it. Despite this assertion, he was known on occa-

sion to refer to Jews as "kikes," but this can be attributed to his earthy nature.

Empathy with the Distressed

Although Truman often was powerless to act because of the opposition of his advisers in the State Department and U.S. military to his Middle East policy, unlike his predecessor Truman displayed genuine concern over the fate of Jews and others suffering in Europe. In an April 14, 1945, speech, just two days after assuming the presidency, Truman spoke with great passion:

> Merely talking about the Four Freedoms is not enough. This is the time for action. No one can any longer doubt the horrible intentions of the Nazi beasts. We know that they plan the systematic slaughter throughout all of Europe, not only of the Jews but of vast numbers of other innocent peoples. . . . Their

Harry Truman taking his early morning walk.

present oppressors must know that they will be held directly accountable for their bloody deeds. To do all this, we must draw deeply on our traditions of aid to the oppressed, and on our great national generosity. This is not a Jewish problem, it is an American problem—and we must and we will face it squarely and honorably.

Despite Truman's intentions to help Jewish victims of Hitler, he faced vast difficulties upon the defeat of Germany and Japan and the unfolding Cold War with Russia. Nevertheless, he did express the hope that one hundred thousand displaced persons could be admitted to Palestine and, in his October 4, 1946, address to Congress, urged the liberalization of the immigration laws so that more displaced persons could be admitted to the United States "including Jews."

His advocacy of allowing more Jewish refugees to enter Palestine was met by the stubborn opposition of his advisers in the State Department as well as the Joint Chiefs of Staff and the Foreign Office in Great Britain. Yet, when on May 14, 1948, Israel would declare its independence as a sovereign state, Truman would extend it de facto recognition within the first half hour of its existence.

Truman himself summed up his deep-felt abhorrence for the Nazi program of exterminating innocent human beings when he wrote in his autobiography, *Mr. Citizen*: "I do not hunt animals and I do not believe in shooting at anything that cannot shoot back." The Nazi attack upon innocent, unarmed civilians riled every fiber of his being.

Contention on Two Flanks

Not only did Truman have to battle anti-Zionist advisers within his administration, but he was forced to contend with Zionist leaders who were constantly pressuring him to act more promptly in addressing the plight of the refugees in support of Palestine as a homeland for dispossessed Jews.

Harry Truman celebrates his unanticipated victory.

As hard as Truman tried to assure Rabbi Abba Hillel Silver, Stephen S. Wise, and other Zionist leaders that he was deeply concerned with the fate of the Jews of Nazi Germany and that he would do all that was in his power to fight for the establishment of a Jewish homeland in Palestine, they constantly doubted him and urged him to act more vigorously. This lack of faith in his integrity aggravated and angered the president greatly. To Eleanor Roosevelt, Truman wrote: "The action of our U.S. Zionists will eventually prejudice everyone against what they are trying to get done."

Finally, as the inhumane conditions under which Jewish refugees were forced to live began to appear in dispatches from foreign correspondents, and as the American public became aware of how badly Hitler's victims were faring at the hands of their U.S. liberators, Truman felt impelled to examine the situation more closely. In the summer of 1945, he sent Earl G. Harrison, dean of the University of Pennsylvania Law School and former U.S. commissioner of immigration, to investigate conditions in the displaced persons (DP) camps of Europe. Joseph J. Schwartz, European director of the Joint Distribution Committee, was assigned to be his assistant.

After receiving Harrison's report, which ironi-

Harry Truman en route to his inaugural.

cally revealed that the German prisoners of war were being treated much better than their victims, Dwight D. Eisenhower, Army chief of staff, created the position of adviser on Jewish affairs. Chaplain Judah Nadich was the first such appointee. His assignment was to visit all DP camps in the American Zone in Germany and DP centers and communities in cities and towns, and to make recommendations directly to General Eisenhower and his chief of staff, General Walter Bedell Smith.

Truman also was distressed by Harrison's report and vowed that such conditions "could not be allowed to continue." Only by securing Palestine as a homeland for the displaced persons, Truman felt, could the DP problem be solved.

At an August 10, 1945, press conference, Truman endorsed the proposal that ten thousand refugees be admitted to Palestine by the British. "The American view of Palestine is that we want to let as many of the Jews into Palestine as is possible," he said. ". . . Then the matter will have to be worked out diplomatically with the British and the Arabs, so that if a state can be set up there, they may be able to set it up on a peaceful basis."

British prime minister Clement Atlee reacted by saying: "No major change in Palestine would be made against their [Arab] will."

Undaunted by the reaction of Atlee, on August 31, 1945, Truman sent the following directive to General Eisenhower regarding displaced persons: "I know you will agree with me that we have a particular responsibility toward those victims of persecution and tyranny who are in our zone. We must make clear to the German people that we thoroughly abhor the Nazi policies of hatred and persecution."

Ben-Gurion and Eisenhower

Chaplain Judah Nadich arranged for David Ben-Gurion to travel to Germany and meet with the displaced persons. On October 29, 1945, General Walter Bedell Smith introduced Ben-Gurion to General Eisenhower. After the meeting with Ben-Gurion, Eisenhower remarked to Smith that he considered Ben-Gurion to be "a top-notch statesman and a man of brilliant intellect."

David Niles and Clark Clifford

Despite the lack of support Truman received from administration members who opposed his efforts to solve the Jewish predicament, two men on his staff stood steadfastly by his side. One was Clark Clifford, a bright, young, non-Jewish attorney who had been selected to be Truman's special assistant. The other was David K. Niles, known as the "House Jew," who had been appointed years earlier by Franklin Roosevelt to be his administrative assistant. When Truman became president, Niles became one of his trusted aides. The president depended upon these two men to outline for him the case to be made for recognition of the Jewish state when it would come into being, as indeed it did on May 14, 1948. It was a difficult assignment because Secretary of State George Marshall, along with most of the top brass of the State Department, opposed recognition.

Truman strongly favored recognition because, as Niles was able to observe firsthand, the president truly and sincerely empathized with the fate of the oppressed Jews of Europe. At one point, Niles recalled the speech that Truman had made in Chicago on April 14, 1945, in which he emphasized that the problem of the victims of Nazism was an American problem, implying that America had to help solve it. Niles went on to comment that Roosevelt never would have uttered such words, and went as far as to say: "There are serious doubts in my mind that Israel would have come into being if Roosevelt lived." This observation was made despite Niles's full knowledge of the one thousand refugees brought to Oswego, New York, from Italy in June 1944 as "guests" of President Roosevelt.

Journalist Ruth Gruber's book *Haven: The Dramatic Story of 1,000 World War II Refugees and How They Came to America* presents a different picture of Roosevelt's attitude toward the refugee problem. She writes that despite the quota that was imposed limiting immigration, President Roosevelt allowed one thousand refugees from eighteen different countries to board an army transport ship that was carrying American soldiers who had been wounded in the battles of Anzio and Cassino, in Italy, to Oswego, New York. These refugees, he declared, were entering as his "guests."

Chaim Weizmann and the President

In late July of 1947, some one hundred thousand letters flooded the White House urging positive action on the Palestine issue. Truman was so annoyed by the pressure being put on him that when Chaim Weizmann (who had been instrumental in having the Balfour Declaration issued and was of great help in Britain's war efforts against the Nazis) arrived in the United States, the president refused to entertain a visit by the elder Zionist statesmen. "Jesus Christ couldn't please them when he was on earth," Truman is reported to have cried out, "so how could anyone expect that I would have any luck!"

It required special pleading by his old friend Eddie Jacobson to persuade the president to allow the Weizmann visit. According to volume two of Truman's White House memoirs, the conversation between Jacobson and the president went something like this:

> Harry, all your life you have had a hero. You are probably the best read man in America on the life of Andrew Jackson. . . . Well, Harry, I too have a hero, a man I never met but who is, I think, the greatest Jew who ever lived. . . . I am talking about Chaim Weizmann. He is an old man and a sick man, and he has come all the way to America to see you. Now you refuse to see him because you were insulted by some of our American Jewish leaders. . . . It doesn't sound like you, Harry.

Truman finally acquiesced, saying, "All right, you bald-headed son of a bitch, I'll see him."

In an interview with Merle Miller, whose oral biography of Harry S. Truman was published in 1973, one year after Truman's death, the president recalled that meeting in a slightly different fashion. Zionist leaders, who were not welcome in the White House because the president could no longer stand the pressure they were exerting upon him, prevailed upon Truman's old friend and business partner Eddie Jacobson to come to Washington and urge the president to grant Weizmann an interview.

The president recalled that when Jacobson spoke to him on the phone, he said: "Eddie, I'm always glad to see an old friend, but there is one thing you've got to promise me. I don't want you to say a word about what's going on over there in the Middle East. Do you promise?" He did.

Truman then recalled that when Eddie Jacobson entered the Oval Office, tears began streaming down his face. "Eddie, you son of a bitch," said Truman, "you promised me you wouldn't say a word about what's going on over there."

Jacobson responded: "Mr. President, I haven't said a word about what's going on over there, but every time I think of the homeless Jews, homeless for thousands of years, and I think about Dr. Weizmann, I start crying. I can't help it. He's an old man, and he's spent his whole life working for a homeland for the Jews, and now he's sick, and he's in New York and wants to see you. Every time I think about it, I can't help crying."

"Eddie, that's enough. That's the last word."

"And so we talked about this and that," Truman told Miller, "but every once in a while a big tear would roll down his cheek . . . I said, 'Eddie, you son of a bitch, I ought to have you thrown out of here for breaking your promise; you knew damn well I couldn't stand seeing you crying.'"

Truman Reconsiders

On March 13, 1948, a one-hour secret meeting was held, enabling Weizmann to solicit Truman's aid in fighting the ban issued by the British government on further immigration to Palestine. The meeting went well, and afterward Truman remarked: "I called him Cham [not remembering how to pronounce Chaim]. He liked it. He was a wonderful man, one of the wisest people I think I ever met. . . . a leader, one of a kind you read about."

Weizmann's visit had helped deflate the pressure Truman had been subjected to by overzealous Zionist leaders. Despite the opposition of Secretary of the Navy James Forrestal, who warned that favoring the Zionist cause would imperil the flow of Arab oil from Middle Eastern countries, and that the Arabs would "push the Jews into the sea," Truman did not waver in his pro-Zionist leanings.

The Partition Vote

On Saturday, November 29, 1947, the United Nations General Assembly, by a vote of twenty-three to thirteen, with ten abstentions, accepted the principle of establishing two states in Palestine, one Jewish and one Arab. In the United States, Harry Truman prevailed over the State Department, which opposed it. Even the Soviet Union, which for many years opposed the Zionist goal, voted for partition, mainly to minimize Britain's long-held control over the Middle East. Great Britain, which had endorsed the Balfour Declaration, abstained. And even though as a result of partition Jews ended up with a tiny homeland (5,500 square miles for Jews and 4,500 for Arabs), they greeted the decision with great joy and danced in the streets of Jerusalem all night long. Isaac Herzog, chief rabbi of Palestine, announced cheerfully: "After a darkness of two thousand years the dawn of redemption has broken."

A State Is Born

Five and a half months later, on Friday, May 14, 1948, David Ben-Gurion, head of the Jewish provisional government, issued Israel's Proclamation of Independence. At the White House, President Truman called a hurried meeting of his Cabinet to advise him about recognition of the new country. Secretary of State George C. Marshall argued against it and Clark Clifford argued in favor. The president followed Clifford's advice and on behalf of the United States government immediately recognized Israel's statehood, the first nation to do so.

The president's remarks on that occasion represented his deep and abiding faith in the course that he had pursued. He said:

> One of the proudest days of my life occurred at 6:12 P.M. on Friday May 14 [1948] when I was able to announce recognition of the new state of Israel by the government of the United States. In view of the long friendship of the American people for the Zionist ideal, it was particularly appropriate that our government should be the first to recognize the new state.

After being elected Israel's first president, Weizmann visited the White House to thank Truman for all that he had done. "You will never know what this means to my people," Weizmann said to the president. "We have waited and dreamed and worked for this moment for two thousand years." He then presented President Truman with an Israeli Torah scroll as a gift of appreciation from the Jewish people.

During the presentation, Weizmann jocularly added: "You may not be aware of this Mr. President, but I am a more important president than you." Truman looked at him in mild astonishment. "I don't quite understand," he said.

"Well, Mr. President," continued Weizmann, "you are the president of one hundred seventy million people; but I am the president of a million presidents." Remembering his difficulties with the highly volatile American Zionist leaders, Truman roared with laughter.

In 1949 Israel's chief rabbi called upon President Truman and expressed his gratitude with these words: "God put you in your mother's womb so that you could be the instrument to bring about the rebirth of Israel after two thousand years."

Several years after the state was founded, David Ben-Gurion met with Truman, and later reported: "I told him that his courageous decision to recognize our new state so quickly and his steadfast support since then had given him an immortal place in Jewish history. As I said that, tears suddenly came to his eyes and his eyes were still wet when he bade me goodbye."

Jewish Friends and Supporters

Aside from Eddie Jacobson, there were few Jews who could be described as close friends of Truman. Though defeat seemed certain in the 1948 race for the presidency against Republican Thomas E. Dewey, a number of affluent members of the Jewish community had stood beside Truman. Foremost among these supporters were Dewey Stone, a prominent businessman and Zionist leader; Arthur Krim, a movie mogul who headed United Artists; and Philip Klutznick, a lawyer and communal leader who would later become international president of B'nai Brith, a member of the United States delegation to the United Nations, and, from 1979 to 1981, secretary of commerce under President Jimmy Carter.

A good friend of the first family during their White House years was singer Robert Merrill. He was the vocalist selected to sing before both houses of Congress on the first anniversary of Franklin D. Roosevelt's death. At the time, Margaret Truman, the president's daughter, whose ambition it had been to become a concert singer, sang many duets with Merrill as

the president accompanied them on the piano.

Truman tried to befriend Bernard Baruch, the wealthy Jewish financier from South Carolina who had been a close adviser to Franklin D. Roosevelt, but he was unsuccessful. At one point Truman asked Baruch to serve on the finance committee of the Democratic Party, but he refused. The unexplained rebuff infuriated Truman. "A great many honors have passed your way," he said to Baruch, "but when the going is rough, it is a one-way street."

Feinberg and Rosenman

One of Truman's loyal supporters was entrepreneur Abraham Feinberg (1908–1998), a New York businessman and philanthropist. He and his family led many fundraising drives during Truman's

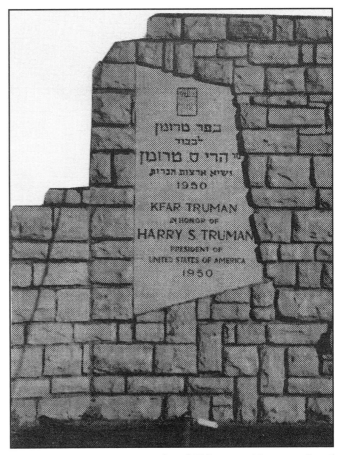

Because Harry S. Truman conferred U.S. recognition upon Israel minutes after it became a state, the small village of B'nei Har-el, near Israel's international airport, was renamed Kfar-Truman in 1950. This monument commemorates that event.

Truman with Chaim Weizmann.

His relationship with President-elect Eisenhower was not amicable, but that did not hinder him from doing what he felt was right and proper.

While waiting in the room of the sergeant-at-arms before going out to the rotunda for the swearing-in ceremony, Eisenhower noticed that his son, John, who was on active duty in Korea, was present.

Addressing the entourage that had accompanied him to the inaugural podium, Eisenhower said sharply: "I wonder who is responsible for my son, John, being ordered from Korea to Washington! I wonder who is trying to embarrass me."

Truman replied: "The president of the United States ordered your son to attend your inaugural. The president thought it right and proper for your son to witness the swearing-in of his father to the presidency. If you think somebody was trying to embarrass you by this order, then the president assumes full responsibility."

Shortly after leaving office, Truman visited the University of Missouri to dedicate a plaque honoring his friend and one-time business partner, Eddie Jacobson.

In retirement Truman devoted time to teaching, lecturing, and preparing his memoirs: *Year of Decisions (1955) and Years of Trial and Hope* (1956). He then turned his attention to establishing the Truman Library in Independence, Missouri. The groundbreaking ceremony was held on his seventy-first birthday, May 8, 1955, and attended by 150 invited guests. True to the ecumenical spirit that always pervaded his being, Truman invited the Catholic archbishop to conduct the ceremony, a Protestant minister to offer the invocation, and a rabbi to pronounce the benediction. The library building was completed and dedicated on July 6, 1957; Eleanor Roosevelt was the guest speaker.

whistle-stop campaign for election in 1948. In 1960, when Mr. Feinberg was honored by B'nai B'rith as its Man of the Year, Mr. Truman observed that in addition to the good works by Mr. Feinberg that had been made public, "I could name two or three times as many that he has done anonymously, without personal credit and always at sacrifice to himself."

Judge Samuel J. Rosenman was another close associate of Truman, as he had been of Roosevelt. He served as special counsel to both presidents and was Truman's personal attorney. After the president left office, Rosenman reviewed a codicil to Truman's will that Truman had written himself and pronounced it pretty good. He said it would have stood up legally. Nevertheless, when there were new developments in the family that the president wanted to take into account, Rosenman wrote the codicils.

Final Years

In 1952 Truman chose not to run for reelection to a third term because he felt it important to restore the tradition of a two-term presidency.

The Perennial Student

Rabbi Jack H. Bloom, of Fairfield, Connecticut, recalls in a memoir detailed in *Conservative Juda-*

ism magazine how the ex-president happened to attend a weekend convocation at the Jewish Theological Seminary in September 1957.

Louis Finkelstein, then chancellor of the Seminary, had organized a weekend in which scholars of a variety of denominations would come together to study biblical and talmudic texts with an ethical message so as to create a better appreciation of Judaism. One of the invited guests was Chief Justice of the Supreme Court Earl Warren (1953–1969).

When Warren arrived at the seminar and the door of his limousine was opened, everyone was amazed to see former president Harry S. Truman seated next to him. When asked why the president was coming to the sessions, Truman is reported to have replied, in his usual jocular manner, that Warren had said to him: "Harry, I've been invited uptown for a good Jewish meal. Want to come along?"

Truman was greatly impressed by the learning sessions and particularly by the lecture of Professor Shalom Spiegel on the subject "Amos vs. Amaziah." In a letter to Chancellor Finkelstein dated September 17, 1957, Truman wrote:

> Dear Mr. Finkelstein,
>
> You do not know how much I appreciated the privilege of being present at a luncheon with the Chief Justice of the United States.
>
> I more than enjoyed the talk on the chapter [seven] of Amos quoting, "Amos, what seest thou?" And I said, "A plumbline."
>
> I have known that entire passage word for word for a long time, and I wish you would tell that able and distinguished rabbi that I have never had a more pleasing experience than listening to his lecture.
>
> Sincerely yours,
> Harry S. Truman

By the end of the 1960s, President Truman's health had begun to fail. At age eighty-eight, on December 5, 1972, he was hospitalized for lung congestion, and on December 26 Truman's life slipped away. His body lay in state in the library he had built, and he was laid to rest on the grounds of the library.

Truman participated in the cornerstone laying of the Washington Hebrew Congregation.

No one has summed up the purpose and goal of Harry Truman's life better than did the president in a prayer that he himself composed, one copy of which he carried with him at all times and another copy which he kept on his desk in the White House. The prayer concluded:

> O, almighty and everlasting God, creator of heaven and earth and the universe:
> Help me to be, to think, to act what is right, because it is right.
> Make me truthful, honest, and honorable in all things.
> Make me intellectually honest for the sake of right and honor, and without thought of reward to me.
> Give me the ability to be charitable, forgiving, and patient with my fellow man.
> Help me to understand their motives and their shortcomings—even as Thou understandest mine. Amen.

[A.J.K.]

Dwight D. Eisenhower

Served from 1953 to 1961

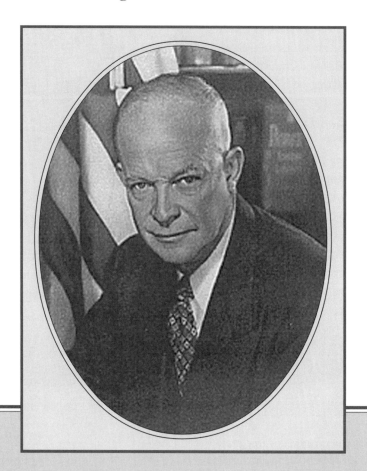

Born on October 14, 1890, in Denison, Texas

Member of the Presbyterian denomination

Married Mamie Geneva Doud on July 1, 1916

Father to one son

Candidate of the Republican Party

Vice president under Eisenhower: Richard M. Nixon

First Inaugural Address delivered on January 20, 1953
Second Inaugural Address delivered on January 21, 1957

Died on March 28, 1969, in Washington, D.C.

Thirty-Fourth President of the United States

LTHOUGH DWIGHT DAVID EISENHOWER joined the Presbyterian Church later in life, his antecedents, who came to America by way of Switzerland, were members of a group known as Brethren in Christ, akin to Quakers. When the Brethren migrated to Kansas, Eisenhower's grandfather, Jacob, joined them. In the 1880s Dwight's father, David, a construction engineer, and his wife, Ida, moved to Denison, Texas, where Dwight David was born. In 1892 the family returned to Kansas and settled in Abilene.

When Dwight and one of his five brothers (a sixth died as a baby), Edgar, attended grade school, the two boys were nicknamed Ike: Edgar was called "Big Ike" and Dwight, "Little Ike." Like many youngsters, Dwight earned pocket money delivering papers and doing odd jobs, and used his leisure hours to swim, fish, and hunt when he was not playing football and baseball on school teams. His particular area of interest in high school was history, and his classmates predicted that he would become a history professor at Yale University.

At first, Dwight planned to further his education at the University of Kansas, but a friend suggested that he apply to the United States Naval Academy. Dwight followed this advice but was rejected by the academy because he was too old. His parents, who were Quakers, opposed the choice of careers, but this did not deter Dwight from applying to the United States Military Academy at West Point, to which he received an appointment. He graduated in 1915, 61 out of a class of 164, and then began his career as a second lieutenant; within a year he was promoted to first lieutenant. Advancing quickly through the ranks, by 1942 Dwight Eisenhower had reached the grade of lieutenant general.

The Jewish Association

Growing up in Denison, Texas, where the Jewish population was scant, Dwight had virtually no contact with Jews. But his parents did not fail to imbue him with a positive attitude toward the Jewish people. He was raised to believe that Jews were the chosen people and that "they gave us the high ethical and moral principles of our civilization." Many years later, when campaigning for the presidency, he reiterated these same sentiments to Chicago's wealthy Jewish leader Maxwell Abbell: "The Jewish people could not have a better friend than me." (Lyndon B. Johnson would use almost identical words when he met with Jewish leaders after the assassination of President Kennedy.)

Because names like Ike and Eisenhower had a Jewish ring to them, quite possibly people were led to believe that Dwight and his family were Jewish. This unfounded claim, which persisted throughout his life, did not disturb Eisenhower, and he dismissed it with considerable ease.

Ike's first experience with those who thought they were disparaging him by calling him a Jew occurred in his senior year at West Point. Next to his picture in the yearbook someone scrawled, "David Dwight Eisenhower, the terrible Swedish Jew."

Ike's brother Milton reported that he had had a similar experience. Once, at a cocktail party in Washington, one of the old dowagers said: "What a pity it is that you Eisenhowers are Jewish!" Milton looked her straight in the eye and responded: "Ah, madame, what a pity it is that we are not."

In President Eisenhower's *Crusade in Europe*, he described a similar rumor that had spread in

Morocco and Tunisia when they were under Nazi occupation during World War II:

> For years the uneducated population had been subjected to intensive Nazi propaganda calculated to fan their prejudices. The country was ridden, almost ruled by rumor. One rumor was to the effect that I was a Jew, sent into the country by the Jew Roosevelt to grind down the Arabs and to turn over North Africa to Jewish rule.

Displaced Persons

In August 1945, Rabbi Stephen S. Wise requested that General Eisenhower assign a liaison officer to coordinate the various efforts in behalf of displaced persons. Believing that the appointment of such an officer would not be helpful, the general denied the request.

However, after President Truman received a report from Dean Earl G. Harrison of the University of Pennsylvania, whom he had sent to report on conditions in DP camps in Europe, Eisenhower was advised of it and he reversed his attitude. Harrison reported:

> Beyond knowing that they are no longer in danger of the gas chambers, torture and other forms of violent death, they see—and there is—little change . . . As matters now stand, we appear to be treating the Jews as the Nazis treated them except that we do not exterminate them. They are in concentration camps in large numbers under our own military guards instead of SS troops. One is led to wonder whether the German people, seeing this, are not supposing that we are following or at least condoning Nazi policy.

Soon thereafter, Eisenhower assigned Chaplain Judah Nadich to his headquarters to be special adviser on all matters pertaining to the welfare of Jews in DP camps and surrounding areas. When Nadich left his post, he was succeeded by a number of civilians, beginning with Judge Simon H. Rifkin. Their efforts led to the creation of separate DP camps for the Jews, where the educational, cultural, and spiritual needs of the former concentration camp inmates—as well as their physical problems—were addressed.

That Eisenhower truly empathized with the mass suffering of Jews was evident from the compassion he showed towards the displaced after the Nazis were defeated. In 1945, unannounced, he attended a Yom Kippur service being held for more than one thousand displaced persons at a camp in Feldafing, Germany. When called upon to speak, he said:

> I feel especially happy to be in a Jewish camp on this holiest day of your year. You are only here temporarily. You must be patient until the day comes—and it it will come—when you leave here for the places you wish to go. The American army is here to help you. The part you must play is to maintain good and friendly relations with your appointed authorities. I know how much you have suffered. I believe that a sunnier day will soon be yours.

The sincerity of Ike's concern for the welfare of the displaced persons was proven not long afterward when he received a report describing how the American military police who were stationed at the gates of the DP camp, under the command of General George Patton, would allow Germans who worked in the camp to come and go at will, while Jewish DPs had to apply for and present passes.

Eisenhower, who as of November 19, 1945, was chief of staff of the U.S. Army, replacing General George C. Marshall, called Patton into his office and asked him: "George, why aren't you doing something for these Jewish displaced persons?" Patton's abrupt response was: "Why the hell should I?"

"Because I am ordering you to do so!" Eisenhower shot back.

Somewhat earlier, after visiting the Nazi concentration camp at Ohrdruf, in Germany, on April 4, 1945, Eisenhower revealed the following about Patton to Army Chief of Staff George C. Marshall:

> The visual evidence . . . of starvation, cruelty and bestiality were so overpowering as to leave me a bit sick. In one room, where there were piled up twenty or thirty naked men, killed by starvation, [General] George Patton

would not even enter. He said he would get sick if he did so. I made the visit deliberately, in order to be in a position to give firsthand evidence of these things if ever, in the future, there develops a tendency to charge these allegations merely to "propaganda."

In 1948, with the war fully behind him, Eisenhower shared with the world his innermost feelings. "I am the most intensely religious man I know," he said. "Nobody goes through six years of war without faith."

Differences with Israel

Despite the many friendly gestures and pronouncements that revealed Eisenhower's respect and admiration for the Jewish people, they did not always coincide with the concerns of the newborn state of Israel. Abba Eban, Israel's first representative to the United Nations, recorded in his autobiography Prime Minister David Ben-Gurion's assessment of Eisenhower: "Eisenhower's contact with our [Zionist] cause had been superficial. Yet, it included something which Ben Gurion was never to forget—a reaction of cold fury to the horrors of Nazism which unfolded before him when the forces under his command entered the Concentration Camps."

Israelis were convinced that Eisenhower was greatly influenced by his secretary of state, John Foster Dulles, who never failed to go out of his way to cultivate the goodwill of the Arabs, par-

Dwight D. Eisenhower with David Ben-Gurion.

ticularly Egyptian president Gamal Abdel Nasser, at the expense of Israel. The usually effective efforts of the pro-Israel lobbyists in Washington did not succeed in counteracting the influence of Dulles on Eisenhower.

Following the advice of Dulles, Ike went out of the way to placate the Arabs, who had been humiliated in the 1956 Sinai Campaign, when Israel took control of Sinai and the Gaza Strip. In a February 1957 nationwide radio and television speech, the president insisted that Israel withdraw, unconditionally, from Gaza and Sharm el-Sheikh, and if it did not, sanctions would be applied.

The Lobbyists

The most effective group in Washington engaged in promoting Israel's interests was organized by I. L. Kenen in the 1950s. Known as AIPAC (American Israel Public Affairs Committee), it had succeeded in mobilizing Congressional support for Israel by convincing congressmen and senators that a strong Israel served best the interests of the United States, in that it could be a buffer against Nasser's dream of expansion.

In a campaign to counteract the views of Dulles, AIPAC urged a cross section of Republican and Democratic legislators to send a strong letter to Dulles, making it clear that they did not agree that sanctions should be placed against Israel or pressure put on Israel to withdraw unilaterally from the Sinai and Gaza.

The success of the Jewish lobbyists in winning over members of Congress so incensed Dulles and Eisenhower that they went so far as to consider disallowing private assistance to Israel via United Jewish Appeal (UJA) donations and the purchase of Israeli bonds. When Kenen's AIPAC members learned of the scheme and reported it to members of Congress, it resulted in such an adverse reaction that Eisenhower was compelled to drop the idea.

Senate Majority Leader Lyndon Johnson, a Democrat, wrote to the secretary of state opposing such "coercion" and arguing that it was damaging to the friendly relationship that had been established with Israel. The Senate minority leader, Republican William Knowland, likewise opposed applying sanctions against Israel. After all, he reasoned, sanctions had not been leveled against the Soviet Union for its military intervention in Hungary.

Reacting to the pressure, Eisenhower tried to placate David Ben-Gurion, writing the prime minister in March 1957 that "Israel will have no cause for regret" if it withdraws its forces. He also promised that Israel would be rewarded for bringing calm to an inflammatory situation. Israel relented and accepted Eisenhower's assurances, in which the secretary of state concurred. Golda Meir, the Israeli foreign minister, then went before the United Nations General Assembly and announced, in a statement jointly drafted by United States and Israeli officials and personally approved by John Foster Dulles, that Israel would completely withdraw from the Sinai on three conditions: (1) the UN Emergency Forces would remain in the Sinai Peninsula and Gaza Strip until a peace accord was reached, (2) Fedayeen raids would cease, and (3) the Straits of Tiran would be freely accessible to Israeli shipping.

Eight years later, in 1965, Max Fisher (1908–) of Detroit, a longtime leader of the UJA and a major financial supporter of Eisenhower's Republican Party, called on the retired president at his farm in Gettysburg, Pennsylvania. Fisher had been sent by the UJA to obtain the former president's agreement to accept a medal acknowledging his role in the liberation of the German concentration camps at the end of World War II. As Fisher prepared to depart, Eisenhower said to him pensively: "You know, Max, looking back at Suez, I regret what I did. I should never have pressured Israel to vacate the Sinai." And then, almost as an afterthought, Eisenhower added: "Max, if I had had a Jewish adviser working for me, I doubt I would have handled the situation the same way."

These revelations, which are reported in Peter Golden's *The Quiet Diplomat*, were corroborated by President Nixon in a later interview with Golden. Nixon recalled: "Eisenhower . . . in the 1960s told me—and I am sure he told others—that he thought the action taken [at Suez] was one he regretted. He thought it was a mistake." Had there been no capitulation at Suez, there would not have been a costly, albeit successful, 1973 Yom Kippur War.

Lewis L. Strauss

Lewis L. Strauss, one of Eisenhower's closest Jewish advisers, had also been a trusted friend and adviser to President Herbert Hoover. Strauss had served as special assistant to the secretary of the Navy in World War II and had beome a rear admiral in 1945. Over the next decade, Strauss would play an instrumental role in shaping American atomic energy policy.

In July 1946 Strauss resigned his partnership in the Wall Street firm of Kuhn, Loeb & Co. to

Lewis Strauss was the third Jew in history to serve as a member of a presidential Cabinet. The first was Oscar Straus, who was secretary of labor and commerce in the Theodore Roosevelt Administration.

Eisenhower was presented with a Torah scroll by representatives of the Jewish Theological Seminary of America. The meeting took place in the Oval Office on February 4, 1960. From left to right: Eisenhower, Louis Finkelstein, Bernard Mandelbaum, Joseph S. Wohl, and Isaac Klein.

accept President Truman's offer of an appointment to the newly created Atomic Engery Commission (AEC). In 1953 President Eisenhower appointed Strauss chairman of the commission, and more than any other individual Lewis Strauss shaped the atomic energy policy of the United States in the years 1953 to 1958.

During his tenure as chairman of the AEC, Strauss urged the revocation of the commission's security clearance to J. Robert Oppenheimer, father of the atomic bomb and one of the nation's most eminent physicists. Supposedly, Oppenheimer had past associations with Communists, and he was also suspect because of continued opposition to the development of the hydrogen bomb. In a controversial and much criticized 1954 decision, the AEC ruled that Oppenheimer was a security risk and would henceforth be denied access to classified information on U.S. atomic energy policy.

In a White House ceremony on July 14, 1958, President Eisenhower awarded Strauss the U.S. Medal of Freedom. Shorly thereafter, Eisenhower offered Strauss the Cabinet post of secretary of commerce and, on October 24, 1958, announced

Strauss's appointment. When the Strauss nomination was sent to the Senate for confirmation in January 1959, it met the strong and unrelenting opposition of the Democrat-controlled Senate. In June of 1959, Strauss's nomination as secretary of commerce was defeated by a Senate vote of forty-nine to forty-six. To this day, Strauss is the only Jewish Cabinet nominee to be denied Senate confirmation.

The Rosenberg Spy Case

One of the most difficult decisions faced by Eisenhower during his presidency concerned the fate of Julius and Ethel Rosenberg, who had been tried as spies and sentenced to death during the Truman Administration. Along with two other defendants, including Ethel's brother David Greenglass, the couple had been charged with conspiracy to commit espionage, in violation of the Espionage Act of 1917, by spying for the Soviet Union and supplying them with information vital to the advancement of their atomic energy program. The trial, under the aegis of Judge Irving Kaufman and being prosecuted by Irving Saypol, had begun in March 1951 in New York City. All four defendants had been found guilty, and on April 15, 1951, Judge Kaufman sentenced both Julius and Ethel Rosenberg to die the week of Monday, May 21, 1951, and remanded the other two defendants to prison.

A number of prominent individuals and organizations felt that imposing the death penalty was excessive. Almost all Jewish organizations, as well as the American Civil Liberties Union, protested the Kaufman ruling, charging that it had been imposed simply because the Rosenbergs were Jewish, despite the fact that the prosecutor and the judge were also Jews.

Others viewed the imposition of the death penalty as a means of deflecting public disappointment with the course of the Korean War. Although troops had been committed by President Truman in June 1950 to help defend South Korea against the attacks of the North Korean communists, by 1953, when thirty-four thousand American soldiers had fallen in battle, it became Eisenhower's war. Avowed communists, the Rosenbergs, it was argued, were convenient scapegoats.

After many postponements, with appeals reaching the Supreme Court, the president finally had to address the question of clemency for the Rosenbergs.

One of the many impassioned voices raised in behalf of thirty-five-year-old Julius and thirty-seven-year-old Ethel, parents of two young sons, was that of Rabbi Abraham Cronbach, a prominent Reform rabbi committed to social justice. The rabbi would later reveal that on June 16, 1953, the forty-seventh anniversary of his ordination, he met with the Chief Executive:

> I conversed with President Dwight D. Eisenhower in the presidential office of the White House Annex. I had been invited to join three Christian clergymen in beseeching the President for clemency toward Julius and Ethel Rosenberg. I remarked, "Mr. President, all of us are dedicated to the interests of America. All of us are solicitous that America shall suffer no harm. Would not America be adequately safeguarded if, instead of death, the penalty

> for the Rosenbergs would be imprisonment, no matter how long? . . . . Life is full of problems that baffle our intelligence. All of us need the guidance of God. Mr. President, may you have the guidance of God!

The president later responsed:

> According to federal law, there is no such thing as "imprisonment no matter how long." State laws provide for long terms of incarceration. With federal law it is otherwise. According to federal law, the Rosenbergs would be eligible for parole in fifteen years. Besides, there are times when nothing but death is a deterrent. After our invasion of Europe the inhabitants of a certain area complained bitterly about the misconduct of some American soldiers. The people had to arm themselves with pitchforks and other makeshift weapons to prevent pillage and rape. All of that stopped after I had two of the malefactors publicly hanged. On one occasion some law-defying soldiers were offered the alternative of imprisonment or service in the front lines. Every one of them chose imprisonment. There are times when death is the only effective penalty.

The president allowed the sentence to stand, and on Friday, June 18, 1953, just a few minutes before sundown, Julius went to the electric chair, followed by his wife.

Cultivating Jewish Friendship

Although Eisenhower lost the Jewish vote in both of his races for the presidency (in 1952, only 36 percent of Jews voted for him while 64 precent voted for Adlai Stevenson; in 1956, 40 percent of the Jews voted for him while 60 percent voted for Stevenson), he did make an effort to cultivate the friendship of prominent Jews. Aside from his close associations with Max Fisher and Lewis L.Strauss, Eisenhower established friendly relationships with Philip Klutznick, Maxwell Rabb, Arthur Burns, and Norman Cousins, among others.

Philip Klutznick (1907-1999), an American-born lawyer, became one of the United States' earliest and most innovative private developers of housing. A captivating speaker, he was deeply involved in Jewish communal affairs and served as international president of B'nai B'rith from 1953 to 1959.

At a 1953 meeting of B'nai B'rith, Klutznick reported that Eisenhower confessed to him that had he been president of the United States in 1948, he was not sure whether he would have been in favor of establishing a Jewish state. Klutznick served as a member of the U.S. delegation to the United Nations from 1961 to 1962.

One of Ike's early important appointments was that of Maxwell Rabb (1901-), whom he selected to be assistant to the president in charge of civil rights matters, immigration, and labor problems. It was Rabb who helped shepherd through Congress the Refugee Relief Act of 1953, which Eisenhower signed into law. It stipulated that for a forty-one-month period an additional 205,000 refugees, orphans, and certain close relatives of American citizens and aliens would be admitted to the United States, above the regular quotas that were in place.

Rabb also served as secretary to Eisenhower's Cabinet from 1956 to 1958 and as liaison to the Jewish community.

Another Jewish appointee of the president was Austrian-born Arthur Burns (1904-1987), who taught economics at Columbia University and Rutgers and served as an adviser on numerous presidential commissions concerned with economic affairs. From 1953 to 1956, he served as chairman of the President's Council of Economic Advisers. (In 1969 Nixon would appoint Burns to serve as his economic adviser.)

Norman Cousins (1915-1990), editor of the *Saturday Review*, was another good friend and adviser to the president. When Eisenhower decided against delivering his final State of the Union Address in person, he did so on radio and television at the suggestion of Cousins.

Post-Presidential Years

After Kennedy was inaugurated as president in 1961, Eisenhower and his wife, Mamie, whom he had married in 1916, left the White House quietly and went to the F Street Club in Washington, D.C., where Lewis Strauss and his wife hosted a farewell dinner for Eisenhower.

When Eisenhower vacated the White House, he was far from a wealthy man. Fortunately for him, however, Congress restored the president to his former five-star general status, which gave him a larger pension and other health benefits—advantages he had had to forego when he assumed the presidency and became commander in chief. The new income enabled him to purchase a working farm in Gettysburg, Pennsylvania, where he devoted himself to agriculture and animal husbandry.

After moving to Gettysburg, the former president's son, John, helped manage his business affairs. A diplomat and author, John was a West Point graduate like his father.

On December 22, 1968, Ike, with Mamie at his bedside, enjoyed (via closed-circuit television) the marriage of their young grandson David Eisenhower to Julie Nixon, daughter of President-elect Richard Nixon and his wife, Pat. Ike had been hospitalized for another heart attack, having suffered his first while still in office and several more thereafter. He died three months later, on March 28, 1969, at Walter Reed Army Medical Center, in Washington, D.C. According to his son, Ike's last words were: "I want to go. God take me."

Throughout his many decades of public service, some actions in regard to Israel notwithstanding, Dwight D. Eisenhower's genuine, warm feeling toward Jews never wavered. The sentiments he expressed in 1962, seven years before his death, in a message he wrote upon the publication of *Rabbis in Uniform*, reflected his true feelings to the Jewish community at large:

> It is a privilege to present a word of greeting and congratulations to the American Jewish community and its spiritual leaders on the occasion of the celebration of the centennial of the commissioning of the first rabbi as a chaplain in the American Armed Forces . . . May this centennial book, recording the achievements of American chaplains of the Jewish faith, help to keep alive the memory of all who have served our country well in times of war and peace. May it help to strengthen our faith in the enduring values which lie at the heart of all our national and spiritual endeavors.

[A.J.K.]

John F. Kennedy

Served from 1961 to 1963

Born on May 29, 1917, in Brookline, Massachusetts

Member of the Roman Catholic denomination

Married Jacqueline L. Bouvier on September 12, 1953

Father to one daughter and one son

Candidate of the Democratic Party

Vice president under Kennedy: Lyndon B. Johnson

Inaugural Address delivered on January 20, 1961

Assassinated on November 22, 1963, in Dallas, Texas

Thirty-Fifth President of the United States

THE FIRST AMERICAN PRESIDENT BORN in the twentieth century, John Fitzgerald Kennedy was also the youngest man ever elected to the presidency. Kennedy categorized himself in his Inaugural Address as one of "a new generation of Americans—born in this century, tempered by war, disciplined by a hard and bitter peace."

As the first Roman Catholic elected to the presidency, Kennedy's electoral victory in 1960 was hailed by American Jews as a triumph over the same religious bigotry to which they had been subjected.

Born in Brookline, Massachusetts, in 1917, Kennedy was the grandson and namesake of John F. "Honey Fitz" Fitzgerald, who had served as a United States congressman and as mayor of Boston. John F. Kennedy's father, Joseph P. Kennedy, a multimillionaire businessman and an early supporter of Franklin D. Roosevelt for the Democratic presidential nomination in 1932, had served Roosevelt as the first chairman of the Securities and Exchange Commission (1934-1935) and, more controversially, as ambassador to Great Britain (1938-1940), openly opposing U.S. participation in World War II.

Entering Politics

Shortly after graduating from Harvard in 1940, John F. Kennedy entered the U.S. Navy and earned a purple heart for his heroism as the commander of a torpedo boat in the South Pacific. Following his discharge from the Navy in 1945, he returned to Boston to campaign for the Democratic nomination for Congress, for the same House seat that his grandfather had once held. As a war hero, and with the unlimited financial backing of his father, Kennedy handily defeated nine opponents in the 1946 Democratic primary and his Republican opponent in the November election. After being reelected to Congress in 1948 and 1950, he won a Senate seat in 1952, defeating the incumbent, Henry Cabot Lodge, Jr., by seventy thousand votes. In winning reelection to the Senate in 1958, with 74 percent of the vote, he received the highest plurality given a candidate in Massachusetts to date—and soon became a leading contender for the 1960 Democratic presidential nomination.

Kennedy's Catholicism loomed large for many voters in the early months of his presidential campaign. He confronted the issue head-on in a speech before the Ministerial Association of Houston, Texas, on September 12, 1960, by declaring that he believed "in an America where the separation of Church and State is absolute, where no Catholic prelate would tell the president (should he be a Catholic) how to act. . . . I do not speak for my Church on public matters, and the Church does not speak for me."

Zionism and Israel

On June 15, 1947, as the General Assembly of the United Nations was about to debate the partition of Palestine, Representative John F. Kennedy, the newly elected congressman from Boston, had opened the annual convention of the New England Region of the Zionist Organization of America by voicing his unequivocal support for the creation of a Jewish state:

> It is my conviction that a just solution requires the establishment of a free and democratic

Jewish commonwealth in Palestine, the opening of the doors of Palestine to Jewish immigration, and the removal of land restrictions, so that those members of the people of Israel who desire to do so may work out their destiny under their chosen leaders in the land of Israel. If the United States is to be true to its own democratic traditions, it will actively and dynamically support this policy.

Throughout his years as a congressman and senator, Kennedy's record indicates that, with the singular exception of his opposition to economic aid for Israel and the Arab states in 1951, he consistently took a pro-Israel position. He publicly questioned the 1954 U.S. arms shipments to Iraq and supported U.S. aid to Israel when the Soviets armed Nasser of Egypt. In a letter dated March 5, 1956, addressed to Secretary of State John Foster Dulles, Senator Kennedy strongly opposed the United States arms embargo imposed on the State of Israel.

The following month, addressing thousands gathered at New York's Yankee Stadium to celebrate the eighth anniversary of the founding of the Jewish state, Senator Kennedy declared: "It is time that the nations of the world, in the Middle East and elsewhere, realize that Israel is here to stay; she will not surrender, she will not retreat, and we will not let her fall."

The 1960 Presidential Campaign

Kennedy's presidential candidacy was initially greeted with suspicion by many Jewish leaders, some of whom had close ties with his more liberal opponents for the nomination, Adlai Stevenson and Hubert Humphrey, while others were disturbed about Kennedy's failure to speak out forcefully against Senator Joseph McCarthy. But most disturbing was the touchy issue of the candidate's father, Joseph P. Kennedy, who, as ambassador to Great Britain during the late 1930s, was alleged to have been openly anti-Semitic and a vocal supporter of Neville Chamberlain's policy of appeasing the Nazis. The charge that Joseph P. Kennedy was an anti-Semite surfaced in different forms and places during his son's presidential campaign.

Aware of these accusations and the effect they would have on his candidacy, Kennedy agreed to meet with an influential group of Jewish leaders on August 8, 1960, at Abraham Feinberg's Pierre Hotel apartment in New York City. At this private meeting, organized by Feinberg and Philip Klutznick, prominent Jewish communal leaders and Democratic Party fundraisers who were early supporters of his presidential candidacy, Kennedy reassured Jewish supporters of his unequivocal support for the safety and security of Israel, while promising those in attendance that, if elected, his door would always be open to them.

In contrast to the Eisenhower years, when Jewish leaders had been given little access to the White House, this was a commitment to be valued. Kennedy convincingly reassured his listeners that his father's opinions on Jews and Nazi Germany were not his own. The meeting was a success. Those present pledged $500,000 to Kennedy's campaign and promised to mobilize further Jewish support for his candidacy.

This John F. Kennedy pin was distributed during his presidential run.

The presidential election of 1960 was one of the closest in American political history. Kennedy won the popular vote by less than 120,000 votes out of the more than 68 million votes cast. Despite his razor-thin margin of victory over Richard Nixon within the electorate as a whole, Kennedy won overwhelmingly in the Jewish community, receiving an estimated 80 percent of the Jewish vote. The Jewish vote, moreover, played an influential role in Kennedy's victory. In New York, though the Democrats won by only 384,000 votes, Jewish precincts gave Kennedy a plurality of 800,000. In Illinois, Jewish votes were critical to Kennedy's slim victory as well.

At Kennedy's first meeting with Israeli Prime Minister David Ben Gurion at the Waldorf Astoria in New York in the spring of 1961, Ben Gurion had renewed Israel's request for the purchase of surface-to-air Hawk missiles, which the Eisenhower Administration previously had refused. Israel's deepest worry was the growing Arab military arsenal being supplied by the Soviet Union. Kennedy's decision to supply Israel with Hawk antiaircraft missiles for Israel's defense against Arab air attack was an important—indeed, historic—departure from previous American policy. Kennedy was the first American president to agree to sell arms to Israel, overruling both the State Department and the Pentagon. In so doing, the Kennedy Administration ushered in a new era in American-Israeli relations. As president, Kennedy further demonstrated his political debt to American Jews, and his continued friendship for the Jewish state, by tripling the amount of American financial assistance to Israel.

The Plight of Soviet Jewry

One of John F. Kennedy's first acts after taking his seat in the U.S. Senate had been his cosponsorship, in February 1953, of a Senate resolution condemning the persecution of Jews in the Soviet Union. Throughout his presidency, Kennedy remained actively concerned about the plight of Soviet Jews and, on more than one occasion, raised the issue of Soviet mistreatment of Jews with Soviet leader Nikita Khrushchev.

While addressing the General Assembly of the United Nations on September 20, 1963, President Kennedy proclaimed that the Declaration of Human Rights is "not respected when a [Soviet] synagogue is shut down." Two months later, just prior to his assassination in Dallas, Kennedy met in the White House with his old friend and political supporter from Boston, Lewis H. Weinstein, who would soon become president of the Conference of Presidents of Major Jewish Organizations, to discuss what the Kennedy Administration could do to actively protest the increasing persecution of Soviet Jews. When Weinstein told him that no American president since Theodore Roosevelt had intervened with Russian authorities concerning their treatment of Jewish minorities, Kennedy had replied: "Well, here's one president who's ready to do something." As Weinstein left the White House, Kennedy promised him that upon his return from his imminent "political" trip to Texas (to prepare for the 1964 presidential election) he would convene a conference in Washington, with American Jewish leaders, to discuss the problems of Soviet Jews who were being denied their right to practice their religion freely.

Jewish Cabinet Appointees

President Kennedy was the first American president to appoint two Jews to his Cabinet: Abraham Ribicoff as secretary of health, education and welfare, and Arthur Goldberg as secretary of labor.

Abraham Ribicoff

One of the most popular vote-getters in Connecticut history, Abraham Ribicoff (1910-1998) is the only American Jew to have served in both houses of Congress, as governor of a state, and as a member of a presidential Cabinet. Born in 1910 in a tenement district of New Britain, Connecticut, the son of impoverished East European Jewish immigrants, Ribicoff graduated from the University of Chicago Law School during the depths of the Great Depression. Returning to Hartford, where

Flanked by John F. Kennedy and Lyndon B. Johnson, Rabbi Nelson Glueck offers the invocation at JFK's inauguration.

he began to practice law, Ribicoff became a friend and political ally of another young Hartford attorney, the future Democratic Party leader John M. Bailey. In 1948 Bailey persuaded Ribicoff, who at the time was a Hartford police court judge, to run for Congress, although it was widely assumed that no Democratic candidate could defeat his Republican opponent in a year when the G.O.P. candidate for president, Thomas E. Dewey, was expected to trounce President Truman. On election day, Ribicoff won an upset victory, becoming one of nine Jews elected to the House of Representatives that year.

During the four years when they were both young Democratic Congressmen from neighboring New England states, Ribicoff and Kennedy became close friends and political allies. In 1954, when Ribicoff was running for the Democratic nomination for governor of Connecticut, it was Senator John F. Kennedy who gave the keynote address at the Democratic state convention at which Ribicoff was nominated by acclamation. At the Democratic National Convention in 1956, Ribicoff delivered the speech nominating Kennedy, who lost to Estes Kefauver, to run for vice president. Meeting with Kennedy after the

balloting was over, Ribicoff assured him that "in four years, we'll go all the way." In 1960 Ribicoff played a pivotal role in Kennedy's campaign, serving as convention floor manager at the Democratic National Convention that nominated Kennedy for president.

After his election, Kennedy offered Ribicoff his choice of Cabinet positions, and Ribicoff chose to become secretary of health, education and welfare. In 1962 he left the Kennedy Administration to run successfully for the first of three successive terms as U.S. senator from Connecticut.

Arthur J. Goldberg

Chicago-born Arthur J. Goldberg (1908-1990) was one of eleven children of poor Russian Jewish immigrants. He worked his way through Northwestern University Law School, graduating at the top of his class in 1930. Specializing in labor law, he became the preeminent labor lawyer in the United States.

During World War II, Goldberg was appointed head of the labor division of the Office of Strategic Services (O.S.S.). In this capacity, he helped establish operations with anti-Fascist trade union leaders behind Nazi lines to sabotage Nazi production.

In 1948 Goldberg became general counsel for the Congress of Industrial Organizations (CIO) and helped draft the historic agreement merging the American Federation of Labor (AFL) and the CIO in 1955. For the next six years, prior to entering the Kennedy Administration, Goldberg served as special counsel for the AFL-CIO. A sought-after labor negotiator, he also played a major role in mediating strikes in the steel, automobile, and airline industries during the 1950s.

An early supporter of John F. Kennedy's presidential candidacy, in 1961 Goldberg was appointed secretary of labor. In 1962, when Justice Felix Frankfurter announced his retirement from the Supreme Court, President Kennedy appointed Goldberg to fill the vacancy. In so doing, Kennedy continued the tradition of the "Jewish seat" on the Supreme Court that had begun with Woodrow Wilson's appointment of Louis Brandeis in 1916 and had followed with the presidential appointments of Justices Cardozo and Frankfurter.

Other Jewish Appointees and Advisers

Several Jews also held important sub-Cabinet and advisory positions in the Kennedy Administration.

Eugene V. Rostow, a law professor, economist, and former adviser to the State Department who had been appointed dean of the Yale Law School in 1955, served as a member of the advisory council of the Peace Corps and as a consultant to the undersecretary of state from 1961 to 1966. He would serve as undersecretary of state from 1966 to 1969 and would be one of President Lyndon Johnson's closest advisers during the Six-Day War.

The younger brother of Eugene Rostow, Walt W. Rostow was a distinguished professor of economics at the Massachusetts Institute of Technology and author of several influential books on economic history and international affairs, prior to his service in the Kennedy Administration. In 1961 he was appointed deputy special

assistant for national security affairs to President Kennedy and counselor to the Policy Planning Council of the State Department. He would serve as special assistant for national security affairs to President Lyndon B. Johnson from 1966 to 1969.

Wilbur J. Cohen, a social welfare policy expert, had served as a Social Security Administration official, a social policy adviser to the Israeli government, and a professor of public welfare at the University of Michigan. In 1961 he was appointed assistant secretary of the Department of Health, Education and Welfare in the Kennedy Administration.

A distinguished professor of Constitutional Law at the Harvard Law School, Paul A. Freund had served as a clerk to Supreme Court Justice Louis Brandeis and as a special assistant to the attorney general of the United States. During the Kennedy Administration, he served as legal adviser to the president and to the State Department. He turned down President Kennedy's offer to appoint him solicitor general and was on President Kennedy's "short list" of possible candidates for appointment to the U.S. Supreme Court.

Jerome B. Wiesner was a professor of electrical engineering at the Massachusetts Institute of Technology and a member of President Eisenhower's Science Advisory Committee. In 1961 Kennedy appointed him special assistant for science and technology. From 1962 to 1964, he served as director of the Office of Science and Technology in the Kennedy and Johnson administrations. In 1971, he would become president of the Massachusetts Institute of Technology, the first Jew to be appointed to that position.

Philip M. Klutznick, one of the foremost figures in post-World War II American Jewish life, had served as international president of B'nai B'rith, general chairman of the United Jewish Appeal, and president of the American Friends of the Hebrew University and the World Jewish Congress. Long active in Democratic Party politics and fundraising, Klutznick had been appointed federal housing commissioner by Presidents Roosevelt and Truman. An early supporter of John F. Kennedy's presidential candidacy, Klutznick was appointed ambassador to the United Nations Economic and Social Council, and

The swearing-in ceremony of President Kennedy's Cabinet, which included Abraham Ribicoff, secretary of health, education and welfare.

served as chief deputy to Adlai Stevenson, U.S. ambassador to the United Nations. In 1980 President Jimmy Carter would appoint Klutznick secretary of commerce.

Abraham Feinberg, who had hosted the important 1960 Pierre Hotel meeting between Kennedy and Jewish leaders that solidified Jewish support for Kennedy and raised $500,000 for the Kennedy campaign coffers, remained a close adviser of Kennedy throughout his administration. A prominent Jewish business executive and philanthropist who had served as chairman of the Board of Trustees of Brandeis University, Feinberg was a major financial supporter of the Weizmann Institute for Science and for many years had served as chairman of Israel Bonds. He had been the Democratic Party's preeminent Jewish fundraiser for several decades. In 1948 Feinberg had played an influential role in helping to finance President Harry S. Truman's successful whistle-stop campaign for reelection, raising a great deal of money for Truman when he needed it most,

and mobilizing Jewish financial support on Truman's behalf, for which Truman was always grateful.

Myer Feldman, a Washington lawyer who had been one of John F. Kennedy's legislative aides on his Senate staff, handling Israeli and Jewish affairs, was appointed a deputy special counsel to the president. In this capacity, he held the "Jewish portfolio," serving as President Kennedy's liaison to the American Jewish community and adviser on U.S.-Israeli policy. In 1961 Kennedy sent Feldman on a secret mission to Tel Aviv to promise Israel protection by the U.S. Sixth Fleet and the sale of the Hawk missiles that Kennedy and David Ben Gurion had discussed at their Waldorf Astoria meeting earlier in the year.

Richard N. Goodwin, who had graduated first in his class at Harvard Law School and had served as a law clerk to Supreme Court Justice Felix Frankfurter before working on the staff of a Senate subcommittee investigating the television quiz-show scandals, had joined John F. Kennedy's

Senate staff as a speechwriter in 1959. During the Kennedy presidential campaign, Goodwin wrote speeches on Latin America, coining the term "Alliance for Progress," and subsequently, as a member of the White House staff, wrote the speech that President Kennedy delivered on this subject in March of 1961. In late 1961, at the age of twenty-nine, Goodwin was appointed deputy assistant secretary of state for inter-American affairs. In 1964, during the Johnson Administration, Goodwin would rejoin the White House staff as a speechwriter on Latin America and urban affairs. He would work as a speechwriter for Robert F. Kennedy during his 1968 presidential campaign and would later marry the Pulitzer Prize-winning historian and presidential biographer Doris Kearns Goodwin.

The Assassination

During his short tenure as president, John F. Kennedy captured the imagination of the nation with his vision of a "new frontier." In his 1961 Inaugural Address, Kennedy had prophetically warned that his far-reaching program would not be completed "in the life of this administration, nor even perhaps in our lifetime on this planet." To the grief and horror of the nation, these words came tragically true when, on Friday, November 22, 1963, President Kennedy was assassinated in Dallas after having served in office for only two years and ten months. He left behind a grieving widow, Jacqueline, and two small children, Caroline and John Jr.

On the Saturday and Sunday following the Kennedy assassination, more Jews and Christians attended synagogue and church than on any other day in the nation's history. Throughout the country, Jews who had not planned to attend Sabbath services came to synagogues to find comfort in their shared grief. Rabbis put their sermon notes aside and spoke extemporaneously, reaching out for the words to express their shock and sorrow.

Rabbi Levi Olan, spiritual leader of Dallas's largest synagogue, Temple Emanu-El, eulogized the fallen president with stirring spontaneity and depth, generated out of both the guilt and grief felt by his congregants and the entire Jewish community of their city.

In Washington, D.C., the following week, the newly-inaugurated president, Lyndon Johnson, attended a community-wide interfaith Thanksgiving Day Service at which Rabbi Stanley Rabinowitz, of Washington's Adas Israel Congregation, delivered the sermon. Entitled "Out of Evil," the sermon expressed the idea, based on an observation of Rabbi Akiba, that evil can be redeemed, that every evil situation contains within it the opportunity to extract from it a blessing.

The following day, Lady Bird Johnson, the first lady, called Adas Israel to ask for a copy of the text of the sermon. When President Johnson spoke at the dedication of a synagogue in Austin, Texas, four weeks after the assassination, he reiterated his commitment to carry out the ideas and ideals of President Kennedy's unfinished program, and then quoted Rabbi Rabinowitz's words, which, he said, "I have remembered so vividly ever since Thanksgiving Day," thus reminding those in attendance of its theme that out of evil can come unanticipated blessings and achievements.

[D.G.D.]

The John F. Kennedy Memorial in Jerusalem. The structure consists of fifty-one spokes, representing the fifty states and the District of Columbia.

Lyndon B. Johnson

Served from 1963 to 1969

Born on August 27, 1908, near Stonewall, Texas

Member of the Disciples of Christ denomination

Married Claudia Alta "Lady Bird" Taylor on November 17, 1934

Father to two daughters

Candidate of the Democratic Party

Assumed the presidency on November 22, 1963 following the assassination of
John F. Kennedy; elected to a full term on November 3, 1964

Vice president under Johnson: Hubert Humphrey (second term)

Inaugural Address delivered on January 20, 1965

Died on January 22, 1973, near San Antonio, Texas

Thirty-Sixth President of the United States

ALTHOUGH HE HAD SERVED AS JOHN F. Kennedy's vice president for three years, Lyndon Baines Johnson's name was not well-known to most Americans prior to November 22, 1963. Suddenly, following the tragic events of that day, when the life of the popular, youthful President Kennedy was suddenly cut short by an assassin's bullets in Dallas, Texas, Johnson was catapulted into the limelight.

Johnson, however, was an old hand at politics, a career he aspired to from the time he was a very young man. He was able to trace his ancestry back to a great-great-grandfather, John Johnson of Georgia, who fought in the American Revolution, as well as to other relatives who fought in the Civil War. His father was a farmer who, although not prosperous, served as a member of the Texas House of Representatives in the early 1900s.

Lyndon Johnson's early childhood was not a luxurious one, and to help his family, which often was in financial straits, he would earn money as a hired hand on neighboring farms. He also would shine shoes in barber shops and go off to trap animals so that he might sell their skins.

In 1918, when his father was running for re-election for the Texas House, Lyndon went along on the campaign trail. It was then that the urge to pursue a political career took hold and, as he confided to a friend, "Someday I'm going to be the president of the United States."

Johnson's first teacher was his mother, who taught him to read when he was only four years old. He attended elementary and high school in Johnson City. After graduating in 1924, he roamed around for two years and then, at the urging of his mother, enrolled in Southwest Texas State Teachers College, from which he graduated in 1930. During this period, Johnson's interest in politics

remained strong, so much so that he and a friend crashed the 1928 Democratic National Convention, which was being held in Houston, Texas.

In 1934, while serving as a secretary to a Texas congressman, Lyndon Johnson met and married Claudia Alta "Lady Bird" Taylor. He was twenty-six, she twenty-one. She encouraged him to pursue a political career, and in 1937 he won the congressional seat in the Tenth District of Texas. In 1941, in a special election, he tried to win an open Senate seat, but lost to Governor W. Lee "Pappy" O'Daniel, while retaining his seat in the U.S. House of Representatives.

In 1940, with war beginning to rage in Europe, Johnson joined the naval reserve. During World War II he served on active duty as a lieutenant commander in the U.S. Navy from December 1941, when Japan bombed Pearl Harbor, to July 1942. At that point, President Roosevelt ordered all members of Congress in the military to return to Washington and resume their duties as legislators.

In 1949 Johnson was elected senator over Governor Coke Stevenson by a mere eighty-seven votes, and served in that capacity until Democratic presidential nominee John F. Kennedy chose him to be his running mate in 1960.

In November 1963, with attention still focused on the slain president, Lyndon Johnson was somehow able to assert himself and take hold of the reins of government. Five days after the assassination, with the nation in shock and in grief, Johnson felt it appropriate to assure American citizens that the country would survive the tragedy and would forge ahead on the path President Kennedy had mapped out. On November 27, 1963, in an address to a joint session of Congress, he told the nation, through its legislature, that he would pursue the progressive and farsighted policies of John F. Kennedy, and that the agents of hate and violence would not prevail.

Johnson was not sure how well his message had been received, but his spirit was elevated when he and his family attended a citywide, non-denominational Thanksgiving service, held on Thursday, November 28, 1963, at the Mount Vernon Place Methodist Church in Washington, D.C. The designated preacher for the occasion was Rabbi Stanley Rabinowitz of Adas Israel Congregation.

In his sermon, Rabbi Rabinowitz praised the new president for his courage in addressing the nation so soon after this national trauma and for his hopeful message that the American people could look forward to an end to the teaching of hate, evil, and violence.

President Johnson was so impressed with the rabbi's sermon that he wrote him immediately:

> Dear Rabbi Rabinowitz:
>
> Your sermon was eloquent and compassionate and so very much to the point in these somber times. It comforted me greatly and I thank you for that. You would please me so much if I could have a copy of the sermon.
>
> Sincerely,
> Lyndon B. Johnson

One month later, another letter arrived from the president:

> Dear Rabbi:
>
> Thank you for copies of your wonderful Thanksgiving Day sermon. Your sincere expression of interest during these days of transition has provided a source of strength for me. I am deeply grateful for your thoughtfulness. My best wishes.
>
> Lyndon B. Johnson

With Lyndon Johnson's spirits renewed, he put his trademark wheeler-dealer skills to work and began resuscitating many of Kennedy's programs, ultimately bringing them to fruition. Among the slew of legislative proposals Johnson was able to push through Congress were the most comprehensive civil rights and antipoverty programs the country had ever known or expected. Many Jewish advisers and supporters were by his side during this remarkably creative period.

Earliest Jewish Contacts

A number of Jews had been supportive of Johnson as he made his way up the political ladder. One of his earliest financial backers was fellow Texan James Novy, who became treasurer of Johnson's first successful 1949 campaign for a Senate seat. Not far behind was Arthur Krim, chairman of the board of United Artists.

Another early staunch supporter of LBJ was Abraham Feinberg, who served as chairman of the Board of Trustees of Brandeis University. Feinberg was a staunch Zionist who, in the 1940s, headed an American group that provided arms for Jewish settlers in Palestine. He had been instrumental in winning over the Jewish vote during the Kennedy presidential campaign, and Johnson, in turn, would reap similar benefits from his close association with Feinberg.

These positive contacts left Johnson with a warm, sympathetic feeling toward Jews and their concerns, which translated into consideration for the welfare of the young state of Israel. When a group of Jewish leaders called upon Johnson soon after he was elevated to the presidency, he said to them: "You have lost a good friend [in Kennedy], but you have found a better one in me."

The Fortas Phenomenon

No one individual was more responsible for Johnson's rise to political power than Abe Fortas (1910-1982). Born in Memphis, Tennessee, the son of a cabinetmaker, Fortas proved himself a brilliant student by the time he graduated from Southwestern College in 1930 and from Yale Law School in 1933. Upon graduating from Yale, he was immediately asked to join its law faculty.

In 1937 Fortas caught the eye of William O. Douglas, who had been called to Washington by President Roosevelt to head the Securities and Exchange Commission. (In 1939 Roosevelt would

Lyndon Johnson makes an emphatic point with Abraham Fortas.

appoint Douglas to the Supreme Curt seat vacated by Justice Brandeis.) Believing that Fortas was "the most brilliant legal mind ever to come out of Yale," Douglas prevailed upon him to become his assistant and chief legal counsel.

From 1942 to 1946 Fortas served as undersecretary of the interior. In 1945 he was an adviser to the American delegation at the San Francisco conference at which the United Nations was founded. It was during this period that Fortas became friendly with Lyndon Johnson who, though a freshman member of the House of Representatives, had become chairman of the Naval Affairs subcommittee investigating waste in the conduct of the naval war. President Roosevelt was impressed by Johnson's handling of the assignment, as was Fortas. In time, Johnson and Fortas became close friends.

In 1946 Fortas became a partner in Arnold,

Fortas, & Porter, which was one of the most respected and influential law firms in Washington. Two years later, when Lyndon Johnson defeated Governor Coke Stevenson in the Texas Senate race by eighty-seven votes, Stevenson contested the election, and Johnson called upon his friend Fortas to represent him. Fortas was victorious, and Johnson earned the amusing nickname "Landslide Lyndon."

While the friendly association between President Johnson and Abe Fortas was of little significance at the outset, it became newsworthy when, two years before the Israeli-Arab Six-Day War, Johnson appointed Fortas to a vacant seat on the Supreme Court.

Reaching Out to Israel

David Ben-Gurion, Israel's first prime minister, recalled meeting Lyndon Johnson when he was Senate majority leader. Ben-Gurion was impressed with the senator's self-confidence and maturity, and the deft manner in which he exercised his considerable power. He also was impressed with Johnson's compassion, as reported in *Moshe Pearlman's Ben-Gurion Looks Back*:

> When I told him [Johnson] about our immigrants from backward or oppressive countries, how we took them in, housed them, trained them for productive lives, he reacted as if he was himself living the process, as if the man in him could feel all they went through. The politician in him could understand our administrative problems, and the statesman in him could recognize the grandeur of the human adventure.

Abba Eban, who was Israel's first ambassador to the United States, had a similar reaction when he first met Lyndon Johnson. After entertaining Senator Johnson in his Washington home, Eban observed: "He seemed to know nothing about Israel in the beginning, but he probed away with all the tenacity of a ruthless dentist and with about the same amount of clinical amiability."

Learning of the dramatic story of the rise of Israel directly from the lips of the "fathers" of

COURTESY OF THE NEW YORK PUBLIC LIBRARY

President and Mrs. Johnson greet Prime Minister and Mrs. Eshkol at a reception given by Israeli Ambassador and Mrs. Harmon in Washington, June 1964.

Having defeated Republican Barry Goldwater in the 1964 presidential election by a large margin, Johnson was well aware that an estimated 90 percent of Jewish voters supported him. In 1966 Johnson invited Israeli president Zalman Shazar to the White House, and later, when Johnson met with the Israeli ambassador to the United States, British-born Abraham Harman, Fortas joined them. Harman had been instructed by Prime Minister Levi Eshkol to request that the United States form a military alliance with Israel. Johnson told Harman that there was no need for such a treaty since the United States was already committed to the security of Israel, and that the Egyptians and Russians were well aware of the fact.

On May 22, 1967, in a speech to the Knesset, Eshkol, eager to avoid war with Egypt, stated categorically that Israel had no intention of attacking Egypt or any other Arab country or of undermining their security. Yet on May 22, Egyptian president Gamal Abdel Nasser closed the Strait of Tiran to Israeli shipping and to all vessels bound for Israel carrying "strategic materials."

Johnson inquired of former president Eisenhower how, in 1957, the U.S. government viewed the right of Israel to free passage through the strait and reported Eisenhower's response: "General Eisenhower sent me a message stating his view that the Israelis' right of access to the Gulf of Aqaba was definitely part of the 'commitment' we had made to them." Johnson then reaffirmed that "the Gulf of Aqaba is an international waterway and that the blockade of Israeli shipping is, therefore, illegal."

When Israeli foreign minister Abba Eban visited with the president, he expressed pleasure at Johnson's explicitly stated position but was profoundly disappointed by the attitude of Secretary of State Dean Rusk, who was more worried about the Soviet Union's reaction than Israel's welfare. Johnson did not share Rusk's view and, encour-

Israel tended to make the president think of Israelis as modern-day Texans repulsing the Arabs like Sam Houston did the Mexicans in 1836.

There were few pro-Israel advocates in the high echelons of the Johnson Administration. After agreeing to do an interview with *The New York Times*, Johnson consulted McGeorge Bundy, who had been national security adviser under Eisenhower. On Thursday, February 6, 1964, the two men had the following telephone conversation:

> BUNDY: I would hold my fire very carefully, Mr. President. . . . You know as well as I do what kind of a crowd they are.
> LBJ: No, I don't.
> BUNDY: Well, the *Times* editorial page is a soft page, Mr. President. It makes Walter Lippmann look like a warmonger. They're clever, but they don't have a whole lot of judgment. You've got to show them you're a man of peace without letting them call the tune, I think, and you're damned good at that. . . . They've been good to the administration, but I think they're going to be watching a little bit. They're not Zionists, but they're influenced by Zionists.

Abba Eban conferring with President Johnson in 1967.

ington that any unidentified ships in the war zone would be attacked, Washington failed to respond. And when as a result of the attack over two hundred American sailors lost their lives, Israel informed Washington immediately of the "mistaken action" and offered to compensate the victims and their families. But this explanation did not satisfy Secretary of State Dean Rusk and Thomas H. Moore, chairman of the Joint Chiefs of Staff. Even Clark Clifford, at the time chief of the American Foreign Intelligence Board and always a strong advocate of Israel, called the attack "inexcusable" and said that Israel should be held "completely responsible."

President Johnson was far less condemnatory, agreeing with Undersecretary of State Eugene Rostow that to attribute ulterior motives to the Israeli attack "made no goddamn sense at all." American Jews were pleased with Johnson's attitude and display of support for Israel.

aged by Walt Rostow, whom the president had appointed as his national security adviser in 1966, and by Walt's brother Eugene, who was undersecretary of state, Johnson approved the sale of weapons to Israel. Ultimately, Israel assumed the initiative and took decisive military action on June 5, 1967. Within six days Israel had defeated the Egyptian and other Arab armies, and the president as well as the secretary of state were delighted.

The USS Liberty Saga

While Israel was victorious in the Six-Day War, which resulted in the occupation of the Gaza Strip, the Sinai, the Golan Heights, and the reunification of the Old City of Jerusalem, it came at a high cost of soldiers killed and injured. It also led to hurt feelings between members of the Johnson Administration and top Israeli officials.

On June 8, 1967, the fourth day of the Six-Day War, Israeli jets and missile boats opened fire on the *USS Liberty*, an American surveillance vessel that was plying the waters off the coast of Gaza, in the Mediterranean. Although at the outset of the war the chief of staff of Israel's Defense Forces, General Yitzhak Rabin, notified Wash-

Emanuel Celler

While serving as a senator, Johnson was deeply impressed by the courage of Brooklyn-born congressman Emanuel Celler (1888–1981), who, from his freshman term in 1922, had become involved in immigration legislation and civil rights issues. By 1948 Celler had gained sufficient seniority to become chairman of the House Judiciary Committee, a position he used to deny funds to the House Committee on Un-American Activities led by the anti-Semitic Democratic congressman John R. Rankin of Mississippi. Rankin never passed up the opportunity to demean his fellow Democrat by referring to him as "the Jewish gentleman," and when Celler objected, Rankin would say he wondered whether Celler was objecting to being called "Jewish" or a "gentleman." (In June 1941, Rankin had indirectly been the cause of the death of Representative M. Michael Edelstein, a Democrat from New York. After responding to a vicious anti-Semitic attack by

Rankin, Edelstein collapsed and died of a heart attack.)

Lyndon Johnson appreciated and acknowledged the efforts of Emanuel Celler, who was a prime mover of the Voting Rights Bill of 1965. Johnson considered the passage of this historic legislation to be the greatest accomplishment of his administration. In his *Means of Ascent: The Years of Lyndon Johnson*, Robert A. Caro concurred: "Abraham Lincoln struck out against the chains of black Americans, but it was Lyndon Johnson who led them into the voting booths."

To accomplish his goal, Johnson exerted pressure on Celler. After the president delivered his January 4, 1965 State of the Union address, which set forth his goal of creating in America a "Great Society," Johnson cornered Celler, then seventy-six years old, and said, "Manny, I want you to start hearings tonight [on voting rights legislation]."

Celler protested: "Mr. President, I can't push the committee or it might get out of hand. I'm scheduling hearings for next week."

Johnson's eyes narrowed. He stared at Celler with a piercing look, jabbed his pointed index finger at the congressman's face, and said sternly: "Start them this week, Manny! And hold night sessions, too!"

Celler followed orders, and in August 1965 Johnson signed into law the Voting Rights Bill, which secured full voting rights for blacks, primarily by eliminating literary tests, poll taxes, and other obstacles.

Arthur J. Goldberg

One of the great legal minds of the United States in the mid-1900s was Chicago-born Arthur Goldberg. In 1948 he had been appointed counsel for the United Steelworkers of America and the CIO. Noted for his skill as a mediator in labor disputes, President Kennedy appointed him Secretary of Labor, a position he held for two years (1960–1962) before being appointed to the Supreme Court.

On November 22, 1963, after Vice President Johnson was sworn in as president of the United States, he flew back immediately from Dallas to Washington. As he stepped out of *Air Force One*, Johnson spotted Goldberg, who was among those assembled at the airport to greet the new president. Later that evening, as was revealed on Johnson's White House Tapes, the president called Goldberg and said:

> I want you to be thinking about what I ought to do to try to bring all these elements together and unite the country to maintain and preserve our system in the world, because if it starts falling to pieces . . . why, we could deteriorate pretty quick.
>
> I want to give some thought, by the way, whether we ought to have a Joint Session of Congress after and what would I say to them. I want you to think about . . . how I ought to do it without . . . I mean, with dignity and reserve and without being down on my knees, but at the same time letting them know of my respect and confidence . . .

In July 1965, Lyndon Johnson would persuade Goldberg to resign from the Supreme Court and replace Adlai Stevenson, who had died of a heart attack, as U.S. ambassador to the United Nations. Abe Fortas was then appointed to the Supreme Court to succeed Goldberg.

Sheldon Stanley Cohen

When President Kennedy was assassinated and Lyndon Johnson was sworn in, Sheldon Cohen (1927–) was one of the first persons to whom the newly sworn-in president turned for assistance.

Born in Washington, D.C., Cohen graduated from George Washington University in 1950 with the highest of honors, and in 1952 he was awarded a doctorate in jurisprudence. Cohen served as legislative attorney in the office of the chief counsel of the Internal Revenue Service from 1952 to 1956 and as chief counsel from 1963 to 1965. In 1965 he was appointed commissioner of the Internal Revenue Service, a position he held from 1965 until his retirement in 1969.

The night of the Kennedy assassination, Johnson called Sheldon and requested that he

President and Mrs. Johnson attending the wedding of Cokie Boggs and Steve Roberts. From left to right: Barbara Boggs Sigmond, Hale Boggs, President Johnson, Mrs. Johnson, Steve Roberts, and Cokie (Boggs) Roberts.

Intermarriage Wedding

To placate the objections of Jewish journalist Steve Roberts, who did not want his marriage to Cokie Boggs to take place in a church, the couple decided to hold the ceremony in the home of the bride's father, Congressman Hale Boggs of Louisiana. In attendance, in addition to President Johnson, were more than three hundred Democrats from the House of Representatives. Cokie's uncle, a priest, presided over the ceremony. Since a rabbi could not be found to co-officiate, the couple turned to Arthur J. Goldberg, the former Supreme Court justice who at the time was U.S. ambassador to the United Nations. Goldberg recited some Hebrew prayers and then addressed the couple. The ceremony ended with the traditional Jewish custom of the groom breaking a glass underfoot.

assist in putting Johnson's personal affairs in order. Sheldon agreed, and around eight o'clock, as he was about to leave for Friday night synagogue services, he received a call from Abe Fortas, asking that they meet at Fortas's home.

Present at the meeting, which would take place shortly thereafter, were Walter Jenkins, Johnson's personal assistant, and Fortas's wife, a tax attorney, in addition to the president, Fortas, and Cohen. After analyzing the president's financial portfolio, they proceeded to prepare a series of trust instruments and gifts, as well as a transfer of assets. On the following Thursday, the president signed the documents that had been prepared. It was the same day on which Johnson heard the sermon delivered by Rabbi Stanley Rabinowitz at the Washington interfaith Thanksgiving service.

In the spring of 1967, when the Egyptians ejected the United Nations Emergency Force from the Sinai and Israel was fretful over its survival, Sheldon Cohen was approached by leading Jews in Israel and in the United States to use his influence with the president and urge him to extend military aid to the Israelis. At first Sheldon balked, but he finally decided to compose a letter asking the president to intervene for the sake of peace:

May 31, 1967
Dear Mr. President:

Since taking office, I have written to you very seldom, usually in the course of government business. For the first time I feel impelled to write to you on a subject which has no relationship to my official position.

I am an American citizen today by the grace of God and the foresight of my grandfather, who immigrated to this country 60 years ago. This country has nurtured its immigrants, and they and their descendants have helped to make the country strong with the vigor of their spirit and a blend of their diverse cultures. My father arrived here at the age of five—now I occupy a position of great responsibility in our government, thanks to you.

When my grandfather and others like him ventured forth to the United States, many of his friends and relatives stayed behind. Those who did so either met death in a Nazi crematorium, or, because of a miracle of survival, sought freedom and hope in the new land of Israel. Those who were lucky enough to make it to Israel now face a new tyrant with a new crematorium. This time there is no place to which they can run.

I know your burdens are heavy and I do not wish to add to them, but I feel I must tell you that when I think of the Israelis, I think that there, but for the grace of God, goes me and Faye and my children.

As an American I feel we must stand by the only democratic ally we have in the Near East. President Eisenhower pledged that the sea routes to Israel would remain open. It was only in the light of these assurances that Israel removed its troops from its position in Sinai. We must find a way to help Israel defend itself—hopefully without bloodshed or harm to any of its neighbors, but aggression must be stopped.

Please forgive this emotional appeal, but you know I am sincere in everything I do and I feel very strongly about this matter.

Best personal regards.
Faithfully yours,
Sheldon S. Cohen

Lyndon Johnson responded as follows:

June 15, 1967
Honorable Sheldon S. Cohen
Commissioner of Internal Revenue
U. S. Treasury Department
Washington, D. C.

Dear Sheldon:

Thank you for sharing your thoughts with me during the tensions of the Middle East crisis. You know that I share your concern.

Now we must all do what we can to try to produce stable peace in that deeply troubled area.

Sincerely,
Lyndon B. Johnson

Lesser-Known Figures

Johnson's formal education was not particularly extensive. He attended Southwest Texas State College from 1927 to 1930 and studied law briefly at Georgetown University from 1934 to 1935. Upon assuming the presidency, he realized that in order to make his dream of a Great Society a reality, he would have to create a task force of intellectual giants who, as he put it, "possess a gift of originality and imagination." These experts would help him craft a legislative program that he could submit to Congress in January 1965.

One of the men Johnson selected in 1964 was Eric Frederick Goldman. Born in Washington, D.C., Goldman was a professor of history at Princeton University. Johnson named him special consultant to the president.

While serving at the White House, Goldman also served as a member of the academic council of the American Friends of the Hebrew University. In 1966 he tendered his resignation to the president and two years later published *The Tragedy of Lyndon Johnson*. The "tragedy" related to what happened on June 14, 1965, when a group of authors and others in the arts were invited to participate in a White House program. The idea backfired when poet Robert Lowell and novelist John Hersey read selections from their writings critical of the war in Vietnam, lamenting the immorality of allowing it to continue. Johnson's wife, Lady Bird, who was always at his side as a loyal helpmate, was so incensed at these performances that she labeled the day "Black Tuesday."

Among others who served on Johnson's elite intellectual task force were Professor David Riesman (1909–) of Harvard University and Milwaukee-born Wilbur Cohen, a social welfare authority who, from 1936 to 1956, was employed in the Social Security Administration. Cohen became undersecretary of the Department of Health, Education and Welfare during the Johnson Administration, and it was during Cohen's tenure that the Medicare and Medicaid health programs were enacted.

The Fortas Scandal

One year after the Six-Day War ended, a second opportunity arose to reward Abe Fortas for his counsel, loyalty, and friendship. In June 1968, after Earl Warren had announced his intention to resign as chief justice of the Supreme Court, having served in that position for fifteen years, Johnson nominated Fortas as Warren's successor. Opponents of the nomination dug into Fortas's past and discovered that while sitting on the high court, Fortas had been consulted by the president and had advised him on a host of political matters. When it also was discovered that while serv-

ing on the bench Fortas was being paid, contrary to law, an annual fee of twenty thousand dollars for serving as trustee of financier Louis E. Wolfson's charitable foundation, and that Wolfson was serving a prison sentence for stock manipulation, objections to Fortas's nomination mounted. In response, President Johnson immediately withdrew Fortas's nomination, and on May 14, 1969, Fortas resigned as a justice of the Supreme Court.

Aside from Abe Fortas, Johnson came to depend upon many talented American Jews to fulfill his vision of America. Among those who helped him most in formulating policy and carrying out his programs were Emanuel Celler and Arthur Goldberg.

Post-Presidential Years

Although Johnson had won the 1964 election in a landslide victory over Barry Goldwater, he announced in March 1968 that he would not seek another term. By then, the Vietnam War had crushed his spirit. The perpetual hounding of antiwar activists had grown intolerable. In addition, Johnson's popularity waned to the point that he could no longer be sure that the Democrats would renominate him, especially in view of the growing popularity of Bobby Kennedy.

On Monday morning, January 19, 1969, the outgoing president accompanied Richard Nixon to the Capitol for Nixon's inauguration. A few hours later, the Johnsons were driven to Andrews Air Force Base, where *Air Force One* was waiting to fly them to their ranch in Texas.

Four years later, on January 22, 1973, while traveling from the LBJ ranch to San Antonio, Texas, Johnson was stricken by his third heart attack and died en route to the hospital.

[A.J.K.]

Abe Fortas, U.S. Supreme Court justice (left), with Israel Supreme Court Justice Moshe Landau.

Richard M. Nixon

Served from 1969 to 1974

Born on January 9, 1913, in Yorba Linda, California

Member of the Quaker denomination

Married Thelma Catherine Patricia Ryan on June 21, 1940

Father to two daughters

Candidate of the Republican Party

Vice presidents under Nixon: Spiro Agnew, resigned in 1973
Gerald Ford replaced Agnew

First Inaugural Address delivered on January 20, 1969
Second Inaugural Address delivered on January 20, 1973

Died on April 22, 1994, in New York City

Thirty-Seventh President of the United States

HEN RICHARD MILHOUS NIXON WAS elected vice president of the United States in 1952, he became the youngest Republican ever to serve in that office. When President Dwight D. Eisenhower was convalescing from a heart attack in 1955, Nixon became the first vice president to preside over Cabinet White House meetings. The road from the vice-presidency to the presidency was an arduous one for Nixon, but after many failed attempts, he finally achieved his goal.

Of Scotch-Irish heritage on his father's side and German-English-Irish on his mother's side, Richard Nixon grew up amid poverty in Yorba Linda, California; in 1922 his family moved to Whittier, California. Richard decided early on that he wanted to be a lawyer. Legend has it that when he was ten years old and the Teapot Dome scandal of the Harding Administration was making headlines, he said to his mother, "I would like to become a lawyer—an honest lawyer who can't be bought by crooks."

When his younger brother, Arthur, died of tuberculosis, Richard made up his mind that he would ease the anguish of his parents by making them proud of his accomplishments. A hard worker and outstanding student in elementary and high school, at Whittier College (1930–1934) he majored in history and was captain of the debating team. Graduating second in his class of eighty-five students, Nixon then received a scholarship to Duke University Law School, where he excelled once again, graduating third in a class of twenty-five students. In 1937 he was admitted to the California bar.

After practicing law in Whittier for five years, Richard Nixon served a four-year stint (June 1942 to March 1946) in the U.S. Navy, rising from lieu-

tenant junior grade to lieutenant commander. Upon his discharge, Nixon's interest in politics peaked, and in 1946 he defeated Democratic Representative Jerry Voorhis for his congressional seat. Two years later he was reelected without opposition and in 1950 defeated Democratic representative Helen Gahagan Douglas in a bitter battle for an open Senate seat. Nixon flooded the state with five hundred thousand "pink sheets" falsely linking Douglas with the Communist Party and earning himself the nickname Tricky Dick. He won the Senate seat but never lived down the epithet.

Because of Nixon's strong advocacy of vigilance against Communist infiltration of the U.S. government, and because of his status as senator from a large western state, Dwight D. Eisenhower chose Nixon as his running mate in the 1952 presidential election. After serving as vice president for two terms under Eisenhower, Nixon had hoped to inherit the presidency, but in the 1960 election he was narrowly defeated by John F. Kennedy, the Democratic senator from Massachusetts.

In 1962 Nixon sought elective office as governor of California, but again he met defeat, this time at the hands of Democratic incumbent Edmund G. (Pat) Brown. In acknowledging the loss, Nixon lashed out at reporters: "For sixteen years, ever since the [Alger] Hiss case, you've had a lot of fun [attacking me]. Just think how much you're going to be missing. You won't have Nixon to kick around anymore, because, gentlemen, this is my last press conference."

This was hardly Nixon's last press conference— or his last bid for public office. Six years later, like the phoenix in the ancient Egyptian myth that lived in the Arabian desert and every five hun-

This Richard Nixon pin was distributed during his run for the presidency.

dred years consumed itself in flames, only to rise again from its own ashes, Nixon's doomed career was revived. In 1968 he managed to win the Republican nomination for president over such popular contenders as Governor Nelson Rockefeller of New York and Governor Ronald Reagan of California, and he went on to defeat Democratic candidate Hubert H. Humphrey. In 1972 Nixon, again the nominee of his party, roundly defeated liberal Democrat George S. McGovern in the general election.

Nixon chose Spiro T. Agnew of Maryland as his running mate in 1968 and again in 1972. During Nixon's second term, Agnew would resign after pleading "no contest" to income tax evasion. He would be replaced by House minority leader Gerald R. Ford, making the Ford succession the first time a president would avail himself of the twenty-first amendment to the Constitution, which allowed the president to fill a vacancy in the office of the vice president.

As early as 1950, in his race for the Senate seat in California against Helen Gahagan Douglas, Nixon felt that Jews did not support him sufficiently. Though he won the election, the fact that he did not receive the Jewish vote would vex him throughout his political life.

In August 1960, as the Republican candidate for president, Nixon remarked: "The preservation of the State of Israel is what I regard as one of the essential goals of United States foreign policy." Even so, the Jewish vote went overwhelmingly to Kennedy.

The Jewish community largely distrusted Nixon throughout his political career. Despite Nixon's intense effort to woo Jewish votes through pro-Israel speeches, Jewish support continued to be weak in both of his presidential campaigns. In 1968, 80 percent of the Jewish vote went to Hubert Humphrey, 17 percent to Nixon, and 2 percent to George Wallace. In the 1972 race, 65 percent went to George McGovern and 35 percent to Nixon.

Four hundred forty-five hours of White House tapes, recorded in 1971 and made public in the summer of 1999, reveal Nixon's view of Jews as antipathy bordering on paranoia. When laying the groundwork for reelection to the presidency in 1972, Nixon believed it was important to expose his "enemies," including Jews. On September 13, 1971, he ordered his chief of staff, H. R. Haldeman, to instruct the Internal Revenue Service to "go after" prominent Democratic campaign donors. "Please get me the names of the Jews," he ordered. "You know, the big Jewish contributors of the Democrats. . . ."

On another tape Nixon instructs Haldeman to "look at any sensitive areas [of government] where Jews are involved . . . Generally, you can't trust the bastards. They turn on you . . . . [Put] someone in charge who is not Jewish," Nixon instructed, to review all key agencies.

As Nixon became more and more fearful that the high rate of unemployment in the United States might affect his standing in the polls, he ordered the removal of Julius Shiskin, head of the Bureau of Labor Statistics. He then ordered a

Richard Nixon delivers his Inaugural Address on January 29, 1969.

report on the ethnic background of all of that bureau's employees. When Nixon received the report, he asked in amazement: "They are all Jews?" To which aide Charles Colson responded: "Every one of them."

The Jekyll and Hyde Syndrome

Despite Nixon's uncomplimentary comments about Jews as a whole, in his personal dealings Nixon's bias generally remained disguised. The need to succeed at all costs made the president eager to reach out to the brightest and most talented Jews and convince them to work in his administration.

Among the prominent Jews selected by Nixon were Leonard Garment, Nixon's chief political adviser; Herbert Stein, head of the President's Council of Economic Advisers; Austrian-born Arthur Burns, chairman of the Federal Reserve; William Safire, speechwriter; and German-born Henry Kissinger, national security adviser and later secretary of state.

Leonard Garment

As the Watergate crisis would grow more ominous and begin to overwhelm President Nixon, he would turn to Leonard Garment (1924-), among others, for counsel and advice. Garment, who had been denied entry into Columbia University Law School because of its Jewish quota, received his law degree from Brooklyn Law School in 1949 and then joined the prestigious law firm of Mudge Rose Guthrie and Alexander, which specialized in litigation. Garment befriended Nixon when the latter joined the law firm in 1963, and Nixon would often visit Garment in his Brooklyn Heights home. Nixon loved to play piano, and Garment, a jazz enthusiast, organized a group called Lenny Garment and His Orchestra.

Although Garment was a liberal Democrat, when Nixon announced that he was seeking the Republican nomination for president, Garment joined his campaign staff, heading the media division. When the president was elected, Garment helped Nixon select his Cabinet and later was asked by the president to become White House

Richard Nixon with Lyndon B. Johnson.

adviser on minority problems. When the Watergate scandal was at its apex, Garment advised Nixon to fire H. R. Haldeman and John Ehrlichman, the president's close White House aides who were implicated in the coverup. Nixon then asked Garment to replace John Dean as White House counsel and help mount a defense on the Watergate matter.

When Garment was denied access to the presidential tapes, he felt that he could no longer serve as Nixon's lawyer and tendered his resignation. Nixon then blamed him for not burning the tapes.

Garment would return to Washington when President Gerald R. Ford asked him to represent the United States on the United Nations Human Rights Commission.

In *Crazy Rhythm*, published in 1997, Garment describes his long relationship with Nixon and his activity as White House lawyer during Watergate.

Herbert Stein

An expert in monetary policy as well as tax and budget issues, Herbert Stein (1916–) did his undergraduate work at Williams College, where he earned a bachelor's degree, and postgraduate work at the University of Chicago, where he was awarded a doctorate in economics.

From 1972 to 1974, Stein was chairman of the President's Council of Economic Advisers. In 1974 he became a professor of economics at the University of Virginia, where he would teach for the next ten years. During that time, he was a member of the White House Economic Policy Advisory Board (1981–1989).

During the Clinton Administration, Stein would be invited to join the President's Commission to Study Capital Budgeting.

Arthur Burns

Arthur Burns (1904–1987), born in Stanislau, Austria, immigrated to the United States with his family when he was ten years old. They settled in Bayonne, New Jersey.

Burns earned a doctorate in economics from Columbia University in 1934. Between 1927 and 1944, he was engaged at Rutgers University as an instructor in economics and from 1944 to 1969 he served as professor of economics at Columbia.

President Eisenhower called upon Burns in 1953 to act as chairman of his Council of Economic Advisers, a position he held until 1956. When John F. Kennedy became president, Burns was invited to be a member of his Advisory Committee on Labor-Management Policy.

In 1968, as he pursued the Republican nomination for president, Nixon asked Arthur Burns to be his economic adviser. Burns was instrumental in helping Nixon capture the nomination over Nelson Rockefeller and Ronald Reagan. From January 1969 to January 1970, Burns served as Nixon's White House counsel and in February 1970 was rewarded for all his efforts in behalf of Richard Nixon by being appointed chairman of the Board of Governors of the Federal Reserve System, a position he held until March 1978, and in which he advocated fiscal and monetary restraint. Burns would later (1981–1985) serve as ambassador to West Germany.

William Safire

William Safire (1929–), born and raised in New York City, worked as a reporter for *The New York Herald Tribune* and later for radio and television before entering the public relations business.

Safire worked on Eisenhower's first presidential campaign. He volunteered to write speeches for Nixon during the 1968 presidential campaign, and when Nixon was elected president, Safire was hired as a special assistant. Safire's book *Before the Fall* (1975) is a history of the Nixon White House before the scandal that brought down the Nixon presidency.

In 1973 Safire joined *The New York Times* editorial staff. His Pulitzer Prize-winning columns have been a feature of that newspaper ever since.

Henry Kissinger

Henry Kissinger (1923–), the foreign policy adviser upon whom Richard Nixon relied more than any other, was born in Fürth, Germany. To escape the Nazi persecution of Jews, he and his family fled to the United States in 1938, settling in the Washington Heights section of New York City. Several of Kissinger's relatives who remained in Germany perished in the Holocaust. After graduating from George Washington High School in 1941, where he was a straight-A student, Kissinger spent the next two years studying accounting at City College.

In 1943 Henry became a naturalized citizen and later that year was drafted into the U.S. Army. He was discharged from the Army in 1946 and enrolled in Harvard College, where he majored in government. After receiving his degree in 1950, Kissinger began graduate work in government at Harvard, earning his doctorate in 1954. Joining the faculty of the Harvard government department that same year, Kissinger would become a full professor in 1962. His doctoral dissertation,

A World Restored: Casterleigh, Metternich, and the Problems of Peace, was published in 1957.

In 1954, in response to the growing Soviet nuclear challenge, Kissinger had been appointed director of a Council on Foreign Relations research project to explore alternative methods to full-scale war. His influential book, *Nuclear Weapons and Foreign Policy*, which resulted from this project, became a bestseller and established Kissinger as one of the leading "defense intellectuals" in America. It was this book that first brought Kissinger to the attention of then Vice President Richard Nixon, who, impressed by the study, sent Kissinger a letter congratulating him on its publication.

In 1956 Nelson Rockefeller appointed Henry Kissinger director of a special project of the Rockefeller Brothers Fund. Kissinger's important 1961 book, *The Necessity for Choice: Prospects for American Foreign Policy*, an outgrowth of that project, further enhanced Kissinger's growing reputation in Washington, D.C., foreign policy circles. During the first year of the Kennedy Administration, Kissinger served as an adviser to McGeorge Bundy, President Kennedy's special

Henry Kissinger

assistant for national security affairs. Kissinger also served as a consultant to the Arms Control and Disarmament Agency from 1961 to 1967 and to the State Department from 1965 to 1969.

Kissinger and Nixon

Throughout the 1960s, Kissinger served as a foreign policy adviser to New York Governor Nelson Rockefeller, who had become Kissinger's mentor and friend. During the presidential campaign of 1968, when Rockefeller was Richard Nixon's rival for the Republican nomination, Kissinger was Rockefeller's foreign policy consultant. After Rockefeller lost the nomination, Nixon invited Kissinger to serve as a foreign policy consultant in his campaign for the presidency against Hubert Humphrey. After Nixon's election in November

1968, he offered Kissinger the post of special assistant to the president for national security affairs, to which Kissinger was appointed in January of 1969. Kissinger was the second Jew to serve in this most important foreign policy position on the White House staff.

Kissinger's achievements in this role were many. In July 1971 he became the first American government official to visit China since 1949 and was instrumental in establishing diplomatic ties between the United States and the People's Republic of China, one of the greatest triumphs of the Nixon era in U.S. foreign policy. Kissinger's secret July 1971 trip to Beijing, in which he met with Chinese premier Chou En-lai, led to a rapprochement between the United States and China, ending two decades of American hostility toward the Chinese Communist regime and paving the way for President Nixon's historic visit to China

Henry Kissinger and Abba Eban (second from left). Mrs. Henry Kissinger is standing at far right.

the following February. Kissinger also had a principal role in negotiating the SALT I Agreement with the Soviet Union in May 1972.

One of Kissinger's most notable achievements while serving President Nixon was negotiating a cease-fire with the North Vietnamese in January1973. After months of talks in Paris, Kissinger initiated an agreement that provided for the withdrawal of U.S. troops, bringing about an end to the Vietnam War. For this achievement, Kissinger was awarded the Nobel Peace Prize in 1973. While admirers of Kissinger praised him for his negotiating skills, critics accused him of prolonging the war to make his efforts seem all the more laudable when a cease-fire was accomplished.

In August 1973, Henry Kissinger was appointed secretary of state, the first Jew to serve in that position. While secretary of state, he retained the title of special assistant to the president for national security affairs, the only secretary of state to do so. Most scholars concur that Henry Kissinger was, with Dean Acheson, one of the two most influential secretaries of state in the twentieth century, and he was unquestionably the most powerful and influential Jewish Cabinet member or White House adviser in American history. No Jew has done as much to shape and determine U.S. foreign policy. As one thoughtful Jewish journalist, J. J. Goldberg, has commented: "No Jew in modern times has wielded greater power on the world stage than Kissinger."

During the first Nixon Administration, Kissinger had very little to do with U.S. policy toward Israel and the Middle East, which was formulated and directed primarily by Secretary of State William P. Rogers. With the conclusion of the Vietnam War and his appointment as secretary of state, however, Kissinger would play an increasingly important role in shaping U.S. Mideast policy. In the years since, much has been written about his role during the Yom Kippur War of October 1973.

The Yom Kippur War

On Saturday morning, October 6, 1973, as most Israelis were preparing to observe the Yom Kippur fast, they were unaware that along Israeli borders, Egyptian and Syrian forces were preparing a similtaneous military assault. When Israel realized that war was imminent, the mobilization of its armored corps reserves was ordered. When Kissinger learned of this move, he advised Israel not to launch a preemptive strike. At 2:00 P.M. on that same day, Egyptian and Syrian armies attacked Israel across the Suez Canal and through the Golan Heights. The surprise attack caught Israel off guard, and for more than two weeks fierce battles ensued. The Arabs were unstintingly being supplied with military hardware by the Soviets.

Outnumbered on the ground by twelve to one, Israel suffered many casualties. After learning from Israeli Ambassador Simcha Dinitz of Israel's losses in the Sinai, and that Egypt was winning the war, President Nixon and Secretary of State Kissinger ordered tons of crucial weaponry be sent to Israel. By October 19 the order was filled and the tide of the war turned; Israel went on to achieve victory.

In addition to weapons, Nixon asked Congress for $2.2 billion to cover the cost of military aid to Israel "to maintain a balance of forces and achieve stability in the Middle East."

On October 22 the United States and the Soviet Union jointly sponsored a UN resolution calling for a cease-fire. The fighting came to a complete halt on October 24.

Kissinger's Role During the War

There has been much debate and controversy within the Jewish community over Kissinger's role in the Yom Kippur War. Many Jewish leaders, both in Israel and the United States, have been critical of Kissinger, maintaining that his Jewishness prevented him from being more supportive of Israel than he might otherwise have been. Some of his harsher Jewish critics have gone so far as to question his loyalty to the Jewish people and the Jewish state, alleging that he betrayed Jewish interests during the conflict.

Gold Meir felt that Kissinger might have done more to support Israel during the war. In his

Arafat: A Political Biography (1984), Alan Hart reports that when he asked Golda Meir whether she suspected Kissinger of discouraging Nixon from offering aid to Israel, she replied: "I'm sure that is exactly what was happening."

Hart then writes:

> When Golda had finished her long and detailed account of the Yom Kippur War, I suggested to her that the only conclusion to be drawn was that Henry Kissinger in effect made use of [Anwar] Sadat [of Egypt] to set up the Israelis for a limited war, to teach the Israeli's a lesson, in order for him to begin a peace initiative on his own terms. . . . Without a pause for reflection, Golda replied: "That is what I believe. That is what we believe. But we cannot ever say so . . . what I mean is that we cannot even say so to ourselves."

In Defense of Kissinger

Other Jewish leaders and political analysts do not share Golda Meir's critical assessment of Kissinger's role in the Yom Kippur War, maintaining that in Israel's hour of greatest need Kissinger was a voice of support for Israel within the Nixon Adminis-

Golda Meir

tration. Some of Kissinger's defenders have claimed that Secretary of Defense James R. Schlesinger, a Jewish convert to Christianity, actively opposed Kissinger's efforts to have the Pentagon send Israel the military aircraft it so desperately needed during the war. Kissinger biographer Walter Isaacson has suggested that during the Yom Kippur War Schlesinger shared the anti-Israel position of his deputy secretary of defense, William Clements, "a Texas oilman with pro-Arab sympathies," and that together they precipitated a four-day delay in starting a weapons airlift to resupply Israel after its initial war losses. General Alexander Haig, who served as President Nixon's chief of staff during the Yom Kippur War, concurs: "Defense Secretary [James R.] Schlesinger was not inclined to help the Israelis," says Haig. "Kissinger, on the other hand, was sensitive to the need for prompt assistance to Israel. As J. J. Goldberg has written, "many Jewish activists are convinced to this day that Schlesinger's feelings toward Israel were colored by his ambivalent relationship to Judaism." The fact that Schlesinger was uncomfortable with his Jewish roots led him to bend over backwards to support the Arab position. Kissinger, by contrast, while not a religiously observant Jew, never denied his Jewish identity and, in the foreign policy debates within the Nixon Administration, was more disposed to supporting Israel's security and military needs than was Schlesinger.

At the most critical moment, in October 1973, Kissinger was Israel's friend. As Walter Isaacson would later state: ". . . . deep inside, Kissinger had an emotional commitment to the survival of Israel that led him to be one of its staunchest defenders when its safety was truly at stake . . ." As Kissinger himself would tell Jewish leaders: "How can I, as a Jew who lost thirteen relatives in the Holocaust, do anything that would betray Israel?"

To Golda Meir, however, it was Nixon whom she considered to be Israel's staunchest friend and Israel's "savior" during the Yom Kippur War. This is evident from a letter she wrote to her sister Clara, who lived in the United States and was very critical of President Nixon: "Look, Clara," she wrote, "you're an American. You don't like Nixon. I'm an Israeli. I'll never forget that if it

Moshe Dayan meeting with President Nixon.

hadn't been for Nixon, we would have been destroyed."

Even Nixon himself did not hesitate to declare: "Christ, if it weren't for me, there wouldn't be any Israel. They know that in Israel. Golda knows that, even though they may not know it over here."

Other Prominent Supporters

Aside from the talented Jews who worked with Nixon professionally during the course of his political career, a number of notable wealthy Republican Jews supported him loyally during his presidential years. Notable among them was Bernard Baruch, who had advised presidents on economic issues from Wilson onward. While serving as vice president, Nixon had turned to him for counsel.

Alan Greenspan (1926-), another economist, helped advise Nixon on economic matters during his runs for the presidency in 1968 and 1972. But when Nixon offered him the chairmanship of the prestigious Council of Economic Advisers,

he turned it down. Not until the Ford Administration was he willing to assume this awesome responsibility.

Nixon also turned for support to Milwaukee-born Walter Annenberg (1908-). Walter's father, Moses, had come to America as a child from East Prussia. He became publisher of *The Philadelphia Inquirer*, launched a string of horseracing tout sheets, and acquired several periodicals and other newspapers. To his father's huge fortune, which Walter inherited, he added radio and television stations and popular magazines such as *Seventeen* and *TV Guide*. In 1969, at the beginning of his first term in office, Nixon appointed Annenberg ambassador to Great Britain, a position he held throughout the Nixon presidency.

Walter's Annenberg's mother, Sadie, a wealthy woman in her own right, was a close friend of Bernard Baruch. She became a major contributor to Nixon's campaigns, and after being elected vice president, Nixon hosted a dinner in her honor.

Other large contributors to Nixon's campaigns include philanthropist Ruth Lewis Farkas (1906-

1996), who married George Farkas in 1928 and was mother to his four sons. A well-educated, imaginative businesswoman, Ruth founded Alexander's Department Stores (now defunct), which were named in memory of her husband's father.

A lifelong Republican, Ruth Farkas contributed more than $300,000 to Nixon's reelection campaign and was rewarded with an appointment as ambassador to Luxembourg. Her confirmation was delayed for a time in the Senate because of charges that she had actually paid for the post through her campaign contributions.

Wealthy Detroit industrialist Max Fisher was another Jew of prominence and influence who supported Nixon. Widely known and respected in the Jewish community, Fisher expended great effort in recruiting a large number of wealthy contributors for Nixon's reelection campaign. Rank-and-file Jews, however, contributed limited funds to Nixon, although they did make substantial contributions to his opponent. In 1968 Nixon appointed Fisher to be his special adviser on urban and community affairs.

Nixon and Rabin

Nixon was particularly fond of Yitzhak Rabin, who had commanded the Israeli armed forces in the victorious Six-Day War of 1967. Before becoming president, Nixon had visited Israel, and Rabin, his host, showed him the sights. On January 1, 1968, after retiring from the army, Rabin became the Israeli ambassador to Washington, where he was well received by Nixon, who appreciated Rabin's "quiet, cool demeanor." Nixon was especially pleased when Rabin reprimanded American Jewish leaders for dabbling in domestic policy matters, especially for criticizing the president's handling of the Vietnam War.

Ambassador Rabin subjected himself to vigorous criticism when, in 1972, contrary to accepted protocol, he spoke out openly in favor of Nixon's reelection. Historians believe that Rabin's support and friendship might have been a factor in Nixon's decision to provide arms to Israel during the 1973 Yom Kippur War.

Upon learning of the death of President Nixon on April 22, 1994, Rabin issued the following statement:

> Israel has lost one of its greatest friends. From our point of view, his supreme test came at a time of tribulation, and he proved himself with honor. During the Yom Kippur War in 1973, Richard Nixon was the driving force in mobilizing the airlift to assist us with weaponry at the most difficult of moments. His contribution to reinforcing the security of the State of Israel merits the highest appreciation.

Golda Meir and Nixon

After he left office ignominiously on August 9, 1974, Nixon wrote in his memoirs that what he appreciated most about Golda Meir was that "she conveyed simultaneously the qualities of extreme toughness and warmth" and that "she used her emotions and they did not use her."

Nixon had had an opportunity to size up the newly elected prime minister of Israel when she came to visit him in the White House in September 1969. Despite Israel's victory in the 1967 Six-Day War, Israel's security and military needs required substantial outside support. The need was so urgent and the stakes so high—especially, since the Arab states were receiving substantial assistance from the Soviet Union—that Golda came to Washington with trepidation.

Golda's mind was set at ease when Nixon assured her that he had no illusions about Soviet motives in the Middle East. She was further comforted when her request for low-interest loans, amounting to $400 million per year, was approved.

Nevertheless, within a few months, in December of 1969, Meir was stunned when Secretary of State William Rogers proposed a Middle East settlement known as the Rogers Plan. It called for the withdrawal of Israel from occupied territory conquered in the Six-Day War, in return for which the Arabs would guarantee permanent peace with Israel. National Security Adviser Henry Kissinger raised no objection to the plan, but Israel rejected it. President Nixon agreed with Israel's position

Rabbi Joshua Haberman, of the Washington Hebrew Congregation, at the White House with President and Mrs. Nixon in 1971.

President and Mrs. Nixon escort Prime Minister Golda Meir to a formal affair.

and instructed his assistant, Leonard Garment, to assure Prime Minister Meir that the president would not support the Rogers Plan.

Despite White House assurances that the United States would stand by Israel in its hour of need, Golda Meir was never quite sure what to expect. In a letter dated March 12, 1970, Mrs. Meir wrote to President Nixon: "It is true that our pilots are very good, but they can be good only when they have planes. Lately, some rumors have reached me that your decision may be negative or at best postponed. I absolutely refuse to believe it. If, God forbid, this were true, then we would really be forsaken."

Eleven days later, on March 23, 1970, Secretary of State Rogers, with Kissinger's support, announced that the United States had decided to deny Israel's request for twenty-five more Phantom Jets and one hundred Skyhawks but would extend to Israel $100 million in economic credit. Only after several visits by Prime Minister Meir to the United States did Nixon agree to close the arms gap between the Arabs and Israel.

Massacre at the Olympics

On September 5, 1972, eight Black September Palestinian terrorists entered the Olympic Village in Munich, West Germany, and killed two Israeli athletes, taking nine more hostage. When the German police attempted to free the hostages, all the Israelis were killed. The Games were postponed for twenty-four hours, but the UN took no action; it would not even entertain a U.S. resolution condemning the terrorism. In retaliation for the Munich Olympic massacre, Israeli planes attacked terrorist bases in Syria and Lebanon.

In a statement made at San Francisco's Golden Gate Pier at approximately 1:00 P.M. on September 5, President Nixon revealed that he "had the opportunity this morning before I left San Clemente to call Prime Minister Meir on the phone . . . I talked with her for about seven or eight minutes. . . . I expressed sympathy on behalf of all the American people for the victims of this murderous action that occurred in the Olympic village . . ."

The following day, the president issued the following formal message to the Israeli leader:

Dear Madame Prime Minister:

The heart of America goes out to you, to the bereaved families and to the Israeli people in the tragedy that has struck your Olympic athletes. This tragic and senseless act is a perversion of all hopes and aspirations of mankind which the Olympic Games symbolize. In a larger sense, it is a tragedy for all the people and nations of the world. We mourn with you the deaths of your innocent and brave athletes, and we share with you the determination that the spirit of brotherhood and peace they represented shall in the end persevere.

Sincerely,
Richard Nixon

Watergate

On June 17, 1972, agents of the Committee to Reelect the President had been arrested in the act of burglarizing the Democratic National Committee Headquarters at the Watergate apartment and office complex in Washington, D.C. Nixon became deeply involved in trying to cover up the incident by means of a number of illegal acts. Inquiry into the scandal and all of its ramifications persisted for two years, ending in televised impeachment proceedings conducted by the House Judiciary Committee. The scandal was exposed by *Washington Post* reporters Carl Bernstein and Bob Woodward, who claimed that their source, "Deep Throat," was someone close to the Nixon Administration whose name they had promised not to divulge. Rumor had it that Leonard Garment was the informant, a charge he denied.

Baruch Korff—Nixon's Rabbi

The Jewish leadership as a whole found it impossible to support Richard Nixon as the Watergate scandal unfolded, but one rabbi—Baruch Korff (1914–1995)—made headlines by coming to Nixon's defense and forming, in 1973, the National Citizen's Committee for Fairness to the

Presidency. Its purpose was that of "preserving the office of the presidency."

Although Korff, who had served as rabbi in Rehoboth, Massachusetts, in the 1950s and 1960s, never met Nixon and did not vote for him in 1960 or 1968, he felt that the president was being mistreated. He took out advertisements in support of Nixon in twenty-five newspapers and raised one million dollars for his defense. On May 13, 1974, Rabbi Korff was finally granted an interview with the president, and that became the basis of a book by Korff entitled *The Personal Nixon: Staying on the Summit*, in which he said of Nixon: "I regard him as a man who has been vilified, savaged, brutalized . . . holding out against willful people who are unworthy of polishing his shoes."

When Nixon resigned on August 9, 1974, Korff said: "Now he has made the supreme sacrifice." Years later, in August 1995, Korff said: "The time has come for me to speak the truth," and he revealed that he knew the identity of Deep Throat: television journalist Diane Sawyer, who in 1974 was an assistant in the Nixon press office. Sawyer denied the allegation.

Threat of Impeachment

The case against the president was so overwhelming that impeachment by the House of Representatives was certain and a trial in the Senate inevitable. On August 7, 1974, Nixon met alone with Henry Kissinger and revealed to him his plan to resign. He asked Kissinger to kneel and pray with him.

On August 8, 1974, Nixon appeared on television and, with his family at his side, announced that "for the sake of the office" he would resign. On August 9, 1974, Nixon and his family flew to their estate in San Clemente, California, and the office of president was immediately assumed by Vice President Gerald Ford, who then selected Nelson Rockefeller to be his vice president.

One month later, Nixon received from President Ford "a full, free, and absolute pardon" for all crimes that he "committed or may have committed or taken part in" while president.

Last Years

At San Clemente, Nixon went into seclusion, devoting himself to writing his memoirs, which were published in 1978. Despite the fact that in 1976 a New York State court found that the former president had obstructed justice in connection with Watergate and disbarred him, the former president was determined to rehabilitate himself. He did so by going to great lengths to maintain contacts with national leaders both in the United States and abroad. In the course of the next ten years he traveled to eighteen countries and met with sixteen heads of state. Nixon was delighted to find that his advice was eagerly sought and respected, and over time he was able to transform himself from a disgraced president to an admired elder statesman, although he would never fully shed the stigma of Watergate.

After suffering a stroke and falling into a coma, Richard Nixon died in a New York City hospital on April 22, 1994.

At the funeral, held in Yorba Linda, California, on April 27, 1994, highly placed politicians from the United States and around the world assembled to pay tribute to the thirty-seventh president of the United States. Of all the eulogies delivered, Henry Kissinger's emotional farewell was particularly moving:

> He stood on pinnacles that dissolved in the precipice. He achieved greatly and he suffered deeply. But he never gave up. In his solitude he envisaged a new international order that would reduce lingering enmities, strengthen historic friendships and give new hope to mankind. A visionary dream and possibilities conjoined. . . .
>
> He drew strength from the conviction he often expressed to me: the price for doing things halfway is not less than for doing it completely, so we might as well do them properly. That's Richard Nixon's greatest accomplishment. It was as much moral as it was political.

[A.J.K.]

Gerald R. Ford

Served from 1974 to 1977

Born on July 14, 1913, in Omaha, Nebraska

Member of the Episcopal denomination

Married Elizabeth Anne Bloomer on October 15, 1948

Father to three sons and one daughter

Candidate of the Republican Party

Assumed the presidency following the resignation
of Richard Nixon on August 9, 1974

Vice president under Ford: Nelson A. Rockefeller

Thirty-Eighth President of the United States

GERALD RUDOLPH FORD, WHO WAS BORN Leslie King, Jr., but later assumed the name of his adoptive father, was the first Chief Executive to become president by appointment rather than by succession. Having been appointed vice president by President Richard Nixon in 1973, following the resignation of Spiro T. Agnew, Ford assumed the presidency at the climax of the constitutional crisis over Watergate, which had caused Nixon himself to resign under threat of impeachment. "He was," as his wife, Betty, put it about Gerald Ford, "an accidental vice president and an accidental president, and in both jobs he replaced disgraced leaders."

Ford had not been seriously considered presidential timber before he became the first non-elected vice president. A University of Michigan football star who had worked as an assistant football coach while attending Yale Law School, Ford was widely but unfairly characterized by his political opponents as just another "dumb football jock." Yet, he graduated in the top third of his class at Yale Law School and, beginning in 1949, served for twenty-five years as a highly effective and respected congressman from Michigan. In every election Ford never received less than 60 percent of the vote.

In 1963 Ford was elected chairman of the House Republican caucus. In December of 1963, President Lyndon Johnson appointed him to the Warren Commission to investigate the assassination of President John F. Kennedy. In 1965 Ford was elected Republican Minority Leader of the House, making him in effect the foremost Republican member of Congress. During President Nixon's first term, Ford was noted for his loyal support of the White House.

When Vice President Spiro Agnew resigned in

October 1973, after pleading guilty to federal income tax evasion while governor of Maryland, Gerald Ford was nominated by Richard Nixon to succeed Agnew as vice president. As Nixon would later recount in his memoirs, Ford was his fourth choice for vice president, after Governor John Connally of Texas, Governor Ronald Reagan of California, and Governor Nelson Rockefeller of New York. Nixon concluded that Ford would most easily be confirmed by the Democratic-controlled Congress without causing internal dissension within the Republican Party.

Ford was sworn in as vice president on December 6, 1973. Eight months later, minutes after Richard Nixon resigned on August 9, 1974, Ford was sworn in as president of the United States by Chief Justice Warren Burger in the East Room of the White House. "Our national nightmare is over," Ford said following his swearing-in. "Our Constitution works; our great Republic is a government of laws and not of men."

One month after taking office, President Ford stunned the nation when he granted former President Nixon "a full, free and absolute pardon" for all offenses committed during his administration. The pardon drew an onslaught of criticism. Ford responded that the public humiliation of resigning the presidency in disgrace was punishment enough, "the equivalent of serving a jail term."

Throughout much of Gerald Ford's twenty-nine-month administration the nation suffered through a severe economic recession, with eight million Americans out of work, the highest unemployment rate since the Great Depression of the 1930s. Ford favored increasing unemployment payments to the jobless and other spending programs but did not succeed in his efforts to resolve the country's economic crisis.

Gerald Ford at work in the Oval Office.

mained committed to the cause of Soviet Jewry: "I will continue to seek further progress on the issue of emigration from the Soviet Union," he promised in 1975. "I raised it personally with General Secretary Brezhnev. I have discussed it on many occasions with my former colleagues in the House and in the Senate with the determination to restore the prior rate of emigration."

Visit to Auschwitz

On an official visit to Poland in 1975, President Ford visited Auschwitz. After placing a wreath at the stone memorial to the four million Holocaust victims who perished there, Ford was visibly moved when he said: "This monument and the memory of those it honors should be an inspiration to the dedicated pursuit of peace and the security of all people."

Support for Soviet Jewry

As congressman, Gerald Ford had voiced concern over the plight of Soviet Jewry. He was one of the signers of a congressional declaration condemning the suppression of Jewish religious and cultural life in Soviet Russia. In 1970 he cosponsored a resolution in the House of Representatives calling upon the Soviets to commute the death penalty imposed on two Soviet Jews. Pleased when the death sentences were commuted, Ford was quoted as saying: "Our elation should be tempered by the circumstances which gave rise to the incident . . . the fact that the Soviet Union is holding Jews in that country against their will is unconscionable."

In an impassioned speech delivered at a rally for Soviet Jewry at New York City's Madison Square Garden on December 13, 1971, Congressman Ford presented in considerable detail what he believed Congress and the U.S. government could and should do to help facilitate and increase Soviet Jewish emigration. As president, Ford re-

Ties with Israel

Upon acceding to the presidency on August 9, 1974, Gerald Ford brought to the White House a record of strong support for the state of Israel. During his years in Congress, Ford had been known as one of Israel's staunchest friends amongst Republicans in the House of Representatives. He could always be relied upon to support increased foreign aid to Israel and to sign congressional resolutions on Israel's behalf. On April 24, 1969, Congressman Ford declared in an address to the American Israel Public Affairs Committee:

> I firmly believe that the fate of Israel is linked to the national security interests of the United States. I therefore cannot conceive of a situation in which the U.S. Administration will sell Israel down the Nile. . . .Israel may enter its twenty-first anniversary confident . . .that Americans are aware of her dedication to freedom and of the basic affinity linking Israel

with the United States. . . . Let me reiterate that the Republican leadership in the House of Representatives identifies with your concerns. We are committed to the growth of Israel-American friendship.

As president, Ford reaffirmed his commitment to Israel's safety and security on several occasions. Shortly after taking office, he declared:

> America must and will pursue friendship with all nations. But this will never be done at the expense of America's commitment to Israel. A strong Israel is essential to a stable peace in the Middle East. Our commitment to Israel will meet the test of American steadfastness and resolve. My administration will not be found wanting. The United States will continue to help Israel provide for her security. . . . Commitment to the security and future of Israel is based upon basic morality as well as enlightened self-interest. Our role in supporting Israel honors our own heritage.

Meeting with Jewish Leaders

Max Fisher, Ford's closest Jewish supporter and adviser, organized a meeting of twenty of the most influential leaders in American Jewish life, Republicans and Democrats alike, at the White House on December 20, 1974. The president began by assuring those in attendance that he was committed to maintaining the geographic integrity of Israel. "The Israelis," said Ford, "can count on our economic and military aid. Israel is vitally important to overall American foreign policy in the Middle East." Ford then went on to discuss Secretary of State Henry Kissinger's shuttle diplomacy and the continuing U.S. efforts to bring peace to the Middle East, which had begun during the Nixon Administration.

"Most other countries," Ford said, "including those in NATO, disagree with our policy, and want Israel to return to her 1967 borders. If we go to a Geneva peace conference, the PLO would have to attend, and Israel will not negotiate with the PLO. Negotiations between Israel and the Arabs should be a quid pro quo. If Israel gives something up, she should get something in return."

Ford's message was precisely what American Jewish leaders wished to hear. They saw the new president as one who seemed to have an impressive grasp of the issues and would be a champion of Israel. As the gathering adjourned "in a wave of warm feelings," Max Fisher wrote himself a note that reflected the confidence of these Jewish leaders: "As long as Ford is president, there will never be another Munich."

A Time of Disappointment

To be sure, relations between American Jewish leaders and the Ford Administration were, at times, less congenial. In March 1975, when Secretary of State Henry Kissinger failed to conclude a much-hoped-for Egyptian-Israeli agreement, the United States announced a "reassessment" of its Middle East policy. American Jewish leaders feared that this would be detrimental to future U.S. relations with Israel. Secretary Kissinger was roundly criticized by American Jewish leaders for his pressure on Israel to withdraw from the Sinai.

On September 1, 1975, however, Israel and Egypt signed an agreement. The signing of this new Sinai accord was a high priority of the Ford Administration, and, at a summit meeting between President Ford and Israeli Prime Minister Rabin held in Washington during the summer of 1975, Ford had promised to generously compensate Israel with increased military and economic aid for its "flexibility" and cooperation in signing the agreement. Much to the satisfaction of American Jewish leadership, the Ford Administration more than made good on its promise: the president doubled aid to Israel to $793 million, the largest amount of economic aid that Israel had received since 1948. This high level of U.S. aid to Israel was renewed the following year as well. As President Ford would later proudly recall: "The funds that I proposed for Israel in my first two budgets totaled over $4 billion for 27 months. These figures speak more eloquently than words." Indeed, in just two years President Ford provided Israel with 40 percent of all aid it had ever received from the United States.

COURTESY OF THE JIMMY CARTER LIBRARY

Gerald Ford banters with Henry Kissinger, as Ladybird Johnson (far right) looks on.

Appointment of Ambassador Moynihan

American Jewish leaders also were delighted with President Ford's appointment, in 1975, of Daniel Patrick Moynihan as U.S. ambassador to the United Nations, where he spoke out eloquently against the U.N. resolution equating Zionism with racism. President Ford clearly shared Ambassador Moynihan's outrage at the UN resolution: "I tell you now," declared Ford, "that we will fight any measure that condemns Zionism as racism or that attempts to deny Israel her full rights of membership in the United Nations."

Jewish Appointees and Supporters

Not only did Ford retain Henry Kissinger as secretary of state and Arthur Burns as chairman of the Federal Reserve Board, but he appointed Jews

to other important offices in his administration, notably Edward H. Levi and Alan Greenspan. Although he never formally joined the Ford Administration, Max Fisher of Detroit, one of American Jewry's preeminent communal leaders and philanthropists, and Ford's loyal friend and supporter for two decades, remained one of the president's most trusted advisers on matters relating to the Jewish community and Israel.

Edward H. Levi

Edward H. Levi (1911-2000), an eminent legal scholar and university administrator, was appointed U.S. attorney general by President Ford in 1975, the first American Jew to be named to this Cabinet post. The descendant of one of America's most distinguished rabbinic families, Levi was the son, grandson, and great-grandson of rabbis, as well as the grand-nephew of Rabbi Kaufmann Kohler, who had been the second presi-

232   THE PRESIDENTS OF THE UNITED STATES & THE JEWS

dent of Hebrew Union College. After receiving his undergraduate and law degrees from the University of Chicago, and a doctorate in jurisprudence from Yale in 1938, Levi was appointed to the law school faculty of the University of Chicago, becoming dean of the law school in 1950. He subsequently served as provost and, in 1967, was appointed president of the University of Chicago, the first Jew to hold that position. A founder of the Chicago chapter of the American Jewish Committee, Levi was an active member of Chicago's Sinai Temple, of which his grandfather, Emil G. Hirsch, had served as rabbi from 1880 to 1923.

Hailed by the American Bar Association as a "brilliant nomination," Levi's appointment was the first Cabinet-level change of the Ford presidency. With his reputation for integrity and nonpartisanship, Levi's appointment restored public confidence in the Justice Department, which had been shaken by the Watergate scandals and the personal involvement of Attorneys General John Mitchell and Richard Kleindienst. Sworn in as attorney general on February 7, 1975, Levi served until the end of the Ford Administration and became one of the Cabinet members with whom Ford was closest. When Supreme Court Justice William O. Douglas retired in November 1975, Ford asked Levi to compile a list of potential appointees and relied heavily on Levi's counsel in eventually selecting John Paul Stevens as Justice Douglas's successor.

Alan Greenspan

Alan Greenspan succeeded another Jewish economist, Herbert Stein, as chairman of the President's Council of Economic Advisers. After receiving his bachelor's and master's degrees from New York University in 1950, Greenspan began a doctoral program at Columbia University, where he studied under Arthur Burns, who would serve as Chairman of the Federal Reserve Board from 1970 to 1978. In 1954 Greenspan founded his own consulting and economic forecasting firm, Townsend-Greenspan & Co., and served as its president until joining the Ford Administration in September 1974.

Although Greenspan had worked as an economic adviser on Richard Nixon's 1968 and 1972 presidential campaigns, he had been reluctant to join the government on a full-time basis, and in early 1974 turned down President Nixon's offer of the chairmanship of the Council of Economic Advisers. But after President Ford succeeded Nixon in the presidency, at the urging of Arthur Burns, Greenspan accepted the appointment and it was confirmed by the Senate on September 1, 1974.

Greenspan's ability to foresee with accuracy the fluctuations of the economy made him invaluable to the Ford Administration. One White House official stated in the spring of 1975 that "Greenspan has a unique personal relationship with Ford. . . . Alan spends time alone with the president on economic policy, and on economic policy Alan is a heavyweight." Resuming his private consulting work with Townsend-Greenspan & Co. when President Carter took office in January 1977, Greenspan would return to government in 1987, when he was appointed by President Ronald Reagan as chairman of the Federal Reserve Board.

Alan Greenspan

President Gerald R. Ford presides over an afternoon Cabinet meeting.

Max Fisher

A wealthy Detroit industrialist and Jewish philanthropist, Max Fisher was a longtime friend and political confidant of Gerald Ford. Born in Pittsburgh, Pennsylvania, in 1908, Fisher graduated from Ohio State University in 1930 and moved to Detroit, where he made a fortune in the oil business. He became one of the city's and country's most influential Jewish communal leaders. In the late 1950s and 1960s, he also began to carve out a singular niche for himself in Republican Party politics and fundraising, becoming a valued adviser to Presidents Eisenhower, Nixon, and Ford. According to one political analyst, Fisher "politicized Jewish America as it had never been done" and in the process "defined the new parameters of the Jewish community's relation to the presidency and politics."

Of the three Republican presidents to whose campaigns he had generously contributed, Fisher was closest to Gerald Ford, whom he had known, supported, and advised since the late 1950s. On August 9, 1974, Fisher flew to Washington, D.C., at the invitation of Vice President Ford, to "discuss the economy." But when he arrived, he was told that Nixon was resigning and Ford was to be sworn in as president. Fisher was one of a select few who were in the East Room of the White House where, at noon, Gerald Ford took the oath as the thirty-eighth president of the United States. Fisher was the only Jewish leader in attendance. "History overtakes men," Fisher told an interviewer after the ceremony. "Many times President Ford said his ambition was to be Speaker of the House. The events of our time have changed his life. . . . Ford was the right man at the right time and place."

And so, too, one might say, was Max Fisher, who enjoyed unparalleled access to Ford throughout his presidency. Even President Ford said himself: "Max had access whenever [he] asked for it.

I trusted him and he had as good access as anybody, if not better." Over the two-and-a-half years of the Ford Administration, Fisher officially visited the Oval Office twenty-five times and spoke with the president, on his private line, regularly. Throughout this period, Fisher arranged frequent meetings between Jewish leaders and the president, and remained Gerald Ford's most trusted adviser on Jewish and Israeli affairs.

Fisher played a central role in Ford's 1976 presidential campaign, mobilizing Jewish support on the president's behalf. However, throughout the campaign, as in 1974, questions continued to be raised as to the constitutionality of granting a presidential pardon prior to conviction in a court of law, and speculation continued to be widely voiced that the Nixon pardon was part of a political "deal" by which Ford had attained the presidency.

The many voters who had never forgiven Ford for pardoning Nixon, whom they felt had gotten off too easily, were able to vent their anger and frustration at the polls in 1976. In the November election, Ford narrowly lost the popular vote to Jimmy Carter, becoming the first incumbent president to lose an election since Herbert Hoover's loss to Franklin D. Roosevelt in 1932. The race was so close that Ford did not concede defeat to Jimmy Carter until the early hours of the morning following the November 2 election. Fisher would later describe the realization that Ford had lost "as the most disappointing moment in my life."

In the aftermath of his defeat, Ford told the press that he believed his decision to pardon Nixon had cost him enough votes to account for Carter's victory.

Post-Presidential Years

After attending the inauguration of his successor, Ford and his wife, Betty, settled in Rancho Mirage, California. In retirement, Ford plays golf and tennis, travels on the lecture circuit, and serves on the boards of several corporations. He is also cochairman of People for the American Way, founded by television producer Norman Lear to counter the influence of the Moral Majority.

In the spring of 1981, the $4.3 million Gerald R. Ford Library was dedicated to house Ford's presidential papers on the Ann Arbor campus of his alma mater, the University of Michigan. In September 1981, Ford was honored at the dedication of the $12 million Ford Presidential Museum in his boyhood town, Grand Rapids. Also in 1981, he joined former presidents Nixon and Carter in representing the United States at the funeral of slain Egyptian president Anwar Sadat. More than a decade later, Ford would once again receive considerable media publicity as one of several former presidents to speak at the funeral of his own political benefactor, Richard Nixon.

[D.G.D.]

Jimmy Carter

Served from 1977 to 1981

Born on October 1, 1924, in Plains, Georgia

Member of the Baptist denomination

Married Rosalynn Smith on July 7, 1946

Father to three sons and one daughter

Candidate of the Democratic Party

Vice president under Carter: Walter F. Mondale

Inaugural Address delivered on January 20, 1977

Thirty-Ninth President of the United States

IN THE PRESIDENTIAL ELECTION OF 1976, the bicentennial year of the birth of the nation, the Democratic candidate was James Earl Carter, Jr., or Jimmy Carter, as he insisted on being called. A political "outsider," a former peanut farmer, naval officer, and one-term governor of Georgia with no experience in Washington, Carter was nationally unknown. He was, in fact, so obscure, that when he entered the presidential race, people asked: "Jimmy who?" But Carter made a virtue of being a dark horse. "As far as Washington was concerned," he said, most Americans "are also outsiders."

Carter's boyhood dream was to become a naval officer, and in 1943 he entered the U.S. Naval Academy at Annapolis. After graduating in 1947, he rose rapidly through the ranks as a junior naval officer. After his father's death in 1953, however, he resigned from the Navy and returned to Plains, Georgia, to help his mother run the family peanut farm, which began to thrive under his management. After several years on the local board of education, Carter won election to the Georgia State Senate in 1962 and, in 1970, was elected governor of Georgia, defeating the highly publicized segregationist Lester Maddox. As Carter introduced reforms and brought efficiency to state government, he came to represent the "New South." He was hailed as a humanitarian whose acceptance of racial equality appeared to be genuine, and he won the respect and friendship of black civil rights leaders, such as Andrew Young, who became early supporters of his presidential candidacy.

Because of a state law in effect at the time, Carter could not run for a second, consecutive term as governor of Georgia. In December 1974, before leaving the governorship, he declared his candidacy for the Democratic nomination for president and spent the next two years actively campaigning.

The election of November 2, 1976, was close, with Jimmy Carter defeating Gerald Ford by approximately two percent of the popular vote (50 percent to Ford's 48 percent), and by an electoral vote margin of 297 to 240. In defeating Ford, Carter became the first candidate from the Deep South to be elected president since Zachary Taylor in 1848.

As president, Carter was unique in other respects as well. As a graduate of the U.S. Naval Academy, he was the first Annapolis man in the White House. He also was devoutly religious. A born-again Southern Baptist, and a deacon of the Baptist Church, he made daily prayers and Bible-reading, as well as Sunday school teaching, an integral part of his life in the White House.

Mentor and Friend, Admiral Hyman G. Rickover

As a junior naval officer, in 1951 Carter was assigned to the unit working on the development of the first nuclear-powered submarine. Before he received this assignment, however, he had to be interviewed by the "father" of the Navy's nuclear submarine program, Admiral Hyman G. Rickover (1900–1986). Rickover had immigrated to Chicago with his family from Poland in 1906 and in 1922 was graduated from the U.S. Naval Academy. During and after World War II, Rickover had become convinced of the feasibility of constructing nuclear-powered submarines. Almost alone, against considerable opposition, he persuaded the Navy in 1947 to undertake the effort. By 1954, under his direction, the *Nautilus* and the *Seawolf*, the first two atomic-powered submarines in the world, would be designed and built.

As their lengthy 1951 interview was ending, Rickover asked Carter whether he had done his best at Annapolis. Upon reflection, Carter said that he had not, to which Rickover countered, "Why not?" This unanswered question left a deep imprint on Carter's life: "Why Not the Best?" would be the theme of Carter's drive for the presidency and the title of his campaign autobiography. Carter understood Rickover's question as a challenge that demanded an ongoing process of self-examination.

Rickover invited the future president to join his program and assigned Carter to work on the *Seawolf*. Later, Rickover would select Carter to be the *Seawolf*'s chief engineer.

Rickover would always remain larger than life for Carter, a revered mentor, adviser, and friend. Throughout his years as governor of Georgia and as president, Carter would consult frequently with Rickover. In awarding Rickover the Presidential Medal of Freedom at a White House ceremony in January 1980, President Carter avowed: "With the exception of my father, no other person has had such a profound impact on my life."

A few months after his 1980 electoral defeat by Ronald Reagan, Carter received a letter from Rickover that said in part: "As long as a man is trying as hard as he can to do what he thinks to be right, he is a success regardless of outcome." In a letter of thanks to Rickover, Carter wrote: "As I leave office, my realization of your great contributions are matched only by my thanks for your personal kindness and consideration. I've never gone wrong by following your advice."

Jewish Appointees

During his presidency, Jimmy Carter appointed four Jews to his Cabinet, more than any other president to date.

In 1977 W. Michael Blumenthal (1926–) was named secretary of the Treasury. Blumenthal, who had been born in Berlin, fled Nazi Germany as a child in early 1939 and, after spending the war years in Shanghai, arrived in the United States in 1947. Blumenthal taught economics at Princeton University during the 1950s and in 1961 was appointed deputy assistant secretary of state for economic affairs by President Kennedy. From 1963 to 1967, Blumenthal served as ambassador and chairman of the U.S. delegation to the Kennedy Round of Tariff Negotiations. After ten years as president of the Bendix Corporation, Blumenthal joined the Carter Administration, serving as secretary of the Treasury until July of 1979. In retirement during the 1990s, Blumenthal became increasingly interested in his family's history as German Jews and Holocaust survivors, and wrote a book, *The Invisible Wall: Germans and Jews, a Personal Exploration*. In 1998, Blumenthal would return to his native Berlin to become chairman of the board and director of Berlin's new Jewish Museum.

Harold Brown (1927–), a prominent physicist, educator and government official, had served as a member of the President's Science Advisory Committee during the Kennedy Administration and, from 1965 to 1969, as secretary of the Air Force. In 1969, Brown was appointed president of the California

Yitzhak Rabin confers with President Jimmy Carter.

THE PRESIDENTS OF THE UNITED STATES & THE JEWS

Institute of Technology, as well as a general adviser to the Arms Control and Disarmament Agency. From 1977 to 1981, during the Carter Administration, Brown served as secretary of defense.

Philip M. Klutznick served as president of the World Jewish Congress and was one of the foremost figures in post-World War II American Jewish public life. Long active in Democratic Party politics and fundraising, Klutznick had served as a Federal Housing commissioner under Presidents Roosevelt and Truman and as Adlai Stevenson's chief deputy at the United Nations during the Kennedy Administration. A major financial contributor to Carter's 1976 presidential campaign, Klutznick was nominated as President Carter's secretary of commerce in November of 1979 and served until Carter left office in 1981. At the age of 72, Klutznick became the oldest member of the Carter Cabinet.

Neil E. Goldschmidt (1941–) had been elected mayor of Portland, Oregon, in 1973, at the age of thirty-two, one of the youngest mayors in the country. Long involved in Portland's Jewish communal life, he was an active member of the local Reform congregation. In July 1979, he was appointed secretary of transportation by President Carter, the first Jew to hold this Cabinet post, and served until the end of the Carter Administration.

In addition to these Jewish cabinet appointments, President Carter named four other Jews to major positions in his administration as well:

A prominent lawyer, Max M. Kampelman (1902–) had long been active in Democratic Party politics and had served as legislative counsel to Senator Hubert Humphrey from 1949 to 1955. Kampelman was actively involved in Jewish public life, serving as honorary vice chairman of the B'nai B'rith Anti-Defamation League, as a member of the Board of Governors of Tel Aviv and Haifa Universities, and as chairman of the National Advisory Committee of the American Jew-

Jimmy Carter with Israeli Minister of Defense Moshe Dayan.

ish Committee. During the Carter Administration, Kampelman was appointed ambassador and head of the U.S. delegation to the Conference on Security and Cooperation in Europe (under the Final Act signed in Helsinki in 1975), and would continue serving in this post during the early years of the Reagan Administration.

A prominent young Atlanta attorney and Democratic Party activist, Stuart E. Eizenstat (1943–) had been an early supporter of Jimmy Carter's presidential candidacy. In 1976 he joined the Carter campaign on a full-time basis and after the election was appointed President Carter's special assistant for domestic affairs and policy and director of the domestic policy staff in the Carter White House. As the highest ranking Jew on the White House staff, he served in this capacity until 1981.

Eizenstat was deeply interested in Holocaust-related issues and played an influential role in the creation of the President's Commission on the Holocaust. The establishment of this commission, which President Carter announced in 1979, on the occasion of Israel's thirtieth birthday, laid the groundwork for the U.S. Holocaust Memorial Museum, which would open in Washington, D.C., in 1993. An observant Conservative Jew who kept a kosher home, Eizenstat left work early on Fri-

Carter confers at Camp David with Menachem Begin (right) and Anwar Sadat (left).

day to observe the Sabbath. One year, he and his wife also invited President and Mrs. Carter to one of the Eizenstat family's Passover Seders. Jimmy Carter thus became the first American president to attend a Seder while in office.

Edward Sanders, Los Angeles attorney, Jewish communal leader, and national president of the American Israel Public Affairs Committee at the beginning of the Carter Administration, had been an early Jewish supporter of Carter's presidential candidacy. In the summer of 1978, Sanders was appointed the White House's liaison to the Jewish community and adviser on Middle East affairs to both President Carter and the State Department.

Lloyd N. Cutler (1917–), a graduate of Yale College and Yale Law School and a founding partner of one of Washington's preeminent law firms, served as counsel to President Carter from 1979 to 1981. He had earlier served, from 1977 to 1979, as the president's special representative for

maritime resource and boundary negotiations with Canada. Cutler, who returned to private law practice in 1981, would later serve again on the White House staff as counsel to President Bill Clinton.

The Camp David Accords

Throughout his long and remarkable campaign for the presidency in 1975 and 1976, Jimmy Carter stressed his commitment to preserving the "integrity" of Israel. In a major campaign speech in mid-June of 1976, the Sunday school teacher from Plains, wearing a blue velvet yarmulke, spoke in a synagogue in Elizabeth, New Jersey, and told his Jewish audience: "I worship the same God you do; we [Baptists] study the same Bible you do." Promising strong support for the Jewish state, Carter declared that "the survival of Israel is not a political issue. It is a moral imperative." As presidential candidate and as president, Carter would reiterate this campaign pledge and declare that "the United States will never support any agreement or any action that places Israel's security in jeopardy." To more than one Jewish audience, Carter reaffirmed his commitment to bringing about a "peace in the Middle East" through a treaty that would be based on Arab recognition and diplomatic relations with Israel.

At the presidential retreat at Camp David, Maryland, for twelve tense days in the late summer of 1978, Jimmy Carter, together with Israeli prime minister Menachem Begin and Egyptian president Anwar Sadat, played a historic role in helping to bring about the framework for such a peace treaty between Israel and Egypt. In the weeks and months that followed, Carter shuttled back and forth between Cairo and Jerusalem, winning concessions and compromises from both sides in a successful effort to bring the treaty to fruition. As part of the accords signed at Camp David, Begin agreed to return to Egypt the Sinai Peninsula, which had been under Israeli control since the 1967 Six-Day War, and to remove Israeli air bases and civilian settlements from the Sinai.

For his part, Sadat agreed to modify his earlier demand for an independent Palestinian state and to endorse the accords, which did not refer to Palestinian "self-determination" or mention the PLO. On March 14, 1979, the Israeli Cabinet voted to accept the Camp David accords. Less than two weeks later, Sadat and Begin flew to the United States, where, on March 26, 1979, a formal peace treaty between Egypt and Israel was ceremonially signed on the North Lawn of the White House, with both Sadat and Begin praising Carter's essential role. "Mothers in Egypt and Israel are not weeping today for their children fallen in senseless battle," pro-

claimed a euphoric President Carter. "Peace has come to Egypt and Israel." That evening, Washington, D.C., celebrated the treaty signing with the biggest State dinner in its history, with close to three thousand people in attendance.

The signing of the Camp David accords, which led to the peace treaty ending the thirty-one-year-old state of war between Israel and Egypt, and for which Menachem Begin and Anwar Sadat would jointly receive the Nobel Peace Prize, was hailed throughout the world as a monumental diplomatic accomplishment. For Carter, who had brought Sadat and Begin together and then had been instrumental in hammering out an agreement, the accords reached were a personal triumph and his administration's crowning foreign policy achievement. "It is a great day in your life, Mr. President of the United States," said Prime Minister Begin. "You have worked so hard, so insistently, so consistently, to achieve this goal."

Despite the euphoria of that moment, American Jews were skeptical of the sincerity of Jimmy Carter's professed support for Israel and distrustful of his administration's increasingly "pro-Arab" policies. Carter's plan for a "reassessment" of Middle East policy had aroused suspicions early in his presidency. On March 8, 1977, he indicated that Israel should withdraw from territories ac-

Jimmy Carter exchanges pleasantries with Menachem Begin.

From left to right: Mrs. Begin, Roslyn Carter, Menachem Begin, and Jimmy Carter posing in front of the White House.

quired in the Six-Day War, a position that neither Presidents Johnson nor Nixon had taken. When, ten days later, Carter spoke publicly in favor of a "Palestinian homeland," Yitzhak Rabin termed this "a further dramatic change in traditional U.S. policy." In his support for a Palestinian state, wrote George Ball, former undersecretary of state and no friend of Israel, Carter remained "more Arab than the Egyptians." In the last year of his presidency, Carter became especially vocal in his criticism of Israeli settlements on the West Bank and went so far as to personally order a "yes" vote by the United States on a UN Security Council resolution deploring new settlements in Judea and Samaria. According to National Security Adviser Zbigniew Brzezinski, Carter told Secretary of State Cyrus Vance, "I would be willing to lose my election because I will alienate the Jewish community but . . . if necessary, be harder on the Israelis."

And alienate the Jewish community he did: In the 1980 election, only 45 percent of Jewish voters opted for Jimmy Carter, an unusually low proportion of Jewish support for a Democratic candidate. Indeed, in his unsuccessful bid for reelection, Carter became the only Democratic presidential candidate since the 1920s to receive less than 50 percent of the Jewish vote.

Carter's presidential leadership also suffered irreparable damage during the last two years of his administration when the revolutionary government of Iran seized the American embassy and held its staff hostage for more than fourteen months, despite all of Carter's efforts to free them. His handling of the Iranian hostage crisis has generally come to be regarded as the single most important issue leading to his defeat for reelection in 1980.

Carter's defeat was decisive: As the ninth incumbent president to lose a bid for a second term, Carter received only forty-nine electoral votes, fewer than any other modern president except William Howard Taft in 1912.

Post-Presidential Years

Immediately after the inauguration of Ronald Reagan, Jimmy Carter returned with his family to his peanut farm in Plains, Georgia. In retirement, the former president began teaching at Emory University, raising money for the Jimmy Carter Library and Presidential Center in Atlanta, and writing his memoirs. Over the next two decades, he would write several other books, including one on the Middle East, *The Blood of Abraham*; volumes of poetry; *An Outdoor Journal*, containing musings on his love for the outdoors, and a book of personal reflections entitled *The Virtues of Aging*. He also would give his active support and leadership to Habitat for Humanity, the nonprofit organization that builds homes for the working poor.

Beginning in the mid-1980s, Carter began to speak out frequently on national issues and to criticize the policies and programs of the Reagan Administration. The former president also began to play an increasingly important role as an elder statesman, attempting to mediate the long-running civil war in Ethiopia, monitoring elections in Panama and Nicaragua, and proposing an international peace conference to monitor the Arab-Israeli dispute. Much to the chagrin of many American Jews, he continued to be openly critical of Israel for its refusal to stop building settlements on the West Bank and its unwillingness to grant the Palestinians greater political autonomy.

As Carter reentered the public arena in his post-presidential years, he gained a degree of popularity and stature with the American people that he had not enjoyed when he left office in 1981. In retirement, as a private citizen, according to *Newsweek*, Jimmy Carter had become "the modern model of a successful ex-president of the United States."

[D.G.D.]

Ronald Reagan

Served from 1981 to 1989

Born on February 6, 1911, in Tampico, Illinois

Member of the Disciples of Christ and Presbyterian denominations

Married Jane Wyman on January 26, 1940; divorced 1948
Married Nancy Davis on March 4, 1952

Father to one daughter and one adopted son with Jane
Father to one son and one daughter with Nancy

Candidate of the Republican Party

Vice president under Reagan: George Bush

First Inaugural Address delivered on January 20, 1981
Second Inaugural Address delivered on January 21, 1985

Fortieth President of the United States

A T AGE SIXTY-NINE, RONALD WILSON Reagan was the oldest person ever elected president of the United States; he was reelected to a second term, by a large majority, at the age of seventy-three. Reagan also was the only professional actor to win election to the presidency. Prior to entering politics at the age of fifty-five, when he was elected governor of California, Reagan had appeared in more than fifty movies and was the host of two popular television series. His background, as a future president, was distinctive in other ways as well. Reagan was the only divorced candidate to be elected to the presidency. He also was the only former leader of a labor union to be elected president, having twice served as president of the Screen Actors Guild and having led its members in a long strike against the movie industry.

Ronald Reagan was born on February 6, 1911, in Tampico, Illinois. During the Great Depression, he attended Eureka College, a small Disciples of Christ school near Peoria, Illinois. After graduating in 1932, Reagan became a radio announcer in Iowa, where his distinctive play-by-play coverage of baseball, football, and other sports would attract a wide following, reaching much of the Midwest.

Upon visiting Hollywood in 1937, a friend arranged for Ronald Reagan to have a screen test, and Warner Brothers soon offered him a two-hundred-dollar-a-week contract that he immediately accepted. Reagan's acting career took off in 1940, when he portrayed the dying football player George Gipp in *Knute Rockne—All American*. His movie career reached its peak in 1941 in the acclaimed *King's Row*, in which Reagan starred as a small-town playboy who awakens to find his legs amputated by a sadistic surgeon. His

character's immortal waking line, "Where's the rest of me?" became the title of Reagan's 1965 autobiography.

After serving in the U.S. Army from 1942 to 1945, Ronald Reagan returned to Hollywood and, in 1947, became president of the Screen Actors Guild, a labor union of movie performers. As his film career waned, Reagan began to appear on television, serving as host of the *General Electric Theater* television series from 1954 to 1962 and as master of ceremonies for *Death Valley Days*, a TV Western series in which he sometimes performed, from 1962 to 1965.

A liberal Democrat, Reagan campaigned for Harry S. Truman in 1948 and actively supported Helen Gahagan Douglas in her U.S. Senate race against Richard Nixon in 1950. Though he did not change his voter registration from Democrat to Republican until 1962, Reagan supported the presidential candidacies of Dwight D. Eisenhower in 1952 and 1956, and Richard Nixon in 1960.

As a spokesman for the General Electric Company, Reagan began to espouse conservative political principles, transforming himself from a liberal adversary of big business to one of its most visible champions. Politically, as he would later put it in his autobiography, he underwent a transformation from what he called "a near hopeless hemophiliac liberal" Democrat who "bled for causes" to a staunchly conservative Republican.

It was Reagan's old friend Walter Annenberg, the Jewish publishing tycoon and philanthropist, who had recommended Reagan for the job of host of *General Electric Theater*, which would propel Reagan into Republican politics. Annenberg, a leading Republican Party fundraiser who would later be appointed ambassador to Great Britain by Richard Nixon, had been a friend of Reagan since 1938.

In 1964 Reagan served as cochairman of California Republicans for Goldwater. In the last days of the campaign, he delivered a thirty-minute nationally televised speech on behalf of presidential nominee Goldwater, which raised more money than any other political speech in history. This television address for Goldwater marked a watershed in Reagan's political career, convincing wealthy California conservative Republicans that this man had great potential as a political candidate. In 1966 Reagan easily won the Republican nomination for governor of California and, in the November election, won an upset victory over Democratic Governor Edmund G. (Pat) Brown by nearly a million votes. Reagan was reelected by a sizable majority in 1970.

Less than a year after stepping down as governor of California, Reagan announced his decision to challenge President Gerald Ford for the 1976 Republican presidential nomination. At the Republican National Convention in 1976, Reagan received 1,070 delegate votes, only sixty less than Ford. Despite Reagan's narrow loss in 1976, his impressive showing established him as the frontrunner for the Republican presidential nomination in 1980, at which time he was easily nominated on the first ballot.

In the November election, Reagan won in a landslide, defeating Jimmy Carter by more than eight million popular votes and receiving 489 electoral votes to Carter's 49. American Jews, increasingly concerned over the Carter Administration's policies toward Israel, were less supportive of Carter's reelection than they had been of any recent Democratic presidential candidate.

A 1978 Carter Administration decision to sell advanced weapons to Saudi Arabia and Egypt had convinced a growing minority of Jewish Democrats that Carter was ready to abandon Israel. "If another presidential election were held today," *Newsweek* wrote at the time, "some experts re-

President and Mrs. Reagan.

port that disaffected Jews might turn the tide against Carter in crucial states such as New York, California, Illinois and Michigan." And so they did in part in 1980, when Ronald Reagan, a staunch supporter of Israel since 1948, received close to 40 percent of the Jewish vote. With the third-party candidate, John Anderson, receiving approximately 15 percent, Jimmy Carter became the first Democratic presidential candidate since the 1920s to receive less than 50 percent of the Jewish vote.

Reagan and Israel

Ronald Reagan entered the White House with a strong record of support for Israel. As early as 1967, during the Six-Day War, Governor Reagan began speaking at public rallies for Israel. At a rally held at the Hollywood Bowl in Los Angeles the day after the war ended, Reagan received a standing ovation from the thirty thousand people in attendance for his stirring appeal on behalf of Israel's safety and security. In 1971 Reagan was instrumental in getting the California State Legislature to sign into law a bill authorizing banks and savings institutions to buy and invest in Israel bonds. This was the first such law in the United States and would become the model for similar laws passed in other states.

During his emergence as a presidential candidate in the late 1970s, Reagan's thinking on foreign affairs was strongly influenced by a group of mostly Jewish neoconservative intellectuals and foreign policy analysts, centered around *Commentary* magazine, who reinforced his commitment to the safety and security of Israel as an important strategic ally whose special relationship with the United States needed to be preserved. Once in office, Reagan appointed several of these Jewish neoconservatives—including Elliot Abrams, Eugene Rostow, Max Kampelman, Michael Ledeen, Richard Pipes, and Richard Perle—to positions in his new administration.

During the 1980 presidential campaign, Reagan had left little doubt about his pro-Israel views. He denounced the PLO as a terrorist organization and described Israel as a "strategic asset," a "stabilizing force," and a military offset to Soviet influence. Early in the 1980 campaign, Albert A. Spiegel of Los Angeles, a leading Jewish Republican fundraiser and activist and the former governor's longstanding personal friend and political confidant, organized a reception for some fellow Jews to meet Reagan in New York. At this gathering, Reagan reiterated his support for Israel as a "major strategic asset to America" and as "the only stable democracy we can rely on in a spot where Armaggedon could come." Moreover, promised Reagan, "a strong, secure Israel is clearly in America's self-interest. To weaken Israel is to destabilize the Middle East and risk the peace of the whole world."

Throughout the campaign, Reagan made a point of differentiating his views on Israel from those of President Carter. As he reminded Jewish audiences, he had been appalled by the Carter Administration's decision to abstain rather than veto a UN resolution condemning Israel's proclamation of Jerusalem as its capital. "Jerusalem is now, and should continue to be, undivided," declared Reagan. "An undivided city of Jerusalem means sovereignty of Israel over the city." He also publicly disagreed with the Carter Administration's efforts to characterize Israel's West Bank settlements as illegal and was quick to reaffirm this position shortly after the election.

American Jews were further encouraged by Reagan's appointment of Jeane Kirkpatrick as the new ambassador to the United Nations. Known to be a friend of the Jewish community and a strong supporter of Israel, Kirkpatrick shared Reagan's belief, reiterated throughout the 1980 campaign, that "Resolutions in the United Nations which undermine Israel's positions and isolate her people should be vetoed because they undermine progress toward peace." Her mostly Jewish staff—which included deputy ambassadors Charles Lichenstein and Kenneth L. Adelman; her chief political adviser, Carl Gershman; and her legal counsel to the UN Mission, Allan Gerson—also were friends of Israel.

Despite all this overt support for Israel, once Reagan was in office, his administration encountered issues that caused strains and tensions with the Jewish community. In particular, the administration's controversial decision to sell AWACS (airborne warning and control system) and other advanced weaponry to Saudi Arabia angered many American Jewish leaders and touched off an eleven-month "battle" between the American Jewish community and the Reagan White House.

Although the AWACS presumably were intended to monitor Iranian air operations, they could be used against Israel as well. Virtually all segments of the Jewish community were strongly opposed to the AWACS deal. An influential group of Jewish Republicans even spoke out publicly against the sale, but to no avail. Despite intense lobbying by the American Israel Public Affairs Committee and other Jewish organizations, the Reagan Administration won the AWACS battle, and the U.S. Senate narrowly approved the arms sale to Saudi Arabia in October 1981.

Even with the tensions generated over the AWACS, overall relations between Jewish lead-

Welcoming Prime Minister Shimon Peres.

rael. United States financial aid to Israel increased steadily throughout the Reagan years, reaching an unprecedented $3 billion a year, in loans and grants, beginning in 1986. In 1988 Israeli Prime Minister Yitzhak Shamir declared to reporters: "This is the most friendly administration we have ever worked with. They are determined that the strong friendship and cooperation will continue and even be strengthened despite the differences that creep up from time to time." This statement seems to reflect the reality of the basic relationship between Israel and the United States during the Reagan era: Despite some strains, relations between America and Israel were stronger at the end of the Reagan tenure than before Reagan took office. In Ronald Reagan, most observers concur, the Jewish state had a reliable friend in the White House.

ers and the Reagan White House remained unimpaired. Jewish leaders were grateful that the Reagan Administration had not condemned the Israeli bombing of an Iraqi nuclear reactor the previous June. So, too, they were pleased that the United States did not "overreact" to Israel's incursion into Lebanon and the bombing of Beirut in 1982, and that President Reagan had reassured Israel's ambassador that the United States did not "anticipate any change" or "fundamental reevaluation" of their relationship as a result of these incidents. During his first term, Reagan also became the first American president to formally authorize the signing of a "Strategic Cooperation Agreement" between the United States and Israel, aimed at thwarting greater Soviet influence in the Middle East and affirming the Reagan Administration's intention of enhancing Israel's special relationship with the United States; there was no corresponding strategic pact signed with any Arab state.

Jewish leaders also were grateful to the Reagan White House for its financial assistance to Is-

Lunch with a Rabbi's Family

On Friday, October 26, 1984, during Ronald Reagan's reelection campaign, Rabbi Morris Friedman had invited the president to address his congregation, Temple Hillel in Woodmere, New York. The overflow assembly was pleased to hear the Chief Executive again proclaim his deeply felt concern for Israel. "If Israel is forced out of the United Nations, the United States and Israel will walk together," Reagan affirmed.

After the speech, the rabbi's wife, Adelaide, hosted an intimate pre-Sabbath luncheon for Reagan, which was attended by Secretary of State James Baker and New York Senator Alphonse D'Amato, along with the immediate Friedman family and several close friends.

The menu included petite *challot*, stuffed breast of chicken, apricot-noodle *kugel*, and apple *kuchen*. This was the first time a sitting president of the United States had lunch in a rabbi's home.

Present at the luncheon tendered by Rabbi and Mrs. Friedman were (left to right): Naomi Wolinsky, Rabbi and Mrs. Morris Friedman, Eugen Gluck, Steve Wolinsky, President Reagan, David and Tammy Friedman, Dr. Mark and Rose Friedman, and Mrs. Eugen Gluck.

Rabbi Friedman presents a woven skullcap to President Reagan as Senator Alphonse D'Amato looks on.

Soviet Jewry

During the 1980 presidential campaign, Reagan spoke out frequently on the issue of Soviet Jewry, attacking the Soviet Union for its imprisonment of Jewish dissidents and its curtailment of Jewish emigration. In a major address before B'nai B'rith in Washington, D.C., on September 3, Reagan declared: "The long agony of Jews in the Soviet Union is never far from our minds and hearts. All these suffering people ask is that their families get the chance to work where they choose, in freedom and peace. They will not be forgotten in a Reagan Administration."

Within four months of his inauguration, on May 28, 1981, Reagan met in the White House with Avital Sharansky to discuss the plight of her husband, Anatoly, the Soviet Jewish activist and spokesman for the Soviet dissident movement who had been imprisoned in Moscow since 1977.

Sharansky's plight became a major human rights cause for Secretary of State George Shultz and for Reagan, who successfully pressed for the dissident's release in his much-publicized summit meeting with Soviet prime minister Mikhail Gorbachev in Geneva, on November 19, 1985. When Sharansky arrived in Israel shortly after his release from prison on February 11, 1986, one of the first calls he received was from President Reagan, welcoming him to a land of freedom.

At his subsequent Reykjavik, Iceland, summit with Gorbachev in October 1986, Reagan would again raise the issue of Soviet Jewry and the importance of the Jewish immigration issue to the people of the United States, telling Gorbachev that "because Jews want to freely practice their religion," their freedom to emigrate was imperative.

"Reagan's interest in Soviet Jewry," as Prime Minister Yitzhak Shamir of Israel would later recall, "was immense; it was close to the first issue on the American agenda and was part of the confrontation between the two superpowers." The Soviet Jewry issue was woven, intrinsically, into the Reagan Administration's view of the So-

A warm welcome from President Reagan in the White House.

viet Union as an "evil empire" whose mistreatment and imprisonment of Jews was one of the most visible manifestations. At Reagan's behest, Shultz, who once attended a Passover Seder organized by Jewish refuseniks in Moscow, would frequently raise the issue of the Soviet government's imprisonment of Jewish dissidents. As Elliot Abrams, who served as assistant secretary of state for human rights under Shultz, put it: "The Reagan Administration kept beating the Soviet Union over the issue of Soviet Jews and kept telling them, 'You have to deal with this question. You will not be able to establish the kind of relationship you want with us unless you have dealt with this question—the question of emigration and the question of what you are doing internally.'"

The Bitburg Controversy

In April 1985, the White House announced that while on a state visit to West Germany, President Reagan would stop at a small military cemetery in Bitburg, where forty-seven officers of the Nazi SS (the German division that carried out many of the Holocaust murders) were buried. There, in the company of Chancellor Kohl of West German, President Reagan was to lay a ceremonial wreath, "in a spirit of reconciliation, in a spirit of forty years of peace." President Reagan's decision to visit Bitburg precipitated much public debate and an outpouring of criticism. Fifty-three members of the U.S. Senate and almost four hundred members of Congress sent petitions to President Reagan urging him not to visit the Bitburg cemetery. Polls showed that a majority of Americans, both Democrats and Republicans, opposed Reagan's scheduled trip.

Church groups urged Reagan to cancel his visit out of recognition that the Holocaust was the greatest moral crime of this century. American Jews were especially troubled, and several Jewish leaders condemned the planned presidential visit to a German military cemetery in strongly worded statements and op-ed columns. Elie Wiesel, chairman of the U.S. Holocaust Memorial Council, and a small group of Jewish leaders

met with Reagan and Vice President George Bush in the Oval Office and implored Reagan to cancel the visit. Their appeal, however, was unsuccessful.

On April 19, in what has been described as one of the most dramatic public encounters ever to take place in the White House, Elie Wiesel, on the occasion of being awarded a Congressional Gold Medal of Achievement, turned to President Reagan and virtually begged him to cancel his visit to Bitburg. Noting that the Jewish tradition required the individual to "speak truth to power," Wiesel—whose appearance was carried live by a number of television networks—said, "That place, Mr. President, is not your place. Your place is with the victims of the SS."

Although President Reagan was visibly moved by Wiesel's remarks, he did not cancel his visit to the German cemetery. After the ceremony, however, out of deference to American Jews, it was announced that President Reagan would visit the Bergen-Belsen concentration camp as well.

Until the day of the Bitburg visit, the Israeli government remained silent on the controversy. Afterward, Prime Minister Shimon Peres said: "I believe that President Reagan is a true friend of the Jewish people and the State of Israel....It is precisely for this reason that we feel deep pain at the terrible error of his visit to Bitburg....There can be no reconciliation regarding the past." Following his brief, ten-minute stop at Bitburg, Reagan visited the Bergen-Belsen concentration camp for over an hour. Addressing survivors of the Holocaust at Bergen-Belsen, Reagan said: "Many of you are worried that reconciliation means forgetting. But, I promise you, we will never forget."

Jewish Appointees

Although Reagan was the first president in several decades not to have appointed a Jew to his Cabinet, he relied heavily on the advice of Milton Friedman and other Jewish economists in shaping his economic policy, and he appointed several Jews to other important positions in his administration.

Elliot Abrams

In 1981, at the age of thirty-two, Elliot Abrams (1948-)was appointed assistant secretary of state for international organization affairs, becoming the youngest assistant secretary of state in the twentieth century. A graduate of Harvard Law School and the London School of Economics, and the son-in-law of Norman Podhoretz, editor of *Commentary* magazine, Abrams had served as special counsel to Senator Henry Jackson and chief-of-staff to Senator Daniel Patrick Moynihan, prior to actively supporting Reagan's presidential candidacy in 1980.

Abrams worked in the State Department for all eight years of the Reagan Administration, serving subsequently as assistant secretary of state for human rights (1981-1985) and as assistant secretary of state for inter-American affairs (1985-1988). Abrams cared passionately about the issue of Soviet Jewry and, during his tenure as assistant secretary of state for human rights, Soviet Jewry was a central issue on the agenda of the State Department's Human Rights Bureau, over which he presided.

Throughout his four-year tenure as assistant secretary of state for human rights, Abrams met regularly with Secretary of State Shultz to strategize and formulate ways to help secure visas for Jews wishing to leave the Soviet Union. Abrams met regularly with American Jewish communal leaders and with Avital Sharansky to discuss Soviet Jewish emigration and the plight of inividual Jewish refuseniks imprisoned in the U.S.S.R. On official visits to Moscow, Abrams, like Shultz, met with various Jewish refuseniks and gave Soviet officials lists of those imprisoned Jewish dissidents that the Reagan Administration hoped would be released.

On a 1984 visit to Europe, Abrams went from capital to capital—Vienna, Paris, Rome, London, and Madrid—meeting with foreign ministry officials to discuss Soviet Jewry and what might be done to press the Soviet government to increase Jewish emigration. Both Abrams and Richard Schifter, Abrams's Jewish successor as assistant secretary of state for human rights, would be especially helpful in securing visas for Jews seeking to leave the Soviet Union.

Milton Friedman

Ronald Reagan called the distinguished University of Chicago economist Milton Friedman (1912-) one of his closest and most trusted economic advisers. In his monumental work, *A Monetary History of the United States, 1867-1960*, Friedman argued that "classical" capitalistic ideas have more in common with traditional Judaic principles than do socialist ideas. Friedman, who had served as president of the American Economic Association in the late 1960s and had received the Nobel Prize for Economics in 1976, had been an adviser to British Prime Minister Margaret Thatcher and Israeli Prime Minister Menachem Begin. Under Reagan, Friedman served briefly as a member of the President's Council of Economic Advisers and had easy access to the White House. Upon Friedman's recommendation, Reagan appointed Harvard Economics Professor Martin Feldstein as chairman of the President's Council of Economic Advisers in 1982, the third Jew to serve in that position since the early 1970s.

Ronald Lauder

An heir to the Estée Lauder cosmetics fortune, Ronald Lauder had worked for many years in the European offices of the firm and was chairman of Estée Lauder International, Inc. In 1981 he joined the Reagan Administration and served as deputy secretary of defense for European and NATO policy for three years. Later, from 1986 to 1987, he was President Reagan's appointee as ambassador to Austria.

After leaving the Reagan Administration, Lauder emerged as one of America's most influential Jewish philanthropists and communal leaders. During the 1990s, the Ronald Lauder Foundation actively contributed to the revival of Jewish life in Eastern Europe after the collapse of the Soviet Union. He also would assume the national presidency of the Jewish National Fund and, in 1998, win election to the presidency of the Conference of Presidents of American Jewish Organizations, considered the preeminent leadership position in American Jewish life.

Leonore Cohn Annenberg

The wife of billionaire publishing tycoon, art collector, and philanthropist Walter Annenberg, who had served as ambassador to Great Britain during the Nixon Administration, Leonore Cohn Annenberg was appointed chief of protocol (with the rank of ambassador) by President Reagan. Although not religiously observant Jews, the Annenbergs gave monumental sums (in the tens of millions of dollars) to a wide variety of Jewish philanthropic causes, including Philadelphia's Dropsie College of Judaic and Near Eastern Studies (which was renamed the Annenberg Research Institute), Philadelphia's Federation of Jewish Charities, Yeshiva University's Albert Einstein School of Medicine, the U.S. Holocaust Memorial Museum, and Hebrew University of Jerusalem. As chief of protocol, Leonore Annenberg managed all Washington visits of foreign heads of state, arranged presidential visits overseas, coordinated ceremonial events for the secretary of state, accredited foreign diplomats, and ran Blair House, the official guest residence for visiting dignitaries.

Marshall Breger

After serving as a law professor and, from 1982 to 1983, as a senior fellow in legal policy at the Heritage Foundation, the conservative Washington, D.C., think tank, Marshall Breger (1946–) was named special assistant to the president, and White House liaison to the Jewish community. Breger was the first Orthodox Jew to serve on the White House staff, and he advised President Reagan on Jewish and Israeli affairs, regularly bringing to Reagan's attention the views of Jewish communal leaders on issues of Jewish concern. During his two-year tenure, Breger was both a popular and effective White House liaison. Jewish leaders, including those who strongly disagreed with Breger's conservative political views, believed that he had been instrumental in gaining them unusually good access to President Reagan and his advisers. In 1985, Breger was named chairman of the Administrative Conference of the United States, a presidential appointment that he held until 1991.

Other Jewish Appointees

Other Jews were appointed to important administration positions as well: Alan Greenspan, the influential Wall Street investment analyst who had served as chairman of the President's Council of Economic Advisers during the Nixon and Ford Administrations, and who advised Reagan on economic policy throughout his presidency, was appointed chairman of the Federal Reserve Board in 1987.

Eugene Rostow (1913–), former dean of the Yale Law School, who had served as an undersecretary of state in the Johnson Administration, was named director of the Arms Control and Disarmament Agency by President Reagan. He was succeeded by Kenneth L. Adelman (1946–), who had served as a deputy ambassador on Jeane Kirkpatrick's staff at the United Nations, and who would serve as the Arms Control and Disarmament Agency director from 1983 to 1987.

Max Kampelman (1923–), who had served with ambassadorial rank in the Carter Administration, continued to head the U.S. delegation to the Conference on Security and Cooperation in Europe, in Madrid, and was also appointed by President Reagan as ambassador and head of the U.S. delegation to the Geneva talks on Nuclear Disarmament and Space-Arms Reductions. Kampelman served as counselor to the State Department during President Reagan's second term.

Richard Perle (1941-), who had been a top aide to Senator Henry Jackson of Washington State from 1969 to 1980, was appointed assistant secretary of defense for international security policy in the Reagan Administration, serving from 1981 to 1987. Douglas Feith, a young Washington attorney and Jewish communal leader, served on Perle's staff as a deputy assistant secretary of defense for negotiations policy and as a Middle East specialist on the National Security Council as well. Richard Pipes (1923–), the Baird Professor of Russian History at Harvard University and formerly director of Harvard's Russian Research Center, was appointed director of the East European and Soviet Affairs division of the National Security Council.

Michael Horowitz served as general counsel for the Office of Management and Budget from 1981 to 1985, and subsequently chaired President Reagan's Domestic Policy Council on Federalism.

Morris Abram (1918–), an eminent New York attorney and Jewish leader, who had served as president of the American Jewish Committee, as president of Brandeis University, and as the first general counsel of the Peace Corps, chaired the President's Commission for the Study of Ethical Problems in Medicine and Biomedical and Behavioral Research from 1979 to1983, and was appointed by President Reagan as co-chairman of the U.S. Civil Rights Commission, serving from 1983 to 1986.

William Kristol (1952–), son of the neoconservative author and editor Irving Kristol (1920–) and historian Gertrude Himmelfarb (1922–), taught political philosophy at the University of Pennsylvania and Harvard's Kennedy School of Government before joining the Reagan Administration in 1985 as chief-of-staff to Education secretary William J. Bennett.

Highlights of the Reagan Years

Shortly after taking office on March 30, 1981, President Reagan was wounded in an assassination attempt as he and his presidential entourage were leaving the Washington-Hilton Hotel. "Honey, I forgot to duck," Reagan joked with his wife as he was rushed to a nearby hospital. After two hours of surgery, he enjoyed a speedy and complete recuperation, and was back at his office in the White House less than two weeks later. His press secretary, James Brady, was seriously wounded by the gunfire of the twenty-five-year-old assailant, John W. Hinckley, Jr.

One of Ronald Reagan's notable campaign pledges while running for president was to nominate a woman for a seat on the United States Supreme Court. Six months after the assassination attempt in 1981, President Reagan fulfilled this campaign pledge when the Senate confirmed Sandra Day O'Connor, an Arizona Appeals Court judge, to be the first woman justice on the Supreme Court.

During his presidency, Ronald Reagan named two other justices to the Supreme Court, Antonin Scalia and Anthony M. Kennedy, and elevated Justice William H. Rehnquist to the chief justiceship. When Justice Lewis F. Powell, Jr., announced his retirement from the Court in 1987, the president's first two nominees to succeed him failed to be confirmed. After an extraordinary and bitter battle, the first nominee, Judge Robert H. Bork, was rejected by the Senate by a vote of 58 to 42. President Reagan's second nominee, Judge Douglas H. Ginsburg, the first Jewish nominee to the Court since Lyndon Johnson's naming of Abe Fortas, withdrew his name from consideration when it was revealed that he had smoked marijuana as a Harvard Law School professor. Reagan's third nominee for Justice Powell's seat, Anthony M. Kennedy, was quickly confirmed by the Senate.

In the area of foreign affairs, the Reagan Administration's impact and achievements were especially evident in its policies toward the former Soviet Union.

Although they were predicated on the view that the Soviet Union was an "evil empire," a phrase that Reagan coined in a March 8, 1983, address to the annual convention of the National Association of Evangelicals, he also opposed the nuclear arms race between the United States and the Soviet Union, and spoke of a world in which nuclear weapons would be "banished from the face of the earth." At his November 1985 summit meeting with Mikhail Gorbachev in Geneva, Reagan raised the issue of nuclear disarmament and, the following year, at their Reykjavik, Iceland summit, Reagan and Gorbachev came close to agreement on a comprehensive ban on nuclear weapons. It was at these summits that Reagan had pressed so hard to help Soviet Jews.

In December of 1987, an historic arms reduction treaty between the United States and the Soviet Union was signed. Under the provisions of this treaty, both countries agreed to destroy hundreds of medium and short-range nuclear missiles.

Iran-Contra and Israel

In 1985 and 1986, high-ranking members of the Reagan Administration arranged for secret sales of arms to be made to Iran in violation of the Boland Amendment passed in 1982. Profits from these sales, which amounted to thirty million dollars, were sent to Nicaraguan right-wing "contra" guerillas for the purchase of arms to be used against the leftist Sandinista government. The chief negotiator in all these dealings was Lieutenant Colonel Oliver North, a White House military aide to the National Security Council, which was headed by National Security Adviser Robert C. McFarlane, and later by Vice Admiral John M. Poindexter.

The whole idea of selling arms came at the suggestion of the Israeli government because it hoped to improve relations with Iran and secure leverage in the quest for obtaining the release of American hostages held in Lebanon by pro-Iranian terrorists. North set up an entire covert network for supplying funds and military aid to the contras, but Israel denied it was involved in that deal.

When in November 1986 a Lebanese magazine exposed the United States arms deal with Iran, a series of congressional investigations was set in motion culminating, in February 1987, in the creation of the Tower Commission, a special panel headed by Senator John Tower of Texas. In November 1987 it issued a report that found no firm evidence that President Reagan had knowledge of the affair conducted by Oliver North and his associates. It also found Israel blameless. In May 1989, North was tried and convicted of obstructing Congress and the unlawful destruction of government documents.

George Bush, vice president at the time, was also implicated in the scandal but never charged. In December 1992, as president, he issued pardons to North, Poindexter, and others who had participated in the shoddy affair.

Post-Presidential Years

As the most popular outgoing president since Dwight D. Eisenhower, Ronald Reagan was one of the few presidents of this century to be able to bequeath the presidential office to his hand-picked successor. After attending George Bush's inauguration on January 20, 1989, Reagan retired to Southern California, where he worked on his ranch; signed a book contract with Simon & Schuster for his memoirs, which were published in 1990; and was actively involved in the development of the Reagan Presidential Library. During his first five years after leaving the White House, Reagan was also much in demand on the lecture circuit, traveling widely and speaking to political and business groups throughout the country.

In November 1994, Reagan announced that he was suffering from Alzheimer's disease and no longer would make public appearances. "When the Lord calls me home," Reagan said in his letter to the American people at the time, "whenever that may be, I will leave with the greatest love for this country of ours and eternal optimism for its future."

[D.G.D.]

George H. Bush

Served from 1989 to 1993

Born on June 12, 1924, in Milton, Massachusetts

Member of the Episcopal denomination

Married Barbara Pierce on January 6, 1945

Father to four sons and one daughter

Candidate of the Republican Party

Vice president under Bush: Dan Quayle

Inaugural Address delivered on January 20, 1989

Forty-First President of the United States

GEORGE BUSH HAD EMERGED AS RONALD Reagan's principal rival in the 1980 Republican presidential primaries, so he was shocked when Reagan invited him to be his vice-presidential running mate. But it came as a surprise to no one when Bush rode Ronald Reagan's coattails to the presidency in 1988.

Formative Years

Born on June 12, 1924, in Milton, Massachusetts, George Herbert Walker Bush was named after his maternal grandfather, George Herbert Walker. His father, Prescott S. Bush, was a successful and prosperous businessman who settled in Greenwich, Connecticut, in 1924 and became active in Republican politics. In 1952 Prescott defeated Abraham Ribicoff in a special election to fill the Senate seat of the late Brien McMahon.

Bush's mother, Dorothy, was born in Kennebunkport, Maine, a town that would be the location of the summer White House during the Bush presidency. She had married the wealthy Prescott Bush in Kennebunkport on August 6, 1921. (She died just two weeks after her son was defeated in his 1992 bid for reelection.)

Although Bush attended the best private schools, his mother, an accomplished athlete, taught George and her four other children (one daughter had died of leukemia in 1953 at age four) to refrain from being braggarts and to accept responsibility for their actions.

When George turned eighteen, he didn't wait to be drafted for military duty. The United States had entered World War II, and, on June 12, 1942, Bush enlisted in the Navy as a seaman second class. Within a year he had earned his wings, be-

coming the youngest pilot in the U.S. Navy. By 1945 he had been promoted to lieutenant, and shortly thereafter he married Barbara Pierce. He was twenty; she was nineteen. Her father, Marvin Pierce, was the publisher of *Redbook* and *McCall's* magazines.

Upon being discharged from the Navy after the war, Bush, who had been accepted to Yale prior to enlisting, enrolled in Yale's two-and-a-half-year accelerated program, majoring in economics. He graduated Phi Beta Kappa in 1948, but rather than become an investment banker like his father, George headed south with his bride and settled in Odessa, Texas. Over the course of the next eighteen years, he made a fortune in the risky oil business.

Bush's career took many turns on the road to the White House. He served as a Republican congressman from the Seventh Congressional District in Houston, Texas, from 1967 to 1971, after a failed attempt to win a Senate seat in 1964. Under President Nixon, from 1971 to 1973, Bush was U.S. ambassador to the United Nations.

While serving at the United Nations, the Security Council adopted a resolution deploring Israel's failure to honor previous UN resolutions regarding the status of Jerusalem. Ambassador Bush reaffirmed the U.S. position that it did not advocate that Jerusalem be a divided city but rather that it remain a unified city with free access to all. In addition, he restated the U.S. position that the final status of Jerusalem be determined by negotiations between Israel and Jordan in the context of a peace settlement.

In 1974 President Ford had appointed Bush chief liaison officer to China, a position he held for thirteen months. Bush was content to stay in Beijing, but President Ford wanted him to return

COURTESY OF THE NEW YORK PUBLIC LIBRARY

President George Bush with his wife, Barbara.

to the United States and assume the directorship of the Central Intelligence Agency (CIA), a position Bush held for one year. In 1980 Ronald Reagan selected Bush to be his running mate, and as a result of Ronald Reagan's decisive victory over incumbent Jimmy Carter, Bush became vice president. Eight years later, after Reagan had served two full terms, Bush scored a decisive victory over Democratic contender Michael Dukakis and won the presidency.

Religious Faith

Of all the U.S. presidents, George Bush and Jimmy Carter were the most overtly religious. George Bush had been raised in a family that read the Bible aloud at the breakfast table, and he and Barbara recited bedtime prayers together. They attended church services regularly on Sunday and read the Bible daily.

In Bush's acceptance speech at the Republican convention that nominated him, he said: "I am guided by certain traditions. One is that there is a God and He is good; and His love, while free, has a self-imposed cost: we must be good to one another."

The Pollard Case

A little more than halfway through Bush's vice presidency the Pollard spy case erupted. Jonathan Jay Pollard, born in the United States on August 6, 1954, was a U.S. naval intelligence officer who, in 1985, faced arrest on charges of spying for Israel.

Jonathan's father, Morris, was a professor of microbiology at Notre Dame University, in South Bend, Indiana, the town where Jonathan was born and raised. Jonathan's childhood was painful. As the only Jew in his school and not particularly athletic, he was subject to much teasing and other unpleasant experiences.

Pollard first attended Stanford University, where he majored in philosophy and history, and later studied law at Notre Dame University. He rounded out his education by studying politics at the Fletcher School of Law and Diplomacy at Tufts University. Having demonstrated high academic achievement, he was well qualified for the job he was offered as intelligence research specialist at Navy headquarters in Suitland, Maryland.

Jonathan's father was an ardent Zionist, and he imbued Jonathan with a love of Israel and a concern for her welfare. Israel, he was taught, was the haven for the remnant of Jews spared from the Holocaust. As Pollard worked at his job, he became aware of the fact that the United States was not sharing with Israel the intelligence it had been promised under a "convention of responsibility" agreed upon between the two countries. Pollard then took it upon himself, considering it a moral responsibility, to warn Israel of threats to its security.

A turning point in Jonathan Pollard's life occurred in May 1984 when he went to Washington to attend a lecture being given by Aviem Sella, an Israeli air force hero who had led the raid in June 1981 that had destroyed Iraq's nuclear reactor, which had the potential to rain terror on

George H. Bush being sworn in as president on January 20, 1989 as his wife, Barbara, looks on.

Israeli cities and their populations. In a letter he later wrote from prison, Jonathan expressed the feeling that had come over him at that time: "I'd rather be rotting in prison than sitting *shiva* for the hundreds of thousands of Israelis who could have died because of my cowardice."

Overwhelmed and enchanted by Sella's presentation, Pollard arranged to meet with him privately, at which time Pollard offered to provide Israel with useful secret information about Arab and Soviet strengths and weaknesses.

Over the next year and a half Pollard turned over to Sella a mountain of valuable information via a secretary working in the office of Israel's scientific attaché in Washington. In order to protect himself and Israel against future betrayal on the part of Pollard, Sella plied Pollard with generous amounts of cash. Pollard, in turn, did not hesitate to use his newly acquired wealth openly by frequenting the very finest restaurants, showering his wife with jewelry, and enjoying expensive overseas vacations.

When supervisors noticed this unusual change in Pollard's lifestyle, they became suspicious. The FBI was put on his trail. When Pollard became aware that his activities had become known, on November 21, 1985, he and his wife attempted to take refuge in the Israeli Embassy in Washington, but they were denied entry. When officials at the State Department questioned employees at the Israeli Embassy, they denied any knowledge of Pollard.

Feeling totally betrayed by Israel, Pollard agreed to cooperate with United States Attorney Joseph DiGenova, who promised that in return for a confession Anne Pollard would be treated leniently and Jonathan would not be sentenced to life in prison.

Secretary of State George Shultz then telephoned Prime Minister Shimon Peres, who promised to give the United States access to all records pertaining to the matter. Abraham Sofaer, legal adviser to the State Department, was chosen to head the mission to Israel to review all documents and suggest appropriate action against all involved in the spy case.

Ironically, while the investigation was ongoing, Sella was elevated to command Israel's largest air force base. When the United States learned of this promotion, it protested, and Sella was asked to resign. Secretary of Defense Casper Weinberger, whose grandfather was a Jew, insisted that Pollard be given the maximum sentence. When the Pollards appeared before Judge Aubrey Robinson in the United States District Court for sentencing on March 4, 1987, after fifteen months of imprisonment, Weinberger's analysis and recommendation played an important part in the decision to send Pollard to prison for life, and his wife, Anne, to prison for five years. Casper Weinberger's brief against Pollard was never made public.

In a conversation with Meir Rosenne, Israel's ambassador to the United States, Weinberger said: "It is difficult for me . . . to conceive of a greater harm to national security than that caused by the defendant . . . . Pollard should have been shot."

While the activity of Pollard was widely condemned, as was the participation of the Israeli government, many Jews as well as non-Jews were terribly disappointed at the severe punishment that was meted out to Anne Pollard and, especially, to Jonathan Pollard. Many Americans who had spied for foreign countries had not received such harsh treatment, and in this case a Jew who spied to help Israel and who in no way intended to harm the United States was punished to the limit.

Despite concerted efforts by prominent Jews and non-Jews to reduce the sentence imposed upon Pollard, neither Reagan, Bush, nor Bush's successor, Clinton, would take such action. CNN journalist Wolf Blitzer, who at the time was the Washington correspondent for *The Jerusalem Post*, interviewed Pollard in prison. In *Territory of Lies: The Exclusive Story of Jonathan Jay Pollard, the American Who Spied on His Country for Israel—and How He Was Betrayed,* published in 1989, he spells out Pollard's motivations for spying and the Israeli government's attempts to cover the damage to U.S.-Israel relations.

The Intifada

Beginning in late 1987, a series of demonstrations, strikes, and riots were staged by Palestinians against Israeli rule in Gaza and the West Bank. As time went on, Palestinian youths began to stone Israel's security forces and civilians, and the *intifada* (Arabic for "uprising") became increasingly violent.

At first, the leaders of the intifada—primarily members of the Palestine Liberation Organization (PLO)—were battling for the creation of an Islamic state in the whole of Palestine. Later, their demands were reduced: they would allow Israel to coexist with their state. Prime Minister Yitzhak Shamir of Israel would not entertain such a solution, and Israeli diplomat Walter Eytan responded to the PLO demand by warning: "For every incident of stone-throwing by Arab youths, ten settlements should be built. When we have settled the land, all the Arabs will be able to do about it will be to scurry around like drugged roaches in a bottle."

In April 1989, four months after ascending to the presidency, George Bush made it clear to Yitzhak Shamir, through Secretary of State James Baker, that the United States would insist that the intifada be halted by the PLO in return for Israel granting the Palestinians autonomy. For months prior to this declaration, Baker had worked closely—and secretly—with Defense Minister Yitzhak Rabin to achieve a peaceful resolution to the intifada. So as not to expose Rabin's involvement, Baker would always refer to Rabin as "the man who smokes." Shamir knew nothing about this initiative and would never have agreed to meet with the PLO.

Tensions lessened when later that month Prime Minister Shamir conferred with President Bush in Washington. Shamir proposed that the Palestinians hold "free democratic elections" to select representatives to discuss with Israel the future of the West Bank and Gaza. These elections would be followed by a period of time during which coexistence and cooperation between the groups would be tested. If successful, actual negotiations would commence. Bush expressed support for the plan, but Yasser Arafat opposed it. In June 1989, however, ninety-two U.S. senators wrote to Secretary of State Baker in support of Shamir's plan.

By July 1989, Prime Minister Shamir would discover that even his own Likud Party did not support his plan. In response to the pressure, he added four conditions:

1. There will be no participation in the elections by East Jerusalem residents.
2. There will be no elections until the intifada ends.
3. Israel will not give up any territory and no Palestinian state will be created.
4. Jewish settlements will continue to be established in the West Bank and Gaza.

Vice President Dan Quayle, President Bush, and Yitzhak Shamir exchange views at the White House.

By October, when it had become evident to Bush and Baker that Shamir would not compromise Israel's position even if his instransigence meant the downfall of his government, Bush telephoned him to complain: "We've invested a lot in this initiative." But Shamir insisted: "We will not meet with the PLO." To which Baker responded: "If you want a confrontation with the United States, that's fine."

Nevertheless, at the December 1989 meeting of the United Nations General Assembly, Vice President Dan Quayle formally stood up for Israel and favored repeal of Resolution 3379, which defined Zionism as a "form of racism and racial discrimination." In a September 1991 speech at the United Nations General Assembly, President Bush would once again urge the repeal of the 1975 resolution equating Zionism with racism. "This body cannot claim to seek peace and at the same time challenge Israel's right to exist," he said.

The Persian Gulf War

Concern over the Israeli-Arab dispute was placed on the back burner when, on August 2, 1990, Iraq invaded neighboring Kuwait. In December 1990 Prime Minister Yitzhak Shamir met with

President Bush in Washington, D.C., to discuss the developing crisis in the Persian Gulf. At the conclusion of the two-hour meeting, Shamir announced that the president assured him that "there will not be any deal at the expense of Israel." On January 8, 1991, after garnering the cooperation of scores of nations worldwide, Bush asked Congress to authorize the "use of all necessary means" to evict Iraqi forces from Kuwait. On January 12, Congress voted President Bush authority to send U.S. troops into combat.

Though President Saddam Hussein of Iraq was warned that a full-fledged attack was imminent, he refused to back down. Instead, he threatened that, should Iraq be attacked, he would unleash against Israel Scud missiles armed with chemical and biological weapons.

The Israeli government took the threat seriously and urged all its citizens to prepare sealed rooms in their homes where they might remain protected during an attack. In addition, gas masks were issued to the entire population.

Fearful that if Israel were attacked, she would retaliate, Bush sent a mission headed by Deputy Secretary of State Lawrence Eagleburger to Israel to urge Shamir to stay out of the conflict and pledged that the United States would protect her. On Friday morning, January 18, 1991, Iraq launched the first Scud missile attack against Israel. Bush immediately phoned Shamir, urging that Israel exercise restraint and not retaliate. Patriot antimissile batteries, to be manned by American soldiers, were dispatched to Israel.

Between January 18 and February 25, 1991, Iraq fired forty missiles at Israel. In these attacks, one person was killed by a direct hit, twelve deaths resulted from injuries related to the missile attacks, and nearly two hundred Israelis were wounded. Over four thousand buildings were damaged. The United States granted Israel more than $600 million to help cover the damage suffered as a result of the Gulf War.

Bush praised Israel for its "low-profile position" during the crisis, and because of Shamir's cooperation, a turnabout ensued in Israel-U.S. relations. Bush and Shamir never became close friends, but their new alliance opened the door to eventual negotiations between the PLO and Israel.

Bush's Jewish Appointees

It is quite evident from the sparse number of high-level Jewish appointees in the Bush Administration that the president was not comfortable with the Jewish "influence" in Washington. At a September 1991 press conference, President Bush demanded that Congress delay Israel's request for a $10 billion loan to create housing for newly arrived Jews from the Soviet Union until after the Middle East peace conference scheduled for October. Exasperated, Bush said: "I'm against some powerful political forces . . . something like a thousand lobbyists on the Hill . . . ."

Soon thereafter, Bush reconsidered his comment. Feeling that it might be misinterpreted as anti-Semitic, he wrote to the president of the Conference of Presidents of Major American Jewish Organizations: "I am concerned that some of my comments at the Thursday press conference caused apprehension within the Jewish community. My reference to lobbyists and powerful political forces were [sic] never meant to be pejorative in any sense."

Despite his having defeated Michael Dukakis

of Massachusetts in the presidential election of 1988, the fact that the Jewish vote went to Dukakis by a margin of two-to-one must have disturbed Bush greatly. Perhaps this would explain why not one Jew served in his Cabinet. That aside, a number of Jews did occupy important posts in the Bush Administration. Prominent among them were Jay P. Lefkowitz and William Kristol.

Jay Lefkowitz, a graduate of Columbia College and Columbia Law School, who had also studied at Bar Ilan University in Israel, served as director of Cabinet affairs in the Bush White House and was the highest-ranking Jew on the White House staff during the Bush Administration. A religiously observant Jew who belonged to an Orthodox synagogue in Washington during his White House days, Lefkowitz kept a kosher home and left work early on Fridays to observe the Sabbath.

William Kristol, son of Irving Kristol, the eminent neoconservative author and editor, and Gertrude Himmelfarb, the distinguished social historian and authority on nineteenth-century England, and nephew of Milton Himmelfarb, the former longtime editor of the *American Jewish Year Book*, received his Ph.D. from Harvard. Kristol taught political philosophy at the University of Pennsylvania and at the Kennedy School of Government at Harvard before moving to Washington, D.C., in 1985, where he joined the Reagan Administration's Department of Education, eventually serving as chief of staff to the Education Secretary William J. Bennett. With the election of George Bush, Kristol became a top policy adviser and, subsequently, chief of staff to Vice President Dan Quayle. In 1994 Kristol would become the founding editor and publisher of the *Weekly Standard*, which would soon become one of the more influential journals of political opinion in the country. Involved in the Jewish community, Kristol belongs to a Conservative synagogue in Fairfax, Virginia.

Other Jews in the Bush Administration included:

- Robert Strauss (1918-), who, although a former Democratic Party chairman (1972–1977) and President Jimmy Carter's Middle

A destroyed house in South Tel Aviv following an Iraqi Scud missile attack in 1991.

East envoy (1979), was appointed ambassador to Russia (1991–1992)

- Richard Schifter, who continued to serve as assistant secretary of state for Human Rights, the position he had held during the last four years of the Reagan Administration
- Herman J. Cohen, assistant secretary for inter-African affairs
- Bernard Aronson, secretary for inter-American affairs
- Melvin Levitsky, secretary for international matters
- Arnold Kanter, undersecretary for political affairs when Lawrence Eagleburger took over as secretary of state following the resignation of James Baker
- Dennis Ross, director of the Policy Planning Bureau of the State Department
- Fred Goldberg, assistant secretary of the Treasury
- Paul Wolfowitz, who had served as director of the State Department's Policy Planning Bureau and as ambassador to Indonesia in the Reagan Administration, undersecretary of defense for acquisitions

- I. Stephen Goldstein, director of public affairs in the Department of the Interior
- Marshall Breger, who had served as special assistant to the president and liaison to the Jewish community during the Reagan Administration, solicitor in the Department of Labor
- Morris Abram, who had served as co-chairman of the U.S. Civil Rights Commission under Reagan, U.S. ambassador to the European headquarters of the United Nations in Geneva

Retirement

On January 20, 1993, George Bush attended the inauguration of William Jefferson Clinton as the forty-second president of the United States. Immediately thereafter, Bush and his wife left for Houston, Texas, to begin retirement.

[A.J.K.]

Bill Clinton

Served from 1993 to 2001

Born on August 19, 1946, in Hope, Arkansas

Member of the Southern Baptist denomination

Married Hillary Rodham on October 11, 1975

Father to one daughter

Candidate of the Democratic Party

Vice president under Clinton: Albert Gore, Jr.

First Inaugural Address delivered on January 20, 1993
Second Inaugural Address delivered on January 20, 1997

Forty-Second President of the United States

ALTHOUGH BORN IN THE SMALL TOWN OF Hope, Arkansas, where few, if any, Jews lived, William Jefferson (Bill) Clinton brought more Jews into his administration than any Chief Executive before him. As the forty-second president of the United States sailed through his first term, with a growing, healthy economy credited to his efforts, Jews generally admired his accomplishments and were pleased with his stewardship.

As Bill Clinton began his second term in 1997, many Jews, such as New York Councilman Noach Dear, who had campaigned for the president and raised funds for his reelection, praised him lavishly. "He [Clinton] is the first president I've met who truly loves the Jewish people. It's not a political thing. It's something that comes naturally—from his *kishkes* [gut]," said Dear.

But, then, the investigation of Independent Counsel Ken Starr alleged that the president had been imprudently involved with a young White House intern, a charge that was initially vehemently denied. In a memorable moment, Clinton, wagging his forefinger at the American public, declared: "I never had relations with that woman—Monica Lewinsky." The scandal brought the Clinton presidency dangerously close to collapse. Even one of Clinton's closest friends, Senator Joseph Lieberman of Connecticut, felt compelled to chastise the president openly and vigorously.

Early Years

Bill Clinton was born on August 19, 1946, to Virginia Blythe. His father, William Jefferson Blythe II, a salesman of heavy construction equipment, died in a freak automobile accident three months before Bill was born. The thought of losing a father without ever getting to know him weighed heavily on young Clinton, and he was determined never to waste a moment, realizing that life could unexpectedly be cut short.

In the 1950s, Bill's mother married Roger Clinton, whose surname Bill assumed. Together, Bill's mother and stepfather had one son, Roger.

The future president's stepfather was an alcoholic who, when drunk, often beat his wife and created a household filled with contention. Bill's mother, whom he adored, took up nursing and, as the president is quoted as saying in *The Comeback Kid*, "always did a good job as a parent. . . . We had a lot of adversity in our life when I was growing up, and she always handled it well."

Attraction to Politics

Clinton's interest in politics began when he was about ten years old. The family had acquired its first television, and during the summer of 1956 Bill's eyes were glued to the set. He was mesmerized by the goings-on at the Democratic convention, which nominated Adlai Stevenson of Illinois, and then the Republican convention, which nominated war hero Dwight D. Eisenhower. Years later, in an interview with the *Arkansas Democrat-Gazette* (July 15, 1987), Bill recalled how "fascinated" he was by the scene, adding, "I was the only person in my family who sat there and watched it all."

Bill Clinton's young-adult fascination with the world of politics reached its peak when, in July of 1963, he traveled to Washington from Arkansas as part of the American Legion program Boys' Nation. There he met and shook hands with Presi-

Bill and Hillary Clinton during his first term as president.

In 1970, in the midst of his third year at Oxford, Bill was offered a scholarship to Yale University Law School. He accepted and in 1973 earned his law degree. It was in the Yale law library that he first met law student Hillary Rodham, a graduate of Wellesley College, who had been class speaker at her commencement exercises. On October 11, 1975, when Bill was twenty-nine and Hillary twenty-seven, the couple were married in a small private ceremony attended only by their immediate families.

From 1973 to 1976, Bill Clinton taught law at the University of Arkansas. Convinced that his future lay in politics, he made his first bid for public office in 1976, winning the Democratic primary for attorney general of Arkansas. Running unopposed in the general election, he had time to direct his efforts to assist in Jimmy Carter's presidential campaign in Arkansas.

In 1978 Clinton ran for governor of Arkansas and won. However, as governor, many voters found him arrogant and smug, and he went down to defeat when seeking a second term. Admitting that "I made a young man's mistake" and promising to correct his errors, in 1982 Arkansas voters gave him another chance. They returned him to the governorship, where he would serve five consecutive two-year terms. As a result, biographers dubbed him "The Comeback Kid."

Having had years of experience in state politics, Clinton began to take a more active role on the national scene. In 1985 he was chosen to deliver the Democratic response to President Reagan's State of the Union Address.

On October 3, 1991, Clinton announced that he was hoping to be the next Democratic nominee for president. At the Democratic convention the following August, after having his name placed in nomination in a highly praised speech by Governor Mario Cuomo of New York, Clinton

dent John F. Kennedy. From that moment on, Bill's previously stated intention of becoming a doctor receded, replaced by the thought that one day he might become president of the United States.

Georgetown, Oxford, and Yale

Always an excellent student, Bill Clinton chose to attend Georgetown University because of its superior political science and foreign service programs. During his junior year at Georgetown, Clinton worked for Senator J. William Fulbright of Arkansas, chairman of the Senate Foreign Relations Committee and a leading critic of the Vietnam War. Clinton shared Fulbright's opposition to that involvement. Though Clinton had legitimately avoided serving in Vietnam, he was widely accused of being a draft dodger.

Graduating from Georgetown in 1968 with a degree in international affairs, Bill Clinton then went on to pursue his studies as a Rhodes scholar at Oxford University, in England. One of his classmates there was Robert Reich, who would become Clinton's first secretary of labor. Another fellow student was Ira Magaziner, who would later advise Clinton on policy development.

was nominated on the first ballot. He chose Al Gore, the junior senator from Tennessee, to be the vice-presidential candidate, despite the conventional wisdom that it is foolish to select someone from a neighboring state as a running mate. In the general election, held on November 3, 1992, Clinton defeated Republican candidate George Bush and Independent candidate Ross Perot. In 1996 Clinton-Gore easily achieved re-election over Republican challengers Bob Dole and Jack Kemp.

Affinity to Judaism

Early in the Clinton presidency, a story made the rounds about a Jewish staff member who had been assigned the task of decorating the White House for Christmas. When he objected, saying that he felt a Christian should be given this task, one of the fellow Jewish staffers reprimanded him: "You have to do it. Everyone around here is Jewish."

The fact is that by the time President Clinton completed his two terms in office, he had surrounded himself with more Jewish advisers, legal counselors, consultants, and pollsters than any other president. In addition, he had appointed more Jewish ambassadors, Supreme Court justices, and Cabinet members than any of his predecessors. When making selections, Clinton seemed to be interested not in an individual's religious affiliation but in his or her intellectual prowess and ability to produce results.

While religion seemingly played little part in Clinton's choice of political appointees, religion was an important influence in his own life. New York Councilman Noach Dear once said of Clinton, "This guy is brilliant, forgets nothing. The president knows the Jewish Bible and the New Testament practically by heart."

This evaluation was borne out when, in an address to the nation after taking his second oath of office on January 20, 1997, Clinton added the following biblical quotation from Isaiah (58:12) to the words that had been prepared for him by his speechwriters: "Thou shalt raise up the foundations of many generations, and thou shalt be called the repairer of the breach, the restorer of paths to dwell in." He was urging each person to accept personal responsibility for himself and for the nation.

In his five-year association with Bill Clinton, including four years as a White House consultant, George Stephanopoulos observed the president's love of the Bible at close range. In his political memoir, *All Too Human*, Stephanopoulos describes one of the most gratifying days of the Clinton presidency. The night before a peace agreement was to be signed on the White House lawn in 1993 between Prime Minister Yitzhak Rabin of Israel and Chairman Yasser Arafat of the Palestine Liberation Organization, Clinton arose at 3:00 A.M., reached for his Bible, and turned to the Book of Joshua for a description of the fall of Jericho and the Israelite conquest of Canaan. He was searching for words that might be used in his speech and was struck by the closing phrase of chapter eleven: ". . . the land had rest from war."

Jewish Cabinet Members

Seven of the Cabinet members chosen to lead the executive departments during Clinton's terms in office were Jews. These included Madeleine K. Albright, Robert E. Rubin, Lawrence Summers, William S. Cohen, Daniel Glickman, Mickey Kantor, and Robert Reich. In the Clinton Administration (as of October 11, 1999), Cabinet-level rank was also accorded to Jacob J. Lew, director of the office of management and budget, Richard Holbrooke, ambassador to the United Nations, and Charlene Barshefsky.

Madeleine K. Albright

Born in Prague, Czechoslovakia, on May 15, 1937, Madeleine Albright became the first woman ever to serve as U.S. secretary of state.

Madeleine's parents, Anna Speeglova and Josef Korbel, were married in April 1935. Josef's ambition was to be accepted for service in the Czech foreign ministry. However, certain that he would not achieve this if he was identified as a Jew, on

Past and present U.S. presidents in attendance at Yitzhak Rabin's funeral—including Jimmy Carter, George Bush, and Bill Clinton.

never referred to their Jewish past. It was not until 1997 that she learned that her family was Jewish and that three of her grandparents had died in German concentration camps.

From England, the Korbel family moved to the United States, and Josef Korbel became associated with the University of Denver, where he founded a graduate school specializing in international relations. Madeleine became a naturalized citizen and learned to speak English without an accent by the time she graduated from high school. In 1959 she graduated from Wellesley College with a degree in political science.

Shortly thereafter, Madeleine married journalist Joseph M. Albright, a member of a wealthy newspaper family. Since the Albrights were devout Episcopalians who would not intermarry with Catholics, Madeleine agreed to convert to her husband's faith. Ironically, her mother-in-law once said to her: "It would have been much easier if you were a Jew than a Catholic."

The Albrights moved to Long Island, New York, and had three daughters. While raising her children, Madeleine pursued graduate studies at Columbia University where, in 1968, she earned a doctorate in public law and government.

When Joseph Albright became Washington bureau chief of *Newsweek*, one of his family's publications, Madeleine and the children moved with him to the nation's capital, and Madeleine began making the associations that would lead to her eventual political career.

Madeleine Albright's extensive network of social contacts began with Senator Edmund S. Muskie of Maine, whom she advised on policy issues and for whom she raised funds for his unsuccessful bid for the Democratic presidential

every state document that asked his religious affiliation he entered, "without confession." In 1937 Josef received his first assignment as press attaché at the Czech Embassy in Belgrade.

After the Nazis occupied Czechoslovakia in 1939, Madeleine's family fled to London (where other Korbel family members lived) and was baptized in the Roman Catholic Church. Madeleine, who was four years old at the time, said she has no recollection of the event and that her parents nomination in 1972. After Jimmy Carter became president in 1977, she was appointed congressional liaison to the National Security Council, working in tandem with Carter's national security adviser, Zbigniew Brzezinski.

In January 1983, Joseph Albright divorced Madeleine to marry a younger woman. The divorce settlement left Madeleine with an estate worth several million dollars. She then began teaching part-time at Georgetown's school of foreign service.

In 1984, when Walter Mondale became the Democratic nominee for president and three-term Queens congresswoman Geraldine Ferraro was his running mate, Albright began working closely with Ferraro, advising her on issues of foreign policy. Mondale and Ferraro lost the election, but a strong bond had developed between Madeleine and Geraldine, and in 1985 the two women planned a visit to Moscow.

When a rabbi learned of the scheduled trip, he asked Ferraro to take some prayer books and medication to the family of the prominent Jewish refusenik Yosef Begun, who was in prison. Upon reaching the Russian capital, and not wanting to make a call to the family of a Russian dissident from their room, Albright and Ferraro crammed into a tiny public telephone booth to make contact. The next evening, despite the fact that they had been warned that Americans were often given rough treatment by the police for visiting the Beguns, they took a cab to the refusenik's home.

During the intervening years of Republican control of the White House, Madeleine remained active in Democratic politics, and in 1993 Bill Clinton selected her to be U.S. ambassador to the United Nations. In 1994, when Albright had occasion to visit Prague, her first cousin Dasha, who lived there, tried to contact her, but to no avail. Dasha's father and Madeleine's father were brothers, and both had converted to Catholicism. Dasha learned about her Jewish ancestry at an early age, while it apparently remained unknown to Madeleine.

When, in 1997, President Clinton selected Albright to be his secretary of state, Michael Dobbs, a diplomatic reporter for *The Washington Post*, decided to investigate Madeleine's mysterious background. It seemed strange that Madeleine's family in England all knew of their Jewish heritage but that Madeleine did not. When Dobbs presented her with documents revealing the fact that her parents and grandparents were Jews, she admitted having heard of such claims and having received "an occasional letter" about her Jewish ancestry, but denied knowing about the deaths of her grandparents in Nazi concentration camps. The fact that Albright felt safe in helping Geraldine Ferraro in the mission of delivering prayer books to the Begun family in 1985 may lend credence to the claim that she knew nothing of her Jewish past.

Bill Clinton's nomination of Madeleine Albright to succeed Warren Christopher as secretary of state was unanimously confirmed by the Senate. A believer in fighting force with force, she advocated a hard-line approach to international crimes against humanity. She strongly supported NATO's offensive against Yugoslavia and its dictator, President Slobodan Milosevic, a man Clinton called "Europes's last dictator." Albright also played an active role in search of a solution to problems in the Middle East.

Robert E. Rubin

Clinton considered three men to fill the important post of secretary of the Treasury: Lloyd Bentsen, Roger Altman, and Robert E. Rubin. Rubin had been a longtime fundraiser for the Democratic party, and especially for Bill Clinton during the 1992 presidential campaign.

Clinton invited Rubin to Little Rock, Arkansas, on November 24, 1991, where the two men spoke for several hours. Rubin, who was born on August 29, 1938, had graduated *summa cum laude* from Harvard in 1960, majoring in economics, and had received a law degree from Yale. Working on Wall Street, he had become co-chairman of the investment company Goldman, Sachs. Though Clinton was highly impressed with Rubin's astuteness, for purely political reasons he decided to appoint Senator Lloyd Bentsen of Texas as secretary of the Treasury. Later, Rubin admitted that Clinton's choice was a wise one, but Clinton did offer Rubin the directorship of the Council of Economic Advisers, a position equal in rank to that of national security adviser.

On December 6, 1994, hoping to become secretary of defense, Bentsen resigned as Treasury secretary, and President Clinton nominated Rubin to succeed him. On January 10, 1995, Rubin was confirmed by the Senate and is credited with being the architect of Clinton's successful economic policy.

In Rubin's philosophy, economics and trade are America's two most powerful tools, mightier even than diplomacy and military force. He counseled a hands-off policy toward the Federal Reserve Board, giving Chairman Alan Greenspan full rein, a decision that in large measure accounted for unemployment being at its lowest since 1953 and for the GDP (gross domestic product) growing by 22.8 percent. Inflation was at its lowest in decades, and the stock market soared.

On May 12, 1999, Rubin announced that he was retiring from government service and returning to the private sector. He was succeeded by his deputy secretary, Lawrence Summers.

Lawrence H. Summers

A brilliant Jewish economist who was born in New Haven, Connecticut, in 1954, Lawrence Summers received a bachelor of science degree from the Massachusetts Institute of Technology in 1975 and a doctorate from Harvard University in 1982. At the age of twenty-eight he had become a professor of economics at Harvard and taught there from 1983 to 1993.

Prior to serving from 1993 to 1995 as undersecretary of the Treasury for international affairs under Secretary Lloyd Bentsen, from 1991 to 1993 Summers was vice president and chief economist of the World Bank. After Bentsen resigned, Summers continued as deputy secretary of the Treasury under Robert Rubin. When Rubin resigned in 1999 to return to private life, Summers succeeded him and played a leading role on issues relating to international economic and financial policy.

When Lawrence Summers assumed the post of secretary of the Treasury, Stuart E. Eizenstat, who

had been U.S. ambassador to the European Union, became deputy secretary.

William S. Cohen

In 1997 President Clinton nominated William S. Cohen to replace William Perry as secretary of defense. Early in his political career, Cohen had served for three years in the House of Representatives and then, in 1978, was elected Republican senator from Maine. In 1996, disillusioned with partisan politics and fundraising demands that sometimes required underhanded dealings, he decided not to run for a fourth term. Cohen's nomination as secretary of defense was approved unanimously by the Senate, a body that appreciated Cohen's years of devoted service.

Born on August 28, 1940, in Bangor, Maine, William Cohen's father, Reuben, was a baker who had emigrated from Russia and married Irish Protestant Clara Hartley. For a while, William attended after-school Hebrew classes, but his mother's religious influence dominated.

Cohen was graduated from Bowdoin College in Maine in 1962, and in 1965 he received a law degree from Boston University. For a brief period he practiced law in Bangor.

Cohen exhibited tremendous talent and ability when, in 1999, NATO forces confronted Slobodan Milosevic, the Serbian dictator who was engaged in the ethnic cleansing of the Albanians in Kosovo. Cohen's steady hand, clear mind, and patient nature were contributing factors in effecting an end to the conflict, imperfect as it turned out to be.

Dan Robert Glickman

Born in Wichita, Kansas, on November 24, 1944, Daniel Robert Glickman received his bachelor of arts degree from the University of Michigan and a law degree from George Washington University. He served in the U.S. House of Representatives representing Kansas's fourth congressional district, where he demonstrated leadership on the House committee on agriculture, which had jurisdiction over almost 74 percent of the U.S. Department of Agriculture's farm program budget.

By the time Dan Glickman was sworn in as U.S. secretary of agriculture on March 30, 1995, replacing Mike Espy, who had resigned, he was already a recognized leader in food and agriculture policy.

Mickey Kantor

Born in Nashville, Tennessee, on August 7, 1939, Kantor received his law degree from Georgetown University in 1968. In 1978 he served along with Hillary Clinton on the board of directors of the Legal Service Corporation, which dispensed federal funds throughout the United States. When Bill Clinton entered the race for the Democratic presidential nomination in 1992, Kantor joined the campaign, revealing his acute knowledge of the complex global business environment and its implications for U.S. trade policy. Clinton rewarded Kantor by appointing him, on December 24, 1992, U.S. trade representative. In that capacity he helped the president conclude more than two hundred agreements to expand trade.

In 1996, when Secretary of Commerce Ronald H. Brown died in an airplane accident, Kantor replaced him as secretary of commerce.

Kantor coordinated Clinton's entire legal defense team before and during the impeachment hearings that ended in 1999 with the president's exoneration.

Robert Reich

Born in Scranton, Pennsylvania, on June 24, 1946, Robert Reich graduated from Dartmouth College and then attended Oxford University, where he received a master's degree. At Oxford, in 1970, he was a Rhodes scholar and a classmate of Bill Clinton.

Upon returning to the United States, Reich attended Yale Law School, from which he received his doctorate in 1973.

In 1993, while a professor of political economics at Harvard's Kennedy School of Government, Reich was chosen by Clinton to be his secretary of labor. Reich urged the administration to accept the view "that our ability to thrive as a nation depends on the capacity of our people to work productively together—both as participants in an economy and as members of a society." He insisted that "a growing economy will lift all boats, and all American workers will prosper."

Although Reich has been called the "godfather" of Clinton's economic program—which called for more public investment, a higher minimum wage, and pension-plan protection—he is given little credit for America's economic growth during his four years of service as secretary of labor.

After leaving Washington, instead of returning to Harvard, Robert Reich accepted an appointment as professor of social and economic policy at Brandeis University.

Jacob J. Lew

An Orthodox Jew, Jack Lew was appointed in 1996 to be the director of the office of management and budget. Born in New York City in 1955, he received his bachelor's degree from Harvard University in 1978 and a law degree from Georgetown University in 1983. In 1988 he served as issues director of the Democratic National Campaign Committee.

Richard C. Holbrooke

Richard C. Holbrooke was born in New York City on April 24, 1941, the son of two European immigrants. His mother, who divorced Richard's father when the boy was sixteen, often took Richard to Quaker meetings on Sundays. She once remarked: "I was an atheist and his father was an atheist. We never thought of giving Richard a Jewish upbringing."

After receiving a bachelor's degree from Brown University in 1962, Holbrooke began his career as a foreign-service officer. He studied Vietnamese and over the next few years served in a variety of posts in Vietnam, including staff assistant to Ambassadors Maxwell Taylor and Henry Cabot Lodge. In 1966 President Lyndon Johnson recalled Holbrooke to Washington so that he might work on his staff handling the Vietnam War.

In the years that followed, Holbrooke was named a fellow at the Woodrow Wilson School at Princeton and in 1970 was assigned as Peace Corps director in Morocco. From 1974 to 1975 he served as consultant to the president's commission on the organization of the government for the conduct of foreign policy.

In 1976 Holbrooke joined the Carter-Mondale presidential campaign and in 1977 was appointed by President Carter to be assistant secretary of state for Asian and Pacific affairs, a post he held until 1981. During his tenure, the United States established full diplomatic relations with China.

For the next few years Holbrooke was associated with Washington consulting firms that worked with such organizations as Lehman Brothers. In 1993 President Clinton recalled Holbrooke to public service and in 1994 appointed him assistant secretary of state for European and Canadian affairs. In 1995 Holbrooke negotiated a settlement that ended the war in Bosnia.

When Warren Christopher resigned as secretary of state in 1996, Richard Holbrooke had high hopes of being appointed to the position, but Clinton instead chose Madeleine Albright, and Holbrooke became the U.S. ambassador to Germany, the birthplace of Richard's mother.

In May 1998 Holbrooke was sent to Yugoslavia to meet Slobodan Milosevic and try to negotiate peace between the warring factions in Kosovo, a province of Serbia in which 90 percent of its two million inhabitants were ethnic Albanians seeking independence. A Kosovo Liberation Army (KLA) had been formed of Albanian freedom fighters who were battling Milosevic's army, which was intent on denying Kosovo self-determination.

On February 28, 1998, the Serbian army began destroying Albanian villages, indiscriminately killing innocent civilians as they drove them from their homes. The "ethnic cleansing" that resulted compelled the international community to intercede.

Holbrooke was sent by President Clinton to persuade Milosevic to halt the carnage, but his efforts failed. NATO forces, with the support of the United States, finally took action and began bombing Serbia mercilessly. By the end of October 1998, Milosevic agreed to pull his forces out of Kosovo, although he remained in power. Seeking to reward Holbrooke for a lifetime of service to the United States, in October 1998 President Clinton nominated him to be the U.S. ambassador to the United Nations, but the Senate Foreign Relations Committee held up confirmation for fourteen months.

Like Madeleine Albright, Holbrooke was born a Jew but raised a Roman Catholic. His wife, Kati Marton, whose Jewish parents fled from Hungary during the failed anti-Communist revolution of 1956, was raised as a Catholic. Only much later did she learn of her Jewish ancestry and that her grandparents had been killed in Auschwitz by the Nazis.

Charlene Barshefsky

A graduate of the University of Wisconsin in 1972 and in 1975 of the Columbus School of Law at Catholic University in Washington, D.C., Charlene Barshefsky (1950-) earned numerous high honors at both schools. Prior to her appointment as deputy U.S. trade representative from May 1993 to April 1996, she was a partner in the Washington, D.C., law firm of Steptoe & Johnson, where, for eighteen years, she specialized in international trade law and policy.

In her capacity as deputy trade representative, Barshefsky pursued bilateral and multilateral trade agreements with many Asian countries, which culminated in a November 15, 1999, landmark agreement with China that opened the country's markets to American companies by lifting many barriers to trade and investment. The successful seven-year negotiations set forth terms for China's accession to the World Trade Organization. Recognizing her unique ability "as a brilliant negotiator for our country" when she served as deputy U.S. trade representative in 1993, President Clinton appointed her, on December 13, 1996, to the ambassadorial position of permanent trade representative.

Ambassadors and Envoys

Among the Jewish ambassadors and envoys appointed by President Clinton during his eight years in office were: Stuart E. Eizenstat, Martin Indyk,

Daniel Kurtzer, Felix G. Rohaytn, and Dennis Ross.

Stuart E. Eizenstat

Born in Chicago, Illinois, on January 15, 1943, Stuart Eizenstat was an honors graduate in political science from the University of North Carolina in 1964 and from Harvard University in 1967, where he earned a law degree. In 1967 and 1968 he served on Lyndon Johnson's White House staff, and during President Jimmy Carter's administration was chief policy adviser for domestic affairs for four years.

During the Republican presidencies of Ronald Reagan and George Bush, Eizenstat's involvement in national politics was muted. For much of that time he was engaged in his law practice and from 1981 to 1992 was adjunct lecturer at the John F. Kennedy School of Government at Harvard. With the return of Democrats to power in 1993, Clinton appointed him ambassador to the European Union, whose headquarters were in Brussels, Belgium. In 1995 he was appointed special envoy for property claims in Central and Eastern Europe. As deputy secretary of the Treasury beginning in 1999, Eizenstat helped in the effort to promote human rights in Cuba. President Clinton praised him as a public servant who "handled many of our nation's most difficult missions, from successful efforts to lift food and medicine sanctions on trading partners—or nontrading partners—to the struggle for justice and compensation on behalf of the victims of the Holocaust."

Since his years at Harvard, Eizenstat, an observant Jew, displayed a keen interest in Jewish affairs. He would leave his office early enough on Fridays to observe the Sabbath, as did Senator Joseph Lieberman of Connecticut. When Eizenstat served in Brussels, he refurbished his kitchen to make it kosher. The work was paid for with private funds.

When Eizenstat's service in Brussels ended in 1996, Secretary of State Warren Christopher presented him with the Foreign Affairs Award for Public Service, the highest such honor that can be given to a noncareer ambassador.

From April 5, 1996 to June 6, 1997, Eizenstat served as undersecretary of commerce for international trade. On June 6, 1997, he was sworn in as undersecretary of state for economic, business, and agricultural affairs, and served in that position until July 16, 1999. When Lawrence Summers succeeded Robert Rubin as secretary of the Treasury in July 1999, Eizenstat was appointed deputy secretary.

Martin S. Indyk

On March 1, 1995, the U.S. Senate confirmed President Clinton's nomination of Martin Indyk as U.S. ambassador to the State of Israel, the first Jew to serve in that post. Clinton's historic nomination of Indyk countered the State Department's long-held assumption that naming a Jewish ambassador to Israel would raise questions about the evenhandedness of U.S. policy toward Israel and the Middle East. President Clinton's nomination of Indyk, however, enjoyed wide support throughout the foreign policy community, although some critics questioned Indyk's close ties to pro-Israel groups within the Jewish community.

Born in London on July 1, 1951, Indyk was raised and educated in Australia, where he received a doctorate in international relations from the Australian National University and had begun an academic career. While on a six-month sabbatical at Columbia University in 1982, Indyk had been invited to help set up a research department at the American Israel Public Affairs Committee [AIPAC], in Washington, D.C. The following year, with the backing of an AIPAC board member and Jewish financial support, Indyk became the founding executive director of the Washington Institute for Near East Policy, a pro-Israel think tank specializing in Arab-Israeli relations and U.S. Middle East policy, a position he held for eight years.

After serving as an adviser to presidential candidate Bill Clinton during the 1992 campaign, Indyk joined the Clinton Administration in January 1993, serving until 1995 as special assistant to the president and senior director of Near East and South Asian Affairs at the National Security Council. In this capacity, Indyk was principal

President Clinton conferring the Presidential Medal of Freedom on Edgar M. Bronfman, president of the World Jewish Congress.

adviser to the president and the national security adviser on Arab-Israel issues and a senior member of Secretary of State Christopher's Middle East peace team, where he worked closely with Dennis Ross.

During his April 1995 to October 1997 tenure as U.S. ambassador to Israel, Indyk helped strengthen U.S.-Israeli relations, advance the Middle East peace process, and substantially increase the level of trade and investment between the United States and Israel. In October 1997 he was nominated by President Clinton to be assistant secretary of state for Near Eastern affairs, the first Jew to serve in that position. In October 1999 Indyk was renominated by President Clinton for a second term as ambassador to Israel; he was sworn in on January 21, 2000.

Daniel Kurtzer

Born in Elizabeth, New Jersey, on May 14, 1948, Kurtzer received his bachelor's degree from Yeshiva University in 1971 and earned a doctorate from Columbia University in 1976. After serving in the State Department for several years, he accepted an appointment as dean of Yeshiva College, the undergraduate school of Yeshiva University. In 1979 Kurtzer returned to the State Department and served until 1982 as second secretary for political affairs at the American Em-

bassy in Cairo, where his fluency in Arabic (as well as Hebrew) was a valuable asset. This was followed by four years with the State Department, serving in Tel Aviv as a Middle East specialist.

On November 6, 1997, Kurtzer was confirmed by the Senate as ambassador to Egypt, succeeding Edward Wallace, who then became ambassador to Israel. Kurtzer was the first member of the Jewish faith to serve as an ambassador to a major Arab country.

At Kurtzer's swearing-in ceremony at the State Department, Undersecretary of State Thomas Pickering noted that "no one has worked harder, cared more, and done more for Arab-Israeli peace than Dan Kurtzer." And, Pickering added, "No one has logged more miles or eaten more tuna salad." This was in reference to the fact that, as an Orthodox Jew, Kurtzer was a strict observer of the dietary laws.

Thanks to a gift to the U. S. government by philanthropist S. Daniel Abraham, founder of Slim-Fast, Daniel Kurtzer and his wife, Sheila Doppelt, were able to install a fully kosher kitchen in the ambassador's residence in Cairo.

Some Egyptians were critical of the Kurtzer appointment, charging that now the U. S. government had two Israeli ambassadors in Egypt, the other being Zvi Mazel, the incumbent Israeli ambassador. But with the passage of time, Kurtzer's affable disposition dispelled such criticism. Ahmed Mather El Sayed, Egypt's ambassador to the United States, remarked: "I have known Dan as a friend and colleague for a long time and admire his moral and intellectual integrity. He has shown the capacity to be fair, tolerant, and objective even in difficult circumstances . . . . A truly religious man tends to be a better man—perhaps it should be a prerequisite for a good ambassador."

Felix G. Rohatyn

Born in Vienna, Austria, on May 29, 1928, Felix Rohatyn's family fled the Nazis and settled in France in 1938; in 1942 they moved to the

United States. In 1948 Rohatyn graduated from Middleburg College in Vermont with a bachelor of science degree, and that year he joined the investment firm of Lazard Frères and Company in New York.

In 1950 Rohatyn became a citizen of the United States and the following year was inducted into the U.S. Army, serving in Korea from 1951 to 1953. After completing his tour of duty, he returned to Lazard Frères as a partner and became an influential Democratic Party fundraiser and adviser. A noted art collector and patron, Rohatyn served for several years as chairman of the American Friends of the Israel Museum.

From 1975 to 1993 he was the unsalaried chairman of the Municipal Assistance Corporation of the City of New York, helping to pull the city out of its financial crisis of the 1970s.

Felix Rohatyn was appointed by President Clinton to be the United States ambassador to France and has been serving in that capacity since September 11, 1997.

Dennis B. Ross

Dennis Ross, President Clinton's special Middle East coordinator and negotiator, was born in San Francisco, California, on November 26, 1948. After receiving his B.A. and Ph.D. in political science from U.C.L.A., Ross worked in the Defense Department during the Carter Administration and as a member of the State Department's policy planning staff, with responsibility for Middle East issues, during the early years of the Reagan Administration. From 1984 to 1986, Ross served as director of Near East and South East Asian Affairs on the National Security Council.

Prior to joining the Clinton Administration, Ross served as director of the Policy Planning Staff of the State Department during the Bush Administration. In this capacity, he accompanied Secretary of State James Baker on all his trips to the Middle East and played a leading role in formulating and implementing U.S. policy toward the former Soviet Union and the Middle East.

Throughout the first and second Clinton terms of office, Dennis Ross was the State Department's special Middle East coordinator and negotiator,

with the rank of ambassador. As such, he served as the point man for the president and the secretary of state in shaping U.S. involvement in the Middle East peace process. Ross was instrumental in assisting the Israelis and Palestinians in negotiating the September 1995 agreement concluding the first stage of the Oslo Accords and, in intensive shuttle diplomacy, brokered the Hebron Accord of January 1997. In addition, he worked closely with the Israelis and Jordanians as they negotiated their historic peace treaty of October 1994, the second such document Israel has signed since its independence. Ross accompanied Secretary of State Madeleine Albright to her meetings with the Middle Eastern leaders and earlier was at Secretary of State Warren Christopher's side on all his trips to the Middle East.

Ambassador Ross is a member of the board of directors of the U.S. Holocaust Memorial Museum and of the Conservative synagogue Beth El, in Bethesda, Maryland. In 1997 Ross received an honorary doctorate from the Jewish Theological Seminary of America in recognition of his achievements as "a distinguished and indefatigable diplomat and mediator," who had "superbly served the cause of peace as Special Middle East Coordinator."

Supreme Court Appointees

Bill Clinton was the first president to name a Jew to the Supreme Court since Lyndon Baines Johnson nominated Abraham Fortas in 1965. His first appointee was Ruth Bader Ginsburg, a circuit judge of the United States Court of Appeals for the District of Columbia from 1979 to June 1993.

Ruth Bader Ginsburg

Ruth Bader Ginsburg was born in Brooklyn, New York, on March 15, 1933. Her father, the proprietor of a small clothing store, had grown up in the shadow of the Holocaust, and Ruth identified passionately with the suffering of her fellow Jews. As she remarked in an interview with

President Clinton looks on as Ruth Bader Ginsburg accepts her appointment to the Supreme Court.

Eleanor and Robert Slater, authors of *Great Jewish Women*: "Jews fortunate enough to be in the United States during those years could hardly avoid identifying themselves with the cause of the Jewish people."

Ruth Bader graduated from Cornell University in 1954, where she met her husband, Martin Ginsburg, a fellow pre-law student. After they married, she attended Harvard Law School for two years and then transferred to Columbia Law School, from which she received a law degree in 1959, tied for first place in her class. In 1969 she became a full professor at Rutgers Law School and three years later was hired by Columbia Law School, becoming their first female tenured professor.

On June 14, 1993, President Clinton selected Ruth Bader Ginsburg to occupy the Supreme Court seat being vacated by Byron R. White. When she was sworn in on August 10, 1993, as the 107th Supreme Court justice, President Clinton said: "Her words and her judgment will

help to shape our nation today and well into the twenty-first century."

Stephen G. Breyer

Having appointed a Jew to the Supreme Court in 1993, it seemed unlikely that Clinton would nominate a second Jew to that body during the balance of his tenure. But when Justice Harry A. Blackmun announced retirement in 1994, there was little opposition to the president's selection of Stephen G. Breyer.

At the July 13, 1994, Senate Judiciary Committee hearing, Breyer responded with great aplomb to a question put to him by Senator Hank Brown of Colorado regarding Breyer's view of the first amendment to the Constitution, the Establishment Clause:

> I think it's fairly well established in case law that the Establishment Clause means at bottom that the Government of the United States

is not to favor one religion over another. . . . That persons who are agnostic, persons who are Jewish, persons who are Catholic, persons who are Presbyterian, all religions, and nonreligions too, is [*sic*] on an equal footing as far as the government is concerned. That's the basic principle.

The son of an attorney, Stephen Breyer was born on August 15, 1938, in San Francisco, California. He graduated from Harvard Law School in 1964 and for the next two years clerked for Supreme Court Justice Arthur J. Goldberg. From 1967 to 1980 he served as a professor of law at Harvard.

In 1973 Breyer served as assistant prosecutor on the Watergate Special Prosecution Force, and in 1974 and 1975 he was special counsel to the Senate Judiciary Committee. He served as chief counsel to the committee from 1979 to 1981.

Breyer was appointed a Federal Court of Appeals judge for the First Circuit in 1980 and chief judge of the First Circuit in 1990, and he was among those considered by Bill Clinton to fill the United States Supreme Court seat being vacated by Bryon White in 1993. This would allow the president to honor his pledge to appoint the first Jew to the bench since Abe Fortas resigned in 1969. As fate would have it, Breyer was hit by a car two days before his scheduled interview with the president, and Ruth Bader Ginsburg received the appointment instead. However, in 1994, when Justice Harry Blackmun announced his retirement, Clinton choose Breyer as the successor, thus making Breyer the 108th justice of the U.S. Supreme Court.

At one point, Breyer, who had received religious training in San Francisco's Reform Temple Emanuel as a child, was asked how Judaism had affected his career. He responded: "It's a little corny. But I think of what [the first-century sage] Hillel said: 'If I am not for myself, who am I? And If I am only for myself, what am I?' I have always thought of the practical nature of Jewish religious beliefs and the way they're involved in making this world a better place, requiring people to have a sense of justice, and to think of others."

Stephen G. Breyer

Seth Waxman

In November 1997 the U.S. Senate confirmed President Clinton's appointment of Seth Waxman as the nation's forty-first solicitor general. As such, Waxman represents the United States government in cases before the U.S. Supreme Court.

Born in Hartford, Connecticut, in 1952, Waxman grew up in a traditional Conservative family that was active in West Hartford's Emanuel Synagogue and in local Jewish communal life. At the age of sixteen, Waxman spent a summer on Kibbutz Hulda in Israel, and when the Yom Kippur War broke out in 1973, he flew to Israel to fill in for members of the kibbutz who were called up for military service.

After graduation from Harvard College and Yale Law School, Waxman was a litigation attorney with a major Washington, D.C., law firm and, subsequently, for many years, a lawyer in the U.S. Department of Justice. Prior to his appointment as solicitor general, Waxman served as associate deputy.

Advisers and Counselors

Living in Arkansas, Bill Clinton had limited contact with Jews in his youth and during his years as governor. Yet, it is amazing to note how many Jews served in major and minor positions during the eight years of his presidency. In addition to those who served in Cabinet and sub-Cabinet positions, other appointees included Roger Altman, Sandy Berger, Sidney Blumenthal, Lloyd Cutler, Lynn Cutler, Maria Echaveste, Sara Ehrman, Rahm Emanuel, Stanley Greenberg, Alan Greenspan, Mandy Grunwald, Ann Lewis, Ken Lieberthal, Abner Mikva, Dick Morris, Bernard Nussbaum, Alice Rivlin, and Robert Shapiro.

Roger Altman

In 1994 U.S. Senate hearings were convened to investigate the 1992 acquisition by Bill and Hillary Clinton of 230 acres of land along the White River in the Arkansas Ozarks. The deal had been made been with longtime Clinton friends James and Susan McDougal. The venture turned out to be unprofitable, but questions were raised about the financing of the project through James McDougal's Madison Guaranty Bank, a savings and loan institution regulated by the State of Arkansas, of which Bill Clinton was then governor.

It was the purpose of the Resolution Trust Corporation (RTC) to investigate Madison Guaranty and the events surrounding this so-called Whitewater Affair. The RTC was to report to Deputy Secretary of the Treasury Roger Altman, who, in 1968, was a senior at Georgetown University when Clinton was a junior. The two students had shared an interest in politics and became fast friends.

Roger Altman had entered the national political arena in 1976, serving as an assistant secre-

tary of the Treasury in the Carter Administration. Following Jimmy Carter's failed 1980 reelection bid, Altman left Washington for Wall Street, where he became a prosperous investment banker. When Bill Clinton ran for the presidency in 1992, Altman assisted in the campaign, hoping that he would be rewarded with the top economic post. That was not to be, for Clinton selected Lloyd Bentsen to be his secretary of the Treasury. Altman became Bentsen's deputy.

When Altman's close association with Bill Clinton became known, he was convinced to remove himself from the Whitewater probe. His continued participation, argued White House counsel Bernie Nussbaum, might give the appearance of impropriety.

Lloyd Bentsen resigned the Clinton Cabinet in 1994, but Robert Rubin, not Altman, was selected to succeed him. Shortly thereafter, Altman left public service for the private sector.

Samuel Berger

Samuel (Sandy) Berger was born in Sharon, Connecticut, on October 28, 1945, and was raised in nearby Millerton, New York. He received his bachelor's degree from Cornell University in 1967 and a doctorate from Harvard Law School in 1971. After practicing law in Washington, where he was a partner in the law firm of Hogan & Harston and head of its international trade group, Berger served as deputy director of the policy planning staff at the Department of State from 1977 to 1980.

Earlier, in 1972, Berger had met Clinton when the two were working for the reelection of George McGovern, who was running against incumbent president Richard Nixon. Bill Clinton was involved in McGovern's campaign and Sandy Berger was one of McGovern's speechwriters. Clinton and Berger developed a strong friendship, and when Clinton aspired to the presidency in 1992, he selected Berger as his policy adviser.

After winning the election, Clinton appointed Berger deputy assistant to the president for national security affairs, and when Clinton won a second term, Berg was elevated to national security adviser, a position that coordinates relations between Cabinet members and handles the flow of foreign policy information to the president.

Madeleine Albright has said of Berger: "Sandy is the glue that holds us together."

Sidney Blumenthal

Journalist Sidney Blumenthal, a close friend of Bill and Hillary Clinton who had worked for *The New Yorker* magazine, *The Washington Post*, *The New Republic*, and *Vanity Fair*, was brought into the White House in July 1997 as a communications strategist. His primary assignment was to help ward off attacks against the president by what he and Hillary called "a right-wing conspiracy" to denigrate the president. Blumenthal became a prime defender of Clinton against Ken Starr, the independent counsel who testified that the president should be impeached and brought to trial before the Senate for obstructing justice and lying to the grand jury.

At one point Starr subpoenaed Blumenthal to find out who in the White House was leaking negative stories about Starr's staff to the media. Blumenthal declined to answer questions about confidential conversations within the White House, claiming executive privilege. He called Starr "a prosecutor on a mission from God" and a "constitutional illiterate." Judge Norman Holloway Johnson, however, ruled that Starr's need for information outweighed the claim of executive privilege.

Lloyd N. Cutler

Born in New York City on November 10, 1917, Lloyd Cutler began practicing law in Washington in 1946, the year of Bill Clinton's birth. With the creation of the law firm Wilmer, Cutler & Pickering, Cutler's reputation soared, and he was called upon to counsel prominent government officials and even presidents. In 1979 he accepted President Jimmy Carter's invitation to be his White House counsel and help smooth out Carter's relationship with Congress and the press.

In 1994, at age seventy-six, Cutler received a call from Vernon Jordan, the former civil rights attorney and very close friend and confidant of President Clinton, asking if they could meet at Jordan's Georgetown residence. Jordan confided that the president was dissatisfied with legal adviser Bernie Nussbaum and was in need of wise, experienced counsel. After meeting with the president, Cutler agreed to come aboard, but only for six months and only if he could be assured that he would be privy to all information and documents necessary to carry out his assignment effectively.

The year 1994 was crucial in the career of Bill Clinton. The Whitewater Affair, which had begun in 1992 when the president was governor of Arkansas, was still brewing. Cutler wanted to see all documents pertaining to the affair but was blocked from doing so.

In May of 1994, Paula Jones threatened to file a federal lawsuit against the president for improper sexual advances made in a hotel three years earlier. Cutler felt that Clinton needed a more aggressive, pugnacious lawyer to deal with the accusations and suggested Washington attorney Robert S. Bennett, whom Clinton then hired.

Believing that the job of White House counsel was to protect the office of the president and not the person of the president, Cutler decided to leave after his six months were up. In addition to concerns that he was not being kept abreast of all that was transpiring at the White House, Cutler was particularly irked that his advice that White House officials should not criticize the appointment of Kenneth Starr as independent counsel was not heeded.

The president would not agree to Cutler's departure unless a replacement was on hand, and he asked Cutler to recommend a successor. That person was to be Abner J. Mikva, a highly respected and experienced jurist. The president was pleased with the recommendation, and Mikva became the third Jew to serve as White House counsel to Bill Clinton.

Lynn Cutler

Born in Chicago in 1938, Lynn Cutler received her bachelor's and master's degrees from the University of Northern Iowa in the 1960s, after having attended the University of Illinois from 1955 to 1957. In 1981 she became vice chairperson of the Democratic National Committee in Washington, D.C., a position she held until 1993.

Cutler was a member of the Jewish Democratic Study Group, which was deeply concerned with women's rights and welfare. President Clinton chose her to be the permanent White House delegate to the 1995 United Nation's World Conference of Women, in Beijing, China.

Maria Echaveste

The eldest of seven children, Maria Echaveste was born in Harlingen, Texas, in 1954, to a poor Catholic family of Mexican migrant workers.

Despite her humble background, Echaveste graduated from Stanford University with a degree in anthropology. Later, she earned a law degree from the University of California at Berkeley. After becoming a corporate attorney in New York City, she met and married Bronx attorney Stanley Schlein, a Democratic Party activist. She converted to Judaism in 1991 because she "found Judaism to be much more life-affirming. It's about what you do every day, about how you use the blessings that you have every day and what you do with this life now, not what's going to happen to you post-death." She has since divorced Schlein, but Echaveste remains Jewish.

Maria Echaveste became active in Democratic politics and, during the 1992 presidential campaign, left her law firm to become the national Latino coordinator for the Clinton team. In the new administration, she became wage-and-hour administrator, a Labor Department position requiring Senate confirmation.

After Clinton was reelected in 1997, Echaveste became his public liaison. She was responsible for garnering support for presidential policies and initiatives. In the summer of 1998 she was elevated to deputy chief of staff, an influential White House job that involved coordinating the State of the Union speech and planning the Wye River summit to negotiate the Middle East peace effort.

Maria Echaveste was described in the *New Republic* as "sort of a one-woman band of diversity." It then explained: "She's a Hispanic woman, a Jew, a corporate lawyer, a Californian, a Texan, a New Yorker, a marathon runner, and a gardener. Oh yes, she also knits."

Sara Ehrman

A native of Staten Island, New York, Sara Ehrman lived in Washington, D.C., all of her adult life. After her first visit to the Middle East in 1956, she traveled to Israel frequently and sat on the boards of several organizations, including the U.S.-Israel Science and Technology Commission. For her efforts to advance Middle East peace through Americans for Peace Now, of which she is a cofounder, she received the Shimon Peres Peace Award.

A staunch Democrat, Ehrman was deeply involved in American political affairs. She was a legislative assistant in the U.S. Senate, first to Joseph Clark of Pennsylvania and then to George McGovern, for whose presidential campaign she worked in 1972. During the McGovern campaign she became friendly with Bill and Hillary, who were also McGovern supporters. During the Watergate hearings, Ehrman and Hillary shared an apartment in Washington for eleven months.

In 1992 Ehrman was deputy political director of the Clinton-Gore campaign in Little Rock, Arkansas, where she ran the national outreach effort to garner the Jewish vote. In the 1996 reelection campaign she advised the president on issues and positions that would appeal to the Jewish vote.

In 1997 Ehrman became a senior adviser to the Center for Middle East Peace and Economic Cooperation.

Rahm Emanuel

Born in Israel in 1960, Rahm Emanuel served in the Israeli army before moving to Chicago, where he was once described as a "wiry, thin, foulmouthed ballet dancer." In 1991 he moved to Little Rock, Arkansas, as an early adviser to Bill Clinton's campaign. It is reported that Emanuel, an observant Jew, holds private sessions with his rabbi twice monthly.

During his five years as senior adviser to Clinton, Emanuel was ever-present to respond to criticism leveled at the president. He served as

Clinton's defender in 1998 and 1999, when the Monica Lewinsky scandal dominated the news. Before leaving the Clinton Administration, the president thanked him profusely at a crowded farewell ceremony.

After returning to Chicago to work in investment banking and teach a college course, Emanuel tried, in an interview, to place the Lewinsky scandal in context. He said: "This is part of his [Clinton's] moral character, but there is a lifetime of work that no one will ever strip from him. Everyone of us is judged by the totality of our words and deeds, and not just by our fellow human beings, but by God."

Stanley B. Greenberg

An articulate, knowledgeable contemporary of Bill Clinton, Stanley Greenberg had advised candidates seeking a variety of public offices, including Senators Chris Dodd and Joseph Lieberman of Connecticut and Governor Jim Florio of New Jersey. For many years he was also the principle polling adviser to the Democratic National Committee.

After graduating from Harvard University with a doctorate in political science, Greenberg taught at Yale for a decade. In 1980 he founded his own research company, serving clients in the United States and abroad. In 1992 he guided Bill Clinton, helping him achieve his political dream of winning the presidency. In 1999 Greenberg, along with Clinton adviser James Carville, traveled to Israel to guide the campaign of Labor Party leader Ehud Barak, who was challenging the reelection of Prime Minister Benjamin Netanyahu. Barak was victorious, a result that pleased President Clinton very much.

Alan Greenspan

Upon completing high school, Alan Greenspan (1926–) studied music at the Juilliard School and earned a living as a saxophone player in a swing band. But his fertile mind was destined for greater things.

In 1968 Richard Nixon had picked Greenspan to be director of policy research for his presidential campaign. Under President Ford, Greenspan had served as chairman of the President's Council of Economic Advisers. He advised Ronald Reagan on economic matters for many years, and in 1987 Reagan appointed Greenspan chairman of the Board of Governors of the Federal Reserve System, a four-year position he continued to hold through three presidencies. Each time he won easy Senate confirmation.

During Clinton's eight years in office, Greenspan maintained firm control of U.S. monetary policy. By the prudent manipulation of short-term interest rates in 1998, he was able to keep inflation under control, and help wipe out the annual deficit.

On June 20, 2000, Alan Greenspan took the oath of office as Federal Reserve Board chairman, thus commencing his fourth four-year term.

Mandy Grunwald

One of the most important members of President Clinton's inner circle of counselors, Mandy Grunwald was Clinton's media adviser. She sagely counseled the president on the best ways to win congressional support for his economic plan. She urged Clinton to appeal directly to the American people, who would, in turn, make their wishes known to their congressional representatives. "What you say to the American people," she told the president, "bounces back to Congress." And she offered the same type of wise counsel to Senator Daniel Patrick Moynihan of New York, for whom she had also served as media adviser.

Grunwald's association with the president began in 1992 when Clinton first set his sights on the White House. In the midst of the campaign, on January 23, 1992, just before the New Hampshire primary, a tabloid, *The Star*, published the charge by Gennifer Flowers, of Arkansas, that she had had a twelve-year affair with Clinton. Grunwald was there—along with George Stephanopolus, Stanley Greenberg, James Carville, and others—to handle the fallout, even as she would six years later when the Monica Lewinsky scandal engulfed the presidency.

In the year 2000, Mandy was a close adviser to Hillary Clinton during the first lady's run for the U.S. Senate seat being vacated by Daniel Patrick Moynihan of New York.

Ann Lewis

Sister of Massachusetts congressman Barney Frank, Ann Lewis was born in Jersey City, New Jersey, on December 19, 1937. Long a Democratic Party activist, she served as deputy campaign manager for the Clinton-Gore reelection campaign in 1996. In January 1997 she was appointed Clinton's deputy communications director, and in May 1997 she was named its director. In 1998 she participated in the First International Jewish Feminist Conference in Jerusalem.

When the Monica Lewinsky scandal erupted, Lewis was ever present on television and radio, responding to character attacks against the president and promoting his policies.

Ira C. Magaziner

A senior adviser to the president for policy development, Ira Magaziner was born in New York City in 1947 and grew up in a home where liberal politics was a family tradition. After graduating from Brown University in 1965, he entered Oxford University as a Rhodes scholar. There, he struck up a friendship with fellow student Bill Clinton. Both shared a desire to work for social justice and to see an end to the Vietnam conflict.

Magaziner met Hillary Clinton when Bill became governor of Arkansas, and when Bill won the presidency, Magaziner and Hillary undertook the task of reforming the country's $900 billion health-care industry; the effort was unsuccessful. Prior to his White House appointment, Magaziner built two strategy consulting firms that suggested policy direction for major corporations.

In 1995 Magaziner was invited to chair a joint National Economic Council/National Security Council initiative to increase U.S. exports. Toward the end of Clinton's term in office, Magaziner supervised the administration's development of a U.S. government strategy for promoting global electronic commerce on the Internet.

Abner J. Mikva

Born in Milwaukee, Wisconsin, on January 21, 1926, Abner Mikva graduated from the University of Chicago Law School in 1951, where he was editor-in-chief of its *Law Review*. Mikva began practicing law in 1952, and in 1968 was elected to the Illinois legislature. In 1975 he was elected to the U.S. Congress, where he served for two years. Upon his resignation in 1979 he was appointed judge in the United States Court of Appeals for the District of Columbia circuit.

President Clinton was pleased with Lloyd Cutler's recommendation of Mikva to replace him as White House counsel, and Mikva joined Clinton's staff on August 11, 1994, giving up a lifetime appointment to the federal bench.

Dick Morris

A bright political analyst, Dick Morris (1948-) had worked for Democrat congresswoman Bella Abzug of New York and Senator Howard Metzenbaum of Ohio, as well as for conservative Republican Jesse Helms of North Carolina. In 1977, he helped orchestrate Clinton's campaign to regain the governorship of Arkansas. In 1996 Morris was brought in by Hillary Clinton to advise her husband on how best to counter the power of the Republican majority in Congress and win a second term. Morris believed that in politics one should be guided by the polls, a view for which he was widely criticized. He also advised Hillary on how to project a kinder, gentler demeanor. When, in August 1996, the *Star* tabloid revealed Morris's continuing association with a prostitute, he lost credibility and was dropped as a Clinton adviser.

Bernard Nussbaum

In the course of Bill Clinton's eight years in office he hired any number of White House counselors, three of whom were Jewish: Bernard Nussbaum, Lloyd Cutler, and Abner Mikva. A New York attorney, Nussbaum's specialty was corporate takeovers.

At the invitation of President-elect Clinton, on January 8, 1993, Bernie Nussbaum flew to Little Rock, Arkansas, for an interview. He came with a rich legal background, having been manager of the House Judiciary Committee during the Nixon impeachment investigation. Nussbaum was eager and ready to assume the job of chief lawyer to the president of the United States.

What clinched the opportunity was the fact that Nussbaum had known Hillary as far back as 1974, when, as a young lawyer, she had worked under Nussbaum compiling information for the House Judiciary Committee investigating the conduct of President Nixon. Nussbaum convinced Bill Clinton that he would serve him well and was immediately offered the position.

The relationship between the president and his counselor began to sour on the first day of Clinton's presidency. On January 20, 1993, Nussbaum was summoned into the Oval Office to advise the president on a crisis that was developing over Clinton's nomination of Zöe Baird for attorney general. But when it was discovered that Baird had not paid social security taxes for a nanny she had employed, the Senate Judiciary Committee pummeled her with questions, and it appeared that she would not be confirmed. The president had to decide whether to fight for her nomination.

Nussbuam argued in favor of continuing support for the Baird nomination, but George Stephanopoulos, Clinton's communications aide, advised against it. The president rejected Nussbaum's advice and felt a change in White House counsel was needed. In March 1994, after only fourteen months of service, Clinton asked Nussbaum to submit his resignation, and the president replaced him with Lloyd Cutler.

Alice Rivlin

Born in Philadelphia on March 4, 1931, Alice Rivlin, daughter of a nuclear physicist, graduated from Bryn Mawr in 1952 and Radcliffe in 1958. At Radcliffe she earned a doctorate while serving as a staff member of the Brookings Institute, in Washington, D.C. From 1966 to 1969 she was deputy assistant at the Department of Health, Education and Welfare, and then she returned to the Brookings Institute as director of economic studies.

Bernard Nussbaum

In 1993 she was appointed deputy director of the office of management and budget. In this capacity, she worked closely with the chairman of the Senate Finance Committee, Senator Daniel Patrick Moynihan of New York.

James P. Rubin

Born in New York City in 1960, James Rubin received a Bachelor of Arts degree in political science from Columbia University in 1982, followed by a Masters degree in international affairs in 1984. In 1988 Rubin was the recipient of Columbia College's John Jay Award for Distinguished Professional Achievement.

Nominated by President Clinton to be assistant secretary of state for public affairs on May 23, 1997, James P. Rubin, was confirmed by the full Senate on July 31, 1997. On August 4, 1997, Secretary of State Madeleine K. Albright swore him in as assistant secretary and appointed him the department's chief spokesman.

Prior to his presidential appointment as assistant secretary, Rubin had served as a senior adviser to the secretary of state. From August to November 1996, he was director of foreign policy and spokesman for the Clinton-Gore presidential reelection.

Robert Shapiro

A founder and vice president of the Progressive Policy Institute and a principle economic adviser to Clinton in the 1992 presidential campaign, Robert Shapiro became senior adviser to the presidential transition team. Born in 1938 in New York City, Shapiro graduated from Harvard in 1959 and from Columbia University School of Law in 1962. He also holds degrees from the University of Chicago and the London School of Economics and Political Science.

After taking office, Clinton appointed Shapiro to his Advisory Committee for Trade Policy and Negotiations, which provides policy guidance on all matters pertaining to trade agreements.

Prelude to Impeachment

In 1996 Bill Clinton soundly defeated Republican challenger Bob Dole in his bid for a second presidential term. Clinton's presidency continued on a high note for the next two years: the country enjoyed low inflation, low unemployment, and a handsome budget surplus instead of the usual deficit. Then, unexpectedly, Clinton's sexual dalliance in the Oval Office with a twenty-two year-old White House intern named Monica Lewinsky nearly drove him from office.

Monica was born in 1974 in Los Angeles, California, the daughter of Marsha and Bernard Lewinsky, an oncologist. Monica's parents had divorced and both were remarried; Monica was particularly close with her mother.

During her formative years Monica Lewinsky received her religious education at Sinai Temple, a Conservative congregation in Los Angeles, and her secular education at Beverly Hills High, a small $12,000-a-year prep school. She then spent two years at Santa Monica College, after which she switched to and graduated from Lewis & Clark College, in Portland, Oregon.

In 1995 Lewinsky became an unpaid White House intern, but in April 1996 she was transferred to the Pentagon Public Affairs Office when her supervisor noticed that she was spending too much time in the vicinity of the Oval Office. At the Pentagon, Monica became friendly with Linda Tripp, an older career government worker. Monica would often confide in Tripp.

In 1993 Attorney General Janet Reno appointed a special prosecutor, Kenneth Starr, to investigate the Whitewater land deal involving the president and Hillary Clinton. During the investigation, it was revealed that Bill Clinton had been involved in sexual improprieties with Paula Jones and possibly with other women. Starr requested and received permission from the attorney general to expand his inquiry into these allegations. Before long, the name Monica Lewinsky surfaced.

Monica had been having a sexual affair with the president, but they had broken it off in May 1997. She told Linda Tripp about the relationship. On Friday, December 19, 1998, while sitting in her office in the Pentagon, Monica was served with a subpoena to testify in the Paula Jones matter. When Linda learned about the subpoena, she began taping her telephone conversations with Monica.

Tripp then notified Kenneth Starr's office that she had in her possession twenty-four hours of taped conversations with Monica containing much information about Monica's affair with the president. Within the hour, members of Independent Counsel Starr's team arrived at Tripp's suburban Maryland home to listen to the tapes. They then arranged for Linda to invite Lewinsky to lunch the next day at the Ritz-Carlton in Virginia, near the Pentagon. Tripp was wired, and the entire conversation, which lasted three hours, was recorded by FBI agents listening in from an upper floor of the hotel.

Monica signed a sworn affidavit stating, "I have never had sexual relations with the president." Over the next eight months Clinton repeatedly denied the relationship, not only to the public at large, but to his closest associates and advisers. Independent Counsel Starr, however, believed that Clinton was not telling the truth and offered Monica immunity in exchange for her truthful testimony. Clinton attempted to defend himself by claiming that his testimony may have been misleading, but that he did not lie.

Impeachment

On Saturday, January 16, 1999, Henry Hyde, chairman of the House Judiciary Committee, summed up the case for impeachment that had been presented by Kenneth Starr in his voluminous September 9, 1998, report. The House then voted 258 to 176 to impeach the president on two counts: perjury and obstruction of justice. The trial was held before the full Senate and Clinton was exonerated, Senate Republicans having failed to muster the sixty-seven votes (two-thirds of the total) required by law to remove a president from office. All forty-five Democratic senators voted to acquit.

Before the vote in the Senate was taken, the Democrats proposed censuring the president rather than proceed with the trial. The Republicans, however, would not agree to this proposal, maintaining that such a course would amount to a mere slap on the wrist, insufficient punishment for Clinton's misconduct.

While Clinton was not removed from office, some of his closest supporters felt that his immoral conduct deserved serious reprimand.

Joseph I. Lieberman

One of Clinton's closest allies and a friend for over thirty years was Senator Joseph Isador Lieberman, Democrat of Connecticut. Born in Stamford, Connecticut, on February 24, 1942, Lieberman received a bachelor's degree from Yale University in 1964 and a doctorate in jurisprudence (J.D.) from Yale Law School in 1967.

Lieberman entered politics in 1970, running for and winning a Connecticut State Senate seat from New Haven. Bill Clinton, a Yale law student at the time, campaigned for Lieberman's election, and the two have remained friends ever since. Lieberman served in the State Senate for ten years, six of them as Speaker. In 1982 he was elected Attorney General of Connecticut, a position he held until his election to the United States Senate in 1988.

Joseph Lieberman is the first Orthodox Jew to serve in the U.S. Senate. Raised in a modern Orthodox home in Stamford, he has been religiously observant throughout his life. When nominated for the Senate, he videotaped his acceptance in advance: he could not attend the nominating convention, because it was held on Saturday. Throughout Lieberman's tenure in the U.S. Senate, he has refrained from political campaigning, driving a vehicle, or using electricity on the Sabbath, and he has continued to meticulously observe the dietary laws. Because of his level of Jewish observance, unique in the halls of Congress, Joe Lieberman has often been referred to as "Clinton's rabbi."

On March 20, 1983, Lieberman, who had been divorced in 1981, married Hadassah Freilich, a daughter of Holocaust survivors.

During his presidency, Clinton was able to count on Lieberman's support, both being "ideological allies from the centrist New Democratic wing of the party," as Bob Woodward phrased it in his 1999 book, *Shadows: Five Presidents and the Legacy of Watergate*. "They spoke frequently by phone at night. Clinton at times woke up Lieberman from a deep sleep. Lieberman joked that he felt like a fireman."

Senator Lieberman greets a group of Israeli youngsters visiting Washington, D.C.

But when the Monica Lewinsky scandal broke, Lieberman considered Clinton's conduct with the young intern inexcusable, and he broke ranks, openly condemning the president. On September 3, 1998, Lieberman delivered a twenty-four-minute speech on the floor of the Senate, admonishing the president for his "disgraceful" and "immoral" behavior, castigating him for his unwillingness to acknowledge wrongdoing or to ask for forgiveness. And he went on to emphasize: "I fear the president has undercut the efforts of millions of American parents trying to instill in our children the values of honesty." Since the report of Independent Counsel Kenneth Starr had not yet been made public, Lieberman considered it premature and unwise to consider censure or impeachment of the president. Instead, as he said in his speech, the president's behavior was "wrong and unacceptable, and should be followed by some measure of public rebuke and accountability."

On August 8, 2000, one week before the Democratic National Convention was held in Los Angeles, California, presidential candidate Albert Gore, Jr., announced that Joseph Lieberman would be his vice-presidential running mate. This was the first time that a Jew was placed on the national ticket, and the selection was widely hailed as a special day not only for the Jewish people, but all America. Elie Wiesel summed it up simply: "Now the political system is open to men and women of all ethnic origins."

Clinton and the Embassy

Lieberman found fault with Clinton once again in June 1999, when the president issued a waiver keeping the American Embassy in Tel Aviv rather than transferring it to Jerusalem as was required by the Jerusalem Relocation Act, enacted by Congress in 1995. It called for the embassy to be moved to Jerusalem by May 31, 1999, "except if national security reasons prevent the move."

Clinton's behavior was puzzling to Jews. They had always viewed the president as deeply concerned with the welfare of the Jewish state and the plight of the Jewish people.

As president, Bill Clinton visited Israel four times, more than any other Chief Executive in American history, and he enjoyed an especially close friendship with Israeli Prime Minister Yitzhak Rabin. But Jews as a whole were disappointed over his inaction relative to the embassy matter.

Rabin and Clinton

After the 1991 Madrid Peace Conference, when efforts to establish a peaceful arrangement between the Palestinians and Israelis had all but collapsed, a new attempt was made in Oslo, Norway, under the leadership of Prime Minister Shimon Peres. In August 1993, Yitzhak Rabin replaced Peres as prime minister of Israel, and a full agreement with the Palestinians was reached one month later. On September 13, 1993, a Declaration of Principles, known as the Oslo I Agreement, was signed in the White House Rose Garden in the presence of President Clinton, Yasser Arafat, Shimon Peres, Yitzhak Rabin, and a host of dignitaries.

On September 24, 1995, Oslo II was consummated at meetings in Taba, Egypt. An elaborate ceremony was held on the White House lawn four days later at which Arafat and Rabin signed official documents. At the prompting of President Clinton, Arafat and Rabin shook hands, albeit reluctantly on Rabin's part, who was still unable to overcome a lifetime of distaste for the Palestinian leader.

Then, shockingly, less than six weeks later, on November 4, 1995, immediately after addressing a peace rally in Tel Aviv's Municipal Square attended by an overflow crowd of more than one hundred thousand people, a young Orthodox Jew named Yigal Amir fired three pistol shots into the back of the prime minister and ended Rabin's life.

Two days later, on November 6, Rabin was buried in Jerusalem at a state funeral on Mount Herzl attended by leading statesmen and political leaders from around the world. Among the many tributes to Israel's fallen leader, President Clinton's eulogy was most heartwarming and deeply felt.

The president began his tribute with these words:

Today, my fellow citizens of the world, I ask all of you to take a good hard look at this picture. Look at the leaders from all over the Middle East and around the world who have journeyed here today for Yitzhak Rabin and for peace. Though we no longer hear his deep and booming voice, it is he who has brought us together here, in word and deed, for peace.

Then, turning to Rabin's widow, Leah, he said:

Leah, I know that too many times in the life of this country you were called upon to comfort and console the mothers and the fathers, the husbands and the wives, the sons and the daughters who lost their loved ones to violence and vengeance. You gave them strength. Now we are here, and millions of people all around the world in all humility and honor offer you our strength. May God comfort you among all the mourners of Zion and Jerusalem.

Clinton's eulogy ended with the Hebrew words *shalom chaver*, "goodbye friend."

Former AIPAC president, and a Democratic National Committee chairman, Steve Grossman believed that the president did not have a closer and more intimate relationship with any world leader than he had with Rabin. In a May 25, 1998, *Jerusalem Post* statement, Grossman recalled being an overnight guest at the White House in April 1995. He described how at 2:00 A.M. he met Clinton outside the yellow Oval Room on the second floor. Clinton pointed to four gifts presented to him to mark the Israel-Jordan peace treaty. In addition to gifts from Ehud Olmert, Ezer Weizman, and King Hussein, was a tray from Leah and Yitzhak Rabin engraved with a psalm. Clinton, said Grossman, "looked at the tray and said of Rabin: 'I admired that man, a great man, a hero. I so, so admired him.'"

Clinton and Pollard

Despite all the pressure placed upon Clinton to pardon Jonathan Pollard, who had been convicted of spying for Israel and had been imprisoned for more than a decade, Clinton refused. Jews and non-Jews alike sent messages of protest to Clinton on Jonathan Pollard's behalf. In a plea for a reduced sentence, Alan Dershowitz of Harvard University wrote: "He [Pollard] pleaded guilty. He fully cooperated. He helped the government in its damage assessment. He spied for a country which was an ally of the United States. . . . These are not defenses, but they certainly argue against the maximum possible punishment, which is what he got."

In a July 1993 appeal to Clinton that he grant Pollard executive clemency, limited to the seven years already served, Benjamin Hooks, executive director of the National Association for the Advancement of Color People (NAACP), wrote the president:

Dear President Clinton:

I have recently reviewed the facts in the case of Jonathan Pollard and have concluded that the term of his sentence is unduly harsh and unjust. I am therefore respectfully urging you to grant Mr. Pollard executive clemency.

As a lawyer and minister, as well as a former judge and CEO of the NAACP, I have rarely encountered a case in which government arbitrariness was so clear-cut and inexcusable . . . .

As inexcusable as Mr. Pollard's acts were, he was never accused of treason or harming our nation. His crime was limited to aiding a close ally and this should have mitigated against such a harsh punishment.

At a protest meeting held in Washington, D.C., in November 1993, Congressman Gary Ackerman of New York, a strong supporter of President Clinton, said:

The issue no longer is whether justice was done in sentencing, but that justice is not served when Pollard is presently serving more time than any person convicted of spying for a friendly foreign government—unless the U.S. declared war on Israel without telling us.

Like his predecessor, Clinton was not receptive to the pleas of any of these prominent people.

Yitzhak Rabin (left) shakes hands with Yasser Arafat (right) on September 13, 1993, as President Clinton looks on.

Establishing a Legacy

As Bill Clinton's second term in office drew to a close in the year 2000, like most presidents who preceded him, his mind turned to the legacy that might be his, particularly in the area of foreign affairs. His contribution to the well-being of the nation in the economic realm was uncontested, but he had yet to leave a mark in the international area.

From the outset, Clinton knew that the assessment of his performance as president would ultimately be based on his management of foreign affairs as well as his handling of domestic issues. With this in mind, shortly after taking office in January 1993, Clinton invited President Richard Nixon to meet with him at the White House. Nixon was widely recognized as an expert on foreign affairs, and Clinton was anxious to learn whatever possible from the former president. Of that meeting, which took place on March 8, 1993, Clinton said: "It was the best conversation I ever had."

Nixon's message was twofold: (1) In order to be successful in carrying out international negotiations it is imperative for a president to get to know their foreign counterparts on a personal level. (2) It is essential that the U.S. president appreciate the pressures under which foreign leaders operate and of their need to account to their individual constituencies.

This advice served Clinton in good stead as he dealt with President Boris Yeltsin, who came to power in 1991, and with Yitzhak Rabin and Yasser Arafat, whom he brought to the White House on September 13, 1993, to witness the signing of the Oslo I Agreement by Shimon Peres of Israel and Mahmoud Abba of the PLO.

Achievement of a lasting peace in the Middle East had been high on the president's agenda, but seven years after the 1993 signing a genuine peace between Israel and the PLO had still not been firmly established. In one final effort, in July 2000 Clinton invited Chairman Yasser Arafat of the PLO and Prime Minister Ehud Barak of Israel to join him at the presidential retreat at Camp David to negotiate a final peace agreement. Clinton prepared assiduously for the meeting, spending endless hours trying to understand and appreciate the goals and needs of each of the parties and trying to develop proposals that would bridge the gap. "Give me a test on some piece of land anywhere in Jerusalem or Israel. I know the answer," he said. "Ask me to draw a map of the West Bank in my sleep. I can do it."

Bill Clinton had heeded Richard Nixon's advice and sensitized himself to the needs of the respective parties. Nonetheless, he was unable to forge an agreement between Barak and Arafat, and on July 25, 2000, after fifteen days of talks, a fatigued President Clinton admitted defeat. Although the president insinuated that the failure to reach an accord rested in Yasser Arafat's intransigence over the status of Jerusalem, Arafat returned to the Middle East a hero, promising that on September 13, 2000 he would unilaterally declare Palestinian statehood. Ehud Barak, though highly praised by the president, returned to Israel to face an uncertain future.

Summing Up

Although Bill Clinton's two terms as president of the United States were marked by the longest stretch of prosperity in the nation's history, fifty-eight historians surveyed—including Stephen D. Ambrose, Douglas Brinkley, and David Kennedy—have scored Clinton's presidency as "fair to middling." In the overall ranking of Chief Executives from Washington through Clinton, the latter finished twenty-first. In "moral authority," he was ranked even below Richard Nixon, who was forced to resign from office in disgrace.

Joe Lockhart, spokesman for the Clinton White House in 1999 and 2000, stated that it was too early to assess Clinton's leadership ability. With regard to Clinton's morality, he said: "I suspect that that's more a reaction to reading the tabloids than a fair reading of history."

As Clinton's second term neared an end, one of his aides described the president as "wistful" about leaving the White House. He called old friends late at night to reminisce, reportedly saying, "God, I'm going to miss the place."

Few of Clinton's predecessors felt the same way about leaving the presidency. Harry Truman referred to the White House as his prison and wrote in his memoirs that "the pressures and complexities of the presidency have grown to a state where they are too much for one man to endure." John F. Kennedy said: "If they want this job, they can have it. It's no great joy to me." Herbert Hoover called it "a compound of hell." Back in 1809, when Thomas Jefferson approached the end of his presidency, he said: "Five more weeks will relieve me from a drudgery to which I am no longer equal."

Despite the healthy condition of the U.S. economy during the Clinton tenure, historians predict that he will be remembered as one of only two presidents who had been impeached: Andrew Johnson, for removing certain public officials without the consent of the Senate, and Bill Clinton, for moral laxity. In 1932 President Franklin D. Roosevelt defined the presidency: "The presidency is not merely an administrative office. . . . It is pre-eminently a place of moral leadership." And, many historians believe this will likely be the yardstick by which future generations judge President William Jefferson Clinton. Because of his indiscretions, he will be, as Senator Charles (Chuck) Schumer of New York noted, "carrying the mark of Cain on him forever."

This perspective notwithstanding, Jews will likely remember the forty-second president both for his overall support of Israel and his appointment of so large a number of Jews to influential government positions.

[A.J.K.]

Bill Clinton

289

Bibliography

Abraham, Henry J. Justices and Presidents: A Political History of Appointments to the Supreme Court, *second edition. New York: Oxford University Press, 1985.*

Abrahamsen, David. Nixon vs. Nixon: An Emotional Tragedy. *New York: Farrar, Straus & Giroux, 1977.*

Adams, Charles Francis, Jr. Charles Francis Adams, Jr.: An Autobiography, 1835–1915. *Boston: Houghton Mifflin, 1916.*

Adams, Samuel Hopkins. Incredible Era: The Life and Times of Warren Gamaliel Harding. *Boston: Houghton, Mifflin, 1939.*

Adler, Cyrus, and Aaron M. Margalith. With Firmness in the Right: American Diplomatic Action Affecting Jews, 1840–1945. *North Stratford, New Hampshire: Ayer Co. Publishers, 1946.*

Allen, Charles F., and Jonathan Portis. The Comeback Kid: The Life and Career of Bill Clinton. *New York: Birch Lane Press, 1992.*

Alteras, Isaac. Eisenhower and Israel: U.S.Israel Relations 1953–1960. *Gainesville: University Press of Florida, 1993.*

Ambrose, Stephen E. Eisenhower: The President. *Two volumes. New York: Simon & Schuster, 1984.*

———. Nixon, The Education of a Politician. *Volume 1. New York: Simon & Schuster, 1987.*

———. The Victors: Eisenhower and His Boys, The Men of World War II. *New York: Simon & Schuster, 1998.*

———, and Douglas Brinkley. Witness to America. *New York: Harper Resource, 1999.*

Anderson, Patrick. The Presidents' Men: White House Assistants of Franklin D. Roosevelt, Harry S. Truman, Dwight D. Eisenhower, John F. Kennedy, and Lyndon B. Johnson. *Garden City, New York: Doubleday, 1968.*

Anthony, Carl Sferrazza. Florence Harding: The First Lady, the Jazz Age and America's Most Scandalous President. *New York: William Morrow & Co., 1998.*

Bailey, Thomas A. Presidential Saints and Sinners. *New York: Free Press, 1981.*

Bak, Richard. The Day Lincoln Was Shot: An Illustrated Chronicle. *Dallas, Texas: Taylor Publishing, 1998.*

Baker, Leonard. Brandeis and Frankfurter: A Dual Biography. *New York: Harper and Row, 1983.*

Barbarash, Ernest E., compiler. John F. Kennedy on Israel, Zionism and Jewish Issues. *1965.*

Barish, Louis, editor. Rabbis in Uniform. *New York: Jonathan David Publishers, 1962.*

Barnard, Harry. Rutherford B. Hayes and His America. *New York: Russell & Russell, 1967.*

Baron, Salo W., and Joseph L. Blau. The Jews in the United States 1790–1940. *Philadelphia: Jewish Publication Society, 1970.*

Baruch, Bernard. My Own Years. *New York: New York: Henry Holt & Co., 1957.*

———. The Public Years, *1960.*

Bennett, Edward M. Franklin D. Roosevelt and the Search for Security. *Wilmington, Delaware: Scholarly Resources, Inc., 1985.*

Bernstein, Irving. Guns or Butter: The Presidency of Lyndon Johnson. *New York: Oxford University Press, 1996.*

Beschloss, Michael R. Taking Charge: The Johnson White House Tapes, 1963–1964. *New York: Simon & Schuster, 1997.*

Blau, Joseph L., and Salo W. Baron, editors. The Jews of the United States, 1790–1840: A Documentary History. *New York: Columbia University Press, 1963.*

Blitzer, Wolf. Territory of Lies. *New York: Harper & Row, 1989.*

Boller, Paul F., Jr. Presidential Anecdotes. *New York: Oxford University Press, 1996.*

———. Presidential Campaigns. *New York: Oxford University Press, 1984.*

———. Presidential Wives. *New York: Oxford University Press, 1988.*

Bookbinder, Hyman. Off the Wall: Memoirs of a Public Affairs Junkie.*1991.*

Bourne, Peter G. Jimmy Carter: A Comprehensive Biography from Plains to Post-Presidency. *New York: Simon & Schuster, 1997.*

Brinkley, Douglas. The Unfinished Presidency: Jimmy Carter's Journey Beyond the White House. *New York: Penguin, 1999.*

Brodie, Fawn. Richard Nixon: The Shaping of His Character. *New York: W.W. Norton & Co., 1981.*

Brokaw, Tom. The Greatest Generation. *New York: Random House, 1998.*

Brookhiser, Richard. Alexander Hamilton: American. *New York: Free Press, 1999.*

Burner. David. Herbert Hoover: A Public Life. *New York: Alfred A. Knopf, 1979.*

Burt, Robert A. Two Jewish Justices: Outcasts in the Promised Land. *Berkeley: University of California Press, 1988.*

Bush, George, with Victor Gold. Looking Forward: An Autobiography. *New York: Doubleday, 1987.*

Cannon, Lou. Reagan. *New York: Putnam, 1982.*

Cantor, Norman F. The Jewish Experience. *New York: Harper Collins, 1999.*

Cargas, Harry James. Shadows of Auschwitz: A Christian Response to the Holocaust. *New York: Crossroads, 1990.*

Caro, Robert A. Means of Ascent: The Years of Lyndon Johnson. *New York: Vintage Books, 1991.*

Chernow, Ron. The Warburgs: The Twentieth-Century Odyssey of a Remarkable Jewish Family. *New York: Vintage Books, 1993.*

Chidsey, Donald Barr. And Tyler Too. *New York: Thomas Nelson, 1978.*

Cleaves, Freeman. Old Tippecanoe: William Henry Harrison and His Time. *New York: Scribner's Sons 1939.*

Cohen, Michael J. Truman and Israel. *Berkeley: University of California Press, 1990.*

Cohen, Naomi W. A Dual Heritage: The Public Career of Oscar S. Straus. *Philadelphia: Jewish Publication Society, 1969.*

———. Encounter with Emancipation: The German Jews in the United States, 1830–1914. *Philadelphia: Jewish Publication Society, 1984.*

Coolidge, Calvin. The Autobiography of Calvin Coolidge. *New York: Cosmopolitan Book Corp., 1929.*

Cooper, John Milton, Jr. The Warrior and the Priest: Woodrow Wilson and Theodore Roosevelt. *Cambridge, Massachusetts: Harvard University Press, 1983.*

Cunningham, Homer T. The Presidents' Last Years: George Washington to Lyndon Johnson. *Jefferson, N.C.: McFarland & Co., 1989.*

Cunningham, Noble E., Jr. In Pursuit of Reason: The Life of Thomas Jefferson. *Baton Rouge: Louisiana State University, 1987.*

Dalin, David G. and Jonathan Rosenbaum. Making a Life, Building a Community: A History of the Jews of Hartford. *New York: Holmes and Meier, 1997.*

———. "What Julius Rosenwald Knew," Commentary, *April, 1998.*

———. "Mayer Sulzberger and American Jewish Public Life," *in Jeffrey L. Gurock and Marc Lee Raphael (editors)* An Inventory of Promises: Essays on American Jewish History in Honor of Moses Rischin. *New York: Carlson Publishing Inc., 1995.*

Dallek, Robert. Lone Star Rising: Lyndon Johnson and His Times, 1908–1960. *New York: Oxford University Press, 1991.*

———. Flawed Giant: Lyndon Johnson and His Times, 1960–1973. *New York: Oxford University Press, 1998.*

Daugherty, Harry M. The Inside Story of the Harding Tragedy. *New York: Churchill, 1932.*

Davis, John H. The Guggenheims: An American Epic. *New York: William Morrow & Co., 1978.*

Davis, Moshe. With Eyes Toward Zion. *North Stratford, New Hampshire: Ayer Co. Publishers, 1977.*

DeGregorio, William A. The Complete Book of U.S. Presidents. *New York: Wings Books, 1993.*

Dimont, Max. The Jews in America. *New York: Simon & Schuster, 1978.*

Dinnerstein, Leonard. Antisemitism in America. *New York: Oxford University Press, 1994.*

———. Uneasy at Home: Antisemitism and the American Jewish Experience. *New York: Columbia University Press, 1987.*

Dobbs, Michael. Madeleine Albright: A Twentieth-Century Odyssey. *New York: Henry Holt & Co., 1999.*

Doyle, Michael V., editor. Gerald R. Ford: Selected Speeches. *1975.*

D'Souza, Dinesh. Ronald Reagan: How an Ordinary Man Became an Extraordinary Leader. *New York: Free Press, 1997.*

Dubnow, Simon. History of the Jews in Russia and Poland. *Five volumes. Philadelphia: Jewish Publication Society, 1916.*

Eban, Abba. Abba Eban: An Autobiography. *New York: Random House, 1977.*

Ehrman, John. The Rise of Neoconservatism: Intellectuals and Foreign Affairs, 1945–1994. *New Haven: Yale University Press, 1995.*

Eichhorn, David Max. Jewish Folklore in America. *New York: Jonathan David Publishers, 1996.*

Eisenhower, Dwight D. Crusade in Europe. *Garden City, New York: Doubleday, 1948.*

———. Strictly Personal: A Memoir. *Garden City, New York: Doubleday, 1974.*

Ellis, John J. Passionate Sage: The Character and Legacy of John Adams. *New York: W.W. Norton & Co., 1993.*

Encyclopedia Brittanica, *fifteenth edition. New York, 1929.*

Encyclopedia Judaica. *Seventeen volumes. Jerusalem: Keter Publishing House Ltd., 1971.*

Evans, Eli N. Judah P. Benjamin: The Jewish Confederate. *New York: Free Press, 1989.*

Falkner, Leonard. The President Who Wouldn't Retire: John Quincy Adams, Congressman from Massachusetts. *New York: Alfred A. Knopf, 1956.*

Farrer, David. The Warburgs: The Story of a Family. *New York: Stein and Day, 1975.*

Feingold, Henry L. A Time for Searching: Entering the Mainstream 1920 to 1945. *Baltimore, Md.: Johns Hopkins University Press, 1992–95.*

———. The Politics of Rescue: The Roosevelt Administration and the Holocaust, 1938–1945. *New Brunswick, New Jersey: Rutgers University Press, 1970.*

Feldman, Egal. Dual Destinies: The Jewish Encounter with Protestant America. *Champaign: University of Illinois Press, 1990.*

Ferrell, Robert H. The Presidency of Calvin Coolidge. *Lawrence: University Press of Kansas, 1998.*

———, editor. Off the Record: The Private Papers of Harry S. Truman. *New York: Harper & Row, 1980.*

Feuss, Claude M. Calvin Coolidge: The Man From Vermont. *Hamden, Connecticut: Archon Books, 1965.*

Fine, William M., editor. That Day with God, November 24, 1963: The Religious Expression of All Faiths Following the Death of President Kennedy. *New York: McGraw-Hill, 1965.*

Finkelstein, Louis, editor. The Jews: Their History Culture and Religion, *Volume I. Westport, Connecticut: Greenwood Press, 1949.*

Fischel, Jack, and Sanford Pinsker, editors. Jewish-American History and Culture: An Encyclopedia. *New York: Garland, 1992.*

Ford, Betty. Betty: A Glad Awakening. *Garden City, New York: Doubleday, 1987.*

Ford, Gerald. A Time to Heal: The Autobiography of Gerald R. Ford. *New York: Harper & Row, 1979.*

Frankel, Max. The Times of My Life: And My Life with The Times. *New York: Random House, 1999.*

Ganin, Zvi. Truman, American Jewry, and Israel, 1945–1948. *New York: Holmes & Meier Publishers, 1979.*

Garment, Leonard. Crazy Rhythm: My Journey from Brooklyn, Jazz, and Wall Street to Nixon's White House, Watergate, and Beyond. *New York: Times Books, 1997.*

Gartner, Lloyd P. *"The Correspondence of Mayer Sulzberger and William Howard Taft,"* Jubilee Volume of the American Academy for Jewish Research *(1979–1980).*

Gerson, Allan. The Kirkpatrick Mission, Diplomacy without Apology: America at the United Nations, 1981–1985. *New York: Free Press, 1991.*

Gilbert, Martin. The Holocaust: A History of the Jews of Europe During the Second World War. *New York: Henry Holt & Co., 1985.*

Goldberg, J.J. Jewish Power: Inside the American Jewish Establishment. *Reading, Massachusetts: Perseus Books, 1996.*

Golden, Harry. For 2¢ Plain. *Cleveland: World Publishing Co., 1959.*

Golden, Peter. Quiet Diplomat: A Biography of Max M. Fisher. *Cranbury, New Jersey: Cornwall Books, 1992.*

Goodwin, Doris Kearns. The Fitzgeralds and the Kennedys: An American Saga. *New York: Simon & Schuster, 1987.*

Gould, Lewis L. The Presidency of William McKinley. *Lawrence: University Press of Kansas, 1980.*

Graff, Henry F. *"Jews and the Presidents: Some Observations and Reflections."* The Sol Feinstone Memorial Lecture. *New York: The Jewish Theological Seminary of America, 1982.*

Graubard, Stephen R. Kissinger: Portrait of a Mind. *New York: W.W. Norton and Company, 1973.*

Grayzel, Solomon. A History of the Jews. *Philadelphia: Jewish Publication Society, 1968.*

Greenberg, Evelyn Levow. *"An 1869 Petition on Behalf of Russian Jews,"* American Jewish Historical Quarterly 54:3, 1965.

Greenstein, Fred I. The Hidden-Hand Presidency: Eisenhower as Leader. *New York: Basic Books, 1982.*

———. editor. Leadership in the Modern Presidency. *Cambridge, Massachusetts: Harvard University Press, 1988.*

Gribetz, Judah. The Timetables of Jewish History. *New York: Simon & Schuster, 1993.*

Gruber, Ruth. Haven: The Dramatic Story of 1,000 World War II Refugees and How They Came to America. *New York: Times Books, 2000.*

Hamby, Alonzo L. Man of the People: A Life of Harry S. Truman. *New York: Oxford University Press, 1995.*

Hart, Alan. Arafat: A Political Biography. *Bloomington: University of Indiana Press, 1984.*

Healey, Robert M. *"Jefferson on Judaism and the Jews,"* American Jewish History 73, 1984.

Healy, Diana Dixon. America's First Ladies: Private Lives of the Presidential Wives. *New York: Atheneum, 1988.*

Hecht, Marie B. John Quincy Adams: A Personal History of an Independent Man. *New York: Macmillan, 1972.*

Hertz, Emanuel. Lincoln Talks: A Biography in Anecdote. *New York: Viking Press, 1939.*

Herzl, Theodor. The Diaries of Theodor Herzl. *Magnolia, Massachusetts: Peter Smith, 1960.*

Herzog, Chaim. Living History: A Memoir. *New York: Pantheon Books, 1996.*

Hess, Stephen. America's Political Dynasties. *Piscataway, N.J.: Transaction Publishers, 1996.*

Hirsch, H.N. The Enigma of Felix Frankfurter. *New York: Basic Books, 1981.*

Holman, Hamilton. Zachary Taylor: Soldier in the White House. *Two volumes. Indianapolis: Bobbs-Merrill, 1951.*

Holzer, Harold. Dear Mr. Lincoln: Letter to the President. *Reading, Massachusetts: Addison Wesley, 1995.*

Hoobler, Dorothy and Thomas. The Jewish American Family Album. *New York: Oxford University Press, 1995.*

Hoogenboom, Ari. Rutherford B. Hayes: One of the Good Colonels. *Abilene, Texas: McWhiney Foundation Press, 1999.*

Isaacson, Walter. Kissinger: A Biography. *New York: Simon and Schuster, 1992.*

Jaher, Fredric Cople. A Scapegoat in the New Wilderness: The Origins and Rise of Anti-Semitism in America. Cambridge, Massachusetts: Harvard University Press, 1994.

Jewish Encyclopedia. *New York: Funk & Wagnalls, 1901.*

Johnson, Paul. A History of the American People. *New York: HarperCollins, 1998.*

———. A History of the Jews. *New York: HarperCollins, 1987.*

Jones, Charles O., editor. The Reagan Legacy: Promise and Performance. *Chatham, New Jersey: Chatham House Publishers, 1988.*

Kalb, Marvin and Bernard Kalb. Kissinger. *Boston: Little Brown and Company, 1974.*

Karp, Abraham J. Golden Door to America: The Jewish Immigrant Experience. *New York: Viking Press, 1976.*

———. Haven and Home: A History of the Jews in America. *New York: Schocken, 1985.*

Karski, Jan. Story of a Secret State. *Boston: Houghton Mifflin, 1944.*

Katz, Irving. August Belmont: A Political Biography. *New York: Columbia University Press, 1968.*

Kaufman, Andrew L. Cardozo. *Cambridge, Massachusetts: Harvard University Press, 1998.*

Kaufman, Burton I. The Presidency of James Earl Carter, Jr. *Lawrence: University Press of Kansas, 1993.*

Kearns, Doris. Lyndon Johnson and the American Dream. *New York: New American Library, 1976.*

Ketcham, Ralph. James Madison: A Biography. *New York: Macmillan, 1971.*

Kissinger, Henry. White House Years. *Boston: Little, Brown and Co., 1979.*

Klein, Philip S. President James Buchanan. *University Park: Pennsylvania State University Press, 1962.*

Klemperer, Victor. I Will Bear Witness: A Diary of the Nazi Years. *Volume I, 1933–1941; Volume II, 1941– 1945. New York: Random House, 1999.*

Klutznick, Philip M., with Sidney Hyman. Angles of Vision: A Memoir of My Lives. *Chicago: Ivan R. Dee, 1991.*

Konvitz, Milton R. "Benjamin Nathan Cardozo," Midstream, *May–June 1999.*

Koppman, Lionel, and Bernard Postal. Guess Who's Jewish in American History. *New York: Shapolsky, 1986.*

Korff, Baruch. The President and I. *Hoboken, New Jersey: KTAV, 1995.*

Korn, Bertram Wallace. American Jewry and the Civil War. *Philadelphia: Jewish Publication Society, 1951.*

Kunhardt, Philip B., Jr., Philip B. III, and Peter W. The American President. *New York: Riverhead Books, 1999.*

Kurtzman, Dan. Soldier of Peace: The Life of Yitzhak Rabin. *New York: HarperCollins, 1998.*

Laqueur, Walter. The Terrible Secret: Suppression of the Truth About Hitler's "Final Solution." *New York: Owl Books, 1980.*

Lash, Joseph P. Eleanor and Franklin. *New York: Konecky and Konecky, 1971.*

Leech, Margaret. In the Days of McKinley. *New York: Harper & Bros., 1959.*

———, and Harry J. Brown. The Garfield Orbit: The Life of President James A. Garfield. *New York: Harper & Row, 1978.*

Leeser, Isaac. Commemoration of the Life and Death of William Henry Harrison, *1841.*

Lipstadt, Deborah E. "The Bitburg Controversy," in American Jewish Year Book 1987. *New York: American Jewish Committee.*

Lomask, Milton. Andrew Johnson: President on Trial. *New York: Farrar, Straus, 1960.*

Lyman, Darryl. Great Jewish Families. *New York: Jonathan David Publishers, 1997.*

Lynch, Denis Tilden. An Epoch and a Man: Martin Van Buren and His Times. *Port Washington, New York: Kennikat Press, 1971.*

Lyon, Peter. Eisenhower: Portrait of a Hero. *Boston: Little, Brown and Co., 1974.*

Madison, Charles A. Eminent American Jews, 1776 to the Present. *New York: Unger, 1970.*

Maney, Patrick J. The Roosevelt Presence: The Life and Legacy of FDR. *Berkeley: University of California Press, 1992.*

Marcus, Jacob Rader. Memoirs of American Jews, 1775–1865. *Philadelphia: Jewish Publication Society, 1955.*

Margolis, Max L. and Alexander Marx. A History of the Jewish People. *Philadelphia: Jewish Publication Society, 1934.*

Marshall, John. The Life of George Washington. *London: printed for Richard Phillips, 1804–1807.*

Martin, Asa. After the White House. *State College, Pennsylvania: Penns Valley, 1951.*

Martin, Bernard. A History of Judaism: Europe and the New World. *New York: Basic Books, 1974.*

Mazlish, Bruce. In Search of Nixon: A Psychohistorical Inquiry. *New York: Basic Books, 1972.*

McCall, Samuel Walker. Patriotism of the American Jew. *New York: Plymouth Press, 1924.*

McCollister, John. So Help Me God. *Bloomington, Minnesota: Landmark Books, 1982.*

McCoy, Donald R. Calvin Coolidge: The Quiet President. *New York: Macmillan, 1967.*

McCullough, David. Truman. *New York: Simon & Schuster, 1992.*

McDonald, Forrest. The American Presidency: An Intellectual History. *Lawrence: University Press of Kansas, 1994.*

———. The Presidency of Thomas Jefferson. *Lawrence: University Press of Kansas, 1998.*

McFeely, William S. Grant: A Biography. *New York: W.W. Norton & Co., 1982.*

McJimsey, George. The Presidency of Franklin Delano Roosevelt. *Lawrence, Kansas: University of Kansas Press, 2000.*

Mendes-Flohr, Paul R., and Jehuda Reinharz. The Jew in the Modern World: A Documentary History. *New York: Oxford University Press, 1980.*

Miller, John C. Triumph of Freedom, 1775–1783. *Boston: Little, Brown and Co., 1948.*

Miller, Merle. Plain Speaking: An Oral Biography of Harry S. Truman. *New York: Berkley, 1973.*

Miller, Nathan. Star Spangled Men: America's Ten Worst Presidents. *New York: Scribner, 1998.*

Moise, L.C. Biography of Isaac Harby. *Columbia, South Carolina: R.L. Bryan Co., 1931.*

Morgenthau, Henry, Sr. My Trip Around the World, *1928.*

———. Ambassador Morgenthau's Story. *Garden City, New York: Doubleday, 1918.*

Morgenthau, Henry III. Mostly Morgenthaus: A Family History. *New York. Ticknor and Fields, 1991.*

Morris, Edmund. The Rise of Theodore Roosevelt. *New York: Coward, McCann & Geoghegan, 1979.*

Morse, Arthur D. While Six Million Died: A Chronicle of American Apathy. *New York: Random House, 1968.*

Moynihan, Daniel Patrick editor. The Defenses of Freedom: The Public Papers of Arthur J. Goldberg. *New York Harper and Row, 1966.*

Murray, Robert K. The Harding Era: Warren G. Harding and His Administration. *Minneapolis: University of Minnesota Press, 1969.*

Nadich, Judah. Eisenhower and the Jews. *New York: Twayne Publishers, 1953.*

Nagel, Paul C. John Quincy Adams: A Pubic Life, A Private Life. *New York: Alfred A. Knopf, 1997.*

Nash, George H. The Life of Herbert Hoover. *Three volumes. New York: W.W. Norton & Co., 1983–97.*

Neufeld, Michael J., and Michael Benenbaum. The Bombing of Auschwitz: Should the Allies Have Attempted It? *New York: St. Martin's Press, 2000.*

Nevins, Allan, editor. The Diary of Philip Hone, 1828–1851. *New York: Dodd, Mead and Co., 1927.*

———. Grover Cleveland: A Study in Courage. *New York: Dodd, Mead and Co., 1933.*

———. Herbert H. Lehman and His Era. *New York: Charles Scribner and Sons, 1963.*

———. editor. Polk: Diary of a President 1845–1849. *New York: Capricorn, 1968.*

———. The New York Times 2000 Almanac. *New York: Penguin, 2000.*

Newton, Verne W. editor. FDR and the Holocaust. *New York: St. Martin's Press, 1966.*

Nichols, Roy Franklin. Franklin Pierce: Young Hickory of the Granite Hills. *Philadelphia: University of Pennsylvania Press, 1931.*

Noah, Mordecai M. Travels in England, France, Spain, and the Barbary States in the Years 1813–1814 and 1815. *1819.*

Nordlinger, Bernard I. *"A History of the Washington Hebrew Congregation," in* The Record, *a publication of the Jewish Historical Society of Greater Washington (D.C.). November 1969.*

Ogden, Christopher. Legacy: A Biography of Moses and Walter Annenberg. *Boston: Little, Brown and Co., 1999.*

Oren, Michael B. *"The* USS Liberty: *Case Closed," in* Azure, *Spring 5160/2000.*

Panitz, Esther L. Simon Wolf: Private Conscience and Public Image. *Cranbury, New Jersey: Fairleigh Dickinson University Press, 1987.*

Parmet, Herbert S. George Bush: The Life of a Lone Star Yankee. *New York: Scribner, 1997.*

Pearlman, Moshe. Ben-Gurion Looks Back in Talks with Moshe Pearlman. *New York: Simon & Schuster, 1965.*

Peterson, Merrill D. Thomas Jefferson and the New Nation. *New York: Oxford University Press, 1970.*

Pfau, Richard. No Sacrifice Too Great: The Life of Lewis L. Strauss. *Charlottesville: University of Virginia Press, 1984.*

Polenberg, Richard. The World of Benjamin Cardozo: Personal Values and the Judicial Process. *Cambridge, Massachusetts: Harvard University Press, 1997.*

Polsby, Nelson W., and Aaron Wildavsky. Presidential Elections: Contemporary Strategies of American Electoral Politics. *New York: Free Press, 1988.*

Potok, Chaim. Wanderings. *New York: Alfred A. Knopf, 1978.*

Pringle, Henry. The Life and Times of William Howard Taft. *Two volumes. New York: Farrar & Rinehart, 1939.*

Rabinowitz, Stanley. *"A Sermon and a President," in* Adas Israel Chronicle, *1963.*

———. The Assembly: A Century in the History of the Adas Israel Hebrew Congregation of Washington, D.C. *1993.*

Randall, Willard S. Thomas Jefferson: A Life. *New York: Henry Holt & Co., 1993.*

Rather, Dan. Deadlines and Datelines. *New York: William Morrow & Co., 1999.*

Reeves, Richard. President Kennedy: Profile of Power. *New York: Simon & Schuster, 1993.*

Reeves, Thomas. Gentleman Boss: The Life of Chester A. Arthur. *New York: Alfred A. Knopf, 1975.*

Remini, Robert V. Andrew Jackson and the Course of the American Empire 1767–1821. *New York: Harper & Row, 1977.*

———. Martin Van Buren and the Making of the Democratic Party. *New York: Columbia University Press, 1959.*

Rochlin, Harriet, and Fred. Pioneer Jews: A New Life in the Far West. *Boston: Houghton Mifflin Co., 1984.*

Roosevelt, Theodore. Theodore Roosevelt: An Autobiography. *New York: Scribner's Sons, 1913.*

Rosenberg, Elliot. But Were They Good for the Jews? *Secaucus, New Jersey: Birch Lane Press, 1997.*

Rosenstock, Morton. Louis Marshall, Defender of Jewish Rights. *Detroit: Wayne State University Press, 1965.*

Rosenwald, Julius. Papers. *Scrapbook 3. University of Chicago Library.*

Rubinger, Naphtali J. Abraham Lincoln and the Jews. *New York: Jonathan David Publishers, 1962.*

Russell, Francis. Adams: An American Dynasty. *New York: American Heritage Publishing Co., 1976.*

———. The Shadow of Blooming Grove: Warren G. Harding and His Times. *New York: McGraw-Hill Book Co., 1968.*

Sachar, Abram Leon. The Redemption of the Unwanted. *New York: St. Martin's Press, 1983.*

———. The Jew in the Contemporary World: Sufferance Is the Badge. *New York: Alfred A. Knopf, 1939.*

Sachar, Howard M. A History of Israel: From the Rise of Zionism to Our Time. *New York: Alfred A. Knopf, 1979.*

———. A History of the Jews in America. *New York: Vintage Books, 1992.*

———. Israel and Europe: An Appraisal in History. *New York: Alfred A. Knopf, 1999.*

Safire, William. Before the Fall: An Inside View of the Pre-Watergate White House. *Garden City, New York: Doubleday, 1975.*

Samberg, Joel. The Book of Jewish Lists. *Secaucus, New Jersey: Citadel Press, 1998.*

Sarna, Jonathan D. The American Jewish Experience. *New York: Holmes and Meier, 1986.*

———. Jacksonian Jew: The Two Worlds of Mordecai Noah. *New York: Holmes & Meier Publishers, 1981.*

———.editor. The American Jewish Experience. *New York: Holmes and Meier, 1986.*

———, and David G. Dalin. Religion and State in the American Jewish Experience. *Notre Dame, Indiana: University of Notre Dame Press, 1997.*

Schappes, Morris U., editor. A Documentary History of the Jews in the United States, 1654–1875. *New York: Citadel Press, 1950.*

Schechter, Solomon. Seminary Addresses and Other Papers. *Cincinnati: Ark Publishing Co., 1915.*

Schlesinger, Arthur M., Jr. The Age of Jackson. *Boston: Little, Brown and Co., 1946.*

———. The Almanac of American History. *New York: Bramhall House, 1983.*

———. The Imperial Presidency. *1973.*

———. A Thousand Days: John F. Kennedy in the White House. *Boston: Houghton, Mifflin, 1965.*

Schoenbuam, Eleanor W. Profiles of an Era: The Nixon/Ford Years. *1979.*

Schwartz, Jordan A. The Speculator: Bernard M. Baruch in Washington, 1917–1965, *Chapel Hill: The University of North Carolina Press, 1981.*

Seager, Robert. And Tyler Too: A Biography of John and Julia Gardiner Tyler. *New York: McGraw-Hill Book Co., 1963.*

Sharansky, Natan. Fear No Evil. *New York: Random House, 1988.*

Shaw, Peter. The Character of John Adams. *Chapel Hill: University of North Carolina Press, 1976.*

Sievers, Harry J. Benjamin Harrison. *Volumes 1, 2. New York: University Publishers, 1952, 1959; Volume 3. Indianapolis: Bobbs-Merrill, 1968.*

Simonhoff, Harry. Saga of American Jewry, 1865–1914. *New York: Arco Publishing Co., 1959.*

Slater, Elinor and Robert. Great Jewish Men. *New York: Jonathan David Publishers, 1996.*

——. Great Jewish Women. *New York: Jonathan David Publishers, 1994.*

——. Great Moments in Jewish History. *New York: Jonathan David Publishers, 1998.*

Slater, Robert. Golda: The Uncrowned Queen of Israel. *New York: Jonathan David Publishers, 1981.*

Smith, Elbert. The Presidencies of Zachary Taylor and Millard Fillmore. *Lawrence: University Press of Kansas, 1988.*

Smith, Page. John Adams. *Two volumes. Garden City, New York: Doubleday, 1962.*

Smith, Richard Norton. An Uncommon Man: The Triumph of Herbert Hoover. *New York: Simon & Schuster, 1984.*

Sobel, Robert. Coolidge: An American Enigma. *Washington, D.C.: Regnery Publishing, Inc., 1998.*

Solomons, Adolphus. Reminiscences of Abraham Lincoln. *n.d.*

Sorensen, Theodore C. Kennedy. *New York: Harper & Row, 1965.*

Spalding, Henry D. The Nixon Nobody Knows. *New York: Jonathan David Publishers, 1972.*

Spiegel, Steven L. The Other Arab-Israeli Conflict: Making America's Middle East Policy, from Truman to Reagan. *Champaign: University of Chicago Press, 1985.*

Steinberg, Alfred. The First Ten: The Founding Presidents and Their Administrations. *Garden City, New York: Doubleday, 1967.*

Stephanopoulos, George. All Too Human: A Political Education. *Boston: Little, Brown and Co., 1999.*

Stone, Irving. They Also Ran: The Story of Men Who Were Defeated for the Presidency. *Garden City, New York: Doubleday, 1966.*

Straus, Oscar S. Under Four Administrations: From Cleveland to Taft. *Boston: Houghton Mifflin Co., 1922.*

Strauss, Lewis L. Men and Decisions. *Garden City, New York: Doubleday, 1962.*

Strober, Deborah Hart, and Gerald S. Strober, Reagan: The Man and His Presidency. *Boston: Houghton Mifflin, 1998.*

Sussman, Lance J. Isaac Leeser and the Making of American Judaism. *Wayne, Indiana: Wayne State University Press, 1995.*

Tanzer, Lester, editor. The Kennedy Circle. *Washington: Luce, 1961.*

Taylor, John M. Garfield of Ohio: The Available Man. *New York: W.W. Norton & Co., 1970.*

Telushkin, Joseph. Jewish Literacy. *New York: HarperCollins, 1991.*

Teveth, Shabtai. Ben-Gurion and the Holocaust. *Orlando, Florida: Harcourt Brace, 1996.*

Thomas, Helen. Front Row at the White House. *New York: Scribner, 1999.*

Tivnan, Edward. The Lobby: Jewish Political Power and American Foreign Policy. *New York: Simon & Schuster, 1987.*

Tobias, Thomas J. "The Many-Sided Dr. De La Motta," in The Jewish Experience in America, *Abraham J. Karp, editor, Vol. II, 1969, pp. 64–81.*

Trefousse, Hans L. Andrew Johnson: A Biography. *New York: W.W. Norton & Co., 1989.*

Troy, Gil. See How They Ran: The Changing Role of the Presidential Candidate. *Cambridge, Massachusetts: Harvard University Press, 1996.*

Truman, Harry S. Mr. Citizen. *New York: Bernard Geis Associates, 1960.*

——. Memoirs by Harry S. Truman *(Volume I:* Year of Decisions, 1945; *Volume II:* Years of Trial and Hope, 1946–1952*). Garden City, New York: Doubleday, 1955–1956.*

The Universal Jewish Encyclopedia. *Ten volumes. New York, 1939–1943.*

Urofsky, Melvin I. A Mind of One Piece: Brandeis and American Reform. *New York: Charles Scribner's Sons, 1971.*

——. Louis D. Brandeis and the Progressive Tradition. *Boston: Little Brown and Company, 1981.*

——. A Voice That Spoke for Justice: The Life and Times of Stephen S. Wise. *New York: State University of New York Press, 1982*

Voss, Carl Hermann, editor. Stephen S. Wise: Servant of the People. *Philadelphia: Jewish Publication Society, 1969.*

Wallace, Lew. Life of General Benjamin Harrison. *Philadelphia, Chicago: Hubbard Brothers, 1888.*

Werner, M.R. Julius Rosenwald: The Life of a Practical Humanitarian. *New York: Harper & Brothers, 1939.*

White, Theodore. Breach of Faith: The Fall of Richard Nixon. *New York: Atheneum Publishers, 1975.*

White, W. A. A Puritan in Babylon: The Story of Calvin Coolidge. *New York: Macmillan, 1938.*

Whitney, David C. The American Presidents: Biographies of Chief Executives from Washington through Nixon. *Garden City, New York: Doubleday, 1967.*

——, and Robin Vaughn Whitney. The American Presidents. *Eighth edition. Pleasantville, New York: Reader's Digest, 1990.*

Wigoder, Geoffrey. The New Standard Jewish Encyclopedia. *New York: Facts on File, 1992.*

Winik, Jay. On the Brink: The Dramatic Behind-the-Scenes Saga of the Reagan Era and the Men and Women Who Won the Cold War. *New York: Simon & Schuster, 1996.*

Wolf, Simon. The American Jew as Soldier, Patriot and Citizen. *New York: Brentano, 1895.*

——. The Presidents I Have Known, From 1860–1918. *Washington: Press of B.S. Adams, 1918.*

Woodward, Bob. The Agenda: Inside the Clinton White House. *New York: Simon & Schuster, 1995.*

——. Shadow: Five Presidents and the Legacy of Watergate 1974–1999. *New York: Simon & Schuster, 1999.*

Wyman, David S. The Abandonment of the Jews: America and the Holocaust. *New York: Pantheon Books, 1984.*

Young, Klyde H., and Lamar Middleton. Heirs Apparent: The Vice Presidents of the United States. *Freeport, New York: Books for Libraries Press, 1948.*

Zola, Gary P. Isaac Harby of Charleston, 1788–1828. *Tuscaloosa: University of Alabama Press, 1994.*

Index

Baruch, Bernard, 140–41, 142, 165, 171, 176, 185, 223
Battle of New Orleans, 32, 35, 37
Beecher, Henry Ward, 78, 107
Begin, Menachem, 241, 252
Begun, Yosef, 269
Belmont, August, 57, 63, 65, 68
Ben-Gurion, David, 182, 184, 185, 191, 192, 199, 202, 207
Benjamin, Judah P., xi, 60, 69, 84–85
Bergen-Belsen, 251
Berger, Samuel, 278–79
Berlin, Isaiah, 23
Bernstein, Carl, 226
Bien, Julius, 63, 65
Bitburg Cemetery (Germany), 250–51
Black Hawk War, 55
Black September movement, 226
Blackstone, William E., 111, 113
Black Tuesday, 168
Blitzer, Wolf, 260
Bloom, Rabbi Jack H., 186–87
Blumenthal, Sidney, 279
Blumenthal, W. Michael, 238
B'nai B'rith, 89, 91, 94, 185, 194, 195, 201, 250
    Anti-Defamation League (ADL), 239
    Cleveland tribute to, 106
Board of Delegates of American Israelites, 76
Boettiger, Joshua ler, x, 176–77
Booth, John Wilkes, 78
Borah, William E., 162–63
Bork, Robert E., 254
Bosnia, 272
Boston, Massachusetts, 152
    Congregation Ohabei Shalom, 78
Brady, James, 254
Brandeis, Louis D., 133–39, 147, 148, 163, 169, 171
    appointment to U.S. Supreme Court, xii, 134, 136, 143, 201
    Balfour Declaration, 138–39
    and labor movement, 136
    on Zionism, 134–35
Brandeis University, 202, 206, 254, 272
Breger, Marshall, 253, 263
Breyer, Stephen G., 276–77
Brezhnev, Leonid, 230
Brookings Institute, 284
Brooklyn Law School, 217
Brown, Harold, 238–39
Bryant, William Cullen, 35, 73, 74
Bryan, William Jennings, 115, 116, 117, 127
Brzezinski, Zbigniew, 243, 269
Buchanan, James, 66–69
    campaigns and elections, 61, 69
    early life, 67
    and Jewish community, 67–69
    legacy of, 69
    Mortara Case, 67–68
    religious beliefs, 66
    retirement years and death, 66, 69

on slavery, 68, 69
    Swiss Treaty, 67
Buffalo, New York, 105, 119
Bull Moose Party, 123, 125, 127–28
Bundy, McGeorge, 208, 220
Burns, Arthur, xii, 194, 195, 218–19, 232, 233
Burt, Robert A., 170
Bush, Barbara Pierce, 256, 257, 258
Bush, George Herbert Walker, 250, 256–63
    campaigns and elections, 255, 256, 257–58, 267
    early years, 257–58
    Intifada, 260–61
    and Jewish community, 258–63, 276
    Jonathan Pollard case, 258–60
    Middle East policy, 260–62
    military service, 257
    Persian Gulf War, 261–62
    religious beliefs, 256, 258
    retirement years, 263
    as vice president, 244, 250, 255, 256

C
California, 89, 215, 227, 245, 246–47
Cameron, William J., 148
Camp David, 240–43, 288
Cardozo, Benjamin, 162–63, 170, 201
Carolina Israelite, 121
Caro, Robert A., 210
Carter, James Earl, Jr., 236–43, 269, 275
    campaigns and elections, 235, 236, 237, 243, 246, 258, 266
    Camp David Accords, 240–43
    early years, 237–38
    Iranian hostage crisis, 243, 247
    and Jewish community, 185, 202, 237–43, 253, 263, 272, 273, 278, 279
    Middle East policy, 241, 243, 246, 247
    military career, 237–38
    religious beliefs, 236, 237, 240
    retirement years, 236, 243
Carter Library and Presidential Center, 243
Carville, James, 281, 282
Catholicism/Catholics
    anti-Catholic sentiments, 61, 158, 160
    Kennedy election, 197
    Mortara Case, 67–68
    right to vote, 51
Celle
r, Emanuel, 209–10, 213
Charleston, South Carolina, 13, 20
    Congregation Beth Elohim, 20
    early Jewish population in, 4, 5, 19
    Reformed Society of Israelites, 20
Chicago, Illinois, 6, 233
    Kehillath Anshe Ma'Arav (K.A.M.) synagogue, 72
China, 220–21, 258, 272, 273

Christopher, Warren, 269, 272, 273, 276
Cincinnati, Ohio, 72, 78, 88, 127
    Congregation B'nai Yeshurun, 78, 129
Civil liberties issues, 18, 87, 93, 170, 206, 237
Civil Service reforms, 101, 103, 127
Civil War, 57, 61, 73, 83, 97, 111, 134
    ending of, 77, 87
    Jewish participation in, 72–75, 90, 134
    military chaplain issue, 75–76
    onset of, 49, 59, 63, 65, 69
    Order No. 11 controversy, xii, 77, 87–88, 91
    secessionist movement, 49, 52, 60, 83, 84
Clay, Henry, 32, 37, 51, 59, 60, 73
Cleveland, Frances, 105
Cleveland, Grover, 103, 104–109, 167
    on anti-Semitism, 105–106
    campaigns and elections, 104, 105, 107, 115
    early life, 105
    and Jewish community, 105–109, 117, 129
    religious beliefs, 104
    retirement years and death, 104, 108–109
Clifford, Clark, 182, 184, 209
Clinton, Hillary Rodham, 264, 266, 281, 282, 283
Clinton, William Jefferson (Bill), 264–89
    advisors and counselors, 278–84
    ambassadorial appointments, 273–76
    Cabinet appointments, 267–73
    campaigns and elections, 263, 264, 266–67, 281, 284
    early years, 265–67, 279, 281, 282
    impeachment of, 271, 279, 284–86, 289
    Jerusalem Relocation Act, 286
    and Jewish community, 218, 240, 267–84, 286, 289
    Jonathan Pollard case, 260, 287–88
    Kosovo crisis, 270, 272–73
    legacy, 288–89
    Lewinsky scandal, 86, 265, 281, 282, 284
    Middle East policy, 267, 276, 286, 288
    morality issues, 288–89
    religious beliefs, 264, 267
    Supreme Court appointees, 276–78
    Whitewater Affair, 279–80, 285
Cohen, Benjamin V., 171
Cohen, Herman J., 263
Cohen, Michael J., 171
Cohen, Sheldon Stanley, x, 210–12
Cohen, Wilbur J., 201, 213
Cohen, William S., 270
Cold War, 181, 192, 193–94, 218
    Reykjavik Summit, 250, 254
    SALT I Agreement, 221
Colonial America, Jewish life in, xi, 4–6,

campaigns and elections, 92, 93, 94, 115
early years, 93
and Jewish community, 94
legacy, 93
military career, 93
Reconstruction policy, 93
religious beliefs, 92, 93–94
retirement years and death, 92, 95
Hay, John, 123, 125
Hays, John, xii, 25, 43
Hebrew Union College (HUC), 88, 139, 233
Hebrew University, 146, 162, 201, 213, 253
Hebron Accord, 276
Hellman, Herman, 89
Herzl, Theodor, 113, 134, 137
Herzog, Isaac, 184
Hillel, 81, 278
Himmelfarb, Gertrude, 254, 262
Hinckley, John W., Jr., 254
Hirsch, Rabbi Emil G., 233
Hirsch, Solomon, 112, 129
Hitler, Adolph, 165, 172, 173
Holbrooke, Richard C., 271–72
Hollander, Jacob, 118
Holmes, Oliver Wendell, Jr., 162
Holocaust, 172–76, 218, 222, 238, 258
Bitburg Cemetery visit controversy, 250–51
concentration camps, 172, 176, 177, 191, 230, 251, 273
Kristallnacht, 165, 173
President's Commission on, 239
survivors of, 143, 285
U.S. Holocaust Memorial Council, 250–51
U.S. Holocaust Memorial Museum, 239–40, 253, 276
Hone, John, 33
Hooks, Benjamin, 287
Hoover Commission, 165
Hoover, Herbert, 149, 156–65, 289
on anti-Semitism, 159, 165
Benjamin Cardozo appointment, 162–63
campaigns and elections, 156, 158, 159, 160–61, 163, 235
early years, 157, 158
Great Depression, 163–64
humanitarian relief work, 157–60, 165
and Jewish community, 158–63, 165
religious beliefs, 156
retirement years and death, 156, 164–65
Veteran's Bonus March, 164
Horowitz, Michael, 254
House of Burgesses (Virginia), 3, 17
House Judiciary Committee, 283, 285
Houston, Texas, 197, 263
Human Rights Bureau, 252
Humphrey, Hubert H., 216, 220, 239

Hungary, 135, 192, 273
Hussein, Saddam, 261
Hyde, Henry, 285

I
Iceland, 250, 254
Illinois, 72, 245
Illinois Gazette, 145
Illinois Territory, xii, 25, 43
Immigration, 4, 47–48, 75
"Ararat" refugee project, 28, 37
first-hand accounts of, 48, 147
from Russia, 12, 94, 121, 123, 125, 135
German refugee crisis, 165, 172–76, 177, 195
of Jews from Europe, 24, 32–33, 79, 135–36
restrictions to, 12, 61, 106, 147, 151, 153, 169, 173, 177
St. Louis incident, 173
Immigration Act of 1924, 151, 153
Impeachment
of Bill Clinton, 271, 279, 285–86, 289
of Andrew Johnson, 83, 289
and Richard Nixon, 226, 283
Independence, Missouri, 179, 186
Indianapolis, Indiana, 111, 113
Indyk, Martin S., 273
Intermarriage, 55, 211
Internal Revenue Service, 211
"International Jew, The," 131, 147–49
International Red Cross, 103, 141
Intifada, 260–61, 261
Iran-Contra affair, 255
Iranian hostage crisis, 243, 247
Iraq, 198, 248, 259, 261–62
Isaacson, Walter, 222
Israel. *See also* Anti-Semitism; Holocaust; Jews and Judaism; Palestine and Palestinians; *and specific events and people;* 141, 208, 212, 224, 232, 274
Bush Administration policy, 261, 262
Carter Administration policy, 240–43, 246, 247
Clinton Administration policy, 260, 267, 274, 276, 280, 286, 287–88
creation of state, 181–85, 195, 197–98
financial aid to, 199, 208, 209, 212, 221, 222, 224
Ford Administration policy, 230–31
lobbying activities, 191–92
Nixon Administration policy, 217
Reagan Administration policy, 246–48
relations with PLO, 231, 243, 262, 280
Soviet Jewry issues, 159, 199, 230, 250, 252, 262, 269
USS Liberty incident, 209
weapons sales to, 198, 199, 202, 209

West Bank settlements, 243, 247, 260–61
Israel Bond Drive, 171, 191, 202, 247
Israel-Egypt peace treaty (1979), 241
Israelite, The, 78
Israel lobby, 191–92
Israel-PLO peace agreement (1993), 267
Italy, 67–68

J
Jackson, Andrew, 34–37, 39, 67
Battle of New Orleans, 35, 37
campaigns and elections, 31, 33, 34, 35, 37
early years, 35, 37
and Jewish community, 24, 37
military career, 35, 37
religious beliefs, 34, 37
retirement years and death, 34, 37
War of 1812, 35, 37
Jackson, Henry, 253
Jacobson, Edward, 179–80, 183–84, 186
Jay, John, 73
Jefferson, Thomas, 16–21
campaigns and elections, 11, 15, 16, 19
Capitol Rotunda statue, 28–29
Declaration of Independence, 17–18
"Dissenters and Jews" law, 18, 20
early years, 17
on James Madison, 23
on James Monroe, 27
and Jewish community, 12, 18–21
on Judaism, 20–21
Mill Street Synagogue letter, 19–20
on presidency, 289
religious beliefs, 18, 19, 20, 47
retirement years death, 15, 16, 21, 29
on separation of church and state, 18
slavery issue, 17–18
University of Virginia, 20, 25
as vice president, 10
Jenkins, Walter, 211
Jerusalem, 90, 209, 241, 247, 261, 288
Jerusalem Relocation Act, 286
UN resolutions on, 257
Jerusalem Post, The, 260, 287
Jerusalem Relocation Act, 286
"Jew Company," 5
Jewish Advocate (Boston), 134
Jewish Democratic Study Group, 280
Jewish homeland. *See* Zionism
Jewish Institute of Religion, 139
Jewish lobbyists, 191–92
Jewish Museum (Berlin), 238
Jewish National Fund, 253
Jewish Publication Society, 129
Jewish Record, 73
Jewish Theological Seminary of America (New York City), 81, 91, 187
Jewish voting patterns. *See campaigns and elections under specific presidents*
Jews and Judaism. *See also* Anti-

Civil War, 72, 73, 75–76, 77, 88, 90
early years, 71–72
eulogies for, 79, 81
Grant's Order 11 controversy, xii, 77, 88
and Jewish community, 24, 71–79, 81, 90
military chaplaincy issue, 75–76
pardons deserter, 73
on patriotism, 74
Reconstruction policy, 84
religious beliefs, 70, 71–72, 145
on slavery, 78
Lincoln, Mary Todd, 61, 71, 78, 90
Lloyd George, David, 137, 139
Lockhart, Joe, 288–89
Lodge, Henry Cabot, Jr., 142, 197
Loeb, Morris, 148
Louisiana, 60, 69, 93
Battle of New Orleans, 32, 35, 37
Luxembourg, 223

M
McClellan, General George B., 73
McDougal, James and Susan, 279–80
McGovern, George S., 216, 279, 281
McKinley, William, 91, 113, 114–19, 127
annexation of Hawaii, 116
assassination, 114, 115, 119, 122
campaigns and elections, 114, 115, 116, 117, 122
early years, 115
and Jewish community, 116–18, 129
military service, 115
religious beliefs, 114, 119
Spanish-American War, 115–16
Macy's Department Store, 107, 117, 122
Madison, James, 22–25, 27, 31, 32
campaigns and elections, 22
on education, 23
and Jewish community, xi, 13, 23–25
religious beliefs, 22, 23
retirement years and death, 22, 25
slavery issue, 25
University of Virginia, 23, 25
Magaziner, Ira, 266, 282
Magnes, Rabbi Judah, 136
Maine (battleship), 115–16, 117
Marion Star, 145
Marix, Adolph, 129
Marks, Alexander, 37
Marshall, George C., 182, 184, 191
Marshall, Louis, 112, 123, 136, 148, 153–54, 160–61
Maryland, 19, 61
Baltimore Hebrew Congregation, 55
Congregation Beth El (Bethesda), 276
Har Sinai Temple (Baltimore), 79
Massachusetts, 31, 152, 155
Medicaid/Medicare, 213
Meir, Golda, 192, 222, 224–26
Mendes, Rabbi Henry Pereira, 122
Merchant marine, 25

Merrill, Robert, 185
Mexican War, 55, 87
Michtom, Morris and Rose, 121
Mikva, Abner J., 280, 282
Military chaplain issue, 75–76
Militia companies (Revolutionary War), 3, 5
Miller, Merle, 183–84
Mill Street Synagogue (New York City).
See also Congregation Shearith Israel (New York City); 13, 15, 19–20, 24
Milosevic, Slobodan, 269, 270, 272
Missouri, 179
Missouri Compromise, 63
Monroe Doctrine, 29
Monroe, James, 26–29, 31
campaigns and elections, 25, 26
early career of, 27
and Jewish community, xi, 24, 27–29
legacy of, 29
religious beliefs, 26
retirement years and death, 26, 29
Montefiore, Sir Moses, 40, 41
Monticello, 18, 19, 29
Moore, Thomas H., 209
Morais, Sabato, 81
Morgenthau, Henry, Jr., 170–71, 176, 177
Morgenthau, Henry, Sr., 141, 170–71
Morris, Dick, 282
Morse, Arthur, 175
Mortara Case, 67–68
Mount Vernon, Virginia, 9
Moynihan, Patrick, 231, 232, 252, 282, 284
Munich Olympics massacre, 226
Munk, Salomon, 41
Murray, Robert K, 149
Myer, Rabbi Isidore S., 13
Myers, James, 71
Myers, Morris and Katherine, 71

N
Naar, David, xii, 51
Nadich, Judah, 182, 190
Nasser, Gamal Abdel, 191, 198, 208
National Advocate, 24, 25
National Association for the Advancement of Colored People (NAACP), 168–69
National Origins Act. *See* Immigration Act of 1924
National Security Council, 254, 269, 274, 275
National Union Party, 83
Nation, The, 172–73
NATO. *See* North Atlantic Treaty Organization
Naturalization Act, 12
Nazism/Nazi Germany, 165, 172–76, 198
"New Deal" legislation, 170, 171
"New Frontier," 203
New Hampshire, 63, 65

New Jersey, 108, 128, 133, 240–41
New Orleans, Louisiana, 7, 60, 69, 73
Battle of, 32, 35, 37
Newport, Rhode Island, 4, 7–8
New Republic magazine, xii, 280
New South, 237
Newsweek magazine, 243, 246, 268
New York, 39, 41, 59, 61, 68, 105, 121, 123
"Ararat" Jewish refuge project, 28, 37
Congregation Shearith Israel (Brooklyn), 75, 122
governors of, 105, 116, 122, 167, 168, 169
Grand Union Hotel incident (Saratoga Springs), 90
Hebrew Educational Society (Brooklyn), 74
machine politics and patronage, 76, 90, 101
Temple Hillel (Woodmere), 248
New York City, 4, 12, 32, 51, 65, 101, 107, 121, 218
Congregation B'nai Jeshurun, 74, 139
Einstein/Weizmann visit, 146
Free Synagogue, 139, 141
Grant's Tomb, 91
immigrant conditions in, 135–36
Jefferson election, 19
Jewish Theological Seminary of America, 81, 91, 187
Lower East Side, 121, 136, 169
Mayor Jimmy Walker incident, 169
Mill Street Synagogue, 13, 19–20, 24
Rector Ahlwardt incident, 122
Rosenberg spy case, 193–94
Spanish-Portuguese Synagogue, 162
Temple Emanu-El, 139
Triangle Shirtwaist Factory fire, 136, 169
New York Evening Post, 35, 74
New York Evening Star, 44
New York Herald Tribune, The, 219
New York Times, The, 152–53, 163, 208, 219
New York World, 83
Nicaragua, 255
Nicholas II (Czar), 123
Niles, David K., 171, 182–83
Nixon, Richard Milhous, 192, 214–27, 229, 245, 257
and anti-Semitism, xii, 216–17
campaigns and elections, 213, 214, 215, 216, 220, 233, 279
early years, 215
eulogies for, 224, 227, 235
foreign policy, 220–21, 288
impeachment, 226–27, 283
Israeli policy, 217, 221, 222, 243
and Jewish community, 195, 216–24, 226, 233, 245, 253, 281
military service, 215
Munich Olympics massacre, 226

religious beliefs, 214
retirement years and death, 214, 224, 227
as vice president, 188
Vietnam War, 221, 224
Watergate, 216–17, 218, 226–27, 229, 234–35
Yom Kippur War, 221–22, 224
Noah, Mordecai Manuel, ix, 15, 19–20, 23–24, 25, 32, 44
"Ararat" Jewish refuge project, 28, 37
as U.S. consul in Tunis, xi, 13, 24, 27–28
Nobel Prizes, 142, 146, 221, 241, 252
Nones, Benjamin, 5, 12–13
Norfolk Naval Base, xii, 75
North Atlantic Treaty Organization (NATO), 231, 252, 269, 270, 273
North Carolina, 51
Novy, James, 206
Nuremberg Laws, 172
Nussbaum, Bernard, 279, 282–83

O

Occident and American Jewish Advocate, 81
Occident, The, 44
Ochs, Adolph Simon, 152–53
O'Connor, Sandra Day, 254
Office of Economic Stabilization, 171
Office of Management and Budget, 272, 284
Office of Strategic Services (O.S.S.), 201
Office of War Information, 171
Ohio, 87, 93, 95, 97, 115, 145
Ohrdruf Camp, 191
Olan, Rabbi Levi, 203
Olympic Games, 172, 226
Oppenheimer, J. Robert, 193
Order No. 11, xii, 77, 87–88, 91
Ordinance of Religious Freedom (Virginia), 18
Oregon, Congregation Beth Israel (Portland), 112, 139
Orthodox Judaism, 275
Oslo Accords, 276, 286, 288
Oswego, New York, 183
Other People's Money (Brandeis), 134
Ottoman Empire, 139
Oxford University (England), 266, 271, 282

P

Palestine Liberation Organization (PLO), 231, 241, 267
intifada, 260–61
peace talks, 262, 276, 280, 286, 288
Soviet ties, 247
Palestine/Palestinians. *See also* Zionism; 90, 165, 181
autonomy issues, 241, 243
Balfour Declaration, 137–39, 169, 183, 184

displaced persons policy, 181
Fourteen Points program, 142–43
Hebron Accord, 276
immigration restrictions (for Jews), 184
Oslo Accords, 276, 286, 288
partition vote, 184, 197
Wye River Summit, 280
Palko v. Connecticut, 163
Paris Peace Conference, 142, 148, 160, 169–70
Patriot antimissile batteries, 262
Patton, George, 190–91
Peace Corps, 201, 254
Peixotto, Benjamin Franklin, 89–90, 94
Pendleton Civil Service Act, 101
Pennsylvania. *See also* Philadelphia; 37, 67
Congregation Rodef Shalom (Pittsburgh), 128
Peres, Shimon, 251, 259, 286
Perle, Richard, 247, 253
Persian Gulf War, 261–62
Philadelphia Enquirer, The, 223
Philadelphia, Pennsylvania, 4, 11, 13, 24–25, 39
Congregation Mikveh Israel, 5, 24, 81
Court of Common Pleas, 129
military chaplaincy issue, 75–76
Republican Convention of 1800, 12
Philippine Islands, 116, 127, 129
Phillips, Jonas, 24–25
Pierce, Franklin, 61, 62–65
campaigns and elections, 62
early years, 63
and Jewish community, xi, 63, 65, 68
Kansas-Nebraska Act, 63
legacy of, 63, 65
Missouri Compromise, 63
retirement years and death, 62, 65
on slavery, 63
Pinner, Moritz, 75
Pinsk massacre, 159
Pipes, Richard, 247, 254
PLO. *See* Palestine Liberation Organization
Podhoretz, Norman, 252
Poindexter, John M., 254
Poland, 12, 106, 135, 159, 173, 174, 230, 237
Polk, James Knox, 33, 47, 50–53
campaigns and elections, 50, 51
and Jewish community, xii, 24, 51, 52
religious beliefs, 50, 52
retirement years and death, 50, 53
slavery issue, 51
as Speaker of U.S. House of Representatives, 51
Pollard, Anne, 259, 260
Pollard, Jonathan, 258–60, 287–88
Portland, Oregon, 112, 139, 239
Powell, Lewis F., Jr., 254

Prague (Czech Republic), 148, 269
Presidency, views on, 91, 289
President's Council of Economic Advisors, 218, 223, 233, 252, 253, 269, 281
President's House. *See* White House
Princeton University, 108, 128, 133, 213, 238
Proclamation of Independence (Israel), 184
Progressive "Bull Moose" Party. *See* Bull Moose Party
Prohibition, 93, 94
Proskauer, Judge Joseph, 171
Protocols of the Elders of Zion, The, 131, 147–49
Prussia, 12, 29, 31
Puerto Rico, 116, 118
Pulaski, General Casimir, 5

Q

Quayle, Dan, 256, 261, 262

R

Rabbi Akiba, 203
Rabbis, as chaplains, 75–76, 195
Rabb, Maxwell, 195
Rabin, Leah, 287
Rabinowitz, Rabbi Stanley, x, 203, 206, 212
Rabin, Yitzhak, 209, 224, 231, 243, 267, 288
Arafat handshake, 286
assassination, 286–87
Clinton eulogy for, 286–87
intifada, 260
Racism, 147–49
Radical Republicans, 84, 85
Rankin, John R., 10, 209
Raphall, Rabbi Morris J., 74, 78, 79
Reagan Presidential Library, 255
Reagan, Ronald, 43, 67, 229, 244–55, 257, 258, 260, 266
assassination attempt, 254
Bitburg Cemetery controversy, 250–51
Cold War policy, 247, 250, 254–55
early years, 245–46
elections and campaigns, 216, 218, 229, 238, 243, 244, 245, 246, 247
Iran-Contra controversy, 255
and Jewish community, 233, 239, 246–54, 263, 275, 281
legacy of, 254–55
Middle East policy, 243, 246–48, 255
military service, 245
religious beliefs, 244
retirement years, 255
Soviet Jewry issues, 250
U.S. Supreme Court nominations, 254
Reconstruction era, 61, 69, 84, 85, 93
Reconstruction Finance Corporation, 163–64

Reform Judaism, 85, 88, 129, 139, 176, 177, 239, 278
   anti-Zionism, 140
   opposition to, 44
Refugee Relief Act of 1953, 195
Refugees. *See also* Displaced persons
   Oswego (New York) refugee aid, 183
   War Refugee Board, 177
Rehnquist, William H., 254
Reich, Robert, 266, 271
Reisman, David, 213
Religion. *See also* Jews and Judaism *and religious beliefs under specific presidents*
   chaplaincy issues, 23, 75–76, 195
   conversion to Christianity, 32
   Establishment Clause (First Amendment), 277
   freedom of, 51, 60, 130–31, 199
   Houston, Texas, Ministerial Association speech (Kennedy), 197
   intolerance of, 19
   separation of church and state, 18, 23, 47, 48–49, 197
Reno, Janet, 285
Republican Party. *See also campaigns and elections under specific presidents*; 111, 125
   and Abolition movement, 61, 73, 76
   anti-Catholic sentiments, 160
   on gold standard, 115, 117
   Hayes election controversy, 93
   impact of immigration, 75
   Jewish leaders of, 129, 130, 159–60, 161, 192, 223, 233, 245, 247
   machine politics and patronage, 76, 101
   Radical Republicans, 84, 85
   Thomas Jefferson and, 12, 19
Revolutionary War, 4–7, 8, 12, 75
   Jewish participation in, xi, 4–6, 7, 12, 47
Reykjavik Summit, 250, 254
Ribicoff, Abraham, 199–200, 257
Rice, Rabbi Abraham Joseph, 55, 56
Rickover, Hyman G., 237–38
Rifkin, Simon H., 190
Rivlin, Alice, 283
Roberts, Steve, x, 211
Rockefeller, Nelson, 216, 218, 219, 220, 226, 228, 229
Rogers Plan, 224
Rogers, William P., 221, 224
Rohatyn, Felix, 274–75
Romania, 89–90, 94, 135
   anti-Semitic league, 123, 125
Ronald Lauder Foundation, 252–53
Roosevelt, Anna Eleanor, 166, 167, 169, 181, 186
Roosevelt, Franklin Delano, 166–77, 289
   Black Tuesday, 168
   Brain Trust, 168, 169
   campaigns and elections, 145, 164, 167, 180, 197, 235
   death of, 166, 176, 179

early years, 167–68
Holocaust, 174–76, 177
and Jewish community, 168–77, 182, 183, 207, 239
Kristallnacht, 173
legacy of, 177
New Deal programs, 170, 171
religious beliefs, 166
St. Louis incident, 173
World War II, 171, 172–76, 177
Roosevelt, Theodore, 120–25, 142, 167, 199
   on anti-Semitism, 122, 123, 125
   Bull Moose Party, 123, 125, 127–28
   campaigns and elections, 120, 122, 130, 133, 140
   early years, 121–22
   and Jewish community, xii, 113, 116, 118, 121–23, 125
   Kishinev pogrom, 123
   origin of Teddy Bear, 121
   religious beliefs, 120, 122
   retirement years and death, 120, 125
   Rough Riders, 116, 121
   as vice president, 114, 120
Roseanne, Meir, 260
Rosenberg, Ethel and Julius, 193–94
Rosenman, Dorothy, 168
Rosenman, Samuel J., 171, 186
Rosenwald, Julius, 130, 159–60, 161
Ross, Dennis, 263, 275
Rostow, Eugene V., 201, 209, 247, 253
Rostow, Walter W., 201, 209
Rothman, John F., ix, x
Rothschild family, 57, 137
Rough Riders, 116, 121
Rubin, James P., 283–84
Rubin, Robert E., 269–70, 274
Rush, Dr. Benjamin, 18
Russia. *See also* Anti-Semitism; Cold War; Soviet Union; 29, 31, 67, 89, 157, 181, 263
   immigration from, 12, 94, 121, 123, 125, 135
   post-World War I famine, 159
   restrictions on American Jews, 106, 130–31
Russo-American Commercial Treaty, 130–31

S

Sabbath observances. *See under* Jews and Judaism
Sadat, Anwar, 235, 241
Safire, William, 219
St. Louis incident, 173
Salomon, Haym, xi, 6
SALT I Agreement, 221
Salvador, Francis, 5
Samuel, Rebecca, 4
San Clemente, California, 226–27
Sanders, Edward, 240
San Francisco, California, Temple Emanuel, 278

Sapiro, Aaron, 149, 155
Saturday Review, 195
Saudi Arabia, 246, 247–48
Savannah, Georgia, 4, 5, 20, 23, 44
Sawyer, Diane, 226
Saypol, Irving, 193
Scalia, Antonin, 254
Schechter, Solomon, 81
Schiff, Jacob H., 112, 123, 125, 136, 141, 148
Schifter, Richard, 252, 263
Schlesinger, Arthur, Jr., 176
Schlesinger, James R., 222
Schultz, George, 250, 252, 259
Schumer, Charles, 289
Schwartz, Joseph J., 181
Scud missiles, 261–62
Sears, Roebuck and Company, 130, 159
Securities and Exchange Acts, 171
Securities and Exchange Commission, 197, 207
Seixas, Moses, 7–8
Seixas, Rabbi Gershom Mendes, 12, 162
Seligman, Jesse, 48, 89, 112
Seligman, Joseph, xii, 48, 75, 89, 90
Sella, Aviem, 258–60
Serbia, 270, 272–73
Shamir, Yitzhak, 248, 250, 260–62
Shapiro, Robert, 284
Sharansky, Anatoly, 250
Sharansky, Avital, 250, 252
Shazar, Zalman, 208
Sherman Anti-Trust Act, 127
Shimon Peres Peace Award, 281
Shiskin, Julius, 216
Silver, Rabbi Hillel, 161, 181
Simpson, Solomon, 19
Sinai Accord, 231
Sinai Campaign (1956), 192–92, 231
Sinai Peninsula, 191–92, 209, 212, 221, 231, 241
Sinai Temple (Chicago), 233
Six-Day War, 201, 208–209, 224, 241, 243, 246–47
Slater, Eleanor and Robert, 276
Slavery. *See also* Abolitionist movement; 17–18, 25, 39, 52, 68, 69, 78
   Amistad incident, 33
   Compromise of 1850, 59
   extension of, 47, 57, 63
   opposition to, 33, 61, 73, 76, 79, 87
   and secessionist movement, 55, 83
Smith, Alfred E., 136, 158, 160
Sneerson, H.Z., 90
Socialist Party, 135
Social Security Act of 1935, 163
Sofaer, Abraham, 259
Solomons, Adolphus Simeon, 74, 84, 99, 103
South Carolina, 20, 35, 37, 93, 176
Southern Patriot, 27
Soviet Union. *See also* Anti-Semitism; Russia; 184, 192, 208, 209, 219, 224, 248

arms reduction treaties, 254–55
as "Evil Empire," 254
Oppenheimer case, 193
and PLO, 247
Rosenberg spy case, 193–94
SALT I Agreement, 221
Soviet Jewry issues, 159, 199, 230,
    250, 252, 262, 269
"Strategic Cooperation Agreement,"
    248
Yom Kippur War, 221–22
Spanish-American War, 115–16, 121, 129
    battleship *Maine*, 115–16, 117
Speigel, Albert A., 247
Springfield, Illinois, 71
Stanton, Edward M., 84, 88
Starr, Kenneth, 265, 279, 280, 285, 286
States' rights, 17, 69
Stein, Herbert, 218, 233
Stephanopoulos, George, 267, 282, 283–
    84
Stettinius, Edward R., Jr., 179
Stevens, John Paul, 233
Stevenson, Adlai, 194, 202, 210, 239, 265
Stewart, A.T., 90
Stock market, 1929 crash, 163, 168
Stone, Dewey, 185
Straits of Tiran, 192, 208
"Strategic Cooperation Agreement," 248
Straus, Herbert Nathan, 161
Straus, Isidor, 107, 108, 109, 122
Straus, Nathan, 107, 122
Straus, Oscar, ix, xii, 106, 107–108, 112,
    115, 123, 161
    U.S. minister to Turkey, 107, 113,
        117–18, 122, 129
Strauss, Charles Moses, 89
Strauss, Lewis L., ix, 158–59, 161, 165,
    192–93, 194, 195
Strauss, Robert, 263
Suez Canal, 192, 221
Sulzberger, Arthur Hays, 152–53, 170
Sulzberger, Mayer, 123, 129–31
Summers, Lawrence H., 270, 274
Swiss Treaty, 59–60, 67
Syria, 221–22, 226
Szold, Benjamin and Henrietta, 79

T

Taft, William Howard, 74, 84, 125,
    126–31, 142
    on anti-Semitism, 131, 136, 148
    campaigns and elections, 126, 127–
        28, 130–31, 133, 140, 243
    as chief justice, U.S. Supreme Court,
        127, 131
    early years, 127–29
    and Jewish community, 128–31, 136,
        169
    religious beliefs, 126
    retirement years and death, 126, 131
    Russo-American Commercial Treaty,
        130–31
    Sherman Anti-Trust Act, 127

Talleyrand, Charles Maurice de, 11–12
Tammany Hall, 19, 105
Taylor, Zachary, 54–57
    campaigns and elections, 237
    death of, 54, 55, 57, 59
    and Jewish community, 55, 57
    military career, 55
    religious beliefs, 54, 55
    on slavery, 57, 59
Teapot Dome scandal, 149, 151, 215
Teddy Bear, origin of, 121
Tel Aviv, 239, 286
Temperance movement, 93–94
Tennessee, 35, 51, 83, 89
    Order No. 11 issue, xii, 77, 87–88, 91
    Vine Street Temple (Nashville), 85
Tennessee Volunteer Militia (1814), 35,
    37
Tenure of Office Act, 84
Texas, 203, 205, 213
    Temple Emanu-El (Dallas), 203
Thatcher, Margaret, 252
The Hague, 63, 68, 113, 123
Titanic, 108, 122
Touro family, 7
Touro Synagogue (Newport, Rhode
    Island), 7–8
Treaty of Geneva, 103
Treaty of Versailles, 142, 161
Triangle Shirtwaist Factory fire, 136,
    169
Tripp, Linda, 285
Truman, Harry S., xii, 178–87, 289
    and anti-Zionists, 179, 181–82
    campaigns and elections, 178, 200,
        202, 245
    displaced persons, 180–82, 190
    early years, 179–80
    Four Freedoms speech, 180–81
    Israel recognized, 181, 182–85
    and Jewish community, 165, 171,
        181–87
    Korean War, 194
    on Middle East, 183–84
    military service, 179–80
    Palestine partition vote, 184
    religious beliefs, 178, 186, 187
    retirement years and death, 178, 186–
        87
    Rosenberg spy case, 193–94
    as vice president, 166, 178
    on Zionism, 181, 184
Truman Library, 186, 187
Tunis (North Africa), xi, 13, 24, 27–28
Turkey, 107, 112, 141
    Armenian massacre, 118
    "Jewish" ambassador post, 129–30,
        171
    Oscar Straus appointment to, 107,
        113, 117–18, 122, 129
Tyler, John, 46–49
    campaigns and elections, 41, 46
    Confederate House of Representa-
        tives, 49

early years, 47
and Jewish community, 24, 47–49, 74
presidential succession controversy,
    44, 47
religious beliefs, 46, 47
retirement years and death, 42, 49
on separation of church and state,
    48–49
on slavery, 47
on tolerance, 47–48
as vice president, 42, 43, 47

U

Union of American Hebrew Congrega-
    tions (UAHC), 88, 146
Union Army (Civil War), 87, 90
United Hebrew Trades Union, 136
United Jewish Appeal, 171, 191, 192,
    201
United Nations, 141, 202, 207
    "Declaration of Human Rights"
        speech (Kennedy), 199
    Golda Meir statement, 192
    intifada, 261
    and Israeli rights, 232
    on Jerusalem, 247, 257
    Karski statement, 174
    Kennedy "Declaration of Human
        Rights" speech, 199
    Munich Olympics massacre, 226
    partition vote, 184, 197
    Resolution 3379, 261
    U.S. delegation, 185, 195, 210, 232,
        247, 253, 257, 269, 272, 273
    on West Bank settlements, 243
    World Conference of Women (1995),
        280
    Yom Kippur War cease-fire, 221
United Nations Emergency Force, 212
United Nations Human Rights Commis-
    sion, 218
United States Food Administration, 157,
    158
United Steelworkers of America, 210
University of Virginia, 20, 23, 25, 218
U.S. Army
    military chaplain issue, 75–76, 195
    Persian Gulf War, 261–62
U.S. Bureau of Labor Statistics, 216–17
U.S. Constitution, 27
    Bill of Rights, 163
    Fifteenth Amendment, 87
    First Amendment, 18, 277
    rights of Jews under, 37
    Twenty-first amendment, 216
U.S. Defense Department, 199, 222
U.S. House of Representatives, 32, 51,
    67, 200
    Clinton impeachment, 271, 285–86
    Grant military pension, 91
    Hayes election controversy, 93
    Andrew Johnson impeachment, 84
    Nixon impeachment, 226, 283
U.S. Justice Department, 233

U.S. Naval Academy (Annapolis), 103, 129, 237, 238
U.S. Navy, 101, 122, 129, 237–38, 257, 258
    anti-Semitism in, 24, 28, 75
    flogging in, 28, 49, 52, 75
    USS Liberty incident, 209
    USS Seawolf, 238
U.S. Senate, 31, 35, 261, 286
    ambassador confirmations, 193, 269, 273, 275
    AWACS sales to Saudi Arabia, 247–48
    Bitburg controversy, 250–51
    Clinton impeachment, 285–86
    Compromise of 1850, 59
    early Jewish Senators, 52, 60
    Hayes election controversy, 93
    Andrew Johnson impeachment, 83, 84
    League of Nations, 141, 142, 148
    Nixon impeachment, 226
    Supreme Court nominations, 136, 163, 254
    Swiss Treaty, 67
U.S. State Department, 138, 220, 221, 252, 263, 275, 276
    anti-Semitism in, 24, 27–28
    anti-Zionist sentiments in, 179, 180, 182
    Israeli policy, 184–85, 199, 202, 224, 260–61, 286
    Jonathan Pollard case, 259–60
    pro-Arab policy, 191
    shuttle diplomacy, 231, 276
U.S. Supreme Court, 60
    Amistad case, 33
    Brandeis appointment, 136, 147, 163, 169
    Cardozo appointment, 162–63, 201
    Dred Scott case, 69, 78
    first Jewish nomination to, 60, 69
    Fortas appointment, 207, 210, 213, 254, 276, 278
    Frankfurter appointment, 170, 201
    Ginsburg (Douglas H.) nomination, 254
    Ginsburg (Ruth Bader) appointment, 276–77
    Goldberg appointment, 201, 210
    Hayes election controversy, 93
    "Jewish seat" on, 170, 201, 278
    O'Connor appointment, 254
    Rosenberg spy case, 193–94
    Taft appointment, 127, 131

V

Van Buren, Martin, 38–41
    campaigns and elections, 38, 44
    Damascus Affair, 39, 41, 68
    Depression of March 1837, 39
    early years, 39
    and Jewish community, 39, 41
    religious beliefs, 38, 39

    retirement years and death, 38, 41
    on slavery, 39
Van der Kemp, Adrian, 13
Versailles (France), 141–43
Veteran's Bonus March, 164
Veterans Bureau, 149
Vice-Presidency, views on, 11
Vietnam War, 213, 221, 224, 266, 272, 282
Virginia, 17–21, 25, 43, 49, 55
    "Dissenters and Jews" law, 18, 20
    House of Burgesses, 3, 17
    Ordinance of Religious Freedom, 18
Voting rights, 87, 93, 210
Voting Rights Bill of 1965, 210

W

Wallace, Lew, 111
War of 1812, 20, 21, 25, 28, 55, 67
    Battle of New Orleans, 32, 35, 37
Warburg, Felix, 148, 159
Warburg, Paul M, 141–42 148
War Industries Board, 140
War Refugee Board, 177
Warren, Earl, 187, 213
Washington, D.C.
    Congregation Adas Israel, 91, 99, 203, 206
    Jewish Community Center, 153–54
    Washington Hebrew Congregation, xi, 63, 99, 117
    Washington Hospital Center, 99
Washington, George, 2–9
    campaigns and elections, 2
    cherry tree incident, 4
    Chicago statue of, 6
    early years, 3–4
    and Jewish community, xi, 4–9, 19, 162
    on John Quincy Adams, 31
    military career, 3–4, 9, 12
    religious beliefs, 2, 8, 9
    retirement years and death, 2, 9
    Touro Synagogue letters, 7–8
Washington Institute for Near East Policy, 274
Washington, Martha Dandridge Custis, 2, 3, 9
Washington Monument, 57, 103
Washington Post, The, 226, 269
Watergate, 216, 218, 226–27, 229, 233, 278, 281
Waxman, Seth, 277–78
Webster, Daniel, 41, 59, 60, 74
Weekly Standard, 262
Weems, Mason Locke ("Parson Weems"), 4
Weinberger, Casper, 260
Weinstein, Lewis H., 199
Weisner, Jerome B., 201
Weizmann, Chaim, 137–39, 146, 169, 183–85
West Bank settlements, 243, 247, 260–61

West Germany. *See also* Germany; 219, 226, 250–51
West Point Military Academy, 87, 103, 189, 190
Whig Party, 20, 41, 42, 43, 44, 47, 51, 54
    and abolitionist movement, 55, 57, 59, 60–61
White House, 11, 198
    "Black Tuesday" incident, 213
    Middle East peace agreements, 241, 267, 286, 288
    modernization of, 60–61
    temperance movement, 93–94
White House tapes
    Johnson, 210
    Nixon, 216–17, 218
Whitewater Affair, 279–80, 285
Wiesel, Elie, 250–51, 286
Willkie, Wendell, 168
Wilson, Woodrow, 132–43, 146, 147
    on anti-Semitism, 143, 148
    Balfour Declaration, 137–39, 143, 169, 183, 184
    Brandeis Supreme Court nomination, 136, 143
    campaigns and elections, 125, 128, 130, 132, 133, 134, 140
    early years, 133
    European relief programs, 157–58
    Fourteen Points program, 142–43
    hopes for Jewish homeland, 133, 141, 143
    illness of, 142
    immigration issues, 135–36
    and Jewish community, 133–36, 139–43, 160, 171
    League of Nations, 141, 142, 145, 148
    legacy of, 142–43
    Paris Peace Conference, 140–43
    religious beliefs, 132, 133, 142
    retirement years and death, 132, 141, 142
    World War I, 137, 140, 157, 159
Wise, Rabbi Isaac Mayer, 78–79, 85, 88–89, 116, 129, 139
Wise, Rabbi Stephen S., 139–40, 162, 168–69, 190
    Jewish homeland advocacy, 137–38, 141
    support for German Jews, 172, 173, 181
Wolf, Adolph Grant, 91
Wolfowitz, Paul, 263
Wolf, Simon, ix, 73–74, 89, 90–91, 116–17, 129
    U.S. consul general in Egypt, 94, 98, 103, 112
Wolfson, Louis E., 213
Woodward, Bob, 226, 285
Works Progress Administration, 171
World Jewish Congress, 201, 239
World War I, 137, 140, 172